THUNDER RUN

David Zucchino is a foreign correspondent
for the *Los Angeles Times*.
His work has been short-listed for the Pulitzer Prize
on three occasions.

THUNDER RUN

THREE DAYS IN
THE BATTLE FOR BAGHDAD

DAVID
ZUCCHINO

FOREWORD BY
MARK BOWDEN

Atlantic Books
London

First published in the United States of America in 2004 by Grove/Atlantic, Inc., 841 Broadway, New York, NY 10003–4793, USA.

First published in paperback in Great Britain in 2004 by Atlantic Books, an imprint of Grove Atlantic Ltd.

This paperback edition published by Atlantic Books in 2005.

9 8 7 6 5 4 3 2 1

A CIP catalogue record for this book is available from the British Library.

1 84354 283 8

Interior maps by Matthew Ericson.

Printed in Great Britain by Bookmarque.

Atlantic Books
An imprint of Grove Atlantic Ltd
Ormond House
26–27 Boswell Street
London WC1N 3JZ

For my father,
First Sergeant Ernest Joseph Zucchino
(World War II, Korea, Vietnam),
who served with honor

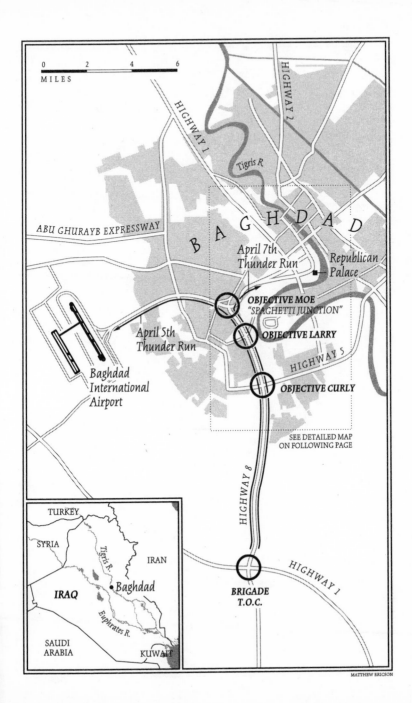

0 2 4 6
MILES

HIGHWAY 1

HIGHWAY 2

Tigris R

ABU GHURAYB EXPRESSWAY

B A G H D A D

April 7th
Thunder Run

Republican
Palace

OBJECTIVE MOE
"SPAGHETTI JUNCTION"

April 5th
Thunder Run

OBJECTIVE LARRY

Baghdad
International
Airport

HIGHWAY 5

OBJECTIVE CURLY

SEE DETAILED MAP
ON FOLLOWING PAGE

HIGHWAY 8

TURKEY

SYRIA

Tigris R.

IRAN

IRAQ

Baghdad

HIGHWAY 1

Euphrates R.

**BRIGADE
T.O.C.**

SAUDI
ARABIA

KUWAIT

MATTHEW ERICSON

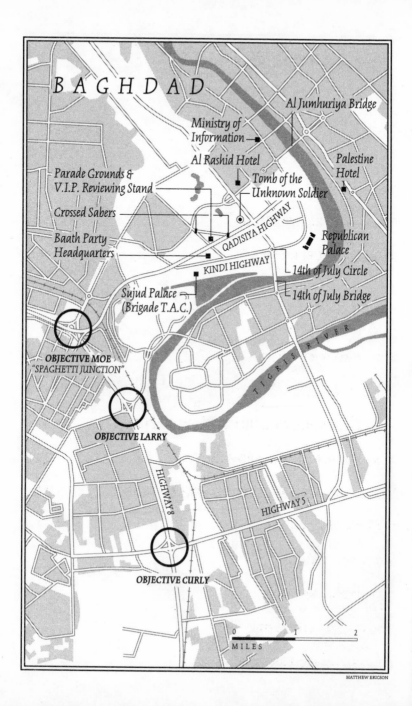

BAGHDAD

Al Jumhuriya Bridge

Ministry of
Information

Al Rashid Hotel

Palestine
Hotel

Parade Grounds &
V.I.P. Reviewing Stand

Tomb of the
Unknown Soldier

Crossed Sabers

QADISIYA HIGHWAY

Baath Party
Headquarters

Republican
Palace

KINDI HIGHWAY

14th of July Circle

Sujud Palace
(Brigade T.A.C.)

14th of July Bridge

TIGRIS RIVER

OBJECTIVE MOE
"SPAGHETTI JUNCTION"

OBJECTIVE LARRY

HIGHWAY 8

HIGHWAY 5

OBJECTIVE CURLY

0   1   2
MILES

MATTHEW ERICSON

CONTENTS

FOREWORD

By far the most important and decisive part of the stunning American sweep of Iraq in 2003 was the surprise armored thrust into the heart of Baghdad. While pundits at home and around the world (myself included) were predicting a potentially bloody, protracted siege of Saddam Hussein's capital, and while the notorious "Baghdad Bob" was before microphones in the Al Rashid Hotel denying that American forces were anywhere near the city, the Spartan Brigade, the Second Brigade of the Third Infantry Division (Mechanized), was blasting its way up the city's central avenues. It was a perfect illustration of how history is usually made, not by planners and critics, but by brave men with their boots on the ground—or, in this case, Abrams tank treads. The Spartan Brigade's thunder run became the turning point of the war both militarily and psychologically.

I have to say that I was not surprised to learn that my friend and longtime colleague David Zucchino was with those men. Zook is one of the best reporters of our generation, and he's been putting himself at risk to get good stories for many years. He's smart, fearless, tenacious, and (thank God) lucky. He survived one serious brush with death covering the war, and dove right back into the action. This book will outshine and outlast the flood of embedded memoirs of that war, because of both where he was and who he is.

We both started as reporters at *The Philadelphia Inquirer* almost a quarter century ago. Zook and I, the late Mark Fineman, Buzz Bissinger, Richard Ben Cramer, Mike Capuzzo, Bob Rosenthal, Lucinda Fleeson, and Joyce Gemperlein were among a group of young reporters at that paper who competed with one another each week to land the "Sunday Strip," the story stripped over the masthead on the Sunday paper. It was the paper's premier showcase for dramatic writing. The Sunday editor then was the late Ron Patel, a dashing man with a lusty appreciation for a lurid tale (for which reason, and others, he was nicknamed the Dark Prince). Philadelphia furnished plenty of opportunities for these stories—cannibal mass murderers, serial rapists, mobsters, animals and damsels in peril, madmen, shipwrecks, mystery, and gore. We called the stories Dirtballs. They were and are the bread and butter of newspaper writing. While other reporters were trying to master the arcana of state budgets or probing for malfeasance in City Hall, we were out looking for the sleazy stuff that would appease the appetite of the Dark Prince. You had to be fast to win the weekly contest, and you had to be good. You had to spot the small item with dirtball potential before anybody else, find the gory details, write it, and have it in Patel's hands whole by Thursday afternoon—he was a stickler for freshness. We all had our moments of glory in this sweepstakes, but I think Zook was the master.

He went on to become the paper's best foreign correspondent, winning a Pulitzer Prize for an amazing series of stories he wrote from South Africa before the overthrow of apartheid. I once had the chance to work with David in the Middle East. We spent a few days together in Jerusalem trying to cover the first Intifada, driving off together into the West Bank and Gaza. He was a veteran by then and I was a rookie. I vividly remember him behind the wheel of our rental at the crack of dawn, heading off from the walls of the Old City into Palestinian territory looking for trouble, remarking gleefully, "Look out, he's got a car!" We always found trouble. Zook had a nose for it. He was getting ready to take off for some other hot spot, and he kindly stuck around for a few extra days to help me get acquainted with the turf.

I thoroughly enjoyed working with him, but I have to admit I was a little relieved when he departed. He was wearing me out. His motor ran in a faster gear than my own. He combined boundless energy with a bottomless appetite for action, and liked to stay up late in the bar drinking beer, swapping tales, and trying to understand the huge story unfolding all around us. I didn't get a full night's sleep until he was out of town.

When I wrote the first draft of *Black Hawk Down* in 1997, Zook had taken a serious career misstep. He had accepted the job of Foreign Editor, chained to a desk through long days and nights, trying to get other people to do what he could do better himself. It worked to my benefit, however, because he became one of the early enthusiasts for my story at the paper, and eventually helped me with it enormously. He edited that first draft into a crisp newspaper serial, so when I sat down to write the book version, I had the inestimable benefit of his earlier guidance. He performed a similar service when I wrote my book *Killing Pablo*, which also first appeared as a Zook-edited serial in the newspaper. I remember him telling me, "Next time, I get the story and you get the damn editing job."

Well, this time Zook gets the story, and I'm lucky enough to have ducked doing the edit—not that he needs any help from me. Already with *Thunder Run* he's got one leg up on my efforts. He was there.

And, as I expected, he has come back with the single best story of the Iraq War. Watching on TV, many of us had the impression that Baghdad's resistance just melted away at the approach of American forces. *Thunder Run* will dispel that illusion. This was the most bitterly contested moment in the war, one that left thousands dead, including some very brave American soldiers. Zook's writing captures the drama, the heroism, the fear, noise, confusion, horror, and, yes, the thrill of battle. It is a masterwork by a master reporter and writer. I'm proud to introduce it to you.

—Mark Bowden

War is neither magnificent nor squalid; it is simply life, and an expression of life can always evade us.

—Stephen Crane, *War Memories*

O N E

CHARLIE ONE TWO

J ason Diaz was worried about his tank. It had taken a terrible beating on the long, swift march up from Kuwait that spring. Roving packs of Fedayeen Saddam, the fanatic Iraqi militiamen in their distinctive black pajamas, had shot it up outside the holy city of Najaf and in firefights along the muddy Euphrates River. The tank's pale tan skin was peppered with holes gouged out by automatic rifle fire and exploding grenades, leaving a splatter pattern of dinks and scrapes and blisters, like a chronic case of acne. The 1,500-horsepower turbine engine had sucked in several pounds of coarse sand and grit. The groaning twin tracks had been ground down by two weeks of firefights and ambushes as Diaz pushed the tank ruthlessly over the hard-pan deserts of southern and central Iraq. He and his crew had been on the move, day and night, for two weeks, and he badly needed a day—or at least a few hours—for maintenance and repairs and sleep.

Diaz was a tank commander, and his life depended on his tank. It was, literally, a mobile home for Diaz and his three crewmen—his gunner, his loader, and his driver. They slept on the decks, wolfed down lumpish MREs—meals-ready-to-eat—inside the turret, hunkered down in the cramped hatches on cold desert nights. The tank's thick steel hull kept them alive; they had stayed buttoned up inside as RPGs, rocket-propelled grenades, exploded with heavy metallic jolts that made the cupola shutter, and as AK-47 rounds beat a steady *ping, ping, ping* on the two-inch-thick steel ballistic skirts. Diaz loved its squat, ugly frame, its bull-shouldered arrogance, even the rank sulfurous stench that permeated the turret each time the aft caps blew off the main gun rounds. The tank was a seventy-ton gas hog, getting a mere one kilometer per gallon, highway or city. It burned fifty-six gallons an hour at full clip and ten gallons an hour while idling. But for all its inefficient bulk, the tank was a $4.3 million killing machine. It was capable of ripping men in half with its coax—its coaxially mounted 7.62mm machine gun—and popping off enemy tank turrets three kilometers away with long sleek rounds from its 120mm main cannon. It was a mobile armory, hauling forty-one main gun projectiles, a thousand fat rounds of .50-caliber ammunition, and more than ten thousand 7.62mm machine-gun bullets. Pitted against an Iraqi army with three-decade-old Soviet tanks, the big pale beast seemed virtually invincible.

The M1A1 Abrams was designed for brutal conditions, and this particular model was a mule. It looked like a junkyard wreck by now, on this cool evening in central Iraq, but it had brought Diaz and his crew all the way from the Kuwaiti desert to the dull gray plains south of Baghdad. The entire Second Brigade of the Third Infantry Division (Mechanized), all four thousand tankers and infantrymen and medics and mechanics, was camped out, eighteen kilometers south of the capital on a grimy stretch of scrub flatlands in the shadow of a soaring highway cloverleaf. The division had just completed the fastest sustained combat ground march in American military history—704 kilometers in just over two weeks, and 300 kilometers in one twenty-four-hour sprint. It was April 4, 2003, and Jason Diaz from the Bronx—budding army lifer, husband of Monique, father of little Alondra and the twins, Alexandra and Anthony—was weary and filthy and longing to go home. But now, on this cold starry night, he was obliged to demand even more from his exhausted crew and his overextended tank. He had just been ordered to take them straight into Baghdad.

Diaz had received the OPORD—the operation order—in the dark that night. At his level in the chain of command, a mere staff sergeant in charge of just three men, he was provided no computer printout, no written battle plan. His platoon lieutenant simply called him over and said, with little elaboration, "We're going into Baghdad at first light." Then the lieutenant felt compelled to add, unnecessarily, Diaz thought, "Be ready for a fight." The whole tank battalion was going—all thirty tanks and fourteen Bradley Fighting Vehicles and assorted armored personnel carriers of the Desert Rogues, more formally known as the First Battalion, Sixty-fourth Armor Regiment, which formed the core of Task Force 1-64. And Diaz's well-traveled tank, part of the lead platoon of Charlie Company, would be squarely in the middle of the armored column.

Diaz was surprised by the sudden operation order, for there had not been the slightest hint that the brigade was going anywhere near downtown Baghdad. No American forces had entered the city; the war's main front was still well south of the capital, where the Medina Division of the Republican Guard was defending the southern approaches. In fact, Diaz and the rest of the battalion had spent most of that day foraging south, blowing up Medina Division tanks and personnel carriers on a sort of combat joyride that some of the tankers were now calling the Turkey Shoot.

Long before "LD-ing," before crossing what soldiers called the line of departure from Kuwait into Iraq sixteen days earlier, Diaz and his men had been told that they would stop short of Baghdad. The Second Brigade, nicknamed the Spartan Brigade, was a heavy-armor unit. The tankers had trained to fight in open desert, not in a city. The U.S. military strategy— as it had been briefed to Diaz, at least—was to surround Baghdad with tanks while airborne units cleared the capital block by block in a steady, constricting siege. The Pentagon brass was still spooked by the disastrous U.S. raid into Mogadishu ten years earlier, when American soldiers were trapped in tight streets and alleys and eighteen men were killed by Somali street fighters. But now, with no warning and with only a few hours to prepare, Diaz was being ordered to take his banged-up tank into a hostile city of 5 million Iraqis, a treacherous urban battlefield of narrow streets and alleyways.

The mechanics worked on the tanks all that night. There were four tanks in Diaz's platoon, and two of them were in worse shape than his. They had debilitating track and battery problems. In fact, they were so degraded that the mechanics couldn't get them battle-ready. They were scratched from the mission in the middle of the night. The platoon would have to go into the city at half strength. Diaz had been up all night with the mechanics, and now he was too agitated to sleep. He didn't know anything about Baghdad. He didn't know anything about the enemy in the city. He wasn't afraid of combat or the enemy. He was afraid of the unknown.

On the same barren field, Eric Schwartz was also having a fitful night. Schwartz was a short, spare forty-one-year-old, the son of a Navy Huey gunship pilot who had won a Silver Star in Vietnam. With his clipped graying hair and studious manner, he looked more like a college professor than a soldier. He had a degree in education and a graduate degree in human resource development. Like most tankers, he was neither tall nor heavyset; trim, compact men fit more comfortably in the tight hatches.

Schwartz had fought as a tank commander in Operation Desert Storm, and now, twelve years later, he had risen to battalion commander. A lieutenant colonel, he was the man in charge of the Rogue battalion, and now he was trying to make it through what was becoming the longest night of his life.

Schwartz had wrapped up the planning sessions for the mission at about 11:30 p.m. He walked out in the dark and climbed up on the deck of his tank to try to sleep. He stretched out there for a while, staring at the stars, his mind racing, and finally he gave up. He climbed down and strolled over to the tank crews. Nobody was sleeping. The tank commanders were talking quietly to their drivers and gunners, laying out details of the mission, their low voices like soft music in the dark. Schwartz went from crew to crew, patting backs, talking about families and food and home. He needed that human contact, and he thought his men did, too. He kept at it for a couple of hours, then went back to his tank deck and tried again to fall asleep. This time, he went down. Thirty minutes later, he woke up. It was nearly dawn. He was ready.

Schwartz had not expected to be preparing to fight his way into Baghdad so soon. His focus had been in the opposite direction, more than thirty kilometers south of the capital, where his battalion had spent most of that day, April 4, lighting up the Medina Division. This was the Turkey Shoot—what amounted to target practice, only with actual enemy tanks and armored personnel carriers instead of the rusted hulks the gunners had fired at on the target ranges in Kuwait and back home at Fort Stewart, Georgia. The Iraqis had hidden their outdated, Soviet-made personnel carriers and tanks—T-55s and T-72s, mostly—in garages, next to homes and schools, and in date palm groves. They were experts in camouflage, and much of the armor had survived coalition air strikes.

Many of the Iraqi regulars manning the vehicles had fled, so the Rogue battalion was firing on quite a few empty tanks and personnel carriers that day. The battalion had absorbed a few stray RPG attacks and small-arms rounds from Iraqi stragglers, but the biggest threat came not from the enemy but from the hot burning metal of exploding Iraqi vehicles. Abrams tanks normally fire at targets two or three kilometers away—the typical kill distance for the American tankers who had destroyed Iraqi tanks in the first Gulf War. But now Rogue's targets were only a few hundred meters away, so close that the gunners could see the curling fronds on the date palm camouflage.

As the Abrams tanks tore into the Iraqi armor, the tanks and personnel carriers exploded. They didn't just pop like firecrackers. They blew like bombs, the tank turrets spinning crazily and chunks of flaming steel and cooked ammunition hissing through the air. A shard of burning metal burned through one of Rogue's Humvee trailers, setting a heap of gear on fire. Several Americans were cut and bloodied by flying metal, none seriously, and the drivers quickly learned to speed up to escape the barrage.

From his tank commander's hatch, Schwartz had spotted an empty T-72. He got on the radio and said, "This one is mine." He told his gunner to fire a SABOT round, a forty-five-pound, armor-piercing projectile with aluminum stabilizing fins and depleted uranium rod—an exceptionally dense metal ideal for penetrating military armor and heating it to molten metal. The round easily punched through the tank's steel skin, but it didn't pop the turret. Schwartz ordered up a HEAT round, a high-explosive antitank projectile tipped with a shaped charge. It turned the T-72 into a bonfire. Schwartz's driver had to speed away to avoid the firestorm.

But at one point Schwartz got tagged. He was passing a burning Iraqi vehicle about 150 meters away, and he told his loader to keep an eye on it. It seemed ready to explode. An instant later, it blew. Schwartz felt a blast of heat and ducked down into the cupola. He popped back up to look around and was slammed down to the bottom of the turret. He briefly lost consciousness. His loader shook him roughly and shouted, "Sir! Sir! Sir! Get up! Get up!" Schwartz came to and looked at his shoulder. A hot shard of metal had smacked into it. The shard burned him and hurt like hell, but Schwartz was okay. He got back up in the turret and moved on.

The shoulder was still aching later that afternoon, when Schwartz got a radio call from Colonel David Perkins, the Second Brigade commander. Perkins wanted to see Schwartz right away at the brigade command tent. Schwartz had just finished the Turkey Shoot, and he and his men were beat. He had hoped to give them time to rest, repair their vehicles, perhaps even grab a few hours' sleep. They had barely slept on the long slog up from Kuwait. Schwartz was a disciplined officer, and when his commander summoned him, he reported right way, no matter how tired and miserable he felt. A slight figure in his green Nomex tanker overalls, Schwartz hustled over to the command post at the edge of the dusty field along the highway.

Inside, Perkins, a slender officer with an erect bearing, was hunched over a map, his head down. Normally, the command post was a loud, busy place, a collection of communications vehicles backed up end to end and covered with canvas. But now it was quiet, and the headquarters staff officers and battle captains were milling around, silent. Schwartz took off his helmet and flak vest. An officer cleared off the map board in front of Perkins. The icons showed Second Brigade's battalions clustered south of the city, the division's First Brigade camped to the west at the airport, and the Third Brigade set up northwest of the capital. A division of U.S. Marines was still on the move southeast of the city, off the map. Baghdad itself was a blank expanse of enemy forces, size and capability unknown.

Perkins looked up. "At first light tomorrow," he told Schwartz, "I want you to attack into Baghdad."

Schwartz heard a whooshing noise in his ears. He felt disoriented. He had just spent several hours in a tank, pushing south, ducking hot shrapnel, and the last thing on his mind was going north into Baghdad. He had always assumed airborne units would clear the capital at some future date, with the Spartan Brigade setting up blocking positions outside the city.

"Are you fucking crazy . . . ?" Schwartz blurted out, then added, ". . . sir?" He waited for the other officers to laugh.

There was silence.

"No," Perkins said. He wasn't the type of commander to kid around. "And I'm coming with you. We have to do this."

Just after dawn the next morning, April 5, the entire battalion was lined up on Highway 8 south of the capital, engines gunning, weapons primed, the squat tan forms of the tanks and Bradleys bathed in gold morning light. Jason Diaz's tank, radio call sign Charlie One Two, was fifteenth in the order of march. He was up in the commander's hatch, awaiting the order to move out, when his driver radioed up from the driver's hole tucked below the turret. "The AIR FILTER CLOGGED light is on," he said.

They hadn't even launched the mission yet, and already the tank was balking. Diaz was anxious enough—and now this. He climbed down to check it out and saw his platoon leader, First Lieutenant Roger Gruneisen, inspecting *his* tank. The lieutenant's right track was damaged and the cooling tubes were worn. Every time the track turned a rotation, it made a horrible clanking sound. Gruneisen looked at Diaz and asked, "You think we'll make it?" Though Diaz was an enlisted man and Gruneisen was an officer, Diaz had more experience as a tank commander. He didn't want to lie. "Really, sir," he said, " I'm not sure." And that was the honest truth.

Diaz respected the lieutenant too much to try to bullshit him. Gruneisen was a platoon leader who trusted his men and let them do their jobs. He was the kind of man that Diaz, a Latino from the Bronx, probably never would have known if he hadn't joined the military. Gruneisen was a white southerner, a pale young twenty-four-year-old, with a shaved head and a soft Kentucky twang. He was a West Point man, focused and resolute, commissioned less than two years earlier.

Diaz, twenty-seven, had already put in eight years and was thinking about becoming an army lifer. He had drifted aimlessly after graduating from John F. Kennedy High in the Bronx, working odd jobs in Puerto Rico before wandering into an army recruiting station one day. The recruiter showed him videos of various military MOSs, or specialties—medic, personnel, supply. Then he put on the tanker video. Diaz saw the thermal sights and the computerized targeting system and all the other high-tech turret gadgets. He watched a tank pulverize targets, spitting out awesome bursts of orange fire from the main gun tube. He thought it would be cool to blow things up. He signed up to be a tanker.

Diaz had a deep affection for his current Abrams, which he had trained on and fought in for the previous six months. He and his gunner, Sergeant Jose Couvertier, had nicknamed it *Cojone Eh?* The phrase had no literal English translation. Essentially, it meant "Yeah, right"—a skeptic's challenge. All the tankers had spray-painted their main cannons with leering names that suggested a particularly aggressive and retributive brand of patriotism: *Apocalypse* and *Crusader, Courtesy of the Red White and Blue* and *Cry Havoc and Let Slip the Dogs of War*. Charlie One Two's nickname just happened to be more esoteric than most.

Standing next to Diaz on Highway 8, Gruneisen did not seriously consider aborting his platoon's mission. They were only going seventeen kilometers from their staging area south of the city, a straight shot north up Highway 8 and then west on 8 where the highway curved toward the international airport. There, the battalion would link up with the division's First Brigade, which had seized the airport the day before, rechristening Saddam International as Baghdad International.

This was an armored reconnaissance mission. Armor recon was just what it sounded like: the battalion was to smash through Baghdad's defenses, drawing fire and shooting back in order to probe the Iraqis' defenses and tactics—to determine, violently, how Saddam Hussein intended to defend his capital. It was recon by fire.

Gruneisen was surprised by Highway 8. It was a modern, divided superhighway, nothing like the rutted roads and sandy tracks the battalion had plowed through down south. It looked like an American interstate highway. From what he could see, it hadn't been badly damaged by coalition air strikes. It was two lanes wide in some places, three in others. The lieutenant thought his ailing tanks could last seventeen kilometers on that smooth, flat surface.

He turned to Diaz. "Let's give it a shot," he said, as if there were any alternative.

Within minutes, the order came to mount up and move out. The column lurched to life. Foul black smoke erupted from the Bradley engines. The tank tracks tore neat little grooves in the asphalt, clanking and grinding, and the roadway was milky white with blowing dust. The lead tank chugged past the final American checkpoint and a voice came over the radio net: "You are now entering Indian Country."

Diaz gave his driver the order to pull forward, with Gruneisen on his wing. Already, they could hear the soft pop of small-arms fire up ahead. They had been in combat for the previous sixteen days, off and on, but still they felt that tight, queasy spasm in their bellies that always rose up, urgent and bitter, just before a fight. It passed quickly, and Gruneisen fell easily into the order of march. The final checkpoint was fading into the yellow dust behind them when the driver radioed the lieutenant that the oil filter warning light had suddenly started flashing.

At the head of the column, First Lieutenant Robert Ball scanned the roadway, left to right, right to left, searching for threats. As the commander of the lead tank, he felt as though he were perched on a slow seventy-ton target, especially standing up in the cupola, his head and shoulders exposed. He wore a CVC—a combat vehicle crew helmet—made of bullet-resistant Kevlar and a small tanker's flak vest, but he knew a single well-placed round from an assault rifle, so useless against a tank, was more than enough to kill him in an instant.

Ball had been selected to lead the column not because he had a particularly refined sense of direction but because his tank had a plow. The battalion was expecting obstacles in the highway. Like any motorist, Ball had been lost a time or two while driving in the States. Even so, he thought of himself as pretty good with a map, and he had carefully studied his 1:100,000 military map of Baghdad and Highway 8. He could see how the highway bent west toward the airport, cutting a slice through southwest Baghdad. But the map had no civilian markings—no exit numbers, no neighborhoods. Ball was concerned about missing his exit to the airport at what everybody called the spaghetti junction, a maze of twisting overpasses and on-ramps on the cusp of downtown Baghdad. He found himself longing for a simple AAA tourist map.

Ball, twenty-five, had never been in combat prior to the firefights in the southern Iraqi desert. He was a slender, soft-spoken North Carolinian with a girlfriend back home and a twin brother in the service. He had spent two years in the North Carolina Army Reserves before entering West Point and earning a commission in 2001. He had been promoted to first lieutenant just four months earlier, and now he was a platoon leader in the same company that Rick Schwartz had commanded in the first Gulf War.

Ball had killed a man for the first time a few days earlier. In fact, he and his crew had killed quite a few enemy fighters down south, and he found it an unnerving experience. He couldn't remember them all, but for certain ones he recalled the most curious details—the stunned look on the dying man's face, the smell, the hazy air, the intense emotional attachment to the intricate ballet of combat. He felt an abiding sense of regret, which he had anticipated. He had met with a chaplain in Kuwait several times, seeking reassurance. The chaplain had told him that killing the enemy was part of a just cause; it would actually save lives in the long run and improve the prospects of thousands of Iraqis. The little sessions with the chaplain had put Ball at ease, and now he was primed for the fight.

Ball's map was clipped to the top of the commander's hatch, next to his .50-caliber machine gun, as he led the column up the highway. It was an unremarkable stretch of roadway. In the early morning light, everything was bathed in a monochrome grayish tan—the overpasses, the access roads, the squat houses and multistory apartment buildings set far off the highway. On either side were open stretches of packed dirt and dust-choked weeds, providing clear fields of fire.

Ball had been rolling only a few minutes when his gunner, Sergeant Geary LaRocque, spotted the first targets of the morning. A dozen Iraqi soldiers in green uniforms were leaning against a building, chatting, drinking tea, their weapons propped against a wall. They were only a few hundred meters away, but they seemed oblivious to the grinding and clanking of the approaching armored column.

"Sir, can I shoot at these guys?" LaRocque asked.

The rules of engagement said anyone in a military uniform or brandishing a weapon was a legitimate target. They didn't say anything about announcing yourself before firing.

"Uh, yeah, they're enemy," Ball replied.

In southern Iraq, the men Ball's crew had killed were murky green figures targeted at great distances by the tank's thermal imagery system. Their body heat gave them away, creating eerie human shapes on the thermals. But now these soldiers highlighted against the dark building along Highway 8 were in living color. Through the tank's magnified sights, Ball could see their eyes, their mustaches, their steaming cups of tea.

LaRocque mowed them down methodically, left to right. As each man fell, Ball could see a puzzled expression cross the face of the next man before he, too, pitched violently to the ground in a pink spray. The last man managed to flee around the corner of the building. But then, inexplicably, he ran back into the open. The gunner dropped him.

The clattering of the tank's coax, its rapid-fire medium machine gun, seemed to awaken Iraqi soldiers posted up and down the highway. Gunfire erupted from both sides—AK-47 assault rifles and rocket-propelled grenades, followed minutes later by recoilless rifles and air defense artillery in direct fire mode.

Ball was surprised by the sudden intensity of fire. He was accustomed to the way the Iraqis had fought down south, which was mostly pop up, shoot, run, and hide. But now, on Highway 8, they were standing their ground—and the column had only traveled about a mile beyond the final checkpoint. Ball could now see that the Iraqis had built an elaborate network of trenches and bunkers on both sides of the highway. He saw bright white muzzle flashes, little sparks of light all the way up the shoulders of the highway. From alleyways and rooftops, men with RPGs were launching grenades toward the column, flaming red balls of light trailed by spirals of gray smoke.

The first main tank round of the mission was fired by Sergeant Jeffrey Ellis, an easygoing Alabamian who was the gunner on the third tank in the column. Ball had radioed back to Ellis that a group of armed men had just fired an RPG and then ducked into a tiny cinder-block hut on the right side of the highway. He wanted them taken out. Sergeant First Class Ronald Gaines, the tank commander, radioed the company commander, Captain Andy Hilmes, and said, "We've got some guys running into a little building. Request permission to fire the main gun." Hilmes responded, "Roger, fire main gun."

Through his magnified sight, Ellis could see men piling into the hut. There were perhaps two dozen of them. The main gun was in battle-carry mode, meaning it was preloaded, in this case with an MPAT round, a multipurpose antitank projectile. It was a new piece of ammunition that had not been used in combat before the Iraqi war. Ellis thought it was just as effective as a HEAT round and a little more versatile. When set to ground mode (it could also be used against helicopters), the MPAT was designed to penetrate a target and explode inside. Ellis traversed the gun tube, got a laser reading of 610 meters, and put the targeting reticle's tiny red crosshatches on the hut. He squeezed the trigger on the gunner's power control handles, which all the gunners called cadillacs, for the original manufacturer, Cadillac Gage. "On the way!" he announced. The MPAT round reduced the hut to dust, unleashing a cloud of gray smoke twice the size of the structure. Even before the crews in the tanks behind him announced over the radio that nothing was moving inside, Ellis knew he had killed them all. Over the net came calls of congratulations: "Great shot! . . . Good shot! . . . Hell of a shot!"

Suddenly trucks and pickups and taxis were speeding toward the overpasses from access roads, dropping off gunmen. They stood at the roadside, completely exposed, and fired AK-47s from the hip. Ball opened up with his .50-caliber machine gun and the gunner unleashed the coax, tearing into the gunmen and sending them tumbling into the dirt. The tank gunners started lighting up the vehicles in fiery red explosions from HEAT rounds, and more HEAT and MPAT rounds tore into the roadside bunkers. The battle was on.

In the command tank a short distance behind Ball, the battalion commander, Rick Schwartz, was determined to keep the column moving. The last thing Schwartz wanted was to get pinned down or be drawn into an extended firefight. The night before, he had instructed his officers and NCOs to keep the convoy moving at fifteen kilometers per hour, with strictly enforced fifty-meter intervals between the vehicles. The drivers were under orders to keep a steady pace; moving faster or slower would break the column and permit enemy vehicles to slice in and attack the tanks in their vulnerable rear exhaust grills. The track commanders and gunners had their own orders: the lead gunners were to try to kill everything they saw, then pass the targets back to the trailing tracks. Schwartz wanted his men talking to one another, describing exactly what they were shooting at and what still needed killing.

Schwartz was still trying to determine exactly what he was up against. The brigade's S-2 shop, the intelligence guys, had not been able to tell him much. In fact, when Schwartz had asked for specifics about enemy strength and positions the night before, he got a vague, long-winded answer. Finally Schwartz said, "So you don't know shit about the enemy in the city, do you?" The intelligence officer told him, "No, nothing really."

Nor were the intelligence officers entirely certain how badly coalition air strikes had degraded Saddam Hussein's forces, what weapons the Iraqis had, or how determined they were to stand and fight. The brigade's scouts, who normally went out ahead to conduct enemy surveillance, had not ventured north. It was too dangerous. And if any Special Forces teams had been into the city, Schwartz certainly didn't know what, if anything, they had discovered. He was on his own.

Schwartz did have satellite imagery providing a black-and-white photographic bird's-eye view of Baghdad. But the imagery was several days old, perhaps a week old or more. Even if it had been shot that morning, it would not have told Schwartz where the enemy was dug in. Satellite imagery could not pick up camouflaged bunkers or RPG teams hiding in alleyways and second-story windows. The division had tried to order up a pass by a UAV, an unmanned aerial vehicle—a spy drone—for real-time battlefield photos, but for various bureaucratic and technical reasons it never happened.

To the best of Schwartz's knowledge, Highway 8 was not blocked by any concerted Iraqi attempt at barricades. The Iraqis certainly had not blown the bridges and overpasses leading into the capital, although American military planners had expected them to try. Based on the most recent satellite imagery, and on reports from American pilots who had flown over the city, the highway was clear and relatively unscathed by coalition air strikes. There was no safer or faster surface for tanks than good old highway asphalt—in this case, asphalt helpfully marked with wide traffic lanes and highway signs in Arabic and English. By all indications, the Iraqis had left the back door to the capital wide open. It was like leaving Interstate 95 and the Capital Beltway open for an enemy tank invasion of Washington, D.C.

In issuing his order to Schwartz, Colonel Perkins had said, "The task is to enter Baghdad for the purpose of displaying combat power, to destroy enemy forces—and to simply show them that we can." Essentially, what Perkins had ordered up was a thunder run, a lightning armored strike straight into the capital. The American military had been conducting thunder runs since the Vietnam War, where the term had originated. The secure artillery fire bases set up in Vietnam in the mid-1960s had been code-named Thunder I, Thunder II, and so on. The Viet Cong, attempting to disrupt U.S. supply convoys plying the highways between the artillery bases, sent out guerrilla teams at night to cut the roads and set up ambushes. To keep the arteries secure, American commanders dispatched columns of tanks and armored vehicles up and down the roads at dusk. The columns moved at high speeds, blasting away on both sides of the highway to draw enemy fire—what the military calls recon by fire. Soon any rapid dash through hostile territory became known as a thunder run.

As the Rogue column came under fire on the morning of April 5, Schwartz got a good look at the enemy. There were hundreds of them, perhaps thousands. Some were in uniform. Some wore civilian clothes, or a mix of jeans and green army vests, with machine-gun coils slung bandolier-style over their shoulders. There were Fedayeen Saddam militiamen in baggy black pajamas and—Schwartz not did realize this until later—Syrian mercenaries brought in by buses from Damascus, their pockets stuffed with Iraqi dinars. Many of the Syrians, along with armed Jordanians and Palestinians, were *jihadis*, Muslim fundamentalists eager to fight a holy war against infidel invaders.

There was an armored personnel carrier here and there, but no tanks—and probably nothing capable of destroying a tank or Bradley. But the recoilless rifles could put a serious dent in an armored personnel carrier and were a real threat, especially to the combat engineers firing their

M-4 carbines from the exposed hatches of the M113 armored tracks. Schwartz had ordered the engineers to fire at snipers in upper-story windows or on rooftops. The tanks had trouble elevating their gun tubes that high. If any of his guys were going to get killed, he feared, it would be the engineers.

The Iraqis seemed to have no training, no discipline, no coordinated tactics. It was all point and shoot. A few soldiers would pop up and fire, then stand out in the open to gauge the effects of their shots. The big coax rounds from the tanks and Bradleys sent chunks of their bodies splattering into the roadside.

Nor did the Iraqis seem to appreciate the lethal and accurate firepower of the tanks and Bradleys. The gunmen fired from bunkers, their muzzle flashes exposing their positions. From hundreds of meters away, nearly out of sight, the tank gunners peered through their optical sights and fixed the red aiming dots and crossed hash lines of their reticles—their targeting systems—on the bunkers. They squeezed red trigger buttons on their cadillacs and the bunkers exploded with a heavy *whump* and a shudder as the HEAT rounds detonated.

Few of the Iraqi fighters demonstrated much command of basic combat maneuvers. They would bunch up in the alleyways, firing wildly. The tank loaders would shove an MPAT round into the breech and set the proximity fuse for ten or twelve meters. The gunners would fire into the mass of men and the broad arc of the explosion would send their shattered bodies airborne.

Gunmen crouched behind walls made of brick or cinder block, apparently unaware that not only the tanks and Bradleys but also the tank commanders' .50-caliber machine-gun rounds could pound the walls to dust in seconds. The gunners watched the fighters' bodies explode and disintegrate along with whole sections of the walls. Other fighters hid in thick stands of date palm trees, leaping out to launch RPGs. Some of the tank and Bradley gunners had discovered down south that a tree hit with a fifty-pound shell unleashes a wave of flying wood shards. It was wood shrapnel. The gunners tore into the date palms along Highway 8, shattering the trunks and impaling anyone crouched behind them.

The tanks and Bradleys had a rhythm now, pounding, pounding, pounding. They were killing people by the dozens, but still the enemy kept coming. By now, gunmen were up on the overpasses, firing straight down on the tank and Bradley hatches. More and more vehicles were appearing. There were little Japanese sedans and bulky 1980s-era Chevrolet Caprices, some of them stuffed with husbands and wives and kids staring wide-eyed at the column as the cars zoomed past in the southbound lanes beyond the median. But other cars and pickups were packed with soldiers in uniform or men in civilian clothes blasting away with AK-47s poking out the windows. There were tan military troop trucks and "technicals"— white Toyota pickups with machine guns or antitank rockets mounted in the beds.

It occurred to the battalion's S-3, the operations officer, Major Michael Donovan, that the battalion was winging it. They certainly had not trained for urban warfare—much less for this battle, which involved urban areas at the highway's margins, but also stretches of wide-open cross-country highway. It was like fighting on the New Jersey Turnpike. Donovan, thirty-eight, a slender, sharp-featured man, was the son of a Vietnam veteran, a Citadel graduate, and a student of military history. It dawned on him now that Rogue battalion was rewriting the army's armor doctrine on the fly. He himself was certainly rewriting the role of an operations officer. His job was planning and organization. But now he was in the commander's hatch of an Abrams—and firing an M-4 carbine at men in ditches on the side of a superhighway. He thought: *Holy shit, I'm the S-3 and I'm shooting dudes with a rifle!*

This was nothing like Donovan had experienced in Operation Desert Storm in southern Iraq a decade earlier. Back then, his tank never got closer than two kilometers to an Iraqi tank. That was a standoff war, distant, removed, impersonal. This war, Schwartz had warned him the night before, would be unique: "This isn't going to be anything like Desert Storm." Now, on Highway 8, Donovan could see the faces of Iraqi fighters. His father had told him stories of Viet Cong guerrillas smiling as they fired. Now he was seeing young Iraqi faces, and their dominant emotion was fear. They looked terrified. Donovan spotted several armed soldiers in a bunker, just beyond the guardrail. They were huddled and afraid. He didn't want to kill them, but he had to. They were the enemy. He opened up with the M-4 and watched them topple.

More carloads of civilians were beginning to appear, complicating what the tankers called target acquisition. Donovan was worried about civilian casualties—what the military, in its wonderfully clinical articulation, referred to as collateral damage. The civilians were getting into the middle of the fight. The crews were under strict orders to identify targets as military before firing. They were supposed to fire warning shots, then shoot into engine blocks if a vehicle continued to approach. Some cars screeched to a halt. Others kept coming, and the gunners and tank commanders ripped into them. Some vehicles exploded. Others smashed into guardrails, their windshields streaked with blood. The crews could see soldiers or armed men in civilian clothes in some of the smoking hulks. In others, they weren't sure. Deep down, they knew they were inadvertently killing civilians who had been caught up in the fight. They just didn't know how many. They knew only that any vehicle that kept coming at the column was violently eliminated.

At one point, a white minivan sped alongside Donovan's tank. The driver, a middle-aged man in civilian clothes, made eye contact and gave Donovan a manic "don't shoot" gesture. Donovan motioned for him to get out of the way. As the van pulled away, Donovan saw that three uniformed soldiers with guns were lying in the rear bed. He radioed ahead to the front of the column. Minutes later, he watched one of the gunners with the fire support team pulverize the minivan as it tried to escape down an exit ramp.

At the next interchange, Donovan spotted a technical—a red Nissan pickup with a Soviet-made heavy machine gun mounted in the truck bed. A young man was firing the gun at the column, his black hair blowing wildly, as the Nissan sped across an overpass. Donovan screamed, "Oh, shit!" and yelled for the loader to open up with his M-240 medium machine gun. Donovan fired his M-4. They missed, and the technical got away.

The technical vehicles worried Lieutenant Colonel Schwartz because the drivers seemed so fearless and reckless. A few seemed determined to ram the column, driving straight toward the massive tanks and Bradleys before the coax rounds shattered their windshields and sent the vehicles careening into the guardrails. Schwartz was worried, too, about antitank weapons. He thought he had spotted a couple of American-made TOW missiles—tube-launched, optically tracked, wire-guided missiles—lethal weapons designed to destroy armored vehicles including American tanks and Bradleys.

Still, he felt confident. The lead tracks were radioing back to other tracks, giving them "triggers" to prepare to fire on technicals speeding up from the rear flanks. Schwartz's air liaison officer was in his ear all morning, radioing with updates from the air force pilots circling overhead, tracking technicals and trucks pouring in from the crowded neighborhoods on either side of the highway.

The column was moving steadily. Nobody was stopping or even slowing. The tracks were passing on targets, handing off, just as Schwartz had ordered. Every single vehicle in the column had been blistered by RPGs or recoilless rifle rounds and thousands of rounds of small arms, but everybody was still intact and moving. Some of the RPGs had detonated on the gear and rucksacks stored on the tracks' external bustle racks, and now the stuff was on fire. Most of the crews just let it burn.

Schwartz was laying down suppressive fire with his .50-caliber, shouting into his radio microphone. He was repeating himself now, but he wanted his message drummed into his soldiers' brains: "Pass 'em off . . . pass 'em back . . . keep moving . . . keep the momentum." The column, still intact, still paced and measured, rumbled up Highway 8. The staff officers back at the brigade operations tent could mark its progress on their computer screens, the column represented by tiny blue icons that inched, slowly, inexorably, north toward Baghdad.

T W O
THE RIGHT
THING

As their tank approached the final checkpoint on Highway 8, Lieutenant Gruneisen's crew was blasting the heavy metal song "Creeping Death" by Metallica on speakers inside the turret. They had nicknamed their Abrams *Creeping Death* because they all loved the song, which they thought evoked something sinister and lethal. That's how they felt going in that morning. Even so, the mood was oddly buoyant inside the turret—buoyant, but also focused and determined, with just a whiff of sweaty anxiety. The crewmen always cranked up the music going into a mission to jack them up, to blow away the butterflies and get them in the mood to destroy the enemy.

It seemed to the crew's gunner, Sergeant Carlos Hernandez, that they had been killing people for a long time, even though it had been barely two weeks. Hernandez had never been at war before, but he had discovered down south that time slowed down in combat. So many things happened all at once that it was almost as though time had to somehow pause and expand in order to accommodate it all. This enabled Hernandez to recall with utter clarity what it was like to kill a man. After the very first time, outside Najaf, he was pumped up and mournful at the same time. That conflicted feeling stayed with him even after he'd killed a few more people, but after a while he just got numb.

Other guys in his company had different reactions. Once, also outside Najaf, they were pounding an Iraqi bunker complex with tank cannons when they saw an Iraqi soldier leap up, throw down his weapon in disgust, and stalk off. The man had almost escaped the kill zone when an American mortar crashed down right on top of him, a direct hit. The soldier's body disintegrated. Everybody laughed—not necessarily at the man's brutal death but at fate, and how a guy who had decided to just walk away from a fight got nailed anyway.

Hernandez had thought a lot about death back in Kuwait. He was Catholic—not exactly a churchgoer but enough of a Catholic to be familiar with the phrase, "Thou shalt not kill." He had sought out the battalion chaplain in Kuwait, for he wanted to make sure he was right with God in case he had to kill somebody. He and the chaplain had three or four good heart-to-heart sessions. Hernandez asked why people went to death row in the real world for murder but got medals in war for killing other human beings. The chaplain told him it boiled down to good and evil, and evil had to be conquered. Hernandez asked how the Iraqis justified killing to their God, their Allah. The chaplain sidestepped the question and told him that Saddam Hussein was evil and had killed thousands of his own people. Ending his regime would save lives. He reassured Hernandez and said, "You're doing the right thing."

Hernandez decided then that he was going to do whatever was necessary to keep his crew alive and to get everybody back home safely, himself included. Twenty-seven years old, he was a family man these days, far removed from the restless, drifting kid he had been after he dropped out of high school in Tampa to work as a carpenter on a construction crew. Joining the army had given him structure, and marrying Kimberly, his high school sweetheart, had settled him down. If he had to kill somebody to get home safely to Kimberly and his little boy, Carlos Anthony, and his daughter, Louise Marie, that's what he would do.

As soon as the tank crossed the checkpoint on Highway 8, the crew killed the music. The lieutenant shouted, "Test fire weapons!" and Hernandez fired a few bursts of coax, which relaxed him and reassured him that everything was going to be okay. Then he heard the driver tell Lieutenant Gruneisen that the oil filter light was on. He radioed his buddy in Charlie One Two, Jason Diaz—Hernandez and Diaz and their wives played dominoes together back home at Fort Stewart—and told him, "Man, this doesn't look too good."

Then the crews heard Lieutenant Ball's radio voice at the head of the column announce "Contact!" The gunmen in the bunkers opened up on them, and the crew got straight into the fight. Up in the turret of Charlie One Two, Diaz started working the .50-caliber, pumping rounds into the bunkers and into technical vehicles trying to race up the on-ramps and onto the overpasses. His gunner was hosing down dismounts—foot soldiers—

with the coax, keeping them away from the column. Diaz feared dismounts would try to get close enough to the tank to pitch a grenade down the turret.

They were approaching the first overpass when Diaz felt a concussion rock the tank. He was wearing his CVC helmet, which muffled even the earsplitting booms of the 120mm main tank cannons, but still he could feel a shock wave washing over the turret. It felt like the concussion from a main gun, and he thought that perhaps Lieutenant Gruneisen in Charlie One One—*Creeping Death*—had pulled too close to him and fired over his back deck.

Diaz radioed the lieutenant and asked whether he had fired his main gun.

"Negative," Gruneisen said.

"Can you look at my rear and see if anything's smoking?"

The air was black with smoke from burning vehicles and bunkers and the exhaust from the Bradleys. Gruneisen couldn't see much. Diaz's tank seemed fine.

"Keep going," he told Diaz.

Moments later, Gruneisen heard his ammo loader, Private First Class Donald Schafer, say, "Sir, something has hit One Two."

Gruneisen looked again and saw a trail of gray smoke snaking from the rear grill. Some sort of fluid was dripping underneath the tank.

Inside Charlie One Two, Private First Class Chris Shipley shouted to Diaz from the driver's hole, "The fire warning light is on!" And then, "The emergency lights are on!" The whole driver's control panel was flashing.

Diaz was reporting the malfunction over the company net just as Gruneisen radioed and told him, "It looks like something hit you in the back, right above the grill!"

Diaz wanted to keep going and try to hobble all the way to the airport, but then Shipley radioed again from the driver's hole: "The tank just aborted."

The engine shut down. They were slowing to a stop. Diaz didn't want to stop under the overpass and expose the stricken tank to enemy fire from above. He willed the tank forward, shouting at Shipley to try to keep it moving long enough to clear the overpass. They rolled on and came to a rest just north of the bridge, in the far left lane of Highway 8.

Diaz looked at his rear deck. Orange flames were shooting up out of the grill. He couldn't believe it. He had never pictured an Abrams tank as helpless, as a victim. The entire brigade had had just one tank disabled by enemy fire in the entire war. Two days earlier, a fire in a tank's auxiliary power unit, triggered by an RPG hit, had been quickly put out and the tank recovered and repaired. Even under punishing conditions and chronic parts shortages, the brigade had lost only 15 percent of its tanks to repairs at any given time. But now the back of Charlie One Two looked like a little bonfire. Diaz cursed and gave the order for the fire drill—the same drill they had practiced endlessly at Fort Stewart and in the Kuwaiti desert. He tried to sound calm as he hollered, "Evacuate tank!"

The defining characteristic of combat is chaos. No operation plays out the way it was planned. The purpose of training is to bring order to chaos, to condition men to react in prescribed ways, no matter what the emergency. On Highway 8, the battalion's training kicked in. Diaz's crew evacuated the tank and took up fighting positions. Gruneisen pulled his tank forward to protect the stricken tank's northern flank. The Charlie Company commander, Captain Jason Conroy, moved his tank ahead of Gruneisen's to provide more combat power, and the trail platoon set up a perimeter of armored vehicles to protect the rear.

Diaz and his crewmen were now exposed. It was a shock to be down on the smoky highway, out of the protective cocoon of the tank and its thick steel hull. The air smelled of cordite and burning fuel. It stung their nostrils. The crewmen heard rounds pinging off the sides of the tank and realized they were under fire. Gunmen in the crease of the overpass, where the bridge abutment meets the underside of the elevated runway, were firing down on them. Shipley, the driver, had fired so many M-4 carbine rounds that he was out of ammunition. He saw an AK-47 on the roadway, picked it up, and got it to work. He was firing away toward the overpass when one of the tanks traversed and cut down the gunmen in the crease with a burst of coax.

The tank fire was behaving strangely now. When Charlie One Two aborted, its fire protection system kicked in automatically, spraying the fire with Halon, a chemical retardant designed to rob flames of oxygen. That doused the fire for a moment, but soon it came back to life. Diaz jumped down to the left side of the tank and yanked the red emergency fire handle, setting off another round of Halon. The fire smoldered.

While his crew laid down suppressive fire, Diaz got on the back deck and inspected the rear grill. He opened up the rear compartments and saw that all the VEE packs—ventilation filters made of aluminum and filter paper with stiff, accordion-like folds—were on fire. In the lower compartments, the tank's batteries were melting. Fuel was pouring onto the highway. It was bad, and Diaz knew it. But he also knew an Abrams was nearly invincible, and the only other brigade tank to catch fire in Iraq had been rescued with minimal damage.

He heard a whooshing sound. An RPG screamed over his head and slammed into the roadway beyond the median in a flash of sparks and flame. Diaz hollered for somebody to toss him his M-4 carbine. He grabbed it and squeezed off several rounds at a bunker on the left side of the highway a few hundred meters to the northwest. He could see muzzle flashes, and he knew the gunmen inside had a clear shot at the tank. They were well concealed in a series of trenches next to a low wall.

Diaz's eyes burned and his throat was raw from harsh chemicals released by the flames. He jumped off the back deck and got his first look at the rear engine housing. Something had left a perfect hole the size of a quarter in the shock housing and punctured the right rear fuel cell in the back of the tank, where the protective steel is only about a quarter-inch thick above the Number Six skirt. The projectile went straight through the hull. It was a one-in-a-million shot—probably a recoilless rifle, Diaz thought. The projectile had to have been fired from below to enter at such a low angle. Diaz had seen recoilless rifles in alleyways, firing up at the elevated roadway, but he never imagined a round from one could actually stop an Abrams.

And yet, if they could extinguish the fire, Diaz thought, they could tow the tank the rest of the way. He grabbed the tank's handheld fire extinguishers and doused the flames. The fire went out—then erupted again. Diaz didn't know it, but fuel was pouring onto the tank's superheated turbine engine, bursting into flames each time the previous fires were snuffed out. Even after tank engines are shut down, they remain hot for a considerable time.

By now, the delay was affecting the entire mission. It took a minute or two for word of the disabled tank to move up and down the column, but soon the entire battalion was stopped, spread out and exposed. In his tank, Lieutenant Colonel Schwartz was listening on the radio to events unfolding at the cloverleaf, growing more anxious by the moment. This was the last thing he wanted—to lose momentum, to get bogged down in a street fight with dismounts. But he also was determined not to lose an Abrams. It would be humiliating to have to leave it for the Iraqis, who would certainly haul out foreign TV crews to film a destroyed American tank. He was willing to give the crew a reasonable amount of time to get the fire out and have the tank towed.

Schwartz decided to take advantage of the delay by ordering his crews to reload. They had expended an astonishing amount of ammunition. They had been shooting nonstop since crossing the checkpoint. Some of the .50-caliber barrels were so hot that they were unable to fire, so the crews replaced them with fresh barrels. Schwartz had half the tanks and Bradleys reload and rearm while the other half continued to lay down fire to keep the bunkers and snipers suppressed. The column was much easier to hit while it was stopped.

Seventy meters behind the burning tank, the brigade commander, Colonel Perkins, was in the open hatch of an M113, an armored personnel carrier. His driver had stopped under the overpass, but Perkins ordered him to move back onto the open highway. He didn't want to expose them to anyone hiding on the bridge. A Bradley behind him also pulled back to get a better firing angle on the overpass and to cover the brigade commander's back.

Like Schwartz, Perkins did not want to leave an Abrams in the hands of the enemy. The tankers had a code: you don't leave your crew behind, and you don't abandon your tank. They were like ship captains; they were willing to go down with their ship. So far, the crew of Charlie One Two was doing all the right things, performing the evacuation and recovery drill just as they had been trained. Perkins was willing to give them a little more time.

After Diaz had expended his tank's handheld extinguishers, the order went out for the other tanks to donate their extinguishers. Crewmen hopped out of the hatches, exposing themselves to fire, and delivered armloads of the red extinguishers. Diaz and his crew sprayed the flames. They smoldered, shot back up, and smoldered again.

On Lieutenant Gruneisen's tank, Sergeant Hernandez wanted to fire the main gun into the troublesome bunker, but the lieutenant thought they were too close to Diaz's crew on the ground—the men were stressed enough without the concussive blast of a 120mm round knocking them off their feet. Hernandez was desperate to help. He had made a pact with Charlie One Two's gunner, Sergeant Jose Couvertier: they would always watch each other's backs. Hernandez had taught the fire evacuation drill in Kuwait, so he asked Gruneisen if he could go help. Gruneisen hesitated—their tank would be the tow tank once the fire was out, and he would need help. But after a long pause Gruneisen finally said he could handle the tank alone for the moment.

Hernandez climbed down onto the highway. He was just now getting his first good look at his surroundings. He had seen nothing but desert on the march up from Kuwait, but now he was suddenly in a dense urban area. He was surprised to see homes and apartment buildings and shops. For the first time, he realized that Iraq—at least this part of it—was a modern twenty-first-century nation, with superhighways and late-model cars and congested suburban sprawl. "Oh shit," he yelled up to the lieutenant, "we're in an actual city!" He felt hemmed in, claustrophobic.

Hernandez climbed up onto Charlie One Two and helped Diaz get the VEE packs out. Because the filter packs were burning so furiously, Diaz thought they could rob the fire of fuel by removing them. Hernandez reached down and grabbed one by its heavy aluminum frame. It burned his hand. He cursed and dropped it. Somebody doused it with water from a five-gallon jug. Hernandez and Diaz reached back down and struggled to lift the packs. They were melted and fused together by the heat. Hernandez pounded them with a hammer, broke them apart, and he and Diaz and others lifted them out.

With the VEE packs removed, the fire settled down. Lieutenant Gruneisen backed up his tank to the crippled tank so that his crewman could hook up the tow bar. Gruneisen thought they were almost out of the predicament. It wasn't so bad. Even while towing another tank, his own tank could still fire, so they wouldn't be out of the fight. But as soon as the tow bar was connected, the fire erupted again.

While the crew unhooked the tow bar, Hernandez got into the fight. He had left his 9mm pistol on his tank, so he picked up an M-4 rifle someone had left on top of Charlie One Two. He fired at the distant bunker, emptying the clip. He yelled at a sergeant who had just pulled up in an armored personnel carrier to assist with the evacuation: "You got another mag?" The sergeant offered Hernandez an ammunition magazine, but first he demanded Hernandez's empty magazine—for "accountability." They were supposed to account for their used magazines and turn them in.

"I can't fucking believe you asked me that!" Hernandez screamed. They were in the brigade's worst firefight of the whole war, an Abrams was on fire, and this guy was worried about turning in a used ammo magazine. But the sergeant insisted. Hernandez had to climb down into the turret, where he'd tossed the empty magazine, and fish it out. He handed it over, slammed in the new magazine, and went back to shooting.

On top of the burning tank, Diaz was out of fire extinguishers. He had pumped about two dozen of them onto the fire, which was stubbornly refusing to die out for more than a few seconds at a time. Then the order went out for the tank crews to give up their five-gallon water jugs, so the crewmen ran through the firefight again, lugging the heavy jugs toward Charlie One Two.

Diaz knew they had reached the point of desperation now. If the Halon and the fire extinguishers couldn't kill the fire, why would water be any more successful? It was getting preposterous now. The battalion's executive officer, Major Rick Nussio, was up on Diaz's tank, trying to help. Nussio was the number two man in the whole battalion, behind Lieutenant Colonel Schwartz. Yet here he was, getting his eyebrows burned off while helping to pull out the smoking VEE packs, dumping a five-gallon jug on a raging fuel fire, standing on a burning tank in the middle of a firefight.

The company commander, Captain Conroy, was worried that the situation was getting out of control. When he gave the order for water jugs, for instance, he had not meant for the crews to remain on the ground after delivering the water. He had to order them to get back inside the tanks for cover. Conroy's tank was in front of the burning tank, providing cover fire while giving Lieutenant Colonel Schwartz a blow-by-blow account over the radio. Schwartz was under pressure from Colonel Perkins to resolve the situation, and that pressure was bearing down now on Conroy. He was a smooth-faced twenty-nine-year-old veteran from upstate New York, an energetic and enthusiastic commander. Despite the pressure, he played for time. He knew they couldn't keep the column waiting much longer, but he wanted to give the crew every opportunity to save the tank.

But Conroy was getting conflicting reports from Lieutenant Gruneisen. First the fire was out. Then it was back. Then it was out again.

At one point, Conroy had just told Rogue Six—Schwartz—that the fire had been extinguished and they were hooking up the tow bar. Then Gruneisen radioed and told Conroy, "It's on fire again."

"What do you mean it's on fire? I thought you were putting it out!"

"I know," Gruneisen said, "but it caught back on fire."

Conroy felt a little ridiculous, updating Schwartz with a situation report that reversed itself every other minute. Gruneisen was getting frustrated, too. He felt the captain was sharpshooting him, trying to instruct him on how to fight a tank fire even though he was following the drill to the letter. Hell, his man Hernandez had *taught* the fire evacuation course.

Colonel Perkins was growing impatient. Not only was the entire column stopped and exposed, but the time lag in radio reports was also confusing everybody. It was one of the hazards of combat—radio updates often were outdated at the moment they were issued. From the hatch of his armored personnel carrier stopped on the highway, Perkins was in a position to see the flames. Yet he kept getting radio reports from Captain Conroy, relayed to him by Major Nussio, that the tank fire had been put out. Yet he could plainly see that Charlie One Two was still on fire.

Then the first suicide vehicle appeared. Conroy saw it, a blue truck hurtling down the on-ramp in front of him. He ordered a machine-gun round fired into the engine block as a warning. The round tore into the truck and the vehicle screeched to a halt. The driver, a man in civilian clothes, stumbled out and put his hands up. Behind him, gunmen in one of the bunkers opened fire. Conroy motioned wildly at the driver to get down. The tanks couldn't fire on the bunker without hitting him.

The man dropped down on his belly and one of the tanks fired a main gun round into the bunker. It exploded. Five soldiers emerged from the wreckage, running at the tanks, firing assault rifles. A burst of coax splattered them across the roadway.

Now a white pickup was roaring across the bridge and heading for the on-ramp. At the foot of the ramp, Conroy ordered his gunner to traverse and fire. The gunner yelled that the hydraulic power had suddenly gone out. He was trying to traverse the main gun with a manual crank. Conroy picked up his M-4 carbine just in case, then radioed a Bradley next to him. "Hey, there's a suicide truck coming down."

The Bradley commander picked it up right away. The truck turned sharply and picked up speed, racing down the ramp. Conroy could see three men inside—one in uniform, one in civilian clothes, and squeezed between them a young man wearing a white headband with black Arabic script. They weren't slowing down. They were aiming for Conroy's tank. The Bradley opened up. From his hatch, Gruneisen pumped away with the .50-caliber. Everybody was unloading—coax, 25mm guns. They couldn't stop it. They kept firing. Finally the pickup shuddered, bounced crazily down the ramp, and slammed into a guardrail a few meters from Conroy's tank.

Conroy could see something piled in the pickup bed. He was afraid it was explosives, so he screamed into the radio net for everyone to hold their fire. Then he saw the young man in the headband moving. The other tank crews saw him, too, and everyone thought the same thing: he might be reaching for a remote device to trigger a truck bomb. Conroy gave the order to fire. Rounds slammed into the pickup. It caught fire, and the man in the headband was burned alive.

Behind Conroy, everyone was furiously pouring water onto the fire inside Charlie One Two, with little success. The burning tank had now consumed nearly thirty minutes of precious time, and the level of fire from both sides of the highway was intensifying. Iraqi military trucks were pouring in from the city, dropping off dismounts.

Diaz began to resign himself to losing his tank. He hated the thought of it, but he hated even more the thought of losing one of his men in a futile attempt to put out a fuel fire. The fuel had leaked into the turret by now, and the fire was spreading. Everyone decided not to try to tow the tank for fear that the ammunition loaded inside would detonate, threatening the towing tank.

Diaz had the crew unload the tank, yanking off sensitive items like radios and code boxes and combat manuals. They piled the stuff, along with their rucksacks and weapons, on top of Gruneisen's tank and inside an armored personnel carrier commanded by the company first sergeant.

Gruneisen had been pleading with Conroy for just a little more time, and Conroy had been asking Schwartz, who had been asking Perkins. But now Perkins had heard enough. They couldn't stay exposed any longer. The entire battalion was at risk, not just one tank. It was time to cut their losses. Perkins ordered that the crew prepare to abandon the tank. Charlie One Two would have to be left to fall into enemy hands.

Diaz heard the order. Despite himself, he agreed with it. It was the right thing to do, given the circumstances. Now, after struggling for so long to save the tank, the crew thought they had to destroy it. They had been trained to destroy any abandoned equipment to keep it from falling into the hands of the enemy. In this case, they certainly didn't want the Iraqis to recover anything from a late-model Abrams tank. It was decided that Hernandez would try to burn it with thermite grenades—incendiary grenades filled with aluminum powder and metal oxide.

After the crew had abandoned the tank, Hernandez threw open the ammunition doors to expose the main gun rounds and the ammunition for the coax and .50-caliber machine guns. He cut the fuel lines and turned on the heater. He knew the drill. He had taught the fire evacuation course. He scattered .50-caliber ammunition across the floor of the turret and stuffed a few rounds inside the gun breech. Then he sprayed everything with lubricating oil from the tank's toolbox.

The rest of the crew finished loading gear and weapons onto other vehicles. Diaz hauled himself up to the loader's hatch of Lieutenant Gruneisen's tank, followed by Diaz's gunner, Sergeant Couvertier, who took Hernandez's spot in the gunner's mount. Private First Class Schafer, Gruneisen's loader, jumped into the first sergeant's personnel carrier along with Private First Class Shipley, the driver from the burning tank.

The order came over the radio to pull out. Colonel Perkins wanted the column back on the move right away. But he didn't want the tank destroyed; he planned to try to recover it in the next couple of days. He wasn't aware that the crewmen, following the dictates of their training, believed they were supposed to burn it so that nothing could be recovered by the enemy.

On top of the stricken tank, Hernandez had on his CVC helmet—his radio helmet—but he had no communications. He was on his own now. He was concerned about hustling back to his tank and getting away from the blast before the thermite grenades set off all the ammo and fuel. He was also waving to get the attention of the drivers of two armored personnel carriers behind him, trying to tell them to get out of the way because he was about to blow the tank. Finally, in frustration, he motioned furiously and showed them the thermite grenades.

Perkins, meanwhile, was getting irritated by the delay. He had ordered the tank abandoned. What was taking so long? He had his driver pull up to the burning tank so he could find out what was holding everybody up. He saw Hernandez up top, clutching a couple of primed thermite grenades.

"Get off the tank! Now!" Perkins yelled. Hernandez was shocked. No one had ever heard Perkins raise his voice. He was a calm, controlled commander with a dead level demeanor. Now his face was flushed and the veins in his neck were pumping.

"Leave the tank, get your crew, get off—let's move on!" Perkins yelled again.

Hernandez took that as an order to blow the tank. He pulled the pin on the first grenade, lifted his fingers off the spoon—the cocked handle— and flipped it into the breech. He popped the second grenade and dropped into down onto the turret floor. The grenades hissed and smoldered for several seconds, giving Hernandez time to clamber off Charlie One Two and hustle back to his own tank, *Creeping Death*.

He climbed aboard and saw that his friend Couvertier, the gunner from the burning tank, was now in Hernandez's post in the gunner's mount. Couvertier offered to move but Hernandez he told him to stay there. Diaz was in the loader's hatch, so Hernandez half sat and half lay on the top of the tank, next to the haphazard pile of gear and weapons from the burning tank, in front of Diaz and to the left of Gruneisen. There were now five men on a tank designed for four.

The driver, Sergeant Derek Peterson, got the tank moving. It was urgent now. The rest of the column had already moved out, and the burning tank was about to blow. Flames were spitting out of the tank commander's hatch, where Hernandez had tossed the grenades. But their overloaded tank was blocked now by an engineer vehicle that had stopped in the roadway. Diaz screamed at the engineers: "Move out! Move out! The tank's about to blow!" The engineers, alarmed, gunned their engine and sped away.

Creeping Death, with Hernandez exposed beside the cupola, was pulling up to the tail of the column when a series of muffled explosions rocked the abandoned tank. Diaz looked back and saw the glow of the flames. He felt heartsick. He had been with Charlie One Two since arriving in Kuwait six months earlier. It was like losing a member of his family.

Behind them, Lieutenant Shane Williams was commanding *Crusader II*, the trail tank in the column. He could see that Charlie One Two was still intact, despite the fire and the thermite grenades. He decided to put a HEAT round into the tank to make sure there was nothing left for the Iraqis. Williams was a thirty-three-year-old combat veteran, a slender, light-haired Floridian who had served as a cavalry scout in the first Gulf War. He waited until the other vehicles had cleared out, then ordered his gunner to unleash a round. It hit just over the driver's hatch. Charlie One Two shuddered and rocked. Williams thought to himself: *I'm now the only tank commander in the entire U.S. Army who has killed an Abrams M1A1 tank.* How was that going to look on his résumé?

On *Creeping Death*, Gruneisen was struggling to catch up to the rest of the column. The crew had piled all the gear and rucksacks and extra weapons right in his field of vision. The stuff was like a little mountain in front of his face. He could see to fire the .50-caliber off to his right flank, and he could see behind him and off to his left. But in front of him all he saw was gear and rucksacks. He was under fire, on an unfamiliar highway, trying to catch up to an armored column, and he couldn't see a damn thing.

THREE
DOUBLE TAP

A t the head of the Rogue column, Lieutenant Ball was relieved to be on the move again. Like everyone else in the battalion, he had spent the thirty-minute wait on Highway 8 fighting to keep enemy dismounts away from his platoon's tanks. He found it hard to believe, but a couple of Iraqi soldiers had actually tried to charge the Abrams on foot. *What were they thinking?* Ball tried popping off a few rounds from his M-4, but he wasn't quite capable of the acrobatics required to fire a carbine accurately while talking on the radio and maneuvering his tank. His wingman, the gunner in the tank behind him, took care of the dismounts with a blast of coax. But Ball couldn't stop worrying about some Iraqi fanatic sneaking up his rear end and tossing a grenade into the hatch.

Ball felt much better now that they were back on track and heading for the airport, even though the delay had given the Fedayeen and the Syrian street fighters time to regroup. Ball could see men with weapons jumping off of trucks that were now arriving from the city and from the increasingly congested warrens of houses and commercial buildings along the divided roadway. Air force pilots, circling far above the battle, were warning the battalion's air liaison officer that more vehicles were on their way from the city center. The pilots were warning, too, about a collection of antiaircraft guns in a grove of date palm trees just off the highway—what they called Triple A Park, for antiaircraft artillery. The Iraqis had leveled some of the guns and shot them in direct-fire mode, aiming directly at the tanks and Bradleys. The Rogue crews could hear A-10 Thunderbolt II planes pounding away on the antiaircraft batteries, their 30mm Gatling guns emitting low groans that echoed across the landscape.

Highway 8 was taking Ball closer to the city center now, and the traffic patterns were becoming more complex and confusing. Ball studied the military map pinned to his hatch, checking the coordinates against his Plugger—his handheld global positioning satellite device. He saw highway signs warning of upcoming exits, but his map didn't show exit numbers or the names of major highways or neighborhoods. Even so, he was thankful that someone in the Baghdad roads department had thought to post huge blue highway signs that read, in Arabic and English: AIRPORT. His company commander, Captain Andy Hilmes, had told Ball to look for the signs.

Enemy fire was intensifying as they drew near the city center. Some of the fighters near the roadside bunkers and trenches were trying something new. They would lie next to the ditches, pretending to be dead. After the tanks had passed, they would leap up, aim an RPG tube, and fire grenades at the rear of the tanks. The soldier who had taken out Charlie One Two may have just gotten off a lucky shot, but he also may have known about the tanks' vulnerable rear engine grills. And if he did, then some of these fighters probably did, too.

From the commander's hatch of his Bradley, Captain Larry Burris, the commander of a mechanized infantry company attached to Rogue, spotted two Iraqi fighters in the median. One was waving a white rag and the other had hoisted a white plastic chair over his head. They were making wild "don't shoot" gestures. Burris let them go. But just after he passed them, the two men picked up weapons and opened fire on Burris's trail platoon. The platoon returned fire and killed them, but Burris realized he now had one more complication to deal with. One of his men already had taken a piece of shrapnel to the face from an exploding enemy truck, and Burris's crews were struggling to tell the difference between civilian cars and military vehicles. He thought his men were showing restraint, holding their fire and waving away errant civilians or firing warning shots. But now they had to deal with gunmen in civilian clothes pretending to surrender. Burris was determined to bring all 160 men in his company back home alive. He realized that the enemy tactics were putting both Iraqi civilians and American soldiers at risk, and that angered him.

Over the net, other commanders were complaining about the phony dead men rising up and firing weapons. They wanted permission to make sure people who appeared to be dead really were dead. Lieutenant Colonel Schwartz had heard enough. He got on the net and ordered his men to "double tap." Anything you see, he instructed, don't assume it's dead. Double tap it. Shoot it again—especially anyone near a weapon. Schwartz wanted them to check their work. At the rear of the column, Lieutenant

Shane Williams, who had put the kill shot into Charlie One Two, would do the final check, making sure no threats with weapons survived. He would execute the final double taps.

At one point, one of the tanks lit up a truck that was unloading dismounts. The soldiers were torn apart, and their remains lay in smoking heaps. In the middle of the mess sat a soldier, who at first appeared to be dead but was now moving. He was reaching for an RPG launcher. Captain Conroy spotted him, but the hydraulic system on his tank was still malfunctioning. His gunner couldn't traverse his main gun and coax.

Conroy got on the radio to the Bradley behind him and said, "There's a guy with an RPG," and he indicated the spot. The Bradley opened up with coax but Conroy couldn't tell if the man had been hit. A gunner on one of the tanks saw him moving, so he opened up with his coax. The soldier was rocking back and forth now, still reaching for the RPG tube.

"Would you *please* kill this guy!" Conroy said.

The soldier was still rocking when the Bradley hit him with a blast of Twenty-five Mike Mike—the 25mm Bushmaster chain gun. The man's body blew apart. Nobody worried anymore about the guy playing dead.

On the west side of the highway, Schwartz noticed a series of flower shops and greenhouses. It looked like one of those nurseries commonly seen on highways outside American suburbs. There were drooping awnings, perennials in big plastic pots and trays of annuals, shrubs and hanging baskets, and sheets of plastic blotting out the hot April sun. Behind the plants were rows of heavy clay plots, and behind them were men with automatic rifles and RPGs, crouching and hiding, apparently in the mistaken belief that a half inch of baked clay and a few pounds of dirt would shield them from coax rounds or Twenty-five Mike Mike. They were all reloading, having pelted the front of the column. Now they were setting up to unload on Schwartz and his vehicles. Schwartz was amazed. The gunmen appeared to have no idea how vulnerable they had left themselves.

Schwartz yelled to his gunner, "Spray some ammunition in there." That would get their attention, Schwartz thought. It would keep their heads down until the Bradley gunners behind Schwartz could get a fix on them. Schwartz radioed the Bradley commanders: "There's a florist, a nursery coming up on your left. Destroy that nursery."

The Bradleys obeyed. Schwartz watched the clay pots explode, right down the row, one by one. Twenty-five Mike Mike is a high-explosive round. It hits and pops. The clay pots disappeared, and so did the men behind them. They evaporated in a spray of dirt and clay, their weapons flying. Four of the Bradleys went at it, killing a few, then passing the targets back to the next Bradley, which killed a few and passed the work back. They were finishing their work. They put perhaps a hundred rounds of Twenty-five Mike Mike into the nursery, and then it was gone, and a couple dozen fighters, more or less, were gone, too.

"Okay, you're done," Schwartz said. "Shut it off." The 25mm gun tubes swung back north and the Bradleys plowed forward, the gunners searching through their thermal sights for more targets.

The enemy kept coming. Soldiers and civilian gunmen were arriving now in every available mode of transportation—hatchbacks, orange-and-white taxis, police cars, ambulances, pickups, big Chevys, motorcycles with sidecars. Major Nussio, the battalion executive officer, opened fire on a huge garbage truck with a soldier at the wheel. He was thinking to himself as the soldier keeled over and the truck crash-landed: *A garbage truck? These people are so stupid—stupid but determined.*

They were not giving up. It seemed suicidal—men with nothing more than AK-47s or wildly inaccurate RPGs were charging tanks and Bradleys. It was like they *wanted* to die, or worse, they just didn't care. That disturbed some of the tankers. They weren't trained to fight people who didn't give a damn. Nor were they quite prepared to fight people who didn't have a plan—didn't have a clue. As each RPG team or pack of dismounts attacked with utter disregard for what the *other* Iraqis or Syrians were doing, the tankers kept thinking: *It's all a big trap. They really do have a plan. They're just luring us in with these haphazard, disjointed tactics. Sometime soon, they're going to get organized and attack with some serious tactics.*

At one point, a little white Volkswagen Passat suddenly appeared on the highway. It came off one of the access ramps. Before anyone could react, the Passat turned sharply and smacked into one of the Bradleys. Everyone thought it was a suicide car, but nothing exploded. The driver opened the door and stepped out, his hands raised over his head. He was a portly middle-aged man with a trim black mustache and wavy silver hair. He wore an Iraqi military uniform with a colonel's gold rank on his epaulets. There was a pistol on his hip.

The Bradley commander radioed Captain Hilmes. "Sir, we got an Iraqi general here," he said, misreading the colonel's rank. "He just crashed his car into our Bradley. What to you want us to do with him?"

"Capture his ass," Hilmes ordered.

Several infantrymen climbed out of the Bradley's hull and snatched the colonel and dragged him inside. Later, under interrogation by U.S. military interpreters, the Iraqi said he was the military quartermaster for all of Baghdad. He was a brown shoes guy, a desk officer. He had been driving to work, minding his own business—and suddenly he was involved in a fender-bender with an American Bradley Fighting Vehicle. He told his interrogators that he had had no idea American forces were in Baghdad. From what he had been hearing on government-controlled radio, American forces had been stopped cold below the Euphrates River, well south of the capital. He certainly never expected to see tanks in Baghdad. Every officer he knew was convinced the Americans were afraid to bring tanks into a city.

It was baffling. Senior Iraqi officers in the capital seemed content to believe their own lies, that the war was going well and the Americans were bogged down south of the city. Even many ordinary civilians seemed unaware that there was a war going on. Despite the columns of black smoke from burning vehicles and the thunderous pounding of the tanks and the Bradleys, civilians in family sedans were coasting down the southbound lanes of Highway 8 and along the access roads, like it was just another Saturday morning in the suburbs. For all they knew from listening to government radio, the war was confined to the southern desert, where American forces were being routed. It was only the Fedayeen and Syrians, and unknown numbers of Special Republican Guards, who seemed to understand that American forces were invading the capital. And if these soldiers and fighters and militiamen were disorganized and poorly trained, they did not lack for determination or gall—and there seemed to be an endless supply of weapons and ammunition, and of gunmen eager to fight and die.

Lieutenant Ball was approaching the spaghetti intersection. His map showed the exit ramp splitting into two ramps. He knew he wanted the ramp to the right, the one that hooked west to the airport highway. He tried to focus. He was under fire, worrying about the antiaircraft guns, talking on the radio, checking his Plugger, glancing down at the map, searching for highway signs to the airport. He had been following blue

AIRPORT signs all the way up Highway 8, with their distinctive white airplane symbols, but now black smoke from a burning Iraqi personnel carrier obscured the entire cloverleaf.

In the web of overpasses and off-ramps, Ball found the ramp he wanted, despite the smoke, and stayed to the right. He was halfway down when he noticed that the exit had three ramps, not two. *Dammit*, he should have taken the middle one. Now he was heading east into downtown Baghdad, toward Saddam Hussein's palace complex and government center, the opposite direction from the airport—and the entire column was following him. Everybody was going the wrong way.

It was too late to radio back and stop them and get them to turn around, so Ball called Captain Hilmes and said, "The road forks. I took the wrong one," so that the column would slow down and give him time to think.

Hilmes could sense the anxiety in Ball's voice. He realized that the last thing Ball needed was an ass-chewing for screwing up the turn. Hilmes was thirty, an eight-year veteran, a West Point grad who had served in Bosnia. He was an army brat, the son of a thirty-three-year army lifer who had served two tours in Vietnam. Hilmes's two older brothers were armor officers. He had learned over the years how to deal with men under stress, and so he tried to encourage Ball and to calm him.

"All I need you to do is find a bypass," Hilmes said slowly. "Just take your time and let me know when you've got it."

Ball checked his grid on the Plugger and looked at his map for a bypass. He figured out which highway he was on and realized that all he needed to do was cross the median and head back in the opposite direction. He was reassured when he glanced across the highway and saw a blue sign pointing back the way he had just come: AIRPORT.

There were metal guardrails on both sides of the divided highway, but they might as well have been made of tissue paper. Ball was in a seventy-ton, solid-steel Abrams M1A1 tank, for God's sake. He could go anyplace he wanted. In the U.S. military, officers are constantly under orders to "stay in your lane," to stay out of matters they don't know anything about. This was one occasion when First Lieutenant Robert Ball was not going to stay in his lane. He radioed back to Hilmes: "I'm gonna jump this guardrail and go back left." The driver gunned the engine and the guardrails were crunched under the tracks like cardboard. He swung left, onto the westbound lanes, and they were back on track, headed back through the spaghetti junction and on to the airport, following the blue AIRPORT signs.

Ball got up in the hatch and looked behind him to make sure the rest of the column was following him. He watched the forward tanks flatten the metal of the guardrails, creating a clearly marked U-turn for the rest of the column. He radioed back to check on his platoon and heard Staff Sergeant Stevon Booker's booming voice. Booker was his platoon sergeant. "Hey, I'm right behind you. I'm with you the whole way. I got your back," Booker said. Ball felt himself relax. It was always good to hear from Booker.

The crews had trained for both the expected and the unexpected. They had been taught to maintain what commanders called orientation, their assigned fields of fire, no matter what happened during a firefight—including wrong turns. In any tactical armored movement, the lead tank scans the twelve o'clock sector, or the front. The next vehicle scans to the right, the next to the left, and so on. The rear vehicle turns its weapons to six o'clock, to cover the rear of the column. This established procedure prevents everyone from firing on the same targets, which wastes ammunition and also inflates reports of enemy strength.

As the Rogue column executed the sharp U-turn, there was a risk of "masking fires," one vehicle drifting into the gun sights of another if the gunners did not maintain their assigned orientation. The potential for friendly fire was real. But as each tank and Bradley crunched over the guardrails and banked sharply to the left, the gunners held to their orientations and the column re-formed with all sectors covered without overlap.

Behind the lead tanks, Perkins's command vehicle was following the rest of the column after crossing over Ball's freshly created U-turn. The colonel was trying to make mental notes of the overpasses and exit ramps in and around the spaghetti junction. American forces would be coming back into Baghdad at some point, and since Perkins's men were the first Americans inside the city, he might as well mentally plot the way into the city center. But the smoke from burning Iraqi vehicles was obscuring his vision and burning his eyes.

As the vehicle emerged from the smoke, Perkins caught a glimpse of a truck speeding toward them from the opposite direction. It was an open-bed truck with Iraqi troops clinging to the rails in back and firing assault rifles. Then Perkins realized it was cutting toward the armored vehicle in front of him—Major Rick Nussio's M113. Nussio wanted to shoot, but another American tracked vehicle was in his line of fire. He held off. Behind Nussio and Perkins, Major Kevin Dunlop on a trailing vehicle started pumping shotgun rounds into the truck. Then somebody with a .50-caliber joined in. The driver was ripped apart by the heavy rounds and went down. The truck rode the guardrail down, pitched on its side, and slid to a stop. Several Iraqi troops crawled out and ran for cover under an overpass, but one soldier started sprinting toward Perkins's carrier, firing an assault rifle.

The man in charge of defending Perkins's command carrier was Captain John Ives, a steady, unflappable officer. He was behind a .50-caliber and swung it toward the advancing soldier. He pressed the butterfly triggers. Nothing. He looked down. He was out of ammunition. The soldier kept coming. Ives glanced around in desperation and spotted the empty metal ammo box. He grabbed it, wound up—and flung it toward the Iraqi. The box tumbled into the dirt. The soldier got closer. In Perkins's command hatch, there were no mounted weapons. He was the brigade commander, responsible for four thousand men. He wasn't supposed to be firing weapons. He was supposed to be commanding and controlling the battle. All he had was a 9mm Beretta strapped to his leg. He hadn't fired it the entire war. He thought: *Nobody is engaging this guy!* He pulled out the pistol, locked his wrist, and took aim. He squeezed off several rounds. The soldier went down hard. The carrier plowed on and left him there in the dirt. Perkins looked at the pistol. At that moment he had a sobering thought: *If the brigade commander is taking out enemy with his nine millimeter, we're in serious trouble.*

Roger Gruneisen, hauling Staff Sergeant Diaz and the other crewmen from the crippled tank, had fallen behind during the confusion of loading up his tank at the fire scene and waiting for Hernandez to blow Charlie One Two. Now they were chugging up Highway 8 on Gruneisen's Charlie One One—*Creeping Death*—searching for the rest of the column. They were overloaded. Gear and weapons and sensitive items were piled on the turret and deck. They had five men instead of the usual four. Hernandez was up on the blowout panel, on top of the tank, trying to hold on and still fire his machine gun. It was a perilous position; snipers and RPG teams were still getting off shots, and any sudden lurch by the tank would send Hernandez flying onto the roadway. But Hernandez was focused on the west-side bunker that had given them so much trouble on the ground. He despised that bunker. He was going to take it out.

The crew had unbolted the mounted weapons from Charlie One Two—they were held fast by metal pins—and tossed them onto Gruneisen's tank. Hernandez now had an M-240-Charlie, a medium machine gun, from the burning tank. It was a crew-served weapon—the C stood for cyclic—but also capable of being fired by one soldier. It was a wicked weapon, firing the same 7.62mm ammunition as the coax, and with astonishing speed—five hundred rounds a minute. As the tank clanked up the highway, Hernandez, half-laying, half-squatting, shot from the hip. He pumped round after round into the bunker—hundreds of them. As the bunker faded into the distance, nobody stirred inside. Hernandez felt a sense of delayed satisfaction.

Up ahead was the spaghetti junction, shrouded in black smoke. Captain Conroy radioed back to warn Gruneisen about secondary explosions from an Iraqi vehicle burning under one of the overpasses. The lieutenant took secondary explosions seriously. The day before, a Rogue loader had had two fingers blown off by a flying shard from an exploding Iraqi vehicle that had been lit up by the battalion. Gruneisen decided to play it safe; none of his guys was going to die in this godforsaken country if he could help it. He had heard a lot of soldiers debating the real purpose of the war in Iraq—to make sure Saddam didn't use weapons of mass destruction, to kill terrorists responsible for 9/11, to liberate the Iraqi people, to secure Middle East oil supplies. Whatever the purpose, Gruneisen figured it wasn't worth the life of a single one of his men. He wasn't fighting to liberate Iraq. He was fighting to kill the people trying to kill his men. He gave the order: "Button up!" He wanted everybody inside, the hatches locked. He ordered Hernandez to squeeze down inside the loader's hatch beside Diaz. The two men had to hug the hull to avoid the twelve-inch recoil of the thirty-two-foot main cannon—a violent, explosive thrust that could easily break a man's back. One of the first things a tanker learns is to respect the recoil.

Gruneisen was getting irritated now. It had been an awful morning. He had gone into the fight two tanks short. He had taken off with his tank's warning lights flashing—an ominous development at the time but now a mere annoyance given all that had happened since. He had had a tank burn up on him, then had watched it take a HEAT round from an American tank. Now he was overloaded, separated from the column—and practically driving blind. It had been hard enough to see the roadway from up top with all the gear piled on the turret. But now he was "open-protected," down in the hatch with only a five-inch gap between the hatch lid and the top of the commander's cupola. He couldn't see out his vision blocks or periscope because of all the piled-up gear and weapons. His driver, Peterson, wasn't bothered by the gear because his hatch was down below the main gun. But the smoke from the burning vehicle made it difficult for him to follow the highway. And none of them knew precisely where they were supposed to be going.

As Hernandez scrambled down into the loader's hatch, he saw that Peterson had the tank hugging the right lane, dangerously close to a concrete bridge abutment just up the highway. The gunner, Couvertier, had the main gun tube swung over the right side, pounding bunkers and trenches. Hernandez realized that the tube was heading straight for the abutment. He cried out, "Traverse left! Traverse left!"

Couvertier was wearing his communications helmet and couldn't hear anything except radio calls, especially with the clanking of the tracks and the incessant explosions from both friendly and enemy fire. He kept scanning the right side of the highway for targets. The abutment rushed toward them. Hernandez squeezed down into the loader's hatch and slammed the hatch cover shut, still screaming for the gunner to swing left.

The tank was rocked by an explosion. Diaz thought they had been hit by a tank round. Hernandez knew what had happened: the turret had smacked into the abutment. There was a shower of sparks and a rush of gray smoke. Suddenly, the entire turret was spinning wildly. The four men inside were pressed against the turret walls, paralyzed, pasted in place by centrifugal force. Diaz had the same helpless, out-of-body sensation he had felt as a kid on the gravity ride at the carnival. They kept spinning, spinning. Gruneisen was still clutching the elevation handle for the .50-caliber machine gun. It had snapped off at impact. He rode the turret around and around, his hand in the air. Loose pieces of equipment were flying around with them. They spun and spun, fifteen spins, twenty spins. They couldn't move. They felt sick. Finally, the turret slowed and stopped. The gun tube hung over the front deck, ripped from its mount.

"Everybody okay?" Gruneisen asked. He was dizzy. He flipped a switch to cut the turret power. Diaz was pressed against the radio, stunned.

Hernandez was crumpled against the turret wall, woozy and disoriented. The lieutenant looked at Couvertier. Blood was gushing from his face. His whole uniform was soaked in blood. Gruneisen looked again. It wasn't blood—it was a greenish fluid. Then he realized: it was hydraulic fluid. The turret's hydraulics system had exploded. Something had smacked into Couvertier's face, breaking his nose and splattering him with blood, but otherwise he was fine. Everyone checked themselves for blood or wounds. They were bruised and disoriented. In the few seconds it took to regain their senses, they realized they were, remarkably, just fine.

In the driver's hole, Peterson still didn't know what had happened. When the gun tube plowed into the abutment, the tank had rocked and shuddered, but somehow it had kept rolling. Peterson saw the turret spinning madly over his head and brought the tank to a hard stop. He wasn't sure the crew in the turret was still alive.

The voice of First Sergeant Jose Mercado came over the radio. He was in the personnel carrier behind them. "What the hell happened? You guys all right?"

Gruneisen radioed back groggily, "Yeah, yeah, we're okay."

Gruneisen popped the commander's hatch and looked out. The pile of gear was gone. The impact had sent it flying. It was scattered all over the highway behind them—personal gear, radios, radio code boxes, manuals, rucksacks. He was preparing to climb out and retrieve it when he saw soldiers from the first sergeant's track scramble out and scoop up what they could. They grabbed the sensitive items—the radio and code boxes—but they left the rucksacks. Diaz and Hernandez lost their clothes, their shower kits, letters from home, their CDs and CD players—everything.

Diaz was in a state of disbelief. It was like watching a series of silly mishaps happen to someone in a movie. It was hard to believe that all this was really happening to them. First his tank burned up. Then they crashed into a bridge abutment and took a carnival ride. Now he had lost all his gear—and the crew had no idea which way to go. He was a forlorn figure down there in the turret, a dirty, weary, distressed tank commander without a tank.

Gruneisen had Peterson get the tank rolling again. They had fallen farther behind, and now they had no main gun. The gun tube was useless, which meant that the coax—which was "slaved" to the main gun—was out of commission, too. Gruneisen knew they were at the spaghetti junction, where they was supposed to take a ramp to the airport highway. What he didn't know is that at this very spot, Ball and the rest of the column had followed a ramp to the improvised U-turn and were now rolling westward on the airport highway. Gruneisen looked ahead, hoping to see the tail of the column. There was nothing.

He radioed Captain Conroy, "Where's the turn?"

Conroy told the lieutenant that he had seen a burning motorcycle and a statue of Iraqi soldiers near the off-ramp he had taken to the U-turn. Gruneisen managed to find the proper off-ramp and was headed now toward the smashed guardrails that marked the U-turn. He couldn't see anything that looked like a motorcycle or a statue. The tank rolled past the U-turn and headed northeast—toward Saddam Hussein's palace complex in central Baghdad. A voice came over the radio: "Hey One One—where'd you go?"

Gruneisen checked his grids and realized he had gone too far. They had to turn around right away. But there were bunkers and snipers on this roadway, too, and now the tank was under fire. Hernandez was back up on the M-240, spraying over the left side. Diaz was ripping open ammunition boxes and tossing belts of ammo up to Hernandez. Gruneisen was struggling with the .50-caliber. He couldn't elevate properly because the elevation handle had snapped off. He wasn't really hitting anybody, but at least he was able to keep the enemy fire suppressed while he figured out how to get back on the proper highway.

Suddenly they were rolling into a traffic circle—Qahtain Square in the Yarmouk section of Baghdad. Gruneisen radioed the captain: "Did you go through a traffic circle?"

"Negative."

Iraqi military trucks were parked along the square. Soldiers were milling around. It was a staging area for attacks on the column. The tank rumbled into the square. The Iraqi soldiers stared up at the big tan machine, shocked to see an M1A1 Abrams barreling down on them. The tank crew stared, too. They had never expected to confront the enemy in such a personal way—literally face-to-face. There was a brief, suspended moment.

"Oh, shit," Gruneisen said.

The Iraqi soldiers didn't open fire. They ran—they scattered everywhere. It struck Hernandez as preposterous. There were five Americans surrounded by dozens of Iraqis in the heart of the Iraqi capital, and the

Iraqis were fleeing. He had a mental image of cockroaches scattering when you turn on the kitchen light.

Gruneisen ordered Peterson to speed through the circle. There wasn't enough time to back up and turn around. He wanted to just plow through the circle, past the trucks and soldiers, and head back the way they had come. The soldiers scattered out of the way. Gruneisen couldn't tell whether anyone was firing at them. As they rolled into the circle, Hernandez saw a yellow pickup truck speeding toward them with two men in the front seat. There wasn't time for a warning shot—no time to determine whether these were wayward civilians or militiamen trying to ram them. Hernandez got off a burst from the M-240. He saw a spray of blood stain the windshield and watched the passenger go down. The driver hit the brakes and the pickup spun and went into a skid.

"Stop! Stop!" Gruneisen ordered Peterson. He couldn't stop. There wasn't time. The pickup's doors flew open and the driver stumbled out, smeared with blood. The tank plowed forward, flattening the pickup and crushing the driver. The jolt sent the M-240 flying out of Hernandez's grip. It skittered across the asphalt. "Get that!" Gruneisen yelled to Hernandez. But then he changed his mind. It would be suicide to get out of the tank. They were all alone, with enemy all around. He had Peterson back up to free the tank from the wreckage of the pickup. Then they lurched forward, crushing the M-240 to render it useless to the Iraqis. Hernandez got behind the remaining M-240, the medium machine gun mounted on the loader's hatch.

The tank rumbled out of the circle, the treads chewing into the pavement. Peterson hollered, "I'm not stopping for anything!" He aimed the tank toward a ramp leading back through the spaghetti junction, where Hernandez spotted an Iraqi military truck parked on the shoulder. A wounded soldier was on the ground, next to his rifle. A second soldier was motioning to him to stay still, to pretend he was dead. Hernandez was seized now by an irrational anger. He wasn't afraid. He was beyond fear. He felt only rage—at losing a tank, at losing his weapon, at being lost and trapped, at the enemy playing dead. He felt a remarkable sense of focus and clarity. He had decided that anyone in an Iraqi uniform was going to die. It didn't matter that they were wounded or pretending to be dead. If they had a uniform and a weapon, they were a threat to his crew. He let fly with the mounted M-240 and killed both soldiers.

Gruneisen was pounding away with the .50-caliber, trying to clear the right side. He was checking his grid when he saw a blue highway sign through the smoke: AIRPORT. Then he saw an Abrams tank on the highway. It was Charlie Six Five—Lieutenant Shane Williams, the last tank in the column. Williams had fallen behind after pumping a HEAT round into Diaz's burning tank. He had been listening on the radio to Charlie One One's misadventures, and now he was waiting for Gruneisen to backtrack. He had found the crushed guardrails and assumed this was the place to make the U-turn to the airport, but he wasn't certain. As Gruneisen pulled up, Williams radioed and asked, "This is where we turn, right? The left turn?"

Gruneisen's heart sank. Williams was lost, too! At this point, Gruneisen desperately wanted to believe he had found a way to the airport. He spotted another AIRPORT sign pointing in the direction where the U-turn would take them. "I guess so," he said to Williams. The two tanks lurched over the crushed guardrail and headed west toward the airport. And there, through the black smoke and yellow haze, Gruneisen saw the blocky tan forms of Abrams tanks. They had found the column.

The airport highway cut through the dense, upper-class neighborhoods of the Yarmouk district in west-central Baghdad. The vegetation was much thicker than on Highway 8, with date palms and overgrown shrubbery obscuring the fields of fire on either side of the highway. There were more palms and shrubs in the broad median, making it difficult for the armor crews to see vehicles in the opposite lanes. The Iraqi military had been digging bunkers and trenches along the highway for weeks, anticipating an American attack on the airport. The Third Infantry's First Brigade had seized the airport, attacking from the south two days earlier, but now the bunkers and trenches on the airport's eastern approaches were still manned by Iraqis. State-controlled television and radio were reporting that the airport was still in government hands, so the fighters along the highway were still awaiting an American assault on the facility.

As Gruneisen's tank rejoined the rear of the Rogue column, he could see RPGs launching from the bunkers, marked by their distinctive gray smoke trails. His tank was down to two weapons, his .50-caliber machine gun and the loader's mounted M-240 medium machine gun. But Gruneisen had fired so often that the .50-caliber had just run out of ammunition. He had used up every last one of the six hundred rounds stored inside the turret. There were another four hundred rounds packed in sponson boxes on the big metal bustle racks mounted on the outside of the tank, but Gruneisen wasn't about to stop now and crawl out to retrieve it. He shut down the .50-caliber and pulled out his M-4 carbine.

Hernandez was still firing the mounted M-240, but it was giving him problems. He would squeeze off ten rounds or so, and then the gun would jam. He had to keep pulling the charging handle to clear the chamber, only to have the gun jam again after a few more rounds. Now his Abrams tank, the most lethal ground mobile weapons system in the U.S. Army, was being defended by an M-4 carbine and a few halting rounds from an M-240.

Over the radio, the crew of Charlie One One heard the voice of Lieutenant Jeremy England, a tank commander from their company's Second Platoon. England sounded calm and composed. He said to Captain Conroy, "I've been shot in the head."

"You have? You sound like you're pretty fine," Conroy told him.

England had been in "open-protected" posture, down in the commander's cupola with the hatch lid closed and just a five-inch opening exposed. Something had whistled through the narrow opening and slammed into his communications helmet, jerking his head back.

"No, seriously, something hit me in the head," he told Conroy. He removed his helmet. There, lodged into the Kevlar shell, was a bullet. England's gunner checked him out to make sure he hadn't been hit. There was no blood. England's head hurt, but he was fine.

"You all right?" Conroy's voice asked.

"I guess."

"Keep moving," Conroy told him.

After listening to the exchange, Gruneisen decided to close up shop. They were back in the column now, and the battalion had plenty of firepower without his tank. He didn't want to risk the life of a single crewman by trying to defend a crippled tank with just one jammed machine gun. His depleted two-tank platoon had had one tank burn up and the other practically shot out from under them. They were lucky to be alive.

The lieutenant gave the order: "Shut the house. Button up." *Creeping Death* was out of the fight.

FOUR
PUPPY LOVE

The rocket-propelled grenades exploding against the steel hulls of the tanks and Bradleys on the airport highway produced a terrifying metallic racket, as though somebody were swinging a heavy shovel against a metal garage door. To the crewmen inside, it sounded as though the hulls were cracking. But for all the earsplitting explosions, the hulls suffered only a few nasty dents and abrasions. It was the gear stored in the external bustle racks that took the brunt of the damage. The tankers' rucksacks and duffel bags were like shock absorbers, muffling and swallowing the explosions, and in some cases bursting into flames. Several tanks appeared to be on fire, but actually it was just the tankers' personal gear going down in flames. It was wrenching enough for the tankers to risk their lives on this thunder run into Baghdad. Watching their underwear and CD players and letters from home go up in smoke seemed like a gratuitous insult.

At least four RPGs had slammed into the third tank in the Rogue column, an Abrams commanded by Sergeant First Class Ronald Gaines, a short, wiry, sunburned NCO from Ohio. Each grenade had rocked the big tank before bouncing off and exploding in the dirt along Highway 8. Gaines had followed Lieutenant Ball's lead tank through the spaghetti junction to the U-turn and now was rolling west toward the airport. After the storm of RPGs on Highway 8, it seemed to Gaines that the fighting had suddenly tapered off. The gunshots and explosions had nearly ceased. He began to think that they had survived the worst of it—that they were nearly home free, that the enemy had cut and run. Then he realized that he had somehow jostled the switch on his communications helmet that cuts off all outside noise. The fight was still very much in progress—he just couldn't hear it. He flipped the switch, and the thump of the battle resumed, louder than ever.

Somewhere just west of the spaghetti junction, Gaines heard a tremendous *whump* on the right side of the tank. The crew in the tank behind him saw an orange fireball erupt, and then a spray of gray smoke. An RPG had bounced off the tank's external smoke grenade storage box, then ripped into the smoke grenade launcher. The whole side of the tank was on fire. Gaines had already endured the desperate thirty-minute attempt to put out the fire on Charlie One Two; he wasn't going to take a half hour to snuff out the flames on *his* tank. He grabbed a handheld fire extinguisher from inside the turret, leaned out of the commander's hatch, and sprayed the flames with a burst of white foam. To his amazement, the fire sputtered and died. The smoke grenades and some of the gear in the bustle racks had burned, but there was no damage to the tank itself. Gaines noticed that the nose cone from the RPG was still embedded in the launcher, and this detail struck him as both curious and noteworthy—a war story to tuck away for later.

There was another curiosity up there on the bustle rack. Somewhere in the scorched rack was the crew's lucky stuffed dog—actually, Staff Sergeant Joe Bell's lucky dog, Puppy Love. It was one of those squeeze toys that played a song. Bell's wife had mailed it to him in Kuwait for Valentine's Day from back home in Knoxville, Tennessee. The couple owned Yorkshire terriers, and this toy dog was a Yorkie. It played the tune "Puppy Love." Bell, the tank's ammo loader, had perched the toy on the bustle racks, figuring that if the dog survived, they would survive, too.

This was the fifth RPG to slam into the tank that morning, and now Bell feared the crew's luck was running out. The enemy fire was relentless. His crew had destroyed so many bunkers with main gun rounds that they were now completely out of HEAT and MPAT—the rounds best suited for collapsing bunkers and killing everyone inside. Their coax was jamming, too. In fact, the coax guns on Lieutenant Ball's tank and on Staff Sergeant Stevon Booker's tank were jamming, too. After considerable radio discussion, the crews realized that the problem wasn't the coax guns. It was the men operating them. It finally dawned on them that the brass trays— the metal hoppers that collected spent coax shells—were overflowing. Until they were emptied, the backup of shells would continue to jam the coax guns. The crews had never encountered the problem because they had never fired enough rounds to fill the hopper—not in training exercises, not during battles in the southern Iraqi desert, and not even on the Turkey Shoot against the Medina Division the day before. They dumped the trays on the turret floors, and the coax guns resumed firing with no further problems.

Just ahead of Sergeant Gaines's tank, on a tank designated Alpha One Three and nicknamed *Another Episode,* Staff Sergeant Booker was having .50-caliber problems that were not so easily resolved. The big machine gun kept jamming. Finally, it quit altogether, leaving Booker with a dilemma. Normally, he could have fired the .50-caliber with a remote trigger on the elevation handle even while protected inside the hatch. But now, with the gun malfunctioning, the tank would have one less weapon firing if Booker stayed down in the hatch. He decided instead to stay up top with his M-4 carbine. It meant he was exposed to enemy fire, but Booker wanted to keep dismounts away from his tank and Gaines's tank in front of him. He gave up on the .50-caliber. When the column stopped on Highway 8 to deal with the burning tank, Booker gave all his .50-caliber ammunition to another crew, trading it for M-240 and M-4 rounds.

Booker was a legendary figure in the battalion, and one of its most popular NCOs. He was a big, loud, demonstrative army lifer who loved being in the middle of things. He was the master of the outrageous wise-crack and the profane putdown, the kind of guy who could get even the officers laughing out loud, despite themselves. Booker's men were fond of him, though he drove them hard. They joked that you always heard Booker before you saw him. His booming voice was the first thing they heard every morning and the last thing they heard when they sacked out at night. None of them had been surprised to see Sergeant Booker up and exposed, pumping his .50-caliber, looking like he was enjoying himself.

At one point, Lieutenant Ball was stopped under an overpass and had his driver back up to a safer position. The driver didn't see Sergeant Booker's tank approaching, and the two tanks collided so hard that Booker's tank actually rode up the rear of Ball's tank. Ball said, "Oh, shit, I think I just hurt Three"—Booker. He got on the radio: "Sergeant Booker—you okay?" There was a long delay. Ball's gunner, Sergeant Jeffrey Ellis, braced for an outburst from Booker. He knew Booker better than just about any-body in the unit. They had roomed together back at Fort Stewart. Booker could get prickly if things went wrong. Finally, Booker's voice came over the net. He sounded calm. "I'm good, sir. Don't worry about me. I'm with you," he said.

Ellis realized that his former roommate, the man he called Book, was in *the zone,* that state of intense concentration brought on by sustained combat. Booker was a rabid Pittsburgh Steelers fan, and he tended to view combat as a higher form of athletics. Like an athlete, he got himself keyed up for game day. The thunder run was game day for the tankers. Booker loved action—he embraced it. When the company had received word the night before that they were going into Baghdad, Booker had punched Gaines in the arm and said, "About damn time!" Some of the younger soldiers were anxious and afraid, and Booker had tried to calm them. He reminded them that they would be inside Abrams tanks—virtually indestructible machines equipped with the most lethal weapons systems on any armored vehicle in the world. It was the enemy who should be worried, Booker said, not them. And Baghdad, he told them, was their ticket home. Once they took the capital, they were as good as on the plane back home to Fort Stewart.

That was Booker's public persona—brash, swaggering, confident. But sometimes he revealed a more reflective side. In his rare quiet moments, he talked about his mother and his girlfriend; he sent money to both back in the States. And early that morning, after grabbing a few minutes of sleep before guard duty, Booker had pulled aside his gunner, Sergeant David Gibbons, and confided that he'd had a nightmare about dying in battle. It disturbed him, he said, burdening his mind with nagging doubts he could not articulate. He told his loader, Private Joseph Gilliam, the same thing. Gilliam and Gibbons weren't sure if Booker was serious or just having a little fun with one of his elaborate put-ons. With Sergeant Booker, you could never tell.

Now, on the airport highway, Booker seemed consumed by the fight. He was leaning out of the hatch, firing his M-4 at dismounts crouched behind trees and shrubs along the roadway. Gilliam was up, too, working the loader's M-240 machine gun. He liked the way Booker allowed him to choose his own targets, unlike some tank commanders who tried to micromanage each shot. And Booker would talk to him, asking how he was doing, what he was hitting, like an assistant football coach working the sidelines. But now Booker yelled at Gilliam to get back down in the hatch. Rounds were pinging off the tank's armor. They had been fortunate so far, surviving two RPG hits on the right side. They had also withstood a second jarring collision when the driver accidentally backed into another tank, shearing off a bustle rack and losing Gilliam's rucksack with all his personal gear. But now the rate of enemy fire was intensifying.

Gilliam didn't want to leave his tank commander up there alone, and he protested. He was twenty-one, stocky and round-faced, a sweet-voiced young man from Raleigh, North Carolina, who had joined the army to get off the streets and inject some order and discipline into his life. Gilliam was in awe of Booker, who was thirty-four and who had treated Gilliam like a favored younger brother during the two years they had been together. Booker told Gilliam again to get down in the hatch, and Gilliam obeyed. As he climbed down, he heard Booker telling him, "I don't want to die in this country." They were just a few kilometers from the airport entrance.

Down in the loader's hatch, Gilliam could hear Booker's M-4 popping steadily. Suddenly Booker leaned down into the turret, sweaty and grinning. He hollered at Gilliam, "I just got four of 'em! I'm a *baaad* motherfucker!" Gilliam laughed and went back to jamming tank rounds into the breech for the gunner, Gibbons.

Gibbons was picking up the pace on the main gun, scanning for bunkers on his thermal sights, flicking the laser with his thumb, then sending a HEAT round on its way with a soft squeeze of his fingers against the cadillac triggers. In some strange way, he enjoyed what he was doing. It was fascinating to see the targets come up on the thermals, to watch an enemy soldier's sweaty face glow light green against the dark green background, to see the hot exhaust from an enemy troop carrier define the milky green rectangular shape of the vehicle. Gibbons and some of the other gunners had talked the night before about the exhilaration they had felt during the Turkey Shoot, when abandoned Iraqi tanks and artillery pieces just sat there, plump and gorgeous, and the searing HEAT rounds popped the tops on the tanks, sending the turrets spinning. It was just a big, expensive video game—and so much easier than in training. They had trained for desert warfare, where the targets were two or three kilometers away. The targets Gibbons was hitting now were just a few hundred meters away, so close that on the magnified scope the dismounts and bunkers seemed to be right next to the tank. Some of the dismounts would stand up right in the open. Gibbons would cut them in half with the coax and he and Booker would shake their heads and mutter, "What the hell are these guys *thinking?*"

Gibbons was twenty-two, a tall, gangly young man, more mature than most guys his age. He had been married for three years to a soldier in an army signal outfit. He had known Booker for two years, serving with him in Bosnia. He was impressed with the way Booker networked, the way he seemed to know everybody. Once, in Bosnia, Gibbons ran into a problem with his leave days. The bureaucracy said he had used them all up, but he knew he hadn't. Booker told him he'd take care of it. He talked to somebody who knew somebody and suddenly the problem was solved and Gibbons got his leave.

Now Gibbons was working the main gun and the coax, trying to keep the enemy fire off the column, and off Staff Sergeant Booker up top. As he concentrated on his thermal sights, he felt something bump him from behind. Often, Booker's feet would poke Gibbons in the back as Booker lowered himself into the hatch to reload or shout out orders. An Abrams tank commander stands above and behind the gunner, who fires from the gunner's seat on the floor of the turret. Gibbons felt the bump and heard Gilliam scream and curse. He glanced back at Gilliam, who had a stricken look.

Gilliam had been gathering up M-240 rounds to get back up top and help Booker suppress enemy fire. He had felt something heavy drop next to him and assumed Booker was coming down for more ammunition. Then he saw Booker's face. Part of it was gone—the whole cheek and jawbone. Booker's green Nomex jumpsuit was slick with blood. A heavy-machine-gun round had torn off part of his face. Gilliam let out a stream of curses. He didn't know why he was cursing. It just happened. He couldn't stop cursing.

Gibbons twisted around in the gunner's seat and saw Booker's ruined face and the mass of blood. Booker was slumped awkwardly, like someone had folded him over. Oh, God, Gibbons thought, Sergeant Booker is dead. Gibbons was stunned—and it seemed to him that Gilliam was in a state of shock. Booker's blood was all over Gilliam's Nomex. Gibbons pawed at Gilliam, checking for wounds. "You okay?" he asked. Gilliam seemed to refocus. "I'm good," he mumbled, but Gibbons wasn't so sure.

Gibbons got on the platoon net and radioed his platoon sergeant, Gaines, in the tank behind him. Gaines heard the call from Alpha One Three, but it was distorted by static. He thought it was Booker calling. Then he thought he heard a panicked voice say, "Three has been hit! Three is down!" *Booker's down?* Gaines radioed back, hoping to get a better transmission. He asked Gibbons for a sit rep, a situation report. Gibbons repeated, "Three is down."

Gaines called it up on the company net, to Captain Hilmes, the company commander. He said, very calmly, "Red Three is dead."

Monitoring the net in his armored personnel carrier, Major Nussio heard Hilmes report a TC KIA, a tank commander killed in action. It had to be bad, Nussio thought, for them to come right out and say a TC was dead. Usually they couched it, saying only that they had a man down. Nussio went through a process of elimination, trying to figure out who it was. Then Lieutenant Colonel Schwartz, the battalion commander, came on the net and asked for a name. "Alpha One Three," Hilmes said. He paused and added, "Sergeant Booker."

Men in combat feed off information. It sustains them. They want to know—they *need* to know—what is happening beyond their own intensely personal fields of fire. They crave any scrap of information that might somehow bring the broad sweep of the battle into focus. On this day, on this highway, the information flowing from the radio net had been relentlessly upbeat, a steady beat of kill reports: a bunker destroyed, dismounts down, a technical absolutely wasted. Some of the tankers felt the same giddy rush as the day before, when they had lit up the Medina Division on the Turkey Shoot.

The battalion—in fact, the whole brigade—had not lost a single man to enemy fire on the march up from Kuwait. Now, on the platoon net and then on the company net, came the first word of a KIA. Booker was down. Everybody knew Booker. He was larger than life, and it did not seem possible that such a man could be gone, and so swiftly. The information dropped on the crews like a hammer blow. The radio net fell silent.

Inside Alpha One Three, Gilliam and Gibbons considered trying buddy aid—the basic emergency first aid taught to all tankers: keep air passages open, apply pressure and elevation for bleeding. But it was hopeless. Booker didn't seem to be breathing. The bleeding was massive. Over the radio, Gibbons told Gaines, "He's dead." Gaines ordered Gibbons to prep the tank for a three-man crew. He was now the tank commander.

Gibbons knew he had to take control of the situation. They had trained for this day—trained for the sudden death of any crewman. They were still rolling. He had to reconfigure the tank so that he could get in the commander's hatch and still fire the main gun and coax with the override joystick. That was going to be difficult with Sergeant Booker still there in the turret. Gibbons would have to work around him because there would be no medevac until they reached the airport. He was trying to focus, try-ing to set aside the grief and shock he felt for his tank commander, a man he idolized—to put those feelings in a reservoir inside him and hold it for later. He knew he had to concentrate on getting the rest of the crew to the airport alive. Gaines was talking him through it over the radio, telling him to stay calm and let his training take over.

Hilmes called Gaines and asked if he was certain Booker was dead. "Does he have a pulse?" he asked. Hilmes did not doubt the crew's com-petence. He had always been impressed with the crisp, accurate reports delivered by Gaines's platoon, but it was his job to make sure they were absolutely certain about something as serious as a KIA.

As Gaines got back on the radio with Booker's crew, Gibbons heard Booker struggling to breathe. He was gurgling and wheezing. Gibbons told Gaines, "He's trying to breathe!" He requested a medevac.

Further back in the column, medical Specialists Joe Hill and Shaun Holland were in a medical track, a specially outfitted M113. Over the net, Gaines told them Booker was still breathing and ordered them to speed to the front of the column. Hill thought it was like the Red Sea parting, the way the tanks and Bradleys and tracks gracefully swung to the side to let the medical track push past them. They drove crazily, spinning and heav-ing. They found Alpha One Three, jerked to a stop, and dropped the rear ramp. Hill and Holland sprinted for the hatch, where Gibbons and Gilliam were struggling to lift Booker out of the narrow hatch. They heard auto-matic rifle rounds pinging off the tank hull.

The column was still stopped to deal with Booker when an RPG ripped into the front of a Bradley in Captain Burris's company. It hit just above the driver's hatch and exploded, blowing off the hatch. The impact stunned the driver, Private First Class Sean Sunday. His skin burning, he leaped out of the driver's hole and slammed awkwardly into the roadway, breaking his leg. He was in the middle of the road, exposed to enemy fire. Staff Sergeant Jeffery Empson jumped out of the trailing Bradley and dragged Sunday off the highway. He got him into the rear hull of the stricken Bradley and ordered one of the infantrymen—a soldier Empson knew had trained as a driver—to take over for Sunday in the driver's hole.

Now Schwartz had two medevacs to deal with. His entire column was halted and stretched along the airport highway. They were only a couple kilometers from the airport, but they were being hammered by the most intense barrage they had received all morning. They had also entered the most perilous stretch of terrain on the seventeen-kilometer journey, with trees and foliage obscuring the fields of fire along the median strip and on either side of the highway. Schwartz was desperate to get moving, and he pressed his commanders. The Bradley crews responded. They managed to get the damaged Bradley started again while Sunday was being stabilized. In a matter of minutes, the Bradley was back in the column and ready to haul Sunday to the airport for a medevac.

On his command track, Colonel Perkins had lost radio contact with Lieutenant Colonel Schwartz. He was concerned about the column's getting trapped and surrounded on the highway. He had his driver pull up behind Booker's tank, where the medical vehicle had just arrived. He was impressed that the driver of the medical vehicle had positioned the track in the line of fire to protect the medics and crewmen trying to evacuate Booker. A couple of medics were on top of the vehicle, firing M-16s.

Because of all the buildings along the airport highway, Perkins also had lost radio contact with the brigade command post south of the city. He radioed directly to the division command center at the airport and delivered a situation report to his superiors. He was confronted with a question he had not anticipated: "Do you want to turn back?" Perkins was stopped on the highway, under fire, and in danger of having sections of his column picked off and isolated. But he had no intention of turning around. He considered the thunder run the opening salvo in the battle for Baghdad. To turn back now would not only undermine the brigade's morale but, more important, provide the Iraqi regime with a psychological and strategic victory. He radioed back and told the division that he was moving forward.

On Alpha One Three, Gibbons had found the shoulder strap on Booker's Nomex jumpsuit and was yanking on it, trying to hand Booker off to medics Hill and Holland, who had scrambled up onto the main deck. Gilliam was trying to help, but he had climbed out of the turret without his helmet. Even in this situation, under fire and trying to get treatment for his mortally wounded sergeant, Gibbons surprised himself by noticing such a thing. He told Gilliam to go back down and get his helmet.

Holland asked for Booker's condition. "Half his face is gone and his stomach is hit, too," Gibbons said. Hill took a look and recoiled. It was awful. The medics got Booker out of the turret and onto a litter inside the medical track. They took off again, speeding for the airport, where the first sergeant had radioed ahead for a medevac helicopter. Booker was barely breathing. He had suffered massive wounds. Hill tried to take his pulse but most of Booker's right thumb and wrist was gone. The pulse on his left wrist was faint. Hill and Holland tried and failed to get an air tube down Booker's throat. They cut into his throat and inserted a tube, but it wasn't helping. Booker's lungs were full of blood.

A call came over the radio. The physician's assistant, Captain Mike Dyches, was coming up in his medical track. He would take over. Hill was relieved. Captain Dyches was high speed—he knew his stuff. If anybody could save Booker, the medics thought, it was Dyches. They stopped their track and the physician's assistant's track pulled alongside. Hill and Holland wanted to move Booker into Dyches's track, but when they lowered the ramp gunfire erupted from all directions. *Forget that,* Hill thought. Dyches and a medical sergeant dove into the back of Hill's track. The hatch slammed shut and they took off again for the airport. There wasn't much even Dyches could do for poor Booker. He tried, but Booker was in terrible shape. Finally Dyches got on the radio and said they could slow down now because Sergeant Booker was gone. The medics got the body bag out. Dyches didn't know what else to do, so he covered Booker's face and held his hand all the way in to the airport.

As soon as Gibbons and Gilliam had reconfigured Alpha One Three for a three-man crew, the driver, Private First Class Aaron Hofer, got the tank going again. Gilliam was numb and in shock, but he got back up on the loader's M-240 machine gun and prepared to get back to killing dismounts. That's what he would do, for the crew and for Sergeant Booker. Gilliam was up next to Gibbons, this time with his helmet on. First Sergeant Robert Hay, who had pulled up his track to lay down protective fire for Alpha One Three with his .50-caliber, saw Gibbons in the commander's hatch, trying to compose himself and take charge. Hay felt a little burst of pride. Gibbons was just a kid, but he was performing like a pro. Hay caught Gibbons's eye and gave him a thumbs up. Gibbons tried to look focused and decisive, but he still managed to nod and return the thumbs-up.

Alpha One Three's ordeal on the airport highway—the hit on Sergeant Booker, the initial KIA report, the thrall of hope when Booker's breathing resumed, the final crushing diagnosis by the physician's assistant—had all played out over the radio inside Charlie One One. Everybody in Lieutenant Gruneisen's makeshift crew knew Booker. You couldn't help but know Booker if you were in the Rogue battalion. He wouldn't let you *not* know him. It had been a miserable run for the crew, but until that moment no one had died—and now they heard that Sergeant Booker hadn't made it. Inside the turret, protected from the fight, no one spoke for several long minutes.

They were coasting into the stretch run, hatches locked down, listening to the steady beat of small-arms rounds against the hull, the shattering booms of main tank rounds and the thudding of Twenty-five Mike Mike from the Bradleys. The inside of the turret stank of stale sweat and the rotten-egg odor of the expended cannon aft caps. Diaz and Hernandez were smoking cigarettes, just sitting there, dejected and lost in thought. The first sergeant's voice came over the net: "We've got casualties."

At first, it sounded as though he were talking about Booker and Sunday. But those casualties were from Alpha Company and the Bradley company. This was First Sergeant Jose Mercado—*their* first sergeant, from Charlie Company. Captain Conroy couldn't hear him clearly and asked Mercado to repeat the transmission.

"Casualties," Mercado said again—in a PC, a personnel carrier.

Goddam, Gruneisen thought. Their guys—Chris Shipley, Diaz's original driver, and Don Schafer, Gruneisen's original loader—had been transferred to Mercado's PC.

A moment later, Mercado was back on the net: "Shipley and Schafer." Schafer had been hit in the arm and back, Shipley in the eye and arm. Nobody could believe it. It was like they were some kind of magnet for tragedy—the one-in-a-million shot on Diaz's tank, the raging fire, the wrong turns, the lost gear, and now Shipley and Schafer, who had started the run tucked safely inside tanks, not PCs. Gruneisen felt a sudden stab of anger and regret, and he cursed out loud. He felt helpless; Shipley and Schafer were his guys, and he wasn't there to help them. Inside the turret, he kept muttering, *Damn, damn, damn.*

Shipley and Schafer had been standing in the open rear hatch of the first sergeant's personnel carrier, firing on roadside bunkers with their M-4 carbines. Earlier, both men had helped try to put out the tank fire on the highway while also shooting at approaching Iraqis. They had jumped aboard the personnel carrier as the column was pulling away after Charlie

One Two had been abandoned. Shipley, who had been the driver on the abandoned tank, had no other ride. But Schafer, the loader on Lieutenant Gruneisen's tank, had been headed back to that tank when he saw that some of the Charlie One Two crewmen had already hopped aboard and filled all the spots. He felt that he had been wrongly usurped, and he was still angry about it as he fired from the personnel carrier. He was a tanker, and he wanted to be with his tank.

Schafer was on the personnel carrier, squeezing off a burst from his M-4, when something smacked him in the back. It felt like the kind of hard slap someone gives you when they try to surprise you and then run away. Then something went through his arm. He cried out, "Ow, my arm! What the hell!" Instinctively, Schafer reached out to steady himself and grabbed Ron Martz, an *Atlanta Journal-Constitution* reporter standing next to him. Schafer lifted his arm, and Martz held it. The reporter saw a tiny hole in Schafer's armpit, with crimson blood spurting from the wound. Schafer shouted, "I'm hit!" and he collapsed into Martz's arms. Both men tumbled to the deck.

Schafer saw that Shipley had been hit, too. Shipley was facedown on the deck, bright blood pumping from his face. He looked absently at his hands and saw blood gushing over them and failed to comprehend who was doing this to him or why. It was his last conscious thought, and he remembered nothing beyond that moment. An AK-47 round had torn through Shipley's Kevlar helmet, sliced through his head, and exploded out his right eye. Martz yelled for a medic—the first sergeant's vehicle was the medical track. Shawn Sullivan, a medic who had been firing his own weapon over the right side, bent down to help Shipley.

An AK-47 round had struck Schafer in the back, just off his spine. It had torn into his lung, out his side, and through his upper right arm, shattering the humerus. Schafer was on top of Martz, who had reached across him to hold Shipley's hand. Schafer asked Martz to hold his hand, and Martz squeezed it with his free hand. Sullivan was trying to treat both wounded men, but his medical equipment was trapped beneath a load of gear that had tumbled onto the deck during the firefight.

Schafer was having difficulty breathing. He told Martz he was about to black out.

"No! No!" Martz yelled. "Keep talking!"

Martz was no medical expert, but he knew enough to keep an injured person alert to stave off shock. He told Schafer that he was headed back to cold beer and cute nurses and a hot shower. Schafer said, "Sounds good to me," and he managed a weak smile.

Sullivan found a pressure dressing for Shipley's head wound, then found something to bandage Schafer. He yanked Schafer to his feet in order to get his combat vest off and cut off his uniform. Schafer bellowed in pain. Sullivan got a bandage on him, tied it with a strip of cloth torn from Schafer's uniform, and set him back down.

Martz squeezed Schafer's hand again, and he squeezed Shipley's, too. He felt fairly useless, and he regretted that he had not taken the time back in the States to enroll in a combat lifesaver's course. All he could do now was to keep squeezing and talking, squeezing and talking, as the carrier lumbered toward the airport.

Behind the PC, in Charlie One One, Gruneisen and his crewmen listened later to First Sergeant Mercado trying desperately to guide the track to the airport and a waiting medevac helicopter. The vehicles in the column were still being pounded by small arms and RPGs, but they managed to swing over to one side to let the first sergeant's track speed past them. But once Mercado reached the airport, no one could tell him over the radio how to reach the tarmac where the helicopters had landed. Mercado described a long wall that was blocking his way. He kept asking how to get around it. Nobody could tell him.

Later, listening to Mercado's pleas over the radio, Gruneisen and his men were frantic. They were overcome by feelings of helplessness and rage. Shipley and Schafer were hurt and bleeding—and nobody could find the medevacs. They rolled on, listening and wondering if their bleeding crewmates would ever reach the helicopters.

In the lead tank, Lieutenant Ball was approaching the airport entrance. He and his gunner were still firing at dismounts in the tree lines and on the overpasses. They were almost home free. Ball was relieved that they had not encountered more obstacles. All the platoon leaders had been warned by the S-2, the intelligence guys, to be prepared for mines or obstructions, but it seemed to Ball that the Iraqis had been caught by surprise and had not been expecting a column of tanks and armor to roll right up the main highway into Baghdad.

So far, all the Iraqis had thrown at them in the way of obstacles were a few RPG rounds wrapped in rags. They tossed them onto the highway, apparently believing that they would somehow explode and disable the American vehicles. The tanks and Bradleys rolled right over them, setting off muffled explosions, like polite little belches. The tracks lumbered on, unscathed.

At the final overpass before the airport, Ball saw something in the highway. As he rolled closer, he realized that the Iraqis had dragged concrete highway dividers across the westbound lanes. They were the kind of dividers he had seen on American interstates—what some people called Jersey dividers, after the New Jersey Turnpike. The dividers were about three and a half feet tall and perhaps a foot thick, with a broad, tapered base. Enemy dismounts and RPG teams were dug into fighting holes on either side of the columns supporting the overpass, and on the bridge were more gunmen. It was an ambush.

Ball slowed and radioed back a description of the barriers to Captain Hilmes, who asked if there was any way to bypass them. Ball looked again. The barriers were arranged in solid rows, blocking access to the shoulders on either side of the highway. It was a fairly effective blockade, a rare indication that someone in the Iraqi military actually had come up with something approaching a defensive strategy. Whether the blockage was designed to keep the Americans from breaking out of the airport to the west, or to block the Rogue battalion's charge from the east, was anybody's guess.

"There's no bypass," Ball told Hilmes. "I'm going to ram it and try to create a lane." He thought the tank's seven-ton plow, with its protruding lip and massive steel teeth, might hit the obstacle with such force that it would separate the barriers and allow the tank to crash on through. It seemed to him that the situation dictated brute force and a direct approach. Ball ordered his driver to speed up to forty kilometers per hour and look for "a soft spot." It was an odd choice of words, but it was the only way Ball could think of to describe any potentially vulnerable section on a hunk of solid concrete. The driver hollered back, "Sir, there's no soft spot. I'm just going to ram it."

The gunmen at the barricade opened up with small arms and RPGs. Ball's driver revved the engine and the tank chugged forward. Ball and the rest of the crew were buttoned up inside the turret, hatches locked. Everybody reached for something solid to brace against. The tank's front plow smacked into the barrier at forty kilometers per hour and pitched up. The tank rode up the obstacle, plunged forward, and went airborne. It sailed across the barrier and slammed down with a tremendous jolt. The crewmen rattled around inside the turret. In the driver's hole, the driver's helmet flew off. The plow was bent backward and the end connector on one of the tracks was hanging by two bolts, but the tank survived. Ball was astonished; he had never entirely believed the direct approach would work so well. The driver retrieved his helmet and kept the tank moving forward.

The Iraqis stopped firing, transfixed by the sight of a seventy-ton tank sailing through the air. Then they opened fire again, trying in vain to stop the column. But Ball's tank was pulling away and rolling toward the airport, bullets pinging off its hull. The impact of Ball's tank had sheared off the top of one of the barriers. That provided a lower obstacle for Gibbons. He was now commanding Sergeant Booker's tank equipped with its own mounted plow. Alpha One Three reached ramming speed and collided with the barrier, pitching up and over and slamming back down. The huge machine righted itself, the tracks biting into the pavement, and the tank chugged on toward the airport.

In the third tank, Specialist Joseph Kalinowski had watched from his driver's hole as both tanks in front of him sailed into and over the obstacle. He had been certain that the tanks' tracks were going to snap. He was amazed that they had held together. The barrier was being ground down, and it was by now only a couple of feet high, but Kalinowski was still worried about popping a track, even with a plow up front to absorb most of the impact. It would be just his luck, he thought, for his track to pop, leaving the tank disabled and surrounded by enemy gunmen.

In the commander's hatch, Sergeant First Class Gaines briefly considered flattening the rest of the barrier with a main gun round, but he knew there wasn't time. The entire column was starting to bunch up behind him. He ordered Kalinowski to hit the barrier. Kalinowski sped up to about sixteen kilometers per hour and slammed into the concrete. He hit the brakes and the tank rolled up and over. It landed with a heavy thud, driving Kalinowski's helmet into the driver's hatch and popping it open. The helmet flew off. Kalinowski was dizzy and disoriented, and it took him a few seconds to get his bearings. Then he threw his helmet back on, slammed the hatch shut, gunned the engines, and pulled away.

The barrier was slowly being ground to dust. Each subsequent tank pulverized what remained of the obstacle, and soon the Bradleys and the M113s were grinding and crunching over the mess, harassed by small-arms fire. They were now less than a kilometer from the airport entrance.

Lieutenant Ball was in the stretch run now, clanking toward the airport entrance, still under fire, when his gunner screamed, "Identify tanks!" He had spotted the outlines of tanks through his thermals, the hot engines lighting up in a bright green glow. *Now what?* Intelligence officers had warned tank commanders that some Iraqi units still had functioning tanks under their commands. Ball knew he was within the kill range of a Soviet-made T-72. He ordered his gunner to prepare to fire, then radioed Captain Hilmes: "Contact! Tanks—direct front!"

Hilmes was starting to wonder if this thunder run was ever going to end. "Can you identify if they're enemy or friendly?" he asked. He told Ball to take his time and make a positive identification.

Over the net, Schwartz asked the same question. Schwartz's first thought had been, *So* that's *where they've been hiding their tanks.* But now he was more concerned about friendly fire than a few outdated relics of Soviet armor. With Ball so close to the airport, Schwartz was terrified that he might accidentally blow away one of the First Brigade's Abrams tanks. "Don't pull a trigger until you confirm!" he ordered.

As Ball rolled closer, he could see through his sights that the tanks were low, sleek, and painted desert tan. They were Abrams tanks—the lead element of the First Brigade, manning the airport entrance. Ball took a deep breath. He ordered the gunner to lift the main gun tube to alert the First Brigade tankers to friendly tanks approaching.

Farther back in the column, the battalion operations officer, Major Donovan, had just made radio contact with the First Brigade battalion at the airport entrance to warn that the column was heading in. Donovan was relieved to hear the familiar voice of the operations officer from one of the First Brigade battalions, Major Rod Coffey, an old buddy from a previous assignment.

Ball's tank rumbled on, its gun tube raised. From the tree lines, and from more bunkers along the highway, enemy gunfire intensified. As the tank passed through the airport entrance, past the First Brigade tanks, the gunfire stopped abruptly. Each passing tank and Bradley had the same experience—a final, furious burst of automatic rifle fire and RPGs, then silence. It was like turning off a faucet. They were home free.

On the airport tarmac, the crew of Charlie One One popped the hatch and came out for air. Their faces were smeared with black grime from the fire. Their eyes were red and burning, and the backs of their throats were coated with the fumes of seared chemicals. There was a foul, bitter taste in their mouths—a taste they would remember for months afterward. But as miserable as they felt, they felt worse about Booker, and about Shipley and Schafer. Lieutenant Gruneisen pulled everybody together and ordered the crew to account for all sensitive items, especially those they had tossed on the first sergeant's vehicle or had been retrieved from Highway 8 by the first sergeant's crew. In addition to their personal gear, they had lost their sponson box, the big metal box that held all the tools needed to maintain and repair the tank. They felt defeated and bereft.

The lieutenant, Diaz, and Hernandez went to find out about Shipley and Schafer; they had heard over the radio that the first sergeant had finally located the medevac Black Hawk helicopters after Lieutenant Ball had the other lead vehicles clear the barricades. The three men jogged across the tarmac to the ambulance exchange point. Tanks and Bradleys were still pouring in from the highway. Diaz was shocked at the sight of them. It was the first time he realized just how fierce the fight had been. Every vehicle was shot up with dents and holes and jagged scrapes that peeled the tan paint back. They were leaking oil and hydraulic fluid and trailing smoke from burning bustle racks. A couple of tracks were streaked with blood. There was shattered glass from the windshields of cars that had rammed the tanks and thousands of expended brass ammunition casings that sparkled in the morning sunlight. Diaz ran past the bullet-pocked medic tracks and saw Sergeant Booker's body bag, still and lonesome in the deep shade of the open hatch.

They found the Black Hawk medevacs. One chopper had just taken off with Schafer aboard. The medics had Shipley on a stretcher, strapping him down for the Black Hawk ride to the mobile surgical hospital tent at the brigade operations center eighteen kilometers south of Baghdad. Gruneisen ran up and tried to talk to Shipley. The private's arm was still bleeding and his eye was covered with a bulky bandage. He was conscious but groggy. Gruneisen asked how he was doing, and Shipley mumbled something. Gruneisen grabbed Shawn Sullivan, the young medic, and looked him in the eye. He asked about the condition of his two soldiers. He wanted an honest answer. Sullivan said, "They're both stable. They're gonna be all right." The three tankers walked back to their tank and collapsed in the shade of the turret. Gruneisen waited for a wave of emotion, something like relief or despair or sorrow. But he didn't feel a thing.

The rest of the column was rumbling in and lining up, motor pool–style, on the tarmac. The crews piled out, their Nomex jumpsuits dark with sweat. Some of them searched the scorched bustle racks for undamaged boxes of water. Caught up in the battle, they had forgotten to drink, and now they were severely dehydrated. They had lost all track of time. Some of the crewmen thought they had been fighting for most of the day; they thought it was mid-afternoon. Actually, it was mid-morning. The battle had lasted just over two hours and twenty minutes.

On the third tank in, Joe Bell was drained and exhausted, but he got out and searched the bustle rack for the toy dog his wife had sent him. He found it, slightly scorched but still upright. He squeezed the toy, and out came the silly, sweet strains of the pop tune "Puppy Love."

On Alpha One Three, Gibbons and Gilliam and Hofer were badly shaken. The stress of reconfiguring the tank after Booker had gone down, of trying to fight through relentless enemy attacks with a three-man crew, had kept them focused on the mission. They had been compelled to focus, to function, in order to stay alive. They had not had the luxury of thinking about Sergeant Booker and what it meant not to have him beside them anymore. Now, in the relative calm and quiet of the tarmac, the terrible reality of what had happened crushed them. Gilliam was in the worst shape. For a long time, he couldn't get out of the tank. He sat inside the turret, head down, staring, crouched in the dark with Sergeant Booker's blood splattered everywhere. After a while he climbed out and sat on the tarmac and smoked one cigarette after another. He would not feel whole again until much later, after he had talked to the battalion chaplain and then, much later, after he had relived every sight, sound, and smell during therapy sessions with the army shrinks. He decided right there on the tarmac that he was not going to reenlist, and he wasn't going back into Baghdad.

Colonel Perkins, joined by Captain Hilmes, walked over to Gibbons and Gilliam. The two crewmen leaped to their feet and saluted. Perkins saw that they were still smeared with Booker's blood. He returned their salutes—it was his honor to salute them, he told them—and he said he had never been more proud of any two men. He told them they had played a central role in helping the battalion achieve a defining moment in military history.

Jeffrey Ellis, the gunner who had roomed with Booker, went over to say good-bye to his friend. He found Book's body bag in the hull of the medic's track, and he had a quiet little conversation with his old friend. The two of them had always talked about taking a cruise after the war, just sailing off to Bermuda or Cancún, someplace warm with lots of cold beer. Now Ellis told Book that he would take the cruise for him. He cried a little bit, and that made him feel better. He said good-bye and told Book as he left, "I'll drink a beer for you."

To spare Booker's young crew the ordeal of cleaning up the mess inside their tank, one of the lieutenants from Second Platoon came over with a couple of soldiers carrying buckets and rags and sponges. It was important to get the tank cleaned up right away, before the rest of the battalion came by and saw the whole awful splash of blood and tissue. It took a long time. The inside of a tank turret is a cramped place, with crevices and levers and handles. But finally the lieutenant, Ryan Kuo, and his platoon sergeant, Eric Olson, got it all cleaned out, and the tank was good to go.

Across the tarmac, Captain Hilmes had run over to the medical track that held the bagged remains of Sergeant Booker. He saw the physician's assistant, Mike Dyches, sitting on the ramp and shaking his head. "There was nothing I could do for him," he told Hilmes.

The captain let his emotions rise up and overflow. He didn't try to stop them. He had known Booker for three years. Booker was more than just his best platoon sergeant—he was a good and loyal friend. Hilmes looked up and saw Rick Schwartz, his face caked with tan dust.

"Sir," he said, "Sergeant Booker is dead." And he began to weep. Schwartz put his arms around Hilmes and led him away. Schwartz had fought in the first Gulf War, and he knew what it meant to lose a comrade.

Hilmes was crying, but not just for Booker. He was crying because he felt guilty—guilty for feeling so relieved to have survived, and guilty for the elation that had swept over him as he brought his soldiers back alive, save for one man. It was a confusing, conflicted feeling, and it overwhelmed him. He wouldn't feel right about the whole thing until days later, after he had written a long letter to Booker's mother, after he and his men had sat around and traded stories about Booker, and after he had delivered a eulogy at Booker's memorial service without breaking down.

American military doctrine says tanks cannot fight effectively in an urban environment, but Rogue's thunder run had stood doctrine on its head. The armored column's fight up the highway had shown that, on this day and under these circumstances, tanks could not only fight in urban areas, but prevail. The Desert Rogues battalion had just killed between eight hundred and a thousand enemy soldiers. They had destroyed whole networks of bunkers on both sides of the highway. They had taken out thirty to forty vehicles and unknown numbers of artillery pieces and antiaircraft batteries. It had cost them one dead, several wounded, a burned-out tank, a busted turret, and a damaged Bradley. Schwartz was convinced that they had rattled the Iraqi leadership, hitting their forces in a way they had not expected. They had exposed the limits of Baghdad's defensive fortifications. And now, he knew, they would have to ratchet up the pressure, to go back in for more.

Perkins knew it, too. On the tarmac, Schwartz had saluted Perkins and told him, "Mission accomplished." The two commanders exchanged an awkward hug, their bulky flak vests bumping. Perkins told Schwartz that the next time they came up Highway 8, they were going straight downtown to the palaces. Schwartz gave Perkins a sharp look. This time, he believed him.

At a Republican Guard command center north of the airport highway that morning, Brigadier General Mohammed Daash was dispatched by his commander to check out a report of fighting at the airport. The center had no radio communications with Iraqi units at the airport, and no one knew the situation there. To guard against coup attempts, Saddam Hussein had balkanized his armed forces. Each military unit had a separate chain of command, unconnected to any other unit. The Republican Guards and Special Republican Guards commanded by Quasi Hussein did not communicate with the regular army, which did not communicate with Uday Hussein's Fedayeen Saddam or the Baath Party militia. In fact, the units competed for resources—for the best weapons, the choice supplies, the rare working radios and cell phones. The only glue binding these competing armies were the Saddam cronies and loyalists placed in charge—many of them tribesmen from Saddam's hometown of Tikrit.

For commanders like General Daash, the only source of information at this moment of crisis was the government's bombastic minister of information, Mohammed Said al-Sahaf. That very morning, Sahaf appeared at the Palestine Hotel wearing his trademark beret and pistol. He told the international news media that Iraqi forces had repulsed an American attack, that the airport was still in government hands. But now Daash was told that three or four American tanks had been spotted at the airport. He was ordered to conduct a surveillance mission and report back. He had to find a military vehicle and persuade the driver to venture out into the streets.

Less than an hour later, Daash returned to headquarters in a panic. He stormed through the offices, cursing his fellow commanders. "Four or five tanks!" he yelled. "Are you out of your minds? The whole damn American army is at the airport!"

F I V E
THE PLAN

At the Baghdad airport on the morning of April 5, Major General Buford C. Blount III had watched the progress of the thunder run on Blue Force Tracker, the satellite communications system that depicts friendly forces as blue icons on a computer screen. Blount, a tall, laconic southerner known to close friends as Buff, was the Third Infantry Division commander. He had been up at the airport entrance all morning, ready to send out a rescue battalion from his First Brigade if the Rogue battalion had been overrun. Blount had watched on his screen as the column stopped to deal with the burning tank and when it took the wrong turns at the spaghetti junction. Every time the column slowed or stopped, Blount worried that Iraqi soldiers and Arab guerrillas would cut it in two and isolate a company or a platoon and hammer it. *Another Mogadishu*—that's what he and Dave Perkins had talked about avoiding, and so far they had pulled it off.

Now, as the tankers and the Bradley crews rested in the shade of their battered vehicles, Blount stood on the tarmac next to Perkins and plotted his next move. Blount wanted to keep the pressure on Saddam's regime. He knew the Iraqis would reinforce Highway 8. He knew they would dig in and defend the capital. The Fedayeen Saddam, the Arab volunteers, and some Special Republican Guards—there were several thousand of them still in and around the city—had fought ferociously, even as some Republican Guard and regular army units were throwing off their uniforms and fleeing. Blount expected them to mine the highway and erect barricades.

Fifty-four years old, with thirty-two years in the army, Blount had spent virtually his entire adult life as a tanker—ever since he was commissioned as an armor officer after graduating from the University of Southern Mississippi in 1971. The military was in his blood. His father had been an air force colonel—Buford Blount II was now the mayor of little Bassfield, Mississippi—and an uncle had been an army general. Buff Blount had earned a master's degree in national security and strategic studies, and he believed tanks could do more than a lot of people assumed. They had proved themselves in the south, where they had blown past the main cities and raced directly to Baghdad. They had proved themselves again that morning, ramming past a determined enemy dug in at the edge of a sprawling metropolis and fighting off speeding vehicles on a superhighway. Now Blount wanted to maintain momentum and send his tanks and Bradleys right back into the city.

The general had seen intelligence suggesting that Special Republican Guard units were being sent into Baghdad to reinforce the capital. But in truth, he really didn't have good intelligence. It was too dangerous to send in scouts. Satellite imagery didn't show bunkers or redoubts inside buildings, or camouflaged armor or artillery. Blount's division had access to only one unmanned spy drone, and its cameras weren't providing a whole lot either. Enemy prisoners of war in Najaf and Karbala had told U.S. interrogators that the Iraqi military was expecting American tanks to surround the city with what the Americans called FOBs—forward operating bases—while infantry from the 82nd Airborne and 101st Airborne cleared the capital block by block. And that *was* the U.S. plan, at least until the thunder run that morning changed the equation. The Iraqi quartermaster colonel the battalion had captured that morning was saying the same thing. One of the Arabic translators had just told Blount and Perkins that the colonel had believed his own military's propaganda—that U.S. forces had been stopped cold south of the Euphrates River. Until the very moment that he drove his Passat into a Bradley, the colonel had been convinced that his army was *winning*.

Blount wanted another thunder run, and quickly. He thought his superiors at V Corps would agree, especially after Rogue's charge up the highway that morning. Blount told Perkins that he might send him back into the city in two days, on Monday the seventh. Instead of one battalion, Blount was considering sending in the entire Second Brigade, with two tank battalions and a mechanized infantry battalion. Blount wanted them to test the city's defenses, kill as many troops and equipment as possible, then come back out to prepare for more thunder runs and, ultimately, the siege of the capital. That morning, he sent the proposal up to V Corps and the rest of the chain of command for approval.

At midday, the Rogue column lined up for the short trip back to the brigade operations center south of the city. The crews took the back way, down a secured highway—Highway 1—that led south and east from the airport. The brigade had seized the intersection of Highways 1 and 8 two days earlier and had set up the command post there because the interchange controlled access from the south to the city and the airport. It had been the staging area for Rogue's thunder run that morning, and now it would be the starting point for any subsequent strike into Baghdad's city center, eighteen kilometers north.

As Perkins rode down Highway 1 in his command vehicle, he thought about the best way to put his tanks and Bradleys into the city. Even before talking to Blount, he had anticipated another thunder run. He welcomed the opportunity. Like Blount, he didn't accept the conventional wisdom that tanks were at a disadvantage in urban terrain. That morning's thunder run was proof of that. He was eager to go back into the city, but not for a thunder run. He wanted to stay.

Perkins was a calm, patient, perceptive New Englander with a deceptively placid demeanor. He was six feet tall and, like most tankers, slight of build. He had a smooth face and rosy cheeks that made him look younger than forty-four. But Perkins also had the grave and studious manner—focused, curious, intent on results—of a much older man. He was a devout Catholic, with a wife and a teenaged son and daughter at Fort Stewart. His wife, Ginger, sent him regular issues of *Our Daily Bread* devotionals, which he tried to read daily.

A native of Keene, New Hampshire, he was a West Point officer, graduating in 1980 and commissioned as an armor officer. While in the military, he had attended graduate school at the University of Michigan. He had had a taste of Washington politics in the mid-'90s, accepting a military fellowship to serve on the staff of House Speaker Newt Gingrich. Perkins advised Gingrich's staff on how to apply the military model for organizing a staff and assigning responsibility during a volatile political era in Washington. And although Perkins had served on peacekeeping missions in Macedonia and Kosovo, he had never been in combat prior to crossing the berm into Iraq. He taught mechanical engineering at West Point during Operation Desert Storm, watching the war on CNN like everybody else. Now, rolling down Highway 1, he figured he probably had just one day to devise a tactical plan for a brigade-sized thunder run into a hostile Arab capital of 5 million people.

At the brigade command tent a few hours later, an American reporter asked Perkins what Rogue's thunder run had accomplished. As the brigade commander, Perkins was the unit's chief spokesman. Part of his job was dealing with the media—and with the Pentagon's new embedded-reporter experiment, reporters were always around, asking questions, probing for information. Perkins tended to speak in interviews the same way he spoke to his commanders—in spare, logical, pointed sentences. He told the reporter that the attack was more than just a tactical victory. It was also a "psychological blow," he said, "a way to showcase our ability to go anywhere in the city at any time. The world saw today that the American army is in fact *not* bogged down. We hold the airport and the main highway into the city." He mentioned Saddam Hussein. "This is supposed to be *his* city. But we just got here—and we drove right through it. No part of the city is safe for him anymore."

The reporter asked Perkins about civilian casualties, an issue that was receiving considerable attention in the international media. Some of his tankers had said, without equivocation, that civilians had been killed on Highway 8—either caught in crossfires or fired on when their vehicles failed to heed warnings to stop. Perkins didn't deny it. He blamed the Iraqis for attacking with civilian cars—taxis, sedans, pickups, even ambulances— and for dressing many of their fighters in civilian clothing. "The de facto uniform of combatants here is civilian clothes, so we have to judge people on the battlefields by their actions, not their clothing," he said. "They are putting their populace at risk by not having a clear delineation between civilians and the military. In effect, Saddam has made his civilian populace combatants." He spoke without rancor, and with little evident emotion until he suddenly mentioned his wife and children. "If I put my family in a Humvee and drove them into Baghdad," he said, "I would be to blame if they got blown away."

At the brigade command tent, Perkins reviewed the morning's thunder run with Lieutenant Colonel Eric Wesley, his executive officer. Wesley was a brisk, intense, highly organized officer from southern California, and a committed Christian. Both his father and grandfather had been military men. A West Point graduate, he had been involved almost his entire career in the Officers' Christian Fellowship, a group that helps Christian officers integrate their faith and their profession. He was married and had three young children.

Like Perkins, Wesley had never been in combat before arriving in Iraq; he had been taking an armor officer advanced course at Fort Knox during Operation Desert Storm. Wesley, thirty-nine, had been with the division since 1998, working his way up from battalion operations officer to deputy division operations officer, and finally to brigade executive officer. He had a master's degree in international relations and had spent time in a psychological operations unit. He had been thinking about Iraq—and how to best wage war there—for years, ever since the first Gulf War in 1990. He and Perkins shared similar convictions about the use of armor and the importance of training units to synchronize their movements under simulated battlefield conditions.

Now Wesley was Perkins's right-hand man and confidant. The two officers had been discussing the best way to attack Baghdad for more than six months—since arriving in Kuwait for desert training and prewar planning the previous autumn. It had been to a certain extent an academic exercise, for the role envisioned for the Spartan Brigade was to set up a blocking position at the edge of the capital while infantry and Special Forces cleared the city. But regardless of which units were ultimately designated to take the city, they thought, it should be done not in a slow siege but in a single, violent strike.

Perkins had attended a major military planning conference in Kuwait in January, in which the Forward Operating Base (FOB) model was adopted: armored units would surround Baghdad at strategically located forward bases while airborne infantry conducted raids designed to steadily destroy enemy resistance. Perkins and Wesley were not fans of the approach. It reminded them too much of Vietnam, where U.S. forces bunkered themselves into forward bases and conducted endless thrusts and patrols that left them bogged down and forever under siege. It didn't make sense to keep advancing and retreating, seizing ground only to give it up. They believed that once enemy terrain is seized, it should be held. To retreat not only magnified the loss of life and equipment required to seize terrain, but it also allowed the enemy to portray any withdrawal as a defeat.

Wesley had been monitoring BBC radio that morning to find out how the news of the thunder run was playing. He had listened to al-Sahaf, Iraq's information minister, deliver a taunting news conference at the Palestine Hotel on the east bank of the Tigris, just six kilometers from where Robert Ball had made the wrong turn off the spaghetti junction. Sahaf claimed that no American forces had entered the city and that Iraqi troops had slaughtered hundreds of American "scoundrels" at the airport.

"Today, we butchered the force present at the airport," Sahaf had said. "We are hitting them with rockets and artillery and surprising them with operations that I said are new"—apparently a reference to suicide cars and trucks. "Today, the tide has turned," he went on. "We are destroying them." Sahaf instructed Iraqi civilians to alert the armed forces to any American troop movements and to maintain "calm, good organization—to confront the enemy effectively, conquer them and force them to retreat accursed and defeated."

Wesley related Sahaf's outlandish claims to Perkins. He also told him that the BBC was reporting that its reporters had not seen any American tanks in Baghdad that morning, and had concluded that there had been no American presence inside the capital. Perkins pursed his lips and shook his head. Sahaf was starting to irritate him. It galled him that his soldiers had driven so hard to penetrate the city, only to have a buffoon in a beret belittle them to the world. And the BBC wasn't even disputing Sahaf's rants. Worse, Perkins thought, enemy fighters who had not actually seen his brigade's tanks that day would now believe their own propaganda. That only motivated them to fight harder in a doomed cause. He felt like driving his tanks up to the Ministry of Information in the city center to shut Sahaf up.

Perkins looked at Wesley and said, "You know, this just changed from a tactical war to an information war. We need to go in and stay." At that moment, before a formal order had even been issued, the Spartan Brigade began planning not only to strike fast and deep into Baghdad, but also to stay there and dig in. The top brass expected the brigade's tank battalions to sprint in and then sprint out, but Perkins and Wesley thought they could change the thinking of their superiors once the battalions were established inside the city. They had no intention of turning around after fighting their way into the city. They were going to topple Saddam's regime from within.

That evening, as Perkins had expected, Blount called him from the airport and said the thunder run had been approved for Monday, April 7. Perkins was ordered to take his tanks and Bradleys into the city center, show that American forces could penetrate to the very heart of Saddam's regime, then pull out. It was to be another recon by fire, with the strategic goal of demonstrating to the world that American troops not only were in the Iraqi capital but were able to come and go as they pleased. It would be the first time the brigade's three maneuver battalions were in combat on the same battlefield simultaneously. It was up to Perkins to develop a tactical plan to make it happen.

Rogue's thunder run had taught him two important lessons. First, the interchanges were critical. Perkins didn't want snipers and technicals firing down on his men from the overpasses on this mission. He decided to pound the four main interchanges between the command post and the city center with artillery that would be fired just ahead of the column. Second, momentum had to be maintained—even at the risk of losing a tank. If a vehicle were disabled by enemy fire or mechanical problems, they weren't going to waste time trying to get it going again. If it was burning out of control, they would abandon it. If not, they would tow it right away.

Perkins was still upset about abandoning Charlie One Two—and the issue wasn't entirely settled. V Corps, the brigade's higher command, wanted the air force to bomb the tank to prevent the Iraqis from learning anything about the inner workings of an Abrams. The brigade argued against it, saying the tank had been stripped of all sensitive items—and a demolished tank could be offered by the Iraqis as proof that their forces had destroyed it. Wesley and others believed they could eventually recover the tank. V Corps won out. An air force fighter first tried to bomb the tank that evening—and missed—but then scored a direct hit with a Maverick missile. The next day, minders from Sahaf's Ministry of Information escorted foreign journalists down Highway 8 to Charlie One Two. The reporters interviewed Iraqi soldiers who claimed they had singlehandedly destroyed the tank. The camera crews got dramatic footage of Iraqis dancing and celebrating on the tank's decks. But even after the fire, after the HEAT round from Shane Williams and after the Maverick missile, Charlie One Two still looked like an intact Abrams tank. In dark letters stenciled onto the gun tube was a clearly marked message: *Cojone Eh?*

That night, Perkins and Wesley sat down with the brigade's planners. They came up with a list of objectives—key "nodes," as they called them—that were to be seized and held. It was like planning a Third World coup: you take the presidential palace, the top ministries, the TV station, the security headquarters . . . and boom, the government falls. In the case of Baghdad, these nodes were conveniently centralized in or around Saddam's palace complex, a walled city within a city about three kilometers long and a kilometer and a half wide. Ordinary Iraqis had never seen the complex, which lay in a restricted and heavily guarded zone wrapped around a bend in the Tigris River. Hidden behind its walls were Saddam's main palace and executive seat of government, the massive Republican Palace, which was topped by four, thirteen-foot-high bronze busts of Saddam wearing an elaborate pith helmet. Smaller palaces and mansions contained homes and offices of the Baath Party and Republican Guard elite, all set on manicured lawns and landscaped grounds graced by rose beds and swaying palms.

At the edge of the complex were Saddam's military parade field and reviewing stand, flanked on either end by enormous crossed sabers held by fists said to be modeled on a cast of Saddam's own hands. At the base were scattered hundreds of green helmets taken from fallen Iranian soldiers during the Iran-Iraq war of the 1980s. Many of the helmets were embedded into the pavement like cobblestones. Nearby were Iraq's tomb of the unknown soldier, Baath Party headquarters, the Ministry of Information, another ornate palace built by Saddam a decade earlier, the convention center, and the Rashid Hotel, a meeting place of the Baath Party leadership. All reflected Saddam's love of the severe and forbidding neo-Stalinist architectural style.

The targets had been selected not only for their strategic value as the power centers of the Iraqi regime, but also because they were in open terrain. The palace complex consisted of broad boulevards, gardens, and parks—and very few tall buildings or narrow alleyways that could conceal enemy positions. The tank battalions would be able to set up defensive positions, with open fields of fire in all directions. Blount and Perkins did not want a repeat of Mogadishu, where U.S. forces were trapped and picked off in dense urban slums. The armored column had distinct advantages over the lightly armed Rangers and Delta Force soldiers who had conducted the Mogadishu raid. There would be no soft-skinned vehicles like the Humvees and trucks devastated by RPG explosions in Mogadishu. The tanks and Bradleys and armored personnel carriers had proven, with the exception of Charlie One Two, that they could withstand anything the Iraqis threw at them.

Eric Schwartz's Desert Rogues battalion was assigned the targets just beyond the walled complex. Because Rogue was familiar with Highway 8—and with the main highway leading into the city center, thanks to the wrong turns that morning—it would take the lead. The battalion was ordered to race up Highway 8, follow the Qadisiya Highway into the city center, and seize the parade field and reviewing stand, Baath Party head-quarters, the tomb of the unknown soldier, and other targets.

Everything inside the palace complex, including the Republican Palace, was assigned to the Tusker battalion—the Fourth Battalion, Sixty-fourth Armor Regiment, and the core unit of Task Force 4-64. Tusker would follow the Desert Rogues battalion into the city, peeling off just past the spaghetti junction onto the Kindi Highway and straight into the palace complex. In the heart of the Tusker sector was the Four-teenth of July Bridge, which controlled access to the city center from the south. The bridge also had symbolic value. Named for the day in 1958 that Baathists overthrew King Faisal II, it was Baghdad's first suspen-sion bridge. The battalion intended to block the bridge by seizing and holding a traffic circle at the base of the elevated roadway, where a mas-sive stone arch led into the palace complex. They also planned to seize the Sujud Palace, an ugly cement and granite structure built in 1990 and referred to by the brigade planners as the "new palace," to distinguish it from the older, larger Republican Palace one and a half kilometers to the east.

The Tusker commander was Lieutenant Colonel Philip Draper deCamp, nicknamed Flip, a fast-talking extrovert from Georgia. DeCamp was forty-one, trim and compact in the tanker tradition, with a ruddy com-plexion and a crooked smile. Blessed with enormous energy, deCamp was never still. He rarely seemed to require sleep. He was a drive-by conver-sationalist; he would often discuss several topics at once, bouncing from one to the next in a free-form monologue. Reporters embedded with the Tusker battalion could count on deCamp for vivid quotes and high-speed verbal gymnastics. He was a highly intelligent officer, with a bachelor's degree in physics from the University of Georgia and a Ph.D. in industrial engineering from Georgia Tech. DeCamp had an impish sense of humor and loved a good joke. Some of his officers, overwhelmed by his frenetic personality, joked that deCamp suffered from adult-onset attention defi-cit disorder. But deCamp became a different person in combat, where he was aggressive and focused, his orders loud but also clear and instructive.

DeCamp had a rich military pedigree. Both grandfathers were West Point graduates, in 1917 and 1929. One, Philip Draper, was an All-American tailback and a basketball point guard for Army teams who retired as a two-star general. DeCamp's father was a two-star general and a professor at West Point, and two uncles were West Point graduates. His older brother was an army tanker colonel. Like Schwartz, deCamp had served in the first Gulf War as a tank company commander.

While the Rogue battalion was fighting its way to the airport that day, deCamp had directed Tusker's spirited charge southeast against the remains of the Medina Division. His men had destroyed more than a dozen T-72 tanks, thirteen armored personnel carriers, and twenty technicals, effectively completing the destruction of the Republican Guards' finest division. Now he was trying to get them ready for another charge, this time into the city.

For the attack on Baghdad, Perkins wanted the two tank battalions to create chaos, to strike with such violence and speed that the regime would be incapable of a coherent response. He believed his men had the requisite training and the equipment to operate successfully on a chaotic battlefield. And he knew from that day's thunder run that the Iraqi military had poor command and control. It was clear from the haphazard, if intense, resistance on Highway 8 that many units were unable to talk to one another—or, if they could, they didn't listen. Perkins doubted the ability of Saddam and his military commanders to deploy troops and mount an effective defense, especially after two weeks of pounding by coalition aircraft.

While Perkins was confident that the two tank battalions could hold their ground inside the city, he knew they could not survive without a steady supply of fuel and ammunition. Each tank would suck down 56 gallons of JP8 fuel an hour just rolling up Highway 8 and at least 30 gallons an hour maneuvering inside the city. With a 504-gallon capacity, the tanks would probably need refueling by the end of the day. And based on Rogue's experience on the thunder run, the tank and Bradley crews could expect to fire off most of their ammunition loads as they blasted their way into the city and fought to hold their ground.

No army survives without secure lines of supply. The American march up from Kuwait, in fact, had been slowed by Fedayeen attacks on the vulnerable supply trains trailing the armor columns. For the attack on Baghdad, Highway 8 itself would be the supply line. It was the all-important LOC—pronounced "lock"—the line of communications. It was the only direct route into and out of the city. If the highway wasn't secured, the tank battalions could not spend the night—and they would have to fight their way out while low on fuel and ammunition.

Perkins assigned the job of keeping Highway 8 open to Lieutenant Colonel Stephen Twitty, commander of the brigade's mechanized infantry battalion, nicknamed China, the Third Battalion, Fifteenth Infantry Regiment, and the core of Task Force 3-15. The China battalion would follow the two tank battalions up Highway 8, dropping combat teams at each of three main interchanges. The teams would clear and hold the intersections, keeping open the crucial ten-kilometer stretch of Highway 8 between the brigade command post and the spaghetti junction. The battalion planners, apparently in a jocular mood, had code-named the interchanges Objectives Moe, Larry, and Curly. Once Highway 8 was secured, trucks and tankers loaded with ammunition and fuel would be waiting near the brigade command post for the order to speed north into the city center to supply the tank battalions.

Twitty was in the middle of a firefight south of the brigade operations center on the afternoon of April 6 when he got a radio call from Perkins telling him that he had a mission for him. Perkins didn't say what the mission was; he wanted Twitty to send someone to receive it in person. Twitty pulled his operations officer, Major Roger Shuck, away from the battle to go see Perkins. He couldn't go himself because his battalion had not quite finished destroying the remnants of the Medina Division's Fourteenth Brigade, which was putting up a bit of a fight and actually had crews still manning several T-72 tanks. It took the rest of the afternoon to kill them off.

The fight was still under way when Shuck radioed to tell Twitty that the brigade was attacking into Baghdad the next morning—and that China had been ordered to secure Highway 8. Twitty was surprised to hear that tanks were going into the city. Like other commanders in the brigade, he had been told that airborne units would clear the capital. But he was not surprised to be told that China would go in behind the tank battalions. His guys were infantry, and what infantrymen did was clear and hold ground. They had been ordered two days earlier to hold a key bridge over the Euphrates that had been seized by a tank battalion, and they had been drawn into a nasty little fight when Iraqi units counterattacked. Twitty expected a much worse fight on Highway 8. Just by glancing at a map, he could see that the highway was as significant to the Iraqis as to the brigade.

It was the only direct route into the city, and the regime's last line of defense. The Iraqis would fight to the death to hold it. He was sure of that.

Twitty was a supremely confident man—confident in his abilities as a commander and confident in the capacity of his men to fight and prevail. He was thirty-nine, a polished speaker with a frank, engaging manner. Raised in the tiny town of Chesnee, South Carolina, Twitty had graduated from the military studies program at South Carolina State University and earned a master's degree in public administration from Central Michigan University. A career officer with a wife and fourteen-year-old daughter, he had fought in Operation Desert Storm. That experience, combined with the previous two weeks of firefights in Iraq, had afforded Twitty a certain sureness of purpose in the way he planned a mission. He knew, even before he finished up with the stubborn Fourteenth Brigade and pushed north to the Spartan Brigade command center, that he would require a guaranteed reserve force in case everything went to hell on the highway. And he knew, too, that he would have to meet face-to-face with his commanders to make sure they realized what they were being asked to achieve.

By late afternoon on April 6, the brigade planners had completed the detailed mission orders and Perkins was ready to lay out the attack for his commanders and senior NCOs. The brigade command staff had moved earlier in the day, tearing down its tents and tarps and moving about a kilometer across Highway 8 from the dusty field to an abandoned warehouse compound just off the highway. The warehouses apparently had been used to store agricultural products; huge bales of red and blue plastic grain sacks were stacked in the cement courtyard. The compound was dirty and bedraggled—part of it was still under construction—but it contained a two-story building with a ground-floor room big enough to accommodate Perkins's battle briefing.

The brigade leadership cadre filed into the room, their tan desert boots leaving footprints in the dust of the cracked linoleum floor. Many of the officers were still recovering from the shock of being told that they would be going into Baghdad in a few hours. Even with the thunder run the day before, most of them still assumed that the brigade would serve as a blocking force for airborne units—not as the strike force itself. Now they were suddenly being asked to lead the charge into the capital for the entire coalition. The weight of this responsibility showed in their clenched jaws and in the intense way they studied the operation orders thrust into their hands as they sat down to await the battle briefing.

Flies were buzzing and the late afternoon light was slanting through cracked windows as Perkins walked to the front of the room. The engineers had connected portable generators to the fluorescent lights and ceiling fans, and now harsh shadows accentuated the worry lines in the soldiers' faces and highlighted the dark streaks of caked dirt along their necks. The fans beat the hot air. There was no PowerPoint presentation, no computer graphics. It was just a commander talking to his subordinates in a battle zone. Perkins spoke without notes, the flat pitch of his New England voice dominating the crowded room.

After a brief introduction, Perkins asked the brigade's intelligence officer to describe the enemy. Thirty-six-year-old Major Charles Watson, a slight, studious officer, stood before a satellite imagery map of Baghdad taped to a wall. Watson had marked the areas on the capital's periphery as amber zones—areas that were secured, or at least somewhat secured. The rest of the city was marked red—hostile—including all the targets assigned to the tank battalions. The entire capital was, in essence, a question mark. Watson acknowledged that no one in the coalition had reliable intelligence on Baghdad. The city was still under the control of Saddam's Special Republican Guards, some the same units that had joined with the Fedayeen and Arab volunteers to battle Rogue battalion the day before. The Guards, once believed to number thirty thousand to sixty thousand men, had been reduced by casualties and desertions to perhaps ten thousand, Watson estimated. He did not believe they had many tanks left, but they did have armored personnel carriers, artillery, antiaircraft guns, mortars, and virtually inexhaustible supplies of RPGs and AK-47 assault rifles.

"Their strength is that they are now so well dispersed," Watson said. They would almost certainly be dug into bunkers and trenches, on rooftops and on side streets. If significant numbers managed to mass in a single area and coordinate a counterattack, Watson warned, "we are in serious, serious trouble."

Watson delivered more warnings—familiar by now to the Rogue commanders and to most of the officers who had fought down south, but still worth repeating. Many Republican Guards and ordinary soldiers had thrown off their uniforms and were fighting in civilian clothes, he said, in some cases literally hiding behind civilians but in all instances taking advantage of the confusion caused by civilians wandering in and out of the kill zones. And Iraqi RPG and recoilless rifle teams, Watson said, seemed well aware that the rear grills of the tanks were vulnerable. They knew to let the tanks pass, then hit them from behind.

The biggest unknown, Watson told the group, was the willingness of the enemy to fight and die for Saddam Hussein. Nobody knew. Iraqis—and Syrians and Jordanians and Palestinians, too—had certainly fought and died on Highway 8 the day before. It seemed only logical that they would fight even more tenaciously to hold the capital itself—to keep the palaces and ministries out of American hands.

"They've done an outstanding job of propaganda," Watson said. "Their people actually believe the regime is defeating the United States." That, he said, was reason enough for them to stand and fight.

Perkins was glad Watson had mentioned the propaganda war. He wanted his men to understand how important it was not just to take Baghdad, but to *prove* that they had seized control. They would be performing in front of the world. Theirs was a mission of persuasion as well as force. The thunder run the day before had been a tactical success, but the brigade hadn't managed to refute the regime's claims of an Iraqi victory. Perkins wasn't worried about the tactical details of his Baghdad plan. He trusted his commanders to make sure that their crews knew exactly where to go and what to do. They had been pulling it off since the brigade crossed into Iraq more than two weeks earlier. Perkins thought it was more important to explain to his men *why* they were going into Baghdad. For any commander, tactics are the easy part. Soldiers were trained to follow a battle plan. But what they needed in order to fight—to fight with vigor and determination—was motivation and inspiration. It wasn't enough to know their mission. They had to know their purpose.

Perkins began: "We have set the conditions to create the collapse of the Iraqi regime. Now we're transitioning from a tactical battle to a psychological and informational battle. This is the last big battle tomorrow, gentlemen. They said it would take five divisions to win this war, but there's no question now that we can really do it ourselves tomorrow. We've got to seal the deal *now*."

The Medina Division was gone, he said. So was the Hammurabi Division, another Special Republican Guard unit that had been eviscerated that week by coalition aircraft and American tanks. Baghdad was surrounded. All that held Saddam's regime together was concentrated now in that narrow stretch of palaces and ministries and monuments along the Tigris. "We get all that out of there, it's all political maneuvering from here on out," Perkins said.

The way to convince the world that the regime was falling was to put American tanks and Bradleys in the palace complex overnight, he went on. That was the ultimate goal—to go beyond a thunder run and hold the palace complex for the entire night. And the only way to spend the night in the city was to keep Highway 8 open for fuel and ammunition. Perkins himself would make the call on spending the night at Hour Four—four hours after the launch of the mission at 6 a.m. It all depended on the lines of communications up and down Highway 8. The China battalion absolutely had to keep the LOC open. "That's our lifeline," Perkins told them.

He repeated his order from the first thunder run: go in fast and hard, and don't stop. He reminded his company commanders that they would not stop this time to deal with a downed vehicle. He looked at the tank battalion commanders, Flip deCamp and Rick Schwartz, and said, "Flip, I want you to stay on his ass."

There was a brief discussion of the importance of avoiding friendly fire. Marines, who were fighting their way into Baghdad's southeastern districts, had been advised that the Spartan Brigade would be operating on the west bank of the Tigris, across the river from the marines' assigned zone. The air force had been notified that, along the length of Highway 8, the brigade would not venture beyond the roadway and the main interchanges. Thus "deconflicting" close air support targets on either side of the highway would be quick and straightforward. And, finally, Special Forces A Teams would be driving up Highway 8 to collect intelligence on enemy forces, political maneuvering, and any evidence of chemical or biological weapons. They would be driving two Toyota pickups—dangerously similar to Iraqi technical vehicles—distinguished by fluorescent orange VS-17 panels draped over the hood and roof. Perkins gestured toward several men wearing jeans, boots, and baseball caps at the rear of the room. "Their vehicle is right outside," he said. "Go take a good look at it."

Perkins mentioned Sahaf, the information minister. He had to admit it—he was becoming obsessed with that cocky little functionary in his military costume and beret. Perkins didn't want to spin his own lies and propaganda. He just wanted the truth to get out. "So we're going to the back of the room where they give the news conferences and ask a couple of questions—and ask for validation for parking for a hundred tanks," he said.

Up to this point, the officers and NCOs had worn their battle faces—tight, tense looks of concentration. But now a rumble of laughter rolled through the room, a little exaggerated, but a welcome break in the tension. A minute later, a major piped up and asked Perkins, "Will there be water in the palace swimming pools? We could all use a good bath." Perkins gave a dry, short laugh.

But the light mood passed swiftly, and soon the men bent back over their orders and their briefing books. They all believed that taking Baghdad was their ticket home. Once Baghdad fell, the war would be over. Their job would be done. There had been virtually no talk of postwar reconstruction and nation-building. The division had been given no guidance for the postcombat phase, no orders for what to do with Baghdad once it was in American hands. Their focus was on the next day's mission. They knew people were going to die—a lot of Iraqis and, almost certainly, a few Americans, perhaps someone hunched over a folding chair in that cramped little room under the lazy spinning fans.

"This is not going to be an easy mission," Perkins said. To seize a city of 5 million people defended by thousands of troops, they were sending in about 970 combat soldiers in sixty tanks and twenty-eight Bradleys, plus a few armored personnel carriers. They were sending just thirty Bradleys, fourteen tanks, and a few hundred soldiers to hold ten kilometers of Highway 8. Perkins looked around the room. Outside, the bright spring sun was setting, and the low buzz of mosquitoes stirred the air. "Tomorrow is our last big fight. Good luck, gentlemen." Everyone shouted out, "Hoo-ah!," the military's all-purpose acknowledgment, and the officers and NCOs filed out to brief their units camped in the surrounding fields.

That evening, some of the officers and men squeezed into a darkened room behind the cinder-block room where Perkins had delivered the battle brief. Inside, the brigade chaplain, Father Patrick Ratigan, was setting up his portable altar. Ratigan was a major, an ordained Catholic priest, a stout man with graying hair and solemn eyes. He was wearing an officer's uniform with a major's gold leaf sewn into one collar and a dark chaplain's cross stitched into the other. He unfolded a little camouflaged communion kit on top of an old table he had found in the room. He withdrew a small Bible with an olive drab cover—he had not been issued one of the new, desert tan Bibles—and lit several candles. Father Ratigan was now ready for the sacrament of confession, for the granting of general absolution upon danger of death. It was something he always did for Catholics on the eve of battle.

In the glow of the candles, the priest spoke of courage and faith as the soldiers lined up before a bullet-pocked wall to receive communion. The men bowed their heads and prayed. "Help us overcome war and hardship," Father Ratigan said. "May Almighty God bless you all."

The priest was still conducting the service when an officer burst into the room. "We've got full enemy contact to the south! Everybody's gotta get in full battle rattle!" he yelled. The crunch of mortars sounded in the distance, and then the low drumming of small-arms fire. Everyone bolted from the room, only to have the sounds of fighting suddenly fade away. One of the brigade's units on the far perimeter had absorbed a brief hit-and-run attack, and a nearby convoy returning from a firefight to the south had also been attacked with mortars. One of the battalions had lit up a couple of enemy vehicles, and the ammunition inside them cooked off with a steady *pop pop pop*. It went on that way for the rest of the night—a series of probes and feints by an unseen enemy, firing and moving in the dark. Patrols were dispatched to seek out the enemy while the rest of the officers and men of the Spartan Brigade prepared for the biggest battle of their lives.

Sometime after midnight, Perkins set up his cot in a tiny space behind the room where Father Ratigan had conducted the service. At that moment, he was alone, and it was a startling sensation. A commander in combat is almost never alone; he is constantly besieged by staff officers with updates or by subordinate commanders seeking guidance. Perkins had already conducted a final, top-level review of the mission with Wesley, Schwartz, and deCamp. He outlined which decisions were theirs to make and which were his. He had heard horror stories about command helicopters stacked up in the air over battlefields in Vietnam, jammed with top commanders micromanaging platoons on the ground. He wanted his commanders to know that he would let them make the decisions they needed to make.

Perkins also had identified several key decisions he knew *he* would have to make the next day: whether to spend the night in Baghdad; how to reposition units on the ground as the battle evolved; how to best use artillery and close air support; how to resupply his tank battalions; and when to send the fuel and ammunition convoys up Highway 8. Perkins bore ultimate responsibility for more than four thousand soldiers. He was taking almost a thousand of them into the most heavily defended city in the world. He knew American soldiers would die the next day. It sounded callous, but he told his commanders that the mission's main goal was *not* to avoid getting anyone killed. It was to force the collapse of Saddam Hussein's regime. He could not—and they could not—get distracted by the death of one man or several men. The soldiers and the medics had been trained to treat and evacuate casualties, and the brigade had worked hard to have the forward surgical teams in place. When the battalions began to take casualties the next day, it would be Perkins's responsibility to press forward based on the course of action that best served the mission in the long run, not what seemed right for an isolated situation at a particular instant. The execution had to be hard, fast, and violent. The greater the speed, the greater the violence, the fewer lives that would be lost.

Inside the little room, Perkins took advantage of the solitary moment to pray, and to complete the sacrament interrupted by the mortar attack. He took out his small army-issue Bible and turned to Isaiah 6:8. The brigade's motto, "Send Me," was taken from the verse. Members of the brigade often punctuated their salutes by shouting, "Send me!" Perkins read the verse: *I heard the voice of the Lord, saying, Whom shall I send, and who will go for us? Then said I, Here am I; send me.* He opened an *Our Daily Bread* devotional from his wife and turned to the daily passage for April 7. On the same page was the passage for April 8. It was from Philippians 4:13: *I can do all things through Christ who strengthens me.* He thought the verse fit his situation, and in it he found strength.

Later Eric Wesley set up his cot in the same tight space. The two officers wanted to get a couple of hours of sleep before the dawn mission. Sitting on their bunks in the dark, finishing up the operation order, they discussed the various ways the Fedayeen and Special Republican Guards might attack the palace complex if the tank battalions managed to get in and set up for the night. They did not doubt the wisdom of the goals they had set or the ability of their men to achieve those goals. But they did wonder what it would cost them. Perkins stared out a window and said, "Damn, it's dark out there. If we end up staying tomorrow night, it could get pretty tough." Wesley nodded. There was nothing more to say. They stretched out and tried to steal a bit of sleep.

S I X
A COVERT BREACH

It was hot inside the tent at the battalion command post, so hot that Phil Wolford was having trouble concentrating. The tent seemed to draw in the heat and radiate it back against the flaps, leaving streaks of moisture on the dusty canvas. Wolford stripped off his flak vest. Underneath, his fatigues were soaked through with sweat. He tried to focus on what Lieutenant Colonel Flip deCamp was telling him and the other commanders of Tusker battalion. Wolford was a captain, the commander of Assassin Company, the battalion's lead company on the planned thunder run into Baghdad the next morning, April 7. DeCamp was telling him to lead the way to the Republican Palace—what deCamp called the four-head monster palace for the four bronze busts of Saddam on its roof. "Don't stop and fight on the highway," deCamp told Wolford. "Just hit it, kill it, keep moving. Don't stop for anything, just keep moving."

DeCamp was sweating and talking intently, jabbing at a map of downtown Baghdad spread out inside the command post. It seemed to Wolford that deCamp was trying to frighten his commanders, trying to build up the enemy into something intimidating and lethal—despite the fact that these were part of the same forces the battalion had just obliterated on the wild gun run against the remnants of the Medina Division the day before. If the colonel *was* trying to scare him, it was working. Wolford was a confident combat commander. He had led his company through several harrowing firefights on the march up from Kuwait. But this was Baghdad, the heart of the whole Iraqi regime. As deCamp spoke, Wolford kept thinking, *Holy shit, we're going straight into fucking Baghdad! Are you crazy? What are you thinking?* He didn't say it out loud, of course, but he did admit to himself that the thought of leading his men into this vast, dark unknown left him . . . if not exactly afraid, then very, very concerned.

Wolford was thirty-six, a sturdy, big-boned man, bulkier than most tankers. He had a pale complexion and short, straw-colored hair that was plastered flat against his head in the heat. Growing up in a small farming town in central Ohio, he had always wanted to be a soldier. His father had served with the First Cavalry Division in Vietnam, and his grandfather had fought in World War I. Wolford played with toy soldiers as a child, setting them up in formations and then shooting them down. He read every book on war and military history in the tiny town library. He joined the army in 1987, two years after graduating from Marysville High. He spent six years as an enlisted man, serving as a scout in Operation Desert Storm. Later he went to college and earned a commission. By 1995, he was a second lieutenant. Now, in the spring of 2003, he was in command of a tank company, responsible for the lives of scores of men—and he had about seven hours to figure out how to carry out the most important mission of his career.

That night, six of Wolford's tanks were down for repairs—including his own, which had a bad gyroscope and a turret malfunction. His mechanics had been working on them all day and late into the night. All the battalion's tanks had taken a beating on the 120-kilometer charge against the Medina Division on April 5. Their suspension systems were collapsing and some of the road wheel arms were popping off. The mechanics had torn apart the operations officer's disabled tank, cannibalizing it for parts to repair the other tanks. DeCamp's own tank was down for repairs, and the mechanics worked furiously through the night to get it going again. They had to scrounge around for parts. One of the war's dirty little secrets was the crippling lack of spare parts. They just weren't getting pushed forward to the combat teams. After Tusker's charge attack against the Medina Division, only half the battalion's tanks qualified as "combat capable."

Inside the command operations center, deCamp issued a warning to all his tank commanders: "Guys, I want to tell you right now, if you have a tank you don't think is going to make it, tell me right now and we won't bring it. We're not going in with any tank that's not going to make it." They were going to have enough to deal with in the palace complex without having to sacrifice a working tank from the fight in order to tow a disabled tank. And if they were not able to hold their positions in the city and had to fight their way back out, deCamp certainly didn't want to do it while towing a tank.

DeCamp was also concerned about getting lost on the way into downtown Baghdad, especially after hearing about Rogue's wrong turn at the spaghetti junction on the April 5 thunder run. Even if they successfully negotiated that junction, there was another confusing interchange just to the east, where the main highway into the city center split into two separate roadways. Rogue would take the northern route, the Qadisiya Highway, and Tusker the southern route, the Kindi Highway. DeCamp didn't have any photos from the UAVs, the unmanned aerial vehicles, or spy drones, that were up over Baghdad. He did have satellite imagery, which showed bridges and rooftops in black and white but did not clearly show highway interchanges. He was relying on a road map, which depicted highway exits, and he drew lines on it to indicate the routes and areas of responsibility for the various companies. The battalion's lead tank would be commanded by Lieutenant Maurice Middleton, a sharp young officer who was good with a map. Middleton had studied his 1:100,000 military map, and he knew that he had to take one ramp, then a service ramp, to reach the Kindi Highway, which would take him directly to the palace gates. Middleton had been leading the battalion for much of the war, and he hadn't been lost yet.

There was one more thing deCamp had learned from Rick Schwartz's thunder run: any gear stuffed into the tanks' external bustle racks tended to catch fire and burn when struck by RPGs. While the gear absorbed some of the impact, deCamp didn't want his tankers dealing with fires of any kind. The tanks and Bradleys had proven they could withstand RPGs, so he ordered his crews to download everything off the bustle racks. They would go in naked. The crews could take a few personal items, but the rest of their gear would have to be brought up Highway 8 later with the fuel and ammunition packages.

By the end of deCamp's briefing, Wolford was drenched in sweat. He grabbed the operation order and stepped outside, where there was a hint of a breeze, and then he walked in the dark to his tank to collect his thoughts. For the next half hour, he sat on top of his tank, going over the mission in his head, writing up a time line and a mission order for the company. He thought, too, about what he was going to tell his officers and NCOs. He thought it was important to convey just how important and dangerous this mission was—probably the ultimate mission for their careers, really. But he did not want to betray his own disquiet and alarm or, worse, panic his men. He felt a sense of urgency, and a fear that events were being rushed. In all his training in the United States and in Kuwait, he had never imagined that he would have only a few hours to prepare for the pivotal battle of the war.

There is a certain art to presenting a difficult and dangerous combat mission to young soldiers. The night before the April 5 thunder run, Captain Larry Burris, the infantry commander attached to Task Force 1-64, had wrestled with how to best lay out to his men the jarring news that they had been ordered to attack into Baghdad. Finally he decided to give what's known as a hood-top brief, gathering his men in a simple, straightforward session around the hood of the command Humvee. (Civilians, and even some soldiers, referred to the vehicles as Humvees, although the acronym was actually HMMWV, for high-mobility multipurpose wheeled vehicle). The captain plopped down his military map board in the dark and shone his flashlight on the map title at the top: BAGHDAD. Burris didn't say a word. He kept the flashlight beam steady until the message sank in and his men understood where their mission would take them. Then he briefed the mission.

Now, late at night on April 6, Wolford gave his own hood-top brief. He walked over to his Humvee, spread out his maps, and gathered his key people in a tight little circle. Wild desert dogs were barking in the distance. It was so dark that nobody bothered maintaining "light discipline"—using red-filtered flashlights to avoid "white light" that might attract enemy fire. Several white-light flashlights shone down on the map overlays on the Humvee hood.

Wolford briefed his men on the details, laying out the mission and describing what was expected from each platoon. Then he delivered the speech he had composed in his head—delivered a performance, really, because a combat commander needs to perform for his men, to inspire them and persuade them that the mission at hand is the most important thing on earth at that moment. On this night, on this dusty field in the middle of the night, Phillip E. Wolford needed his men to believe that.

"Men," he began, "we've been through a lot these past few months, and it ain't over yet. We're the Assassins of Fourth Battalion, Sixty-fourth Armor Regiment, and you should be proud of that. Tomorrow morning, we're attacking into Baghdad. We are going into the heart of Saddam's regime and we are going to take it and keep it. The enemy situation is sketchy at best, but higher expects contact as soon as we LD"—the minute they crossed the line of departure past the final friendly checkpoint on Highway 8.

"I have some concerns for tomorrow's fight," he went on. "First, if we have a tank breakdown or a tank get hit, we're going to surround it with other tanks to shield the crew. Then we're going to fire every fucking machine gun we have, we are going to lay down a wall of steel until we get the crew out. No Assassin is going to go down, and you better believe that no goddam Assassin is going to be left behind. If they fire one round at us, we fire a thousand back. If they shoot one of us, we kill them all."

Wolford paused here and mentioned that Tusker Six—deCamp—had ordered each company commander to identify a stretch of terrain big enough to accommodate the entire company and open enough to provide fields of fire in all directions. They would set up in front of the Republican Palace and defend it. But if they came under sustained attack and things started to fall apart, they would drop back to the open beach behind the palace, on the west bank of the Tigris River. It was clearly marked on the maps.

"Fellas—look at me!" Wolford said, and he slammed his fist down on the hood of his Humvee. "If all goes to shit we rally right here on the beach. We get in a three-hundred-sixty-degree perimeter and we fucking fight with everything we've got, and we make them regret the day they joined the Iraqi army. Talk to your soldiers. Let them know what we expect of them. Tomorrow we fight."

It was a hell of a speech—one that some of the men from Assassin would still be quoting six months later. When the officers and NCOs fanned out across the field to brief their crews, Wolford walked around to the positions and spoke quietly in the dark to as many Assassins as he could, as much for himself as for them.

For the men of all three battalions, it was a pivotal moment. They had trained for months, in the piney woods of American bases and in the bleak Kuwaiti desert, to reach this precipice. They had fought for almost two weeks, pushing north through the deserts of southern and central Iraq. They had become conditioned to fear and deprivation, and their lives were narrow and circumscribed. It was difficult for them to look beyond the prevailing operation order because the demands of those orders were so insistent and debilitating. In their rare moments of downtime between missions, when they wolfed down their pasty meals-ready-to-eat and cursed and scratched themselves, there were elliptical discussions of the political and diplomatic forces that had sent them off to war. With a sense of foreboding, some of the men remarked on the president's warning the previous autumn that Iraq could launch a biological or chemical attack in as little as forty-five minutes. There were vague allusions to terrorism and to the brutality of Saddam Hussein's dictatorship, and to the notion of somehow delivering freedom to the Iraqi people. These topics were mentioned often but were not deeply probed, for these were esoteric concepts, too remote and cryptic for young men whose immediate focus was on the twin tasks of destruction and survival. They were fighting for their country, of course, and for the inherent nobility of their profession. But mostly, they were fighting to come home alive and to ensure that the men beside them came home, too. The military works assiduously to build unit cohesion, in part because a man will fight harder beside someone he knows, someone with whom he has built a bond from shared danger and sacrifice and fear. A few men spoke of "getting some," that peculiar, sexually tinged reference to confronting the enemy and killing him. But most of them spoke of getting out of Iraq alive, and their buddies with them.

The men of the combat teams were as tight as brothers now. They had lived in filth for weeks, as each hot, punishing day slid into each cold, unforgiving night. They had pissed in the sand, crapped in slit trenches, burned their own shit. They had gagged on sand and picked it out of their eyes and their ears and their crotches. It was a fine, talcumlike sand that seeped into weapons and engines and radios. Some of the men used pantyhose as a sand filter, and those who had the foresight to pack resealable plastic freezer bags were able to protect their laptops and CD players for a time. But soon the bags were themselves reservoirs of dust and grit, and the dust had conquered all. The men had endured day after day of sweat and grime, weeks removed from a proper shower. They wiped their armpits and asses with sloppy wet Joey wipes, but still they stunk of sour sweat, and the skin between their toes sloughed off and rotted. Guys would sniff the air in crowded Humvees and ask, "Is that *you* or *me*?"

As the days grew hotter, they became more miserable inside their suffocating chemical and biological warfare suits. They had been required to wear the suits until just a few days earlier. After they had breached the so-called red zone around Baghdad without coming under nuclear, biological, or chemical attack, the order had come down to dispense with the suits. The suits were formally known as JSLIST suits, but most soldiers called them MOPP suits, for mission-oriented protective posture, as if a

soldier wearing one could assume a protective posture while still orient-
ing his attention to the mission at hand. It took several minutes to pull on
the heavy, charcoal-lined pants with suspenders, and then the charcoal-
lined jacket, the two pairs of gloves—one cloth, one rubber—the thick
rubber boots with metal clasps, and, finally, a floppy rubber gas mask with
a tangle of head straps. The soldiers bitched about taking them off and
putting them on, about the endless warning sirens in Kuwait that had sent
them diving into trenches until the chemical officers screamed, "All clear!"
Waiting in the trenches, the soldiers would joke about "doing the funky
chicken"—choking on their own blood in the spastic convulsions brought
on by chemical weapons. They killed time by nominating one another for
"least mission critical"—that hapless soldier designated as the guinea pig
to remove his gas mask to test the air after a suspected chemical or biological attack. Sometimes they nominated the embedded reporters.

     They didn't talk much about dying. For some of them, it was bad luck
to speak of such things. For others, there was no point talking about it
because it was a capricious thing, a crapshoot—though some of the Gulf
War vets warned that sometimes it happened to guys who got careless, who
lacked a certain situational awareness. But mostly, dying was something
the enemy did. Even so, they made sure to write their blood types in water-
proof ink on the shoulders of their uniforms, big and bold for the medics.

Not far from Phil Wolford's Assassin Company, Stephen Twitty's China
battalion had run into an ambush while setting up for the night. RPG teams
were firing at Twitty's men from thick groves of date palms at the far end
of the fields that hugged Highway 8 where it intersected Highway 1 south
of Baghdad. Twitty still had not briefed his key commanders on the
Baghdad battle plan, so he had to call them in from the firefight and let
the first sergeants and platoon leaders take over the battle. It wasn't that
big a fight, mostly harassment from Iraqi fighters who fled after squeezing
off a few rounds or launching a series of mortar rounds.

     Under normal circumstances, Twitty briefed a new operation order
over the radio, but not this one. He wanted to look his men in the eye and
tell them what they were up against. Somebody from the battalion had
found an abandoned house that was quickly converted into the battalion
command post. The roof was gone and the windows had been blown out,

so some of the men stretched a tarp over the top and covered the windows; any light escaping from inside could target the building for a mortar attack. The engineers hooked up portable lights to a generator. Folding tables and chairs were set up. Maps were posted. (A combat unit on the move is like a huge traveling circus. Everything is packed and unpacked so many times, and under so many challenging conditions, that each new command post practically sets itself up. Each time, everything—the command table, the laptops, the printers, the coffeepot, the map boards—ended up in its same familiar spot.)

On this night, the company commanders were seated in a row of chairs facing Twitty. He had given quite a bit of thought to what he wanted to say to them. For one thing, he didn't think it was necessary to dwell too long on just how little they knew about the enemy. Twitty didn't even know what kind of buildings lined Highway 8; the satellite imagery didn't give a clear indication. If some of them were higher than four or five stories, that meant he would not be able to elevate his gun tubes high enough to hit gunmen in the windows or on the roofs. He had radioed Rick Schwartz, who put him at ease by telling him that most of the buildings were no more than two stories high. Schwartz also told him about the bunkers, the trench systems, the overpasses, the technical vehicles, the suicide cars, and the streams of pickup trucks, taxis, ambulances, motorcycles, and sedans loaded with gun-toting fighters.

The first time Twitty had looked at Highway 8 on his map, he thought: registered artillery. Certainly the Iraqis had registered the artillery and mortar coordinates at each interchange. That's what he would have done if he were in charge of defending the capital. He also would have fortified each major interchange to block and trap any forces trying to set up there. Twitty knew the brigade's two tank battalions would blow past the intersections. What he didn't know was what the Iraqis would do in the interval before Twitty's own mechanized infantry battalion arrived to seize and hold the interchanges. This uncertainty weighed on him. It didn't help that Colonel Perkins had taken two of Twitty's platoons—about eighty soldiers and eight Bradleys—as a reserve force to protect the brigade command center. It would be left vulnerable once the brigade's three combat battalions pulled away at dawn, so Perkins had to weaken Twitty in order to strengthen his command post. But that left Twitty shorthanded at Objective Curly, the southernmost interchange. He had asked Perkins whether he could call on the two platoons if he got into trouble. "Whatever you need," Perkins had assured him.

Twitty decided to put one of his two full companies on Objective Moe, the northern interchange at the spaghetti junction, which provided access to the city center to the east and the airport to the west. The second full company would take Objective Larry, two and a half kilometers south, where an intersecting highway led to the strategic Al Jadriyah Bridge across the Tigris River to the east. The third company, minus two platoons, would move into Objective Curly, about six kilometers north of the brigade command center and the reserve force.

Now Twitty faced his commanders and staff and laid out the battle plan, with all its unknowns. He could tell that the men were still adjusting to the shock of charging straight into Baghdad—or in their case, straight into the three main interchanges controlling access to the city—after being told for months that they would be setting up blocking positions outside the capital.

"Guys, this is it," Twitty told them. "We're going to take the fight right into Baghdad. And what I'm going to ask you to do is hold some terrain. You have one choice here. You can hold it and be successful. Or you can hold it and die."

Normally, the commanders and staff goofed around during meetings, throwing out asides and wisecracks. Now there was silence. Twitty knew what his men were thinking: *We could lose people on this one.* They'd been lucky so far. They had not lost a single man to combat, and just three men had suffered battle wounds.

Twitty tried to reassure them. "We're going to hold this terrain," he told them. "I want the enemy to die here. The key to your success is, you have to get in there and protect yourself. And the way you protect yourself from these suicide bombers is you cut down all the light posts, you drag all the cars you can find, berm them up around the intersection so the suicide cars can't get through."

Twitty saw looks of concern on the faces of his men and he said: "This is it. We could lose a few people. We'll probably take some casualties on this one, and that's okay. Some of us in this room may die, and that's okay, too. Just know it's for a good cause." Then he offered a short prayer before sending the commanders off into the night to prepare their crews for the fight ahead.

* * *

That afternoon, Major Sean Mullen had pulled up to the last American checkpoint on Highway 8 in a small convoy and asked the soldiers on duty how far ahead the road had been cleared and secured. The sentries told him that, as far as they knew, it had been cleared only to that point. Mullen had been ordered to go farther north and have a look. He was the brigade S-4, the officer in charge of all supplies—from ammunition and fuel to food and water. He wanted to make sure the fuel and ammunition convoys had a secure section of highway to assemble their vehicles while waiting to be sent up Highway 8 the next day to resupply the tank battalions once they had fought their way into the city. Colonel Perkins had made it abundantly clear that getting the R2 package—the refuel and rearm convoy—into the city was crucial.

A short distance north of the checkpoint, Mullen and his men made a discovery that would stir considerable interest at the brigade command center. They came across rows and rows of what appeared to be dirty black spots in the northbound lanes. The spots turned out to be land mines—hundreds of them. Somehow, Iraqi teams had managed to creep out onto the roadway and plant a minefield that snaked four hundred meters up the highway. The entire mission was now at risk. So were Mullen and the little convoy of Humvees and MP vehicles he had led up the highway. Shortly after discovering the minefield, they came under attack by Iraqi fighters in technical vehicles and had to flee back south, past the minefield. Mullen radioed Captain Larry Burris, who sent a platoon of tanks north to assist him. But the Abrams tanks could not move past the minefield, so Mullen's convoy had to outrun the technicals before reaching the safety of the tanks. Along the way, a piece of shrapnel sliced into Mullen's face.

Mullen rushed back to the brigade command center, blood streaming down his cheek, to find Colonel Perkins. The news of the minefield triggered a brief moment of panic. If the Iraqis could sneak in and plant a minefield just a few kilometers from the brigade headquarters, they might also have been able to plant minefields and barriers all the way up Highway 8. There was talk of postponing the mission. The brigade's planners began devising contingencies and alternatives to a thunder run that was now just hours away.

Perkins and Eric Wesley, the executive officer, decided to request a UAV drone for a spy flight over Highway 8. UAVs were in short supply and difficult to obtain on short notice, but division headquarters prevailed on V Corps to put one of the small aircraft up over the highway. While he waited for the UAV report, Wesley asked Perkins what conditions would force him to postpone the thunder run.

Perkins turned to Wesley and said sharply, "Eric, this brigade is going to Baghdad tomorrow morning."

Wesley asked if Perkins would still attempt the mission if the UAV found minefields and obstacles all the way up Highway 8 into the city. Perkins thought for a moment and said, "Then we'd have to delay," but only, he added, if the highway were completely blocked.

It was not until much later—about 4 a.m. on the seventh, or less than two hours before the thunder run was to launch—that division headquarters reported that the UAV had detected four or five barriers on Highway 8 made from burned-out vehicles and debris, but no more minefields.

Wesley asked Perkins if the mission was still on. "Roger," the colonel said.

Earlier in the morning, an emergency call had gone out to the combat engineers and sappers of Second Platoon, Delta Company, of the Tenth Engineer Battalion, commanded by Captain David Hibner. Regardless of what the UAV flight would uncover, the minefield had to be cleared right away. The thunder run was still on pending the UAV report, with a launch time of 5:30 a.m.

Combat engineers tend to be inquisitive and dexterous types, the sort of men who, as children, dismantled small household appliances to find out what made them work. Many of them have survived childhood encounters with firecrackers, chimney fires, and cherry bombs. During combat operations, engineers are asked to lay down bridges or blow them up, to set up minefields or clear them. And early on the morning of April 7, a team from Delta Company was sent racing up Highway 8 to figure out a way to dispose of a minefield before the lead tanks of Rogue battalion rolled through on the thunder run into Baghdad at first light. After considerable discussion at the brigade command center, it had been decided to mount a covert breach—an attempt to clear the highway safely and quietly, without alerting the enemy.

This was not the first covert breach for the company. The engineers had cleared a similar minefield in Najaf a week earlier, so they knew what to expect. That gave them a certain confidence, though the Najaf field had been only about seventy meters deep, not even a quarter the size of this monster minefield. What they did not know, and what weighed on them as the rode north up Highway 8 in the dark, was whether the enemy was out there waiting for them. It was standard U.S. military doctrine to "overwatch" minefields, to make sure that the enemy doesn't tamper with them. The engineers had no idea what Iraqi doctrine dictated, or whether anyone in the Iraqi military paid attention to doctrine. But if enemy soldiers were out there and decided to fire on them, the covert breach would become a breach under fire—the last thing anybody wanted to deal with in the middle of the night on the highway to Baghdad. As an emergency backup, they hauled up a trailer loaded with a MCLC—pronounced *micklick*—a mine-clearing line charge. It looked like a rocket trailed by sausage links. The rocket was designed to be fired into a minefield, scattering links of C-4 plastic explosive that would detonate on impact and clear the field. It created a hell of a mess, and so it was not the preferred method for clearing a highway for a thunder run.

When Sergeant Steve Oslin got his first look at the minefield, he was puzzled. It looked like it had been set up by amateurs. The mines—hundreds of them—had been lined up right on top of the asphalt. Each one had been covered with dirt in what appeared to have been a clumsy attempt to disguise them. It was possible, Oslin thought, that the dirt was hiding trip wires or antihandling devices—sensors that exploded if the mines were disturbed. He realized that, whatever the reason for the dirt, it would have the effect of slowing down the clearing teams. They would have to clear each mine by hand, checking it for antihandling devices or trip wires. Perhaps the Iraqis knew what they were doing.

Whispering in the dark, the sappers unloaded their vehicles. Behind them was a platoon of four Bradleys from Captain Burris's infantry company, the track commanders up in the hatches scanning both sides of the highway through night-vision goggles. Beyond the far northern end of the minefield, across a field east of the highway, they could see a technical vehicle, an antiaircraft gun, and a recoilless rifle. The gunners lined up each target in their thermal sights, ready to hit them with coax if they threatened the sappers. This was a covert breach; the Bradley crews were there to provide security, not to initiate a firefight.

The sappers were not aware of the enemy. Their focus was on the mines—and how they were going to clear them in just a couple of hours. It was after 3 a.m. by the time they set up and unloaded. The armored column was scheduled to launch at daylight, or sometime after 5:30 a.m. Two squad leaders, Sergeant Jason Deming and Staff Sergeant Eric Guzman, decided to test a couple of the mines for antihandling devices. They would "lasso" them. A lasso was a length of engineers' tape made of thick cloth, a long strap, dragged into a minefield to "lasso" mines and haul them in. They had used the technique in Najaf to drag mines from a safe distance to test them for antihandling devices or booby traps. Here on Highway 8, they decided, they would lasso eight mines—the first two rows of four mines each—dragging them across the asphalt to see if they detonated.

Specialist Alfred Hassan, a sapper everybody called Bear, walked slowly onto the highway, tiptoeing between the mines. He carefully draped a length of strap around the first mine. He could see that all the mines were Italian-made antitank mines, powerful enough to flip over a seventy-ton tank. They were about ten inches in diameter and five inches high, roughly the size and shape of a birthday cake. Hassan tied the strap into a slip knot, cinched it tightly around the mine, and slowly made his way back to the rest of the engineer team, careful to avoid getting his feet tangled up in the strap leading back to safety. Now *that* would truly be embarrassing, and probably fatal, he thought—to trip over the strap and set off an anti-tank mine. Hassan made it back to the vehicles, where the rest of the team was lying flat on the highway, staying low for protection in the event of a blast wave. Hassan got down, too. Somebody whispered the countdown . . . one . . . two . . . three . . . and Oslin yanked on the end of the strap. The mine slid across the highway. The men braced for an explosion. There was nothing. The mine came to a rest, still intact.

The sappers repeated the lasso process for seven more mines. Each attempt produced the same result—no explosion. The squad leaders talked it over. They didn't have time to lasso all four hundred mines. That would take all night. They decided to take a chance and assume that none of the mines had trip wires or antihandling devices. They would remove them by hand, checking each one by using a quicker but much more dangerous method—the two-finger sweep, checking for wires or sensors by running two fingers around each mine. If anybody got hurt, the medics would treat the casualties and evacuate them. The company commander would then decide whether to abort the mission or press on. Nobody talked about casualties. Nobody even thought about getting hurt; they had faith in their training. In fact, faith was the fulcrum of their training—faith that if they performed exactly the way they had been trained, nothing bad could possibly happen.

Just four men would go out and remove the mines, checking each one and then lifting it and setting it carefully on the shoulder of the highway. The squad leaders didn't want to risk losing more men if a mine went off. Two more men would follow behind, isolating the cleared areas by creating small berms from trash and debris scattered along the roadside. Two of the squad leaders, Guzman and Staff Sergeant Matthew Oliver, would scan the perimeter through night-vision goggles, providing security. Other engineers would haul out orange traffic cones to mark the cleared roadway for the armored convoy.

Oslin would be clearing the mines. He unshouldered his rifle and removed his fatigue jacket. He didn't want anything flopping down on the mines while he was crouching down to clear them. None of the sappers wore protective gear; it just got in the way and made it difficult to move freely. Oslin took a deep breath, adjusted his kneepads, and walked out to the first row of mines. He got down on his knees and went at it. He carefully cleared the dirt from each mine, slowly running two fingers around the sides and top, ready to stop abruptly if he felt a wire or antihandling device. He tried not to think about what *he* would have done if he had set up the minefield, because he would have drilled holes in the asphalt beneath the mines and booby-trapped them to explode if anyone tried to lift them. But he couldn't *not* think of all that, and it haunted him. He kept thinking about his wife, and he ran through his life insurance policy in his head and thought: *Well, at least she'll be taken care of if I don't come home.* He had those thoughts for mine after mine, dozens of them, as he cleared each one and picked it up and carefully set it down on the other side of a concrete divider on the east shoulder of the highway.

The other sappers worked the field the same way, sweeping, clearing, lifting, walking, setting the mines down. It was a cool desert night, but they were sweating under their T-shirts. All of the mines were covered with dirt, and a few were topped with human excrement. Apparently, at least a few of the Iraqis were not in such a hurry that they couldn't stop and defecate. Nobody knew what to make of it, but they took it as an insult—just a filthy insult, as if they didn't have enough to worry about already.

The sappers worked steadily, silently, row after row. Oslin looked up at one point and felt a sudden stab of fear. He couldn't see the security vehicles. The highway had bent to the right, and now he was out of sight. He could see the dark outlines of burned-out Iraqi vehicles destroyed during Rogue's thunder run. He was worried about someone taking a shot at him. He could see faint streaks of light in buildings in the distance, and the wind was blowing trash all over the highway. At one point Oslin was startled by a loud crashing sound—the wind had torn a section of sheet metal from a roof, and it clanged across the field. Somewhere in the distance, a metal garage door was banging in the wind.

Behind Oslin and the other sappers, in the lead troop carrier at the southern edge of the minefield, Sergeant Tony Raskin was scanning both sides of the highway with his night-vision goggles. His .50-caliber machine gun was primed to fire. He was under strict orders not to fire unless fired upon, but he intended to open up with the .50-caliber if anybody took a shot at his guys crouching and moving at the far end of the minefield. Raskin had spotted three or four people walking around about three hundred meters off the west side of the highway. He couldn't tell whether they were civilians or soldiers, or whether they had weapons. But they made him nervous, and he kept the goggles on them. From time to time, the squad leaders would walk back and give him progress reports to radio back to the platoon leader in the medevac track, First Sergeant Dale Vanormer. The operation was moving briskly, but not as fast as Raskin liked. He wanted to get it done and get out of there.

Ahead of Raskin, Sergeant Deming and Staff Sergeant Christopher Turner were shuffling up the side of the highway, hauling stacks of orange traffic cones. They had their M-16s slung across their backs and their night-vision goggles strapped to their heads, struggling with armloads of cones. In the dark, they looked like eerie fluorescent orange shapes scooting up the highway, shedding bits of orange every fifteen meters as they dropped cones to mark the cleared lanes. Running back and forth to collect cones and drop them off, Deming and Turner had to pass a section of highway that was exposed to an alleyway off to the right. They heard noises from that direction but they couldn't see anything, even with their goggles. They were winded and anxious, and worried about having to stop, drop the cones, and shoulder their weapons if someone took a shot at them. They kept thinking that if somebody got hurt way up there, it would take a while for the medics to run all the way up the highway in the dark. A man could bleed to death before anyone arrived to treat him. They were relieved, and more than a little surprised, when they finished setting up the cones without a shot being fired.

After a little less than two hours, all 444 mines had been cleared, lifted, and moved to the shoulder. The sappers and the squad leaders hustled back down the highway, and everybody performed accountability, counting off in the dark. They felt enormous relief and a sense of pride. They had just pulled off a hell of a thing, clearing a massive minefield in a combat zone, in the dark, with no protective equipment. Deming kept thinking, *Damn, how many guys can say they pulled off a sneaky covert sapper breach in the middle of the night—not in training, but for real, against real live bad guys?* They were all exhausted and drained, but they felt somehow elated and giddy, and each man could tell by the look in the other guys' eyes that they felt it, too.

They got back to the vehicles and unloaded a directional panel, a stretch of canvas marked with a huge white arrow. The armor crews had been instructed to follow the arrow and the cones through the cleared lanes. The engineers set up the panel, tied it down with parachute cord, braced it with dirt, and made sure the arrow was pointing away from the mines. Then everybody loaded back up and the vehicles pulled away, the Bradleys staying behind to cover their retreat back south to the brigade command center. The sun was coming up over the desert. It was 5:40 a.m.

The engineers had been riding south for just a few minutes when they heard a series of explosions. The Bradleys had opened up with their coax and Twenty-five Mike Mike. A week would pass before the engineers learned that, while they had been creeping through the minefield that night, they were being watched by Iraqi soldiers manning two technicals, an antiaircraft gun, and a recoilless rifle. The Bradleys destroyed them all. The engineers knew nothing of this now as they encountered the lead Rogue tanks of the armored column, rolling north at dawn on Highway 8 toward the freshly cleared minefield, bound for the palace complex of Saddam Hussein. The thunder run was on.

S E V E N
THE PALACE
GATES

Before taking off on any mission, Lieutenant Colonel Kenneth Gantt always reached into his pocket and pulled out a piece of Bazooka bubblegum to hand to Dave Perkins. It was a little ritual they had developed during the firefights down south, a sort of prebattle talisman—the passing of the lucky gum. They had done it before the thunder run on April 5, and now, just before dawn on April 7, Gantt reached for his gum.

He had just climbed aboard Perkins's command vehicle, an armored personnel carrier equipped with so many communications antennae that it looked like it was carrying a load of heavily armed fishermen with their poles swaying in the back. Perkins would direct the day's fight from the commander's hatch, talking on various radio nets with the division commander, General Blount; the two tank battalion commanders, Rick Schwartz and Flip deCamp; and executive officer Eric Wesley at the tactical operations center at the intersection of Highways 1 and 8, where the armored column was lined up now, ready to launch on this still, foggy morning south of Baghdad.

Gantt was an artilleryman, the commander of the Battle Kings, the First Battalion, Ninth Field Artillery Regiment. He rode in the carrier's hatch at Perkins's right elbow, working the battalion and brigade fire nets to control all "indirect fires"—all artillery and rockets. Gantt, forty-two, was a tall, long-limbed man with a worldly air. He had a master's degree in Near Eastern studies from Princeton, and he spoke Arabic and Hebrew. He had served a stint as a United Nations military observer in the Middle East, and another stint as a Middle East political-military analyst at the Defense Intelligence Agency. With his knowledge of the region, as well as his expertise in artillery, Gantt was a valuable asset to Perkins, who kept him at his side during battles.

Gantt's big guns were set up now in a farm field just south of the operations center, the long tan tubes of the Paladin howitzers upraised and pointed north through the mist and fog. The Paladin was a 155mm howitzer that had been brought into service after Operation Desert Storm, and the Iraqi war was its first real combat test. Gantt loved the new guns. The Paladins were mounted on tracks and capable of speeds of up to fifty-six kilometers an hour—not quite as fast as the tanks and Bradleys, but impressive for self-propelled artillery. They looked like bulky tanks, but with oversized cannons capable of flinging a ninety-five-pound projectile twenty-four kilometers. They could fire accurately on the move and were designed to "shoot and scoot"—to fire off a series, then speed away to escape counterbattery fire. On this particular morning, a dozen Paladins were lined up across a farmer's field at a place designated Objective Trista, where they were primed and ready. It was Gantt's responsibility to make sure the Paladins laid down accurate fire at several interchanges along Highway 8 precisely ten minutes before the armored column arrived at each overpass. It was a complex, delicate mission requiring exquisite timing and coordination. It was the first time during the war that the brigade had attempted to combine artillery with a fast-moving armored raid.

Gantt had survived the thunder run two days earlier. He had cringed every time the command carrier rolled under an overpass, where Republican Guards and Fedayeen had launched RPGs and fired AK-47s straight down toward the roadway. The Rogue battalion had been fortunate to lose just one man that day. For this thunder run, Perkins wanted those overpasses cleared—but without destroying them or blocking Highway 8 with rubble from the impact of heavy artillery. Gantt and Perkins decided to drop HEPD on the overpasses—high-explosive point-detonating rounds. Their fuses were timed to explode ten to fifteen meters above ground, spraying hot shrapnel straight down. HEPD was like a little neutron bomb. It killed people but left infrastructure intact. The shells would eviscerate any human being within roughly 150 meters of the airburst but spare the overpasses and the highway any serious structural damage. Gantt was confident his crews could pull it off. The Paladins had performed well just the night before, when Stephen Twitty's China battalion was harassed by mortar fire. They had swiftly and efficiently destroyed every last mortar position.

But just before the armored column pulled out, Gantt got another order, for prep fire. The spy drones and the scouts had detected Iraqi mortars and antiaircraft guns a little more than one and a half kilometers north on Highway 8. Gantt would have to eliminate them to clear the way for the column. He ordered a series of strikes from a battalion of multiple rocket launchers posted near the intersections of Highways 1 and 8. The rockets were highly efficient killers; they could destroy everything inside a square kilometer grid in fifteen seconds. Twenty-four rockets screamed from their launchers and exploded in the distance. Minutes later, the forward observers reported back: targets destroyed.

Things were moving quickly. The column lurched to life, rolling up Highway 8 to the final American checkpoint. Minutes later, the Paladins targeted the first interchange, the thirty-nine-inch projectiles erupting from the tubes in bursts of orange flame and black smoke. The shells whined overhead and detonated in the air above the overpass, two overlapping rounds at each corner of the interchange. Gantt wanted a scattershot effect—overlapping concentric circles of 40 meters' diameter each for a kill zone of perhaps 150 meters. He heard the deep thud of impact. He knew that any human being standing anywhere on or near the overpass at Curly was now flat on the ground, dead or mortally wounded. An exploding 155mm round does ghastly things to people, but these people were endangering the lives of his men, and Gantt felt no remorse. He was energized by the mission into Baghdad, eager to prove his battalion's effectiveness in battle, and anxious to finish off things in Baghdad so that he and his men could go home. There was also the matter of propaganda—specifically, Sahaf the information minister. Gantt and Perkins had discussed how satisfying it would be to pull their tanks up to the information ministry and expose Sahaf as a fraud.

Toward the front of the column, Rick Schwartz was up in his cupola, listening to the 155s whistle overhead and then slam down. They were hitting just a kilometer or so ahead of his lead tanks. Schwartz was on the radio to his field artillery officer, who was talking to Gantt's artillerymen back in the farm field. Schwartz was calling out latitudinal grid lines known as northings: "I'm at the seventy-nine, I'm at the eighty. Shoot it!"—telling Gantt and his men precisely when to launch the rounds. Schwartz was pleased by how smoothly the communication was flowing; artillery was treacherous stuff, and if you got careless it could drop right on your head. But even though the brigade had not previously used artillery to cover a speeding armored column, everyone on the combat team had learned to synchronize and communicate during all the firefights down south. Schwartz was able to call in his position and, in less than three minutes, the rounds would crash down right on the mark.

It was a magnificent thing, Schwartz thought—this great humming flow of radios and machinery and weaponry, all flowing north to Baghdad. The mission was playing out as planned. The column had rolled past the cleared minefield without incident, herded into the western lanes by the engineers' orange cones and white directional arrow. Just north of the minefield, the Iraqis had erected a barrier on the highway, stacking up burned-out cars and hunks of concrete and road debris. But the spy drones had picked it up the night before and transmitted the imagery down to the brigade operations center. The information was passed to Schwartz, who had his lead tanks prepare their plows. Lieutenant Bobby Hall's platoon was in the lead again—Captain Andy Hilmes had put him back up front, despite his missed turn two days earlier, telling him, "This is *your* highway." Hall could see that the Iraqis, for some reason, had left convenient two-meter gaps between the barriers. These obstacles were not as effectively placed as the barriers the Iraqis had erected near the airport two days earlier. Hall's plow tanks were able to wedge between the barriers, get low for leverage, and shove the piles of junk and debris off to the side of the highway.

As the column approached the first big interchanges, at Objective Curly, Schwartz could see that the overpass was clear. The artillery had blown everything off the bridge—soldiers, vehicles, debris. But the airbursts had not disturbed the gunmen hiding in the creases, where the underside of the bridge met the support walls. Their RPG launchers were detected by the gunners as they scanned the creases through their magnified sights. Schwartz gave the order to engage, and the Bradley gunners sent Twenty-five Mike Mike rattling up into the creases. The way the rounds exploded and splattered reminded Schwartz of a paintball game. The gunmen simply disappeared in a black curtain of smoke, and the column rolled on.

Back on the open highway, some of the bunkers that Rogue had hit two days earlier had been reseeded. The awful whoosh of RPGs rose up from both sides of the highway, followed by bursts of automatic weapons fire. Schwartz could see technicals and trucks moving into position on the access roads, and it became clear that the Iraqis had not adjusted their tactics over the past two days. They were still trying to break the order of march, still using RPG crews and recoilless rifles and suicide vehicles to hammer sections of the column in hopes of isolating and killing the crews. It seemed to Schwartz that the rate of fire was not as intense as during the first thunder run. He thought Rogue had broken much of the resistance two days earlier. If Saturday's thunder run was a ten on a ten-point scale in terms of enemy resistance, he figured today's was perhaps a six. He felt confident about blowing through the defenses on the highway and straight into the downtown government complex.

Then Joe Bell's tank took a couple of wicked hits. The tank had survived five RPG hits on the first thunder run, and even Bell's toy dog, Puppy Love, had arrived intact. But now Bell, manning the commander's hatch of the column's lead tank, was wondering just how many more RPGs his shrapnel-pocked Abrams could withstand. He had just passed the scorched remains of Charlie One Two, which didn't exactly build his confidence. He felt a little better after he pumped a few rounds from his .50-caliber into a Soviet-made tracked recovery vehicle—basically, a huge tow truck for tanks—that was parked next to Charlie One Two. He couldn't believe it: it was hooked up to the stricken tank. The Iraqis were actually trying to tow an American tank in the middle of a battle. Bell radioed back and warned Captain Hilmes. Just to make sure the recovery vehicle was destroyed, the captain had his tank gunner put a HEAT round into it.

Bell had just passed Charlie One Two when an RPG screamed toward him. It smashed into the right side of his tank, a tremendous blow. The whole tank rocked sideways, and Bell had to hold on tight. From the trailing tank, Sergeant First Class Ronald Gaines radioed Bell, "You just got hit," as if Bell hadn't noticed.

A minute later a second RPG streaked in and ripped through the rear of Bell's tank, straight through the hull. Gaines's voice came over the net again: "You just got hit again. You're leaking real bad."

Lieutenant Ball, the platoon leader, radioed and asked, "Hey, are you guys okay?" Bell's voice came back: "Yeah, we're all okay. We got a small fire going."

The rear compartment was burning. The automatic fire control system doused the blaze with a spray of Halon, and the crew pulled the emergency lever to fire another round of the flame retardant. The fire went out, but the fuel and hydraulic lines had been ruptured. Fuel and hydraulic fluid were leaking onto the highway. The tank rolled another hundred meters, then aborted, shutting itself down.

Bell wasn't particularly alarmed. He knew the drill. Colonel Perkins and Lieutenant Colonel Schwartz had made it clear that the column was not going to be held up by a disabled tank this time around. This time, recovery vehicles were standing by to push forward and tow any disabled tank back to the brigade operations center. Bell's tank was only three and a half kilometers from the center. The rest of the column kept moving, and over the radio Bell heard a voice telling his crew, "Don't worry. They're coming for you." It didn't seem so bad. They didn't have hydraulic power, but they could still fire the main gun, the coax, the loader's machine gun, and their automatic rifles.

The rest of the column pulled away. Bell and his crewmen sat there, buttoned up, a lone tank at the side of the highway. Bell felt even more exposed when the rest of the column moved out of radio range and he couldn't raise anybody on the net to find out when the recovery vehicle was coming. It was like to trying to reach an AAA road repair dispatcher from the side of the interstate. He tried to concentrate on security, to keep the crew focused and alert for the enemy. Sergeant David Gibbons, the gunner who had brought his crew home safely after Staff Sergeant Booker was killed two days earlier, was scanning through the gunner's primary sight, checking to make sure no one was creeping up on them.

At one point, Gibbons spotted three Iraqi dismounts poking around. He killed all three with a sudden burst of coax that startled the crew. There was steady gunfire in the distance. The four crewmen sat there for the next thirty minutes, cut off, scanning, sweating, waiting. At last they heard a sharp banging on the front deck. They looked out the vision blocks and saw a man in a uniform. It was a friendly—a young infantryman from the China battalion. He said, "We got you. Come on out." Within minutes, the tow bar was hooked up and the disabled tank was dragged back to the rear, Bell's Puppy Love still tucked safely into the bustle rack.

Up ahead, inside the commander's hatch of a Bradley from the Tusker battalion, Staff Sergeant Thomas Slago thought the rate of fire was exceptionally intense. He and his crew had survived several fierce firefights down south, but nothing on this scale. He could see muzzle flashes and RPG trails

on both sides of the highway. Slago, thirty-five, was an experienced veteran, a stocky, boisterous NCO with a gift for gab. He loved commanding
a Bradley; he had named his nine-year-old son Bradley, although his wife
had made him abandon the middle name he had selected: Gunner.

Slago's crew had killed quite a few Iraqis down south, and it disturbed
him that after a while killing people had become almost routine. He had
talked to his crew about it, and he had decided to rationalize his feelings
by dehumanizing the enemy. He did not think of the Iraqis there on the
roadway as people but as obstacles. They were in his way; in fact, they were
trying to kill *him*. He was not interested in dying for his country. He wanted
them to die for their country. He wanted them out of his way.

Just before the day's mission, Slago had pulled aside his gunner,
Specialist Gary Techur, who had developed a habit of calling out "Contact RPG!" or "Contact machine gun!" to alert Slago to give the order to
fire. Slago told Techur: "You see anybody in a uniform, anybody with a
weapon, don't ask me for permission to shoot. Just kill 'em. They're enemy.
Take 'em out. *Then* you can yell 'Contact RPG.'"

Slago was anxious about the mission. He had not been able to sleep
the night before. In fact, he had not slept in several days. Maybe it was the
nickname the crew had given the Bradley: *Nocturnal*. Slago could not shake
the feeling that somebody was going to die on the run into Baghdad—
maybe a member of his crew, maybe himself. His wife's parents had mailed
him a Bible, so he stashed it in the Bradley's coax "ready box," the ammo
tray. He felt better just knowing it was there, close by.

That morning, as his crew prepped the Bradley for the mission, Slago
had tried to kid around with Techur, hoping to relax them both. They even
managed to laugh when they passed the minefield and realized that the
Iraqis had just dumped the mines right on top of the asphalt. It seemed so
amateurish, so silly and ineffective. It felt good to laugh. But when Slago
saw the sleeping forms of the guys assigned to the tactical operations center, still snug and warm in their sleeping bags at dawn, he felt a deep longing for sleep.

Slago was also worried about his Bradley. It had taken two frighten-
ing RPG hits down south—hits so jarring that Phil Wolford started calling Slago an RPG magnet. The first time, an RPG had torn through the
front headlight, pierced the Bradley's front armor, and exploded out the
side. Slago was amazed that no one had been hurt. But the second time,

just south of Baghdad three days earlier, a Syrian guerrilla wearing a green headband had launched an RPG that ripped straight through the driver's hatch and sent a fireball exploding through the rear hull. The driver, a nineteen-year-old kid named Robert Sciria, had his back lacerated by shrapnel. One of the infantrymen inside the hull was hit, too, and Techur, the gunner, took a sliver of shrapnel in the thigh. Sciria had saved them, driving madly for a mile and a half out of the kill zone with his back bleeding and his wounds burning. Now, on Highway 8, Slago was confident that his crew knew how to respond to any crisis, but he couldn't help but wonder how many more RPG hits his battered Bradley could withstand.

As soon as they passed the cloverleaf at Objective Curly, Slago heard the RPG teams open up from the roadside bunkers and from alleyways to the east. In an instant, he was focused and alert. He was intrigued by the way the battlefield always shifted so suddenly from calm to chaos. It was like going from zero to 120 mph in one wild burst of energy. One minute he was anxious and apprehensive, and the next he was intense and energized, the adrenaline pumping so hard that his ears pounded. He saw Techur in the gunner's mount, scanning the right side. "Yeah, go for it, Techur!" he hollered. Slago had complete confidence in Techur, who was young—just twenty-three—but tough and decisive, a wiry little guy from the Palau Islands.

Techur had spotted three men coming out of a house and into an alleyway about five hundred meters to the east. He watched them close a gate behind them and lay their RPG launchers on the ground, as though they had all the time in the world. Then one of them reached down, lifted the launcher to his shoulder, and loaded a grenade. The launcher was aimed at the battalion executive officer in a vehicle just behind the Bradley. Techur put his magnified sight right on the launcher and punched up a HEAT round. He was thinking: *Ain't no way you're getting that round off, man.* He squeezed the trigger and the round exploded on top of the three men. Techur couldn't see any blood or body parts. It was a very clinical scene. The men were just gone, evaporated.

In the next alleyway, also to the east, men with RPGs and AK-47s were running back and forth, trying to get into position to fire on the column. Techur had discovered down south that it was virtually impossible to track and hit men who were on the move. Instead, he had learned to ricochet coax rounds off streets and buildings. Now he fired into the pavement and watched the coax bounce crazily through the alleyway, sweeping the gunmen off their feet. They went down and stayed down. It was like bowling with a machine gun. Techur felt no sorrow or even pity. He was killing in order to survive. It was more than a job, more than a mission. It was pure survival.

Even with Techur's spectacular kills, Slago was still uneasy. Slago had been unnerved when his Bradley passed by Bell's disabled tank, and then the remains of Charlie One Two. Slago hadn't heard the story of Charlie One Two. He thought the tank had just been hit. It was a sobering sight. He thought: *Damn, they've already taken out two Abrams tanks! This is incredible. An Abrams is supposed to be indestructible!*

Slago was up in the hatch, his head and shoulders exposed, and now he felt more vulnerable than ever. He had just seen what RPGs or recoilless rifles had done to the two tanks, and now he imagined what a single 7.62 AK-47 round would do to his head. His head would explode. He tried not to think about it. He concentrated on the reports on the radio from the tanks and Bradleys ahead of him. They were providing the coordinates for enemy positions. Slago marked them on his map. He wanted to be able to tell Techur exactly where to lay down his rounds. Nobody was going to get off a first shot at his crew.

Just south of the spaghetti junction, beyond the row of greenhouses on the west side of the highway, Yusef Taha and his brother Ziad were huddled in the rear downstairs room of their two-story stucco home in the shade of the green nursery awnings. The Taha brothers owned one of the greenhouses, which had been shredded by coax from the Rogue Bradleys two days earlier. They had stayed in the war zone to protect their house—not from the Americans, but from the Syrian mercenaries who had arrived several days earlier to seize control of the entire greenhouse complex. The brothers knew that if they fled, the Syrians would have set up snipers' nests on their roof, drawing tank rounds that would have flattened their modest little home. So now they were hunkered down inside with twelve family members—aunts and uncles, in-laws and children—praying that the Americans would pass by quickly and leave their house intact.

Yusef was a heavyset forty-two-year-old, with a thick mustache and the beginnings of a beard. Ziad was twenty-six, thin and handsome and had a trimmed mustache. The brothers had pleaded with the Syrians, begging them to find some other place to fight the Americans. But the Syrians said the greenhouses and nurseries occupied a strategic stretch of territory along the Hillah Highway—Highway 8—controlling access to the airport and to the government palace complex downtown. They set up RPG teams inside the greenhouses, joined by Republican Guard troops in their dark green uniforms with distinctive maroon insignias. It seemed to the Taha brothers that the Syrians were in charge. They were certainly more fanatic and energized than the Republican Guards. They spoke often of jihad, of dying while killing Americans infidels. Some of them strapped packs of explosives to their chests and spoke of ramming suicide cars into the tanks and Bradleys. Some of them brandished swords, like Saladin, the Arab conquerer. The brothers did not particularly welcome the American invasion—and certainly not the devastating firepower brought to bear on their nursery business—but they resented the Syrians, who were invaders in their own right. When the brothers asked one of the Syrian fighters to move away from in front of their house, the man cursed them and asked why they weren't fighting to defend their own country.

During the highway battle two days earlier, several of the Syrians—along with a few Fedayeen fighters in black robes—had died in a horrifying series of explosions behind a row of heavy clay planters. The families of the Fedayeen had arrived later in the day to retrieve what remained of the fighters' corpses, and the Syrians dragged away their own dead countrymen for burial. The Taha brothers had hoped the brutal deaths would discourage the other fighters, but the Syrians and Fedayeen had regrouped for today's fight. They were crouched behind concrete walls and in the cinder-block frames of unfinished homes, armed with RPGs and AK-47s. Across the highway, the Republican Guards had set up inside a cement granary.

When the American tanks appeared through the yellow haze obscuring the highway, the brothers and their family members got down on the floor, below the level of the windows. The floor shuddered as grenades roared from RPG tubes and the automatic rifle rounds beat a steady *thunk thunk thunk*. The blasts of the tank and Bradley cannons rattled the windows and the shells struck with a heavy thud somewhere next to the highway. The Taha family could not see the battle—they could only hear it, and feel it thumping through the floors and walls.

Yusef looked through the front window and saw his neighbor, Saad Fadhil, running into the courtyard toward his car. It was on fire. Machine-gun fire from the American column was tearing through the metal front gate and gouging holes in the stucco walls. Fadhil was splashing the flames with water from a plastic jug when something caused his body to pitch backward and explode. Yusef could see that Fadhil had been killed instantly, but he thought he should try to recover his body before the machine gun mutilated it even more; already, Fadhil's arm was gone and part of his midsection was missing. Yusef crept through the front doorway. The American machine gun opened up again, the rounds slapping against the stucco, and Yusef ran back inside and threw himself back down on the floor.

The brothers' elderly mother was hyperventilating, and Ziad was trying to calm her. He had to shout over the roar of the battle. Some of the date palms in front of the house were on fire now, and the family feared that the flames would spread to the house. The incoming rounds tore the flowering petals from the bougainvillea vines hanging from the second-floor balcony, and the ground outside was covered with a bright scarlet carpet. The family huddled together on the floor for many long minutes, listening to bullets ping against the metal gate and watching the flames flicker and die on the date palm fronds. Then, as suddenly as it had begun, the shooting stopped. The clanking of the tank treads faded and the only sounds were the shouts of the Syrians and Fedayeen. They were collecting their dead.

A half mile up the highway, the helmeted head of Lieutenant Maurice Middleton was visible above the commander's cupola of a tank that had the nickname *Apotheosis* stenciled on the gun tube. Middleton had already passed the greenhouses and was following the tail vehicles of the Rogue battalion. He was commanding the lead tank for Flip deCamp's Tusker battalion. It was Middleton's job to lead the entire tank battalion into Saddam Hussein's palace complex, where his company—Captain Phil Wolford's Assassins—had been ordered to seize and hold the hulking Republican Palace with just seventy men, ten tanks, and four Bradleys.

The night before, Wolford had briefed Middleton on the route into the city center. He had stressed the importance of getting a smooth separation from Rogue battalion, which would split off north along the six-lane

Qadisiya Highway toward Saddam's parade grounds and reviewing stand, and the tomb of the unknown soldier. It was crucial that Middleton split off to the east, along the four-lane Kindi Highway. If he missed the turn-off, Wolford told him, the whole damn battalion would be headed in the wrong direction. There was no way to turn around and go back. Wolford had told Middleton, "Don't . . . fucking . . . miss it."

Middleton was twenty-three, a slender, soft-spoken graduate of Emory University who exuded a quiet confidence. He had only been in the army for two years after being commissioned right out of college, but he had seen enough combat on the march up from Kuwait to feel comfortable leading the column. He knew from his maps and his satellite imagery that just past the spaghetti junction he needed to take a ramp that led to a service ramp, which led in turn to the Kindi Highway. His only concern was the weather. A dust storm had kicked up and the sky was a strange yellowish-gray, streaked with wisps of black from all the gunfire up Highway 8. Middleton was worried about being able to see the exit ramps. He had heard about the Rogue guys getting lost at the junction two days earlier.

Up to this point, Middleton had been concentrating on firing his .50-caliber machine gun into the roadside bunkers. It was so hazy that he couldn't see any enemy dismounts, only their muzzle flashes. He directed his gunner on the coax and main gun while also monitoring the platoon and company nets. At one point, he heard Captain Wolford's voice over the net, screaming, "Watch out for indirect!"—for mortars. An RPG had been fired straight up into the air, like a mortar, and had exploded on the highway next to Wolford's tank, rocking him in the turret. He knew it was an RPG, not a mortar, but he yelled out the warning because it had crashed down just like a mortar. He was intrigued by the bizarre ways the Iraqis used their weapons.

As Middleton rolled past the spaghetti junction, he concentrated on the roadway. He was searching for the spot where the Rogue column would continue on the Qadisiya Highway and Middleton would peel off onto the Kindi Highway. Middleton had marked the turnoff on his maps and had entered the GPS coordinates on his Plugger. The enemy gunfire had died down, so he was able to concentrate—and suddenly there it was, a clearly defined exit ramp exactly where it was supposed to be. Middleton followed the ramp, which led to an access ramp, which took him straight onto the

Kindi Highway, trailed by the rest of the column. It wasn't all that difficult, but still he felt a small sense of triumph.

As the column moved east on the highway, Middleton spotted a series
of bunkers on both sides of the highway. Up ahead, he could see gunmen
leaping from technicals and running into the tree line. And now, speeding
toward the column in the westbound lanes were two cars—an orange-and-
white taxi and a small dark blue sedan. Middleton ordered his gunner to
fire a warning burst of coax at the taxi. Then he got on the radio to his
wingman in the tank behind him, Staff Sergeant Shawn Gibson, and told
Gibson to take care of the other car. The coax from Middleton's tank had
no effect on the taxi, which actually seemed to speed up. The next burst
tore into the passenger compartment. The taxi careened off the highway
and crashed into the guardrail about a hundred meters away. Before
Gibson's tank could fire on the second car, the vehicle skidded to a stop.
The crews didn't have time to stop and determine whether either car contained soldiers or just wayward civilians. They plowed on, toward the
palace.

Two tanks behind Middleton, Sergeant First Class Jonathan Lustig
was surprised to see a Chevrolet Caprice suddenly appear on the roadway. He hadn't seen it coming. It just materialized out of the haze, speeding the wrong way, racing toward Lieutenant Middleton's lead tank. An
Iraqi flag was flapping out one of the windows. Lustig couldn't do much
about it; his turret was broken and he couldn't traverse. He saw Middleton's
gunner fire a burst of coax into the Caprice. The car spun out of control.
It flew off the left side of the highway and sailed into a tree. The impact
launched the driver through the windshield like a man shot out of a cannon. It was a remarkable sight, Lustig thought—like watching one of those
slow-motion car crashes on TV cop shows.

To the left of the roadway, Staff Sergeant Gibson saw something
move in a grove of date palms. He looked closer and saw a turret turning.
It was a BMP, a Russian-made armored personnel carrier, camouflaged
by a layer of palm fronds. It was only about 150 meters away. The Iraqi
gunner was trying to traverse the turret to fire on Middleton's tank at the
head of the column. Gibson yelled at his gunner to fire a main gun round.
The gunner got a laser reading through his sights, then said, "Bad lase!"
The laser reading was flashing all zeros, meaning the target was too close
to get a reading.

"Just squeeze the fucking trigger!" Gibson screamed.

The gunner lined up the targeting reticle on the BMP and fired a round that tore into the vehicle, setting it ablaze and triggering a series of secondary explosions as the BMP's ammunition cooked off. From the tank commander's cupola, Gibson saw a second BMP, also covered by palm fronds. His loader slammed a fresh round into the breech. Gibson didn't bother with a laser reading. He looked through the sights, put the reticle on the BMP's center mass, and squeezed the trigger on the power control handles. The vehicle exploded, sending shards of metal and exploding ammunition across the highway. "Button up!" Gibson yelled. He had heard stories about guys getting whacked by secondary explosions.

The ammunition was still cooking off as the roadway turned straight and flat, and the column picked up speed. Middleton was looking for the Fourteenth of July traffic circle, a roundabout that connected the Fourteenth of July Bridge over the Tigris to the stone archway leading into the Republican Palace complex, which stretched for more than a mile along the river. The column was now taking more and more gunfire from bunkers and from two- and three-story buildings lining the highway. The incoming rounds whipped past the tank as Middleton swung into a traffic circle anchored by a bronze monument honoring Iraqi war dead.

Middleton stopped and checked his map. He was certain he had found the Fourteenth of July circle, but he couldn't find the roadway into the Republican Palace complex. He thought it was the road that jutted off to the east. He radioed Lustig and asked, "Is this the road we're supposed to go on?"

Lustig checked his map. He wasn't sure, either. "It looks like it," he said.

Middleton headed down the roadway. Iraqi soldiers were popping up out of bunkers around the circle. Middleton radioed back to alert the rest of the column, then spotted a stone archway that led directly into the palace grounds. As the archway came into view through the haze, Middleton saw that it was flanked by a pair of recoilless rifles mounted on green Land Rovers—apparently the last line of defense for the entire palace complex. Quickly, Middleton ordered his gunner to lock on to one Land Rover and then told Gibson to take care of the other. The recoilless rifle crews were abandoning the guns just as the breech and barrels were ripped apart, the HEAT rounds exploding on impact.

Smoke from the burning guns obscured the road, but Middleton could still make out some sort of obstacle blocking access to the archway. He rolled closer and saw that heavy concrete planters filled with dirt had been lined up across the roadway. A tall metal gate attached to the archway was sealed by a heavy chain and padlock. As Middleton paused to consider his options, Lustig radioed and said, "Just drive through that shit!"

Middleton thought he might be able to crush the planters and roll right over the top. The Rogue tanks had managed to crash through concrete highway dividers near the airport two days earlier. Middleton had his driver rev the engine, and the tank plowed into the planters. It rode halfway up, but then hung awkwardly at a forty-five-degree angle. The tank's belly was exposed. Gibson's tank was mounted on the front with a heavy plow. Gibson radioed and said, "Come back off and I'll hit it with the plow."

Middleton managed to back up and free his tank from the planters. Behind him, Gibson realized that he needed to hit the obstacle at a higher speed than Middleton had attempted. Because he was farther back, he was able to get a good running start. He intended to maintain his momentum past the planters and smash through the metal gate and chain beneath the arch. His driver had the tank moving at least thirty miles an hour, its plow in the raised position, as the seventy-ton vehicle surged forward and barreled into the planters. The collision crushed the planters and sent them skidding across the pavement. Gibson's tank went airborne for an instant, then slammed back down. Middleton was amazed; he had never seen a tank do that.

Gibson didn't slow down. Middleton watched Gibson's tank lumber straight ahead, its seven-ton plow aimed at the metal gates and chain. The Abrams smashed through, crushing the gate and popping the chain. Gibson's main gun barrel smacked against the stone arch and spun to the rear, but the sergeant was now the first American soldier inside Saddam's Republican Palace complex. It was just past 8 a.m. In slightly more than two hours, Assassin Company had breached the palace gates.

E I G H T

SUICIDE AT THE GATES OF BAGHDAD

On the way up Highway 8 that morning, Captain Jason Conroy ordered his tank crews to conserve main gun rounds. Each tank carried only forty of the big shells—plus one in the tube—and Conroy didn't know how many Iraqi tanks and armored personnel carriers the column might have to confront. In fact, Conroy knew very little about the enemy. The brigade's S-2 shop, the intelligence officers, had provided only vague guidance. They had warned the company commanders to expect several thousand Special Republican Guards, plus Fedayeen militiamen and Arab mercenaries. They had spoken of bunkers and snipers and suicide vehicles—the same sort of resistance Conroy and the Rogue battalion had already encountered on the first thunder run two days earlier.

It seemed to him presumptuous to invade a hostile metropolis of 5 million people—a capital whose city center had never been penetrated by American troops, not even during the first Gulf War—without a detailed breakdown of enemy forces and defenses. In fact, when Conroy had relayed the orders to his lieutenants at Charlie Company the night before, they were so shocked that they dropped their briefing books. Even so, the first thunder run had given Conroy and his men a certain level of confidence, and they believed their tanks and Bradleys could blow through the city center the same way they had blown past the Iraqi defenses along Highway 8 and the airport highway. Whether they would be able to hold their ground and survive through the night was another matter. There wasn't much Conroy could tell his men about that prospect. All he said was, "Guys, plan on spending the night."

Now, after a brief but intense firefight at the nursery, Conroy and the rest of the Rogue battalion had made the turn at the spaghetti junction and were heading east into the governmental complex. The battalion had

been firing mostly coax and .50-caliber, hitting only the most obvious targets and passing off the rest to the Tusker crews behind them before the
Rogue column split off onto the Qadisiya Highway. The resistance was
similar to Saturday's thunder run—sustained small-arms and RPG fire,
some recoilless rifle, occasional artillery and mortars. Conroy thought it
was slightly less intense this time around. His crews had destroyed two
suicide trucks, but the main threats were from bunkers and snipers. Because his company had fired only a few main tank rounds, he felt comfortable about his ammunition reserves. He thought he had enough to last
until nightfall.

Conroy was still uncertain what to expect inside the city, though he
was not particularly surprised when he spotted two Iraqi armored personnel carriers just beyond an overpass. They were backing up and turning
around, trying to get in position to fire on the approaching convoy. The
carriers—they were Russian-made BMPs—were outfitted with 105mm
short-barrel guns, which fired skinny little rounds that were not capable
of penetrating an Abrams's armor but could disable a tank if they struck in
the rear engine compartment. Conroy ordered his gunner to hit one of the
BMPs with a main gun round. Then he radioed back and told a tank commander from his third platoon to take care of the other one. The gunners
squeezed the triggers before the BMPs could turn around. The vehicles
burst into flames. Their ammunition racks ignited and their turrets popped
off—a spectacular show of exploding metal that brought a round of cheers
from the crews.

It was less than four kilometers from the spaghetti junction to
Conroy's assigned target, Saddam Hussein's parade ground and VIP reviewing stand next to Zawra Park. The parade ground was flanked on either
end by a pair of stainless steel crossed sabers, built at the height of the Iran-
Iraq war in 1985 and named the Victory Arches, despite the inconclusive
outcome of the conflict. Conroy was surprised by how quickly the Rogue
column covered the ground, even with a constant barrage of RPGs and
automatic rifle fire.

Just as the dull shine of the towering sabers came into view through
the haze, a white pickup truck emerged from the westbound lanes. It was
bearing down on Conroy's tank. Conroy tried to get his gunner to traverse
the main gun, but there wasn't time. The gunner managed to hit the truck
with a burst of coax, but it kept coming. Conroy felt it plow into the side

of his tank, then careen off into a guardrail. He swung his .50-caliber machine gun around and fired directly into the passenger compartment. The truck exploded. Conroy couldn't see who had been inside, but the intensity of the explosion made him think the truck had been packed with ammunition. He was alarmed at how quickly the pickup had closed in on him, and he began to worry that his luck was running out. His tank had already been rammed on the first thunder run, and now this. He rolled on—and suddenly he realized that he had gone past the parade field. He had to stop and make a U-turn, the whole company following him. They crushed a series of guardrails, crossed an open field, found the access road, and there, shrouded in gray smoke, were the crossed sabers.

Most of the tankers had seen news clips of Hussein standing at attention on the reviewing stand, gazing out past the crossed sabers at passing formations of Iraqi troops and tanks. They had seen him in a military uniform dripping with medals, and in a dark suit and black homburg, his arm upraised and half-cocked in that peculiar cross between a wave and a salute. A few had seen the video of Hussein on the reviewing stand, squeezing off a shotgun blast, one-handed. Now their tanks and Bradleys were rolling toward that very spot—and there was no one there to stop them. The whole vast sweep of the parade grounds, which stretched for more than a kilometer, seemed to be lightly defended. Three Iraqi soldiers bolted from the reviewing stand and ran toward an office complex attached to the stand. One of them was killed by coax; the others escaped. A few hundred meters to the north, Conroy's men destroyed several RPG teams that had been firing from behind a row of electric transformers near the zoo. The fighting had ignited several fuel containers, which sent plumes of black smoke curling into the morning sky.

It was difficult for Conroy to absorb it all. He had expected the Iraqis to mount heavier resistance for such a significant stretch of terrain in the middle of the governmental complex. He found it hard to believe that he—twenty-nine-year-old Jason Conroy from upstate New York—now owned Saddam Hussein's parade grounds and VIP reviewing stand. He looked around. Directly across from the reviewing stand, he saw an impressive statue—a huge bronze depiction of Saddam riding a horse. He felt a strong urge to put a tank round straight through Saddam's chest.

The company set up in defensive positions, with a 360-degree perimeter that provided clear fields of fire in all directions. Other units pushed west, beyond the sabers, where they came under sporadic artillery fire and were fired on by gunmen in speeding cars. Still others moved farther north, through Zawra Park, where Iraqi soldiers were firing RPGs from rooftops and thick stands of palm groves lining a series of small lakes. More Rogue units secured the tomb of the unknown soldier, a circular concrete structure with long sloping sides and a cavern in the center.

From time to time, mortars crashed down on either side of the monument. Even though he had secured the reviewing stand, Conroy knew that Iraqi troops and militiamen were still dug in throughout the park and beyond the tree lines. A few were still on rooftops, manning antiaircraft guns that were firing straight down at the tanks. And from somewhere beyond the park, Iraqi mortar crews were launching rounds that seemed to be inching closer to the reviewing stand. Conroy braced himself for a long day of fighting.

As Conroy's company was securing the parade ground, Lightning 28, a mixed Bradley crew of marines and Third Infantry soldiers, was traveling in the middle of the Tusker column and well behind the lead Rogue tanks. The Bradley was part of Cyclone Company, from the Tusker battalion. The marines inside were from ANGLICO, for Air and Naval Gunfire Liaison Company, a Marine Corps unit that had been attached to the Third Infantry Division. The ANGLICO men were experts on calling in close air support. The seven-man Bradley crew was a hybrid of soldiers and marines, part forward air control team and part combat gun vehicle.

For more than an hour, the men inside Lihghtning 28's rear hull had been listening to thumps and explosions along Highway 8 and struggling to catch glimpses of the battle through the Bradley's vision blocks—three-inch-high rectangular windows made of bulletproof glass. The crewmen could see black smoke spewing from bunkers and bright orange flames spitting from burning vehicles, and they could hear the steady beat of small-arms fire.

Up in the commander's hatch, Marine Major Mark Jewell was working the 25mm main gun, each high-explosive round rattling the steel hull. In the gunner's seat, Sergeant Walter Daniel was squeezing off periodic bursts of coax. From time to time, the men in the back could hear bullets punch the outside of the hull, making a hollow clanging sound. They could have been fired on from anywhere—from bunkers, from rooftops, from alleyways. There was no way to know. The hull was sealed off.

The crewmen went about their work with a furious intensity. The radioman, Marine Sergeant Dennis Parks, was monitoring five separate radio nets after cleaning his radio headset nodes with a pencil eraser. He was feeding information to Major Jewell through the Bradley's intercom and shouting grid coordinates to Marine Captain David Cooper, who was seated next to him. Parks looked more like a tanker than a marine. He was short and muscular, and he moved quickly and nimbly inside the tight confines of the hull. He was only twenty-one, but he had an officer's sense of command. He was quick-witted and decisive—what people in the military call squared away.

Captain Cooper was seven years older and taller and rangier than Parks, but he exuded the same calm efficiency. Leaning back, with his long legs crossed, Cooper had the furrowed, intense look of a man reading a newspaper on a lurching subway car. He was clutching a map in his left hand. With his right hand, he was scribbling map coordinates into a notebook, converting the army's GPS grids to longitude and latitude for the air force pilots. "Just give me a grid and I'll get you aircraft," he said over the radio. Cooper was an air liaison officer, an easygoing officer with a wife and a house full of pets back home in North Carolina. He was relaying potential target coordinates for warplanes attacking in support of the armored column. His long face was flushed and sweaty under his communications helmet, but he seemed strangely content and absorbed in his work.

Matthew Hanks, an army lieutenant, was more animated. He scrambled back and forth between the hull and the upper deck, talking to the gunner and trying to hear the orders shouted down by Major Jewell up in the hatch. Hanks was twenty-three, a tall, brown-haired Virginian who spoke in quick, excited bursts and seemed unable to sit still for more than a few minutes at a time. Parks barked at him a few times, trying to get Hanks to stay put. Hanks kept up a steady chatter.

Across from Parks was Trevor Havens, a twenty-three-year-old marine corporal who was stretching his neck to peer through the rear vision blocks. He was watching the Bradley's "six," its rear six-o'clock position. The Bradley's heavy rear hatch was outfitted with a tiny gun port, and from time to time Havens poked his M-16 through the opening, searching for something to hit. When Havens's gun barrel wasn't jutting through the port,

Parks used it as an ashtray, flicking ashes from his cigarettes through the tiny opening.

Havens bounced his knee nervously as he squinted through the vision blocks. He felt an urgent need to urinate. "I gotta piss bad!" he announced. Parks gave him a disgusted look and reached down for an empty water bottle amid the crumpled MRE pouches littering the steel deck. All the crews carried emergency piss bottles.

"Here," Parks said. "Don't miss."

Havens braced himself against the hull, half-standing, half-squatting, and tried to fill the bottle. It was hopeless. The Bradley was lurching and bouncing. Havens lost his balance and a few drops on the floor. Everyone groaned and cursed. The air inside the Bradley was already hot and stale, saturated with sweat and oil and cordite. Now there was the acidic scent of fresh urine.

As the Bradley drew closer to its destination, the Fourteenth of July traffic circle, the gunfire outside intensified. The crewmen could hear some of the tanks open up with their main gun rounds, and the Bradley shuddered from the concussions. An explosion rocked the vehicle, slamming everyone against the hull. "What the hell was that?" somebody asked. Cooper responded casually, "Secondary explosion." A suicide vehicle had just been incinerated by a tank round, and whatever was inside was cooking off. Voices on the radio net were reporting more technicals and suicide cars nearby.

The Bradley rumbled into the Fourteenth of July circle under fire. Jewell ordered everyone to button up—to stay inside and keep the hatches locked. Jewell had sealed the commander's hatch and ducked down inside. The main gun had jammed, and he didn't have the wrench required to manually crank the ammunition feed system and get the gun working again. With only the coax to defend the Bradley, Jewell had the driver park the Bradley behind a wall of tanks from Cyclone Company that had taken up positions at the foot of the bridge. From the rear vision blocks, the crewmen could see the tan backs of the tanks and a pall of gray smoke obscuring the bridge and the river. It was a startling sight: an American tank company was in the heart of Baghdad.

The Cyclone commander was Captain Stephen Barry, a tall, husky former high school athlete with a shaved head. Barry was a popular commander who was so big and imposing that he was hard to miss. Flip deCamp sometimes referred to him as Big Sexy—a nickname bestowed by another officer's wife. Barry was twenty-eight, a West Point man who had graduated as the top history major in his class. He was determined to shut down the bridge, which provided access to the entire government complex across the Tigris River from the south. He had discussed the importance of the bridge with Phil Wolford of Assassin Company the night before. They were worried about a narrow seam between the sectors assigned to Rogue and to Tusker. Barry wanted to make sure he covered Wolford's rear at the entrance to the palace complex, where a road jutting east from the Fourteenth of July circle led through the archway that had been rammed by Assassin's tanks. About eight hundred meters to his northwest, a road from the circle connected to the Qadisiya Highway near the tomb of the unknown soldier. That was Barry's boundary with Captain Jason Conroy's sector, though there was an unsecured gap between the two units.

Barry was concerned about the poor quality of the intelligence he had received. He had been ordered into downtown Baghdad with no clear sense of what he was up against. Except for the few details he had picked up from Rogue's thunder run two days earlier, he was winging it. He was in the commander's hatch of his tank—nicknamed *Conquer This*—and holding what was almost certainly the most strategic traffic circle in all of Baghdad at that moment. Yet he had no idea where the enemy was, or what weapons they carried. His battalion commander, deCamp, had described the mission as attacking the Iraqi equivalent of the capital mall in Washington, D.C. Barry was now inside Baghdad's version of the national mall, an unfamiliar and unsettling place. He didn't know what it would take to hold his ground. "It could be a breeze, it could be friggin' hard, it could be something in between," Barry had told his crews the night before.

Cyclone Company had been at the circle for just five minutes when a white car streaked across the bridge, bearing down on the traffic circle. Barry could see three men inside. One of them was pointing a machine gun out a window. Barry gave the order to fire. Three tanks opened up, including Barry's own Abrams. The sedan caught fire and crashed. Two men climbed out and both went down, killed instantly by coax. Thirty seconds later, a white Jeep Cherokee sped down the bridge span. Coax and .50-caliber rounds shattered the windshield. The Cherokee exploded. The fireball was huge—so big that Barry was certain the vehicle had been loaded with explosives. He knew the difference between a burning car and the detonation of explosives. This was a suicide car.

And they kept coming—sedans, pickups, a Chevy Caprice, three cars in the first ten minutes, six more right after that. The tanks destroyed them all. It was incomprehensible. Barry kept thinking: *What the hell is wrong with these people?* They were trying to ram cars into tanks. It was futile—absolutely senseless. It was like they *wanted* to die, and as spectacularly as possible. Barry hated slaughtering them. And that's what it was—slaughter. They were the enemy—at least the ones he could see—but it gave Barry no pleasure to kill them. It got worse when smoke from burning vehicles made it difficult to see through the thermals and determine whether the people in the vehicles were armed.

Some of the gunners were distressed by the carnage. They tried to follow the rules of engagement for dealing with oncoming vehicles: first fire into the roadway, then into the engine block, and then, if the car kept coming, into the windshield to kill the driver. The gunners hoped the cars would stop and turn around after the first shots into the roadway. But they kept coming, and the gunners kept killing them.

One car, an old Caprice, surprised everyone by speeding toward the circle from the west, down the same roadway the company had used to reach the circle. A tank gunner, Sergeant Derrick January, fired warning shots. The Caprice kept coming. January fired at least a hundred rounds of coax through the windshield. The Caprice kept coming. Finally January stopped the vehicle with a HEAT round. A middle-aged man in civilian clothes crawled from the wreckage, raising a white towel. His face was burned and blackened and his legs were bloodied, but he was alive. No weapon was visible. The man jabbered in broken English while Sergeant Luther Robinson, a medic, treated his wounds. Nobody could figure out why he had decided to challenge the tanks. Robinson shrugged and said in his North Carolina drawl, "That's the luckiest man I've seen in Iraq yet."

The cars kept coming. After one vehicle was hit and burst into flames on the bridge, the passenger door opened and a man with a pistol stepped out. The gunner on Barry's tank, Sergeant Arnoldo Spangaro, obeyed Barry's order to fire at the man's feet. Then the man starting running toward the tank, aiming his pistol.

"Shoot him!" Barry ordered.

Spangaro hesitated. It didn't feel right. Spangaro was a family man, with an eight-year-old stepson and a four-year-old daughter back home. He wasn't the kind of man who enjoyed killing people, even people with guns in their hands.

"Shoot him!" Barry yelled again. Spangaro opened up with coax, blowing the man apart. The gunner turned to his captain. "That didn't feel too good," he said.

Afterward, Specialist Jarrid Lott, a tank driver, saw one of the tank commanders taking photographs of mutilated bodies in the vehicles. He was appalled. He asked the commander why he wanted to capture such horrible images. The man had his reasons. "If my son says he wants to join the army," he told Lott, "I'll show him this and tell him: '*This* is what the army does.'"

Even after vehicles stopped speeding over the bridge, Cyclone Company was still taking small-arms fire. Barry realized that gunmen were creeping across the bridge along a pair of narrow catwalks below the elevated roadway. The gunners managed to kill some of them, and the rest fled back across the river. After that, things settled down. For the moment, the Fourteenth of July Bridge and traffic circle were secure. For the first time, Barry allowed himself to believe that the war in Iraq was coming to a close—if not that day, then very soon.

Inside Lightning 28, Mark Jewell was still trying to get the Bradley's main gun to work. Jewell was a feisty character, full of energy and good cheer. He was thirty-nine, short and solidly built, his light brown hair clipped into a tight marine crew cut. He had been a marine for fifteen years, commissioned right out of school after graduating from the University of Louisville. Jewell had a wife and three children back in the States, and they were constantly on his mind. He had used a reporter's cell phone to call a friend in the States and have him send a bouquet of flowers to his wife for their wedding anniversary that week.

Now Jewell was struggling with the ammunition feed on the main gun. At one point, the gun accidentally went off, firing a round harmlessly into the tree line. It scared the hell out of Steve Barry, who got on the radio and asked Jewell, "Two Eight, what the hell?" Jewell explained and apologized, and went back to work on the gun.

Jewell wasn't an armor officer. In fact, he had never commanded a Bradley until two weeks earlier. He had received an hour-long training session in Kuwait from Tom Slago, the Bradley commander from the Tusker battalion, but after that he had to learn from on-the-job training during the march up through the desert. He knew enough to realize that he needed a special wrench to crank the ammunition feed chains to clear the jammed main gun. He radioed one of the Cyclone crews and asked to borrow the tool.

Jewell's Bradley was still buttoned up when the crew heard someone pounding on the rear hatch. Parks swung it open. And there in the morning haze, wrench in hand, wearing a decidedly non–military issue helmet and flak vest, stood Geoff Mohan of the *Los Angeles Times*. Mohan was Cyclone's embedded reporter. He had volunteered to deliver the wrench because he desperately needed to get outside in order to crank up his satellite phone and transmit updates to his story in time to meet his paper's final deadline. It was well before midnight in Los Angeles, still time for Mohan to make the April 7 editions. It was a fortuitous arrangement for everyone involved. Mohan got his story, and Jewell got his wrench.

Outside Lightning 28, Lieutenant Hanks noticed an RPG launcher in a grassy expanse of date palms and eucalyptus trees a few steps beyond the Bradley. He walked over and saw a series of bunkers covered by corrugated metal and camouflaged with palm fronds. Jewell yelled at Hanks to stop and wait for help. He didn't want him probing the bunkers alone. He summoned Parks, who volunteered to be, as he called it, a tunnel rat.

Parks took Jewell's 9mm pistol and a flashlight. With Hanks and Corporal Havens covering him, Parks crawled into one of the bunkers. Around a bend in the tunnel, his flashlight lit up the terrified faces of several Iraqi soldiers huddled in the dark, their arms upraised, begging not to be shot. Jewell heard Parks scream, "You *hajji* motherfuckers! Get out of the hole!" Soldiers called all Iraqis, civilian or military, *hajjis*—for *hajj*, the Muslim pilgrimage to Mecca. It was not a complimentary term. Parks emerged from the bunker, his fatigues caked with dirt and his pistol trained on a column of Iraqis in filthy green uniforms. The scarlet insignia on some of the men's epaulets identified them as Special Republican Guards.

Several Cyclone tankers ran over and searched the other bunkers, yanking out more Iraqis, some in dirt-encrusted civilian clothes—eighteen in all. The prisoners got down on their bellies. The tankers hog-tied them with plastic handcuffs and rifled through their pockets, tossing aside cigarettes and wallets. Staff Sergeant Anthony J. Smith, a silver-haired tank commander, screamed at them, "Republican Guard? Yes?" One of the men nodded. In English, he mumbled, "Thank you! Thank you!" Smith grinned at him. "This is a good thing for you. You're going to live," he told him.

A prisoner who had not yet been handcuffed lay on his belly and held out a tiny Koran. Smith motioned for him to flip through the pages to show it wasn't booby-trapped. Then Smith gingerly took the book, inspected it, sealed it in a plastic bag, and gave it back to the prisoner. Still on his belly, the man mumbled his appreciation for this small act of kindness in a war zone.

The Iraqis had been living in filth. The bunkers were dark and strewn with trash and rotting food and flimsy bedding. There were piles of uniforms, berets, and helmets, all of it abandoned by soldiers who had fled. The soldiers had been subsisting on moldy bread and dried dates, but they were well armed nonetheless. The bunkers contained dozens of AK-47s, seven RPG launchers, sixty rockets, forty grenades, and five thousand rounds of ammunition.

Parks stared at the weapons. "They could have easily killed us all," he said. "They could've hit us before we even knew where they were." He seemed more mystified than relieved.

A mile to the west, Colonel Perkins had arrived at the gates of Saddam's modern concrete palace across from the Baath Party headquarters on the Kindi Highway—what the brigade called the New Palace to distinguish it from the older and larger Republican Palace two and a half kilometers to the east. The formal name of the structure was the Sujud Palace, a squat, blocky edifice of pale tan concrete built in 1990 for Saddam's first wife. Part of the ornate entry vestibule, built of pink marble and cascading stalactite molding, had been collapsed by a direct hit during the U.S. Air Force bombing campaign the previous week. The palace was deserted when Perkins, in the hatch of his M113 command armored personnel carrier, arrived on the Kindi Highway in the middle of the armored column.

Perkins had just survived a close call on the highway after the column had come down the ramp off the spaghetti junction. A white Toyota pickup had sped toward Perkins's carrier from the rear, its headlights burning in the early morning haze. Captain Shannon Hume, a Bradley commander from the Tusker battalion, spotted the vehicle and ordered his gunner to fire a warning burst of coax. The pickup plowed ahead, closing to within 150 meters of the command carrier, even after a second round of coax was fired into the pavement. Hume ordered his gunner to fire armor-piercing rounds from the 25mm main gun directly into the pickup. The first round slammed into the engine block. The second tore through the windshield, killing the driver, and the third struck the cab and ignited an explosion that lifted the pickup off the highway. A series of secondary explosions convinced Hume that the truck had been a suicide vehicle packed with explosives.

Attack Company, attached to Tusker and Task Force 4-64 from another battalion, searched and secured the palace and grounds. Perkins set up his TAC—his tactical command post—at the top of a palace ramp that led to a covered walkway and the partially collapsed vestibule. The TAC was Perkins's mobile command post, a set of armored communications vehicles parked back to back to form the brigade's battlefield headquarters. From here, Perkins could direct the fight, talking by radio and satellite phone to General Blount at the airport and Lieutenant Colonel Wesley at the brigade operations center eighteen kilometers to the south.

From his perch at the top of the ramp, past the blooming red and pink roses in the palace's manicured gardens, Perkins could see the hazy outlines of Saddam's entire downtown government complex—from the Republican Guard headquarters to the west and Zawra Park to the north. To the east, obscured by haze and smog, lay the Fourteenth of July Bridge and, beyond it, the Republican Palace. Downtown Baghdad seemed to be on fire. Columns of black smoke swirled on the horizon, fed by oil fires set in ditches by Iraqi forces to obscure targets from American warplanes, and by flaming Iraqi vehicles and bunkers destroyed by tanks and Bradleys. Perkins believed he had accomplished his first goal—to create chaos, to disrupt Iraqi defenses with the speed and violence of the armored thrust. He had managed to cut through the concentric layers of defense, and now his tanks and Bradleys were behind the enemy. The second goal was now attainable—to fight from the inside out, to establish a foothold in the center of the capital and push outward and collapse the regime from within.

The Rogue commander, Rick Schwartz, had seized and secured the Rashid Hotel, the convention center, the parade grounds, the tomb of the unknown soldier, the amusement park in Zawra Park, and the adjacent zoo, where some of the Rogue crews later fed hogs to the neglected and emaciated lions. Rogue was also preparing to seize the Ministry of Information, where Schwartz hoped to encounter Mohammed Said al-Sahaf, the troublesome information minister. DeCamp's men were in the process of taking control of the entire palace complex, from the Sujud Palace east through the Fourteenth of July Circle past the bend in the Tigris River and then north to a small stone archway on a palace roadway that led to the broad Jumhuriya Bridge. DeCamp told Perkins he was prepared to spend the night, assuming he could get his battalion's fuel and ammunition safely up Highway 8.

Perkins was now more determined than ever to spend the night. Steph Twitty's China battalion was still moving up to secure Highway 8, so it was too early to know whether the fuel and ammunition convoys would get through. But things had gone so smoothly that Perkins felt a surge of confidence. He thought he could persuade General Blount to let him stay the night. It would then be up to the general to convince the higher command to shift from a quick-strike thunder run to an overnight occupation of the capital.

The U.S. military had come a long way since Vietnam, Perkins thought. The men directing the Iraqi campaign had come of age during the Vietnam conflict, when the top brass tended to micromanage every firefight, robbing ground commanders of initiative and spontaneity. There was more willingness now to let officers in the field respond and adapt to fluid situations. During the thunder run two days earlier, the command at V Corps—the next level above the Third Infantry Division —had monitored events from a UAV spy plane but had not interfered with Perkins's decisions on the ground.

Perkins had fought Saddam's army all the way up from Kuwait. He had studied the enemy for months, preparing himself for this day. He had punched his way into Baghdad not once but twice, and he had taken the measure of Saddam's defenses. He knew now, more than ever, what was required to topple the regime. If he could hold his positions through the night, he thought, Baghdad would belong to him.

There was also a strategic matter Perkins knew he needed to address. He had to outflank Mohammed Sahaf. He believed the minister was somewhere in the city center, and he anticipated another barrage of claims describing a decisive Iraqi military victory. It wasn't enough for Perkins to set up his command post inside Saddam's palace and government complex. He had to *prove* he was there. He had to compete with Sahaf for the international TV audience. Sahaf had the international press corps at his disposal across the river. Perkins had ... Fox News.

Greg Kelly, Fox's square-jawed, energetic correspondent, had ridden in the back of Perkins's command vehicle. Kelly and his cameraman were embedded with brigade headquarters. As Attack's infantrymen cleared the palace, Kelly set up his camera out front, framing the palace portico as a dramatic backdrop. He was ready to file live from downtown Baghdad. It was mid-morning now, the middle of the night back in the States but the beginning of the workday in the Arab world and in European capitals. Kelly went live—and gestured for Perkins to come over.

Perkins knew exactly what he wanted to convey. He wanted the world to know that American forces were moving at will inside the government complex—and there was nothing Saddam Hussein could do about it.

"What we have in the city now is an entire armored brigade," Perkins began. His helmet strap was pinching at his chin, and his delivery was swift and clipped. "Right now, we really have control of the center of Baghdad and what is the heart of his governmental structure," referring to Saddam.

Kelly asked how long Perkins intended to stay in the city. Perkins thought for a moment, then lapsed into vague military-speak. He didn't want anyone to know he intended to stay overnight—and he certainly didn't want to reveal just how dependent his tank battalions were on keeping Highway 8 open for fuel and ammunition. "We'll continue to develop the situation," he said, gesturing toward the city center. "We'll see what our tactical requirements are and how they fit into the overall situation. There's a lot of ways we can control this ground, a lot of ways we can control entrance and exit."

When Kelly asked if the end of the war was near, Perkins was careful not to claim victory but to make it clear that the U.S. military was dictating the fight. "Tactically, we've obviously already crushed his armed resistance and the American soldier has been victorious from that point of view," he said. His flak vest was cinched tight and his pistol was strapped to his leg. The fight was still very much on. In the background, Perkins could hear the booms of tank cannons and mortars. "We still have resistance throughout the city," he went on. "We're taking our armored forces and pushing all the way through and completely securing this so that we have freedom of maneuver in the city."

When Perkins was finished, Kelly summoned deCamp, who was in a celebratory mood. He was considerably more animated than Perkins. His face was streaked with sweat and grime, giving him a desperate, hooded look. "Saddam Hussein says he owns Baghdad," deCamp said loudly. "Wrong! *We* own Baghdad. We own his palaces, his downtown district, his hotel."

DeCamp grinned and introduced his Attack Company commander, Captain Chris Carter, who described the haphazard and disorganized nature of the resistance by Iraqi irregulars in the city. DeCamp joked about taking a shower in Saddam's palace, then began unfolding a red banner. The Fox News anchor in the United States told his early morning viewers that the tankers were unfurling the brigade's colors. Actually, the banner was a University of Georgia Bulldogs flag. DeCamp and Carter had graduated from the school, and they had hauled the flag through Iraq for this moment. Each man grabbed a corner of the flag and unfurled the school colors.

"How 'bout them Dawgs?" deCamp hollered.

"How 'bout them Dawgs?" Carter yelled back.

"Hoaah!" deCamp said.

Across the Tigris River, barely two miles from the Sujud Palace, Sahaf was putting on his own show for the cameras. He stood at his usual perch, a mezzanine roof on the second floor of the Palestine Hotel conference center. He wore his trademark black beret and a starched olive Baath Party uniform bearing two small medallions—an Iraqi flag and a portrait of Saddam. As he had two days earlier, Sahaf spoke with a flourish, denying that American forces had entered the capital.

"There is no presence of American columns in the city of Baghdad at all," Sahaf said, addressing a crush of reporters. "They were surrounded, and they were dealt with and their columns were smoldered. The American mercenaries will commit suicide at the gates of Baghdad. I would encourage them to increase their rate of committing suicide."

The reporters were openly contemptuous. Some of them had watched through binoculars from their hotel rooms upstairs as Bradleys from Phil

Wolford's Assassin Company rolled onto the riverside grounds of the Republican Palace one and a half kilometers across the Tigris. From across the river came the steady rattle of gunfire and the occasional dull thud of a tank round exploding. *That*, Sahaf explained blithely, was the sound of American soldiers being slaughtered.

And what about the American commanders who had appeared before American cameras at Saddam's palace? It was all an elaborate fraud, Sahaf said; the commanders had been filmed inside the ornate reception hall at the Baghdad airport—a facility Sahaf had said two days earlier was firmly under Iraqi military control.

"They are really sick in their minds," Sahaf said of the Americans. "They said they entered with sixty-five tanks into the center of the capital. I inform you that this is too far from the reality. This story is part of their sickness." He advised reporters not to repeat their lies.

As Sahaf delivered his performance, Salar Mustafa Jaff watched in silence. He despised Sahaf, though he never dared let it show. Jaff's narrow face betrayed no emotion. Jaff was an English speaker, a polite and reserved functionary who worked for Sahaf's ministry as a "minder" charged with monitoring and controlling the movements of foreign reporters. Sahaf had almost gotten Jaff killed two days earlier, when he had ordered him to drive into the city center to translate for Iraqi interrogators questioning American soldiers purportedly taken prisoner during Rogue's battle along the airport highway. Sahaf told Jaff that the interrogations would be videotaped and broadcast on state-run television so that the world could see that the Americans were caged like *ulooj*—an Arabic insult that translated loosely as "animals." Jaff had driven straight into a furious firefight. He managed to turn around and escape, but only with the assistance of wildy gesticulating Fedayeen militiamen. There were no American POWs, of course, but Jaff did not raise the issue with Sahaf; the man carried a pistol, and Jaff had heard rumors that Sahaf had taken shots at underlings. Jaff merely reported to one of Sahaf's aides that he had been unable to locate the American prisoners.

As Sahaf described for the international media an overwhelming Iraqi victory over the American infidels, Jaff glanced around the conference center. He caught the eye of one of his fellow Iraqi minders. The man was snickering, covering his mouth with his hand, trying with all his might to keep from laughing out loud.

N I N E
THE PARTY IS ABOVE ALL

Talal Ahmed al-Doori was up early on the morning of April 7, driving through the narrow streets of the Al Mamoun neighborhood in downtown Baghdad. He had heard rumors that American tanks were approaching the city, and he wanted to make sure his assigned sector was secure. Doori was a Baath Party militia leader, responsible for a tight swath of his neighborhood at the western edge of Highway 8 where it split at the airport and Qadisiya interchanges, or what soldiers from the Second Brigade called the spaghetti junction. In more normal times, Doori's job was rather straightforward. He was to make sure no one challenged or undermined the regime of Saddam Hussein. A hulking man of thirty-two, with a weight lifter's physique and powerful hands, Doori was an intimidating enforcer with a black goatee and a massive shaved head. He was a well-known figure in the neighborhood, the son of a popular soccer coach. He had also worked as a bodyguard for Saddam's son Uday, and he had a certain reputation as a man who was not to be trifled with. He kept his neighborhood under control.

But now, driving through the streets with the sounds of explosions echoing in the distance, Doori felt somehow inadequate. With Baghdad under siege by American forces, his responsibilities had changed. They had become both broader and less precisely defined. He wasn't quite sure what he was supposed to be doing. The previous week, for instance, the Baath Party had issued orders to arrest anyone with a Thuraya satellite phone, for fear that spies would relay global positioning system coordinates to American warplanes. But many senior Baath Party officials had Thuraya phones. Doori wasn't about to confront them. He ignored the order.

There was also the matter of bunkers. Doori was responsible for five bunkers, all of them manned by Baath Party militiamen from his neighborhood. But some of the militiamen had disappeared, and the bunkers were lightly manned. They were supposed to form the core of the neighborhood's limited defenses. Doori had not been supplied with heavy weapons; he and his men had RPGs and AK-47s, but no recoilless rifles or armored vehicles. The Republican Guards had heavy weapons, but Doori had not seen many Guards in his neighborhood since April 5, when the Americans had sent tanks up the airport highway on Al Mamoun's southern rim. Doori had not heard from his immediate superior, a deputy defense minister, since that day. He had heard rumors that the minister had fled with his family to his ancestral village north of Baghdad. Doori had heard, too, that a senior Republican Guard commander had issued orders for troops to take their weapons and go home to await further orders. Things were falling apart.

Driving through the streets, armed only with an AK-47, Doori began to wonder why he had even bothered to venture out. If the Republican Guards weren't capable of protecting his neighborhood, what could he possibly achieve on his own? He had once considered the Guards elite and invincible, but not since April 5. That afternoon, he had been summoned to the airport highway to help shore up Iraqi defenses. But the fight was over, and all Doori could do was help remove Republican Guard corpses from a bus that had been incinerated by an American tank round. He counted twenty-seven bodies. They were burned beyond recognition. They didn't look like human beings. They looked like something you'd clean out of a fireplace.

Doori drove on. The neighborhood was emptying out. Many residents had fled after the highway battle on the fifth, and more were packing up now. He had received no orders to stop anyone from leaving. In fact, he had received no orders at all. He steered the car down a street that dropped down to a dark tunnel beneath a highway overpass. As the tunnel came into view, Doori saw something blocking the road. He looked closer and realized it was a tank—an American tank. He hit the brakes and skidded. He heard the squeal of brakes from the car behind him and felt the jolt of the car skidding into the back of his vehicle. Doori saw the tank's turret swivel slowly toward him. He threw the gearshift into reverse, slammed the other car out of the way, and swung his own car in a sharp U-turn. He sped away, anticipating a sudden blast from the tank. There was nothing. He escaped. He was several blocks away when he decided that a few militiamen in bunkers could not possibly protect Al Mamoun from American tanks. He drove home to wait out the war.

Across downtown Baghdad that morning, the city's concentric circles of defense were collapsing. The chaos that David Perkins had sought to create was reverberating outward from the government complex. It was like watching an onion being peeled. The elaborate series of roadside bunkers that had been dug and reinforced in the weeks prior to the American invasion were emptying, first in the city center, then outward through the residential districts. Soldiers stripped off their uniforms and fled, some with their weapons, some completely unarmed. The graceful tree-lined roadways of Saddam's palace complex were littered with abandoned green uniforms made of poor-quality wool or cheap polyester and Soviet-surplus AK-47s and RPG launchers tossed into the grass. Some uniforms were the thin, plain fatigues of the regular army; others bore the crimson unit patches of the Republican Guards and Special Republican Guards. Black berets dotted the landscape, still pinned with the red, black, and green metal eagle insignia of the Baath regime. Cement huts where the soldiers had bunked were empty except for tubes of toothpaste and plastic bottles of cheap cologne. There were containers of lentil soup and rice, and stale bread, the soldiers' daily rations. (They received meat twice a week.) Some of the men had left behind diaries and duty rosters and snapshots of lovers and wives and children. Certain units had received orders as early as March 27 to change into civilian clothes in order to confuse the Americans. Other units had received no orders at all, deciding on their own initiative to strip down and slip away.

Many commanders did not have maps or radios. Command and control was sporadic. There was little unit-to-unit communication and few orders from the party or military leadership. Even during peacetime, Saddam's disjointed military apparatus barely communicated. Now radios had been banned for many regular army units on the pretext that American warplanes would hone in on the radio signals. The real reason, officers knew, was that Saddam and the senior leadership feared that military units would coalesce and conspire to overthrow the regime. Republican Guard and Special Republican Guard units were issued radios and satellite phones, but only for communication within those units. The Guards did not communicate regularly with the Baath Party militia, which had little contact with the Fedayeen, which had only face-to-face contact with the four thousand to five thousand Arab mercenaries and *jihadis* who had poured across Iraq's borders to join the fight. By the morning of April 7, commanders had been reduced to dispatching soldiers in cars to find out what other units were doing. An officer sent out that morning by Baha Ali Nasr, an air force general, never returned. Nasr found the officer's car later that day, destroyed by an American tank.

The independent military units competed for weapons and supplies. That morning, a regular army captain named Ahmed Sardar was trying to mobilize the thirty men who remained from his original company of eighty when a Republican Guard unit appeared at Sardar's base on Baghdad's southeastern edge and commandeered every last one of his company's working vehicles.

At a warehouse facility in northeast Baghdad, General Omar Abdul Karim, who was in charge of repairing vehicles and equipment, had managed to hold on to most of his unit's supplies. Karim had been told during the last week of March to stand by for orders to deliver vehicles and equipment to units in the city. He waited all day on the seventh, and into the evening, for the orders. They were not issued. The equipment never left the warehouses.

Colonel Raaed Faik was riding with fellow Republican Guard officers on a civilian bus thirty-two kilometers northeast of Baghdad that morning, trying to obey an order to rush to Baghdad to join in the defense of the city. They were to help keep Highway 8 open for a counterattack. Faik was a senior signal officer in the Republican Guard, but he was dressed now in civilian clothes. The chief of staff had radioed an order for his division to fight without uniforms in hopes of mounting an effective guerrilla war against American forces on the streets of Baghdad. But some officers had not received the order, and they were still in their uniforms. They bickered with the plain-clothes officers over how to dress for the battle.

Faik was disgusted. He took pride in being a member of an elite unit, but now they were like women trying to decide what outfits to wear. They were fools led by imbeciles. Their commanders were incompetent. Sometimes they issued several conflicting sets of orders each day. Sometimes they issued no orders at all. That very morning, Faik had overheard the Second Army commander, Fazi al-Lihaiby, cursing into his satellite phone upon learning that one of his brigades had been ordered to disband pending further orders. "Traitors! Cowards!" Lihaiby had screamed.

The capricious and indecisive commands originated at the very top of the chain of command—the supreme commander of the Republican

Guards, Saddam's son Quasi. During the last week of March, Quasi had issued a new order every day for Faik's armored brigade to reposition its tanks. Each handwritten "order for movement" contradicted the order from the day before. And each time the tanks were removed from their bunkers, a few more were exposed and destroyed by American warplanes. At the same time, another armored brigade was ordered to disable its tanks—based solely on Quasi's irrational paranoia that Kurdish militias based hundreds of kilometers to the north might somehow capture the tanks and use them against the Iraqi regime.

Faik had watched helplessly as discipline evaporated. Even as American tanks were moving up from the south, commanders were granting leaves to soldiers who wanted to go to Baghdad to check on their families. With his brigade decimated by leaves and outright desertions, Faik decided that he, too, would request a brief leave to check on his family. He had a wife, two sons, and a daughter in the middle-class Yarmouk district of west-central Baghdad. He arrived home on a six-hour leave on April 5, finding his family safe but his neighborhood under attack by an American armored column firing along the airport highway. On his way back to rejoin his unit, Faik encountered a group of Fedayeen fighters marching through the streets. They were cheering and celebrating, claiming that they had driven the Americans from the airport. They were displaying charred corpses—American soldiers killed, they claimed, in the battle along the nearby airport highway. Faik got a good look at the remains. He was horrified. They weren't Americans—they were Republican Guard soldiers. Faik had spent twelve years in the Guards. He knew a Guard uniform when he saw it—even a badly burned one. When he retuned to his unit and told fellow officers what he had witnessed, they called him a liar. They said they had been told that the Fedayeen militiamen were hoisting American corpses on bayonets and that Quasi himself had been presented with the severed heads of American soldiers.

Now, riding on the bus toward Baghdad on the morning of April 7, Faik was convinced he was being sent into the city to be slaughtered. For weeks, the military command had been preparing for a siege of the capital. Faik and other commanders had been told to prepare to fight street by street against American infantry units they expected to parachute in or unload from helicopters. They even named the units—the 101st Airborne Division and the 82nd Airborne Division. Iraqi forces would fight them from bunkers and rooftops and alleyways, taking advantage of the familiar urban terrain. A long siege would produce steady American casualties and the United States would be forced by American public opinion to negotiate a truce. And Iraqi forces would not have to confront tanks, the commanders were told, because the Americans were afraid to expose tanks to street fighting.

But even though spotty intelligence reports were confirming that American tanks were in the city center, Faik and his fellow officers were being dispatched to confront them as if nothing had changed. They were armed with nothing more than AK-47s and RPGs. They were on a civilian bus; their military vehicles had been stolen by officers intent on repainting them in civilian colors for personal use after the war. Faik was secretly relieved when the bus came to a stop, blocked by a crush of civilians and soldiers fleeing Baghdad. The highway was impassable. The officers on the bus decided there was no point in trying to reach the city. Faik agreed. He was thirty-three, a father of three, a blue-eyed man with a sad, jowly face, the owner of a fine home stocked with modern conveniences—a refrigerator-freezer, a color TV, computer games for his children. He wasn't willing to be butchered in Baghdad for a regime that was collapsing all around him. He got off the bus and started walking home.

Brigadier Baha Ali Nasr spent the morning of April 7 in his military office in north-central Baghdad, awaiting orders. Nasr was an air force commander without an air force. On March 24, he and his fellow commanders had received orders to dismantle their planes and bury them. It was a preposterous order, but they obeyed. Iraq's entire fleet of MIG-23s, MIG-25s, and Mirage fighters had been disassembled and buried underground. Now Nasr, a paunchy man of forty-two with a droopy mustache, was at his post in his office as he listened to explosions from the battle in the city center. He had been told to await orders to move to prearranged battle positions in the government complex. He had arrived at work armed only with his standard-issue 9mm pistol, but a supply of weapons had just arrived. Nasr was issued an RPG launcher and several grenades. He was a desk officer. He hadn't fired an RPG since military school two decades earlier. He felt useless. He didn't see the wisdom of heading into the government complex where, it was rumored, Iraqi forces had abandoned the Republican Guard headquarters, the Baath Party headquarters, and the Presidential Security Services building over the weekend. But if the orders came, he decided, he would obey. He was a professional soldier. He sat and waited the rest of the day.

Inside a sandbagged bunker in north-central Baghdad, Nabil al-Qaisy spent the morning of April 7 trying to find out what was going on in the center of the city. Qaisy was a Baath Party militiaman, a member of the Al Kuds squad, a local civil defense unit charged with defending the neighborhood. He was no soldier. He was a painter and calligrapher who taught art to elementary-school kids. He had joined the Baath Party only because a party card—stamped with the message THE PARTY IS ABOVE ALL—was required for his teaching position at a government-run school. Qaisy was thirty-one, meticulous in dress and manner, with smooth skin, perfect teeth, and the tapered fingers of an artist. Qaisy resented the Baath Party and the demands it made on his time. He had been manning the bunker since March 20, when he was summoned to active duty. He was issued an AK-47 but was required to buy his own uniform. He was supposed to be fed three meals a day, but the money for the food had been appropriated by the local militia commander. He walked home every day for lunch and dinner.

Qaisy had been given no specific orders, other than to man the bunker twenty-four hours a day, except for meal breaks. He and his fellow militiamen—merchants, accountants, office workers—had undergone perfunctory training. They were shown how to fire AK-47s and how to load and fire an RPG. They had been told to anticipate nighttime helicopter and paratroop assaults from the Americans. Their orders were to climb onto rooftops, await a signal—the cutting of the local power supply to plunge the neighborhood into darkness—and then fire their rifles at helicopters and paratroopers. Qaisy didn't think he could possibly hit anything in the dark with an AK-47. He thought it was more likely that the helicopter gunships would kill anyone foolish enough to expose himself on a rooftop in the middle of an air assault.

But now, lounging in the bunker with his fellow militiamen, Qaisy did not feel a particular sense of urgency. His unit had no radio and no way to contact the neighborhood party leader. Qaisy had no idea where the man was. From time to time, a car was dispatched to drive toward the city center to forage for information. There had been rumors of American tanks in the government complex. But even after three forays, no information was forthcoming. Qaisy could hear the distant rumble of tanks and artillery, but in his neighborhood it was a fairly quiet spring morning. Everything seemed so ordinary. He had anticipated a great rush of emotion and fear when the Americans finally invaded. Qaisy settled down with his rifle, waiting for the Americans to descend on his neighborhood—and silently prayed that they would leave it alone.

Just south of the city, near the spaghetti junction, retired army general Juawad al-Dayni had volunteered to help Fedayeen and Syrian fighters manning bunkers along Highway 8. Dayni was fifty-six, retired for the past four years, and streaks of gray were creeping into his black mustache. But as a former officer he felt an obligation to answer the call for volunteers to fight the Americans. He walked from his comfortable two-story stucco home, which was about one and a half kilometers west of the highway, and climbed into a bunker with an AK-47. Dayni had survived the American armored attack along the highway on April 5, but he had been deeply disturbed by the carnage inflicted by the tanks and Bradleys. He had served in the Iran-Iraq war of the 1980s and in the first Gulf War, but he had never seen such lethal weapons. The tanks and Bradleys were remarkable. They were able to fire in a 360-degree radius, and from incredible distances, even while on the move. Their guns reduced some of the Fedayeen militiamen to hunks of meat; their remains had to be slopped into plastic bags for burial.

Dayni was distressed by the way the regime was defending the capital. He thought the highways and bridges leading into the city should have been destroyed to deny the Americans easy access. He had heard from former colleagues in the military that Saddam and his advisers had not originally expected an American invasion; they had expected to delay, to bluff, to negotiate their way out of a military confrontation. But even after the invasion began March 20, Dayni was told, the leadership believed Republican Guard divisions arrayed south of the city would blunt the American advance. The roads and bridges were kept open to allow for supplies of fuel and ammunition, and for commanders to report back into the government complex downtown. Dayni thought the leadership had learned nothing from its humiliating defeat in Kuwait in 1991. The country's leaders seemed to be in denial. They seemed unwilling to accept the hard truth that the American military was vastly superior and could not be defeated in a head-to-head confrontation. It seemed to Dayni that they were repeating the mistakes of a decade earlier.

Now, on the morning of April 7, Dayni was back in the bunker, fearing the worst. When the American column sped up Highway 8 just after dawn, the tanks and Bradleys shot at everything on either side of the roadway. The Fedayeen and Syrians—and a few small units of Republican Guards—fought furiously, but even their recoilless rifles and antiaircraft artillery pieces had little effect on the column. Their technical vehicles were pulverized by tank and Bradley cannons. Dayni could not see anything from inside the bunker, but he could feel the impact of the rounds and hear the cries of men dying. At the far end of his bunker, there was a sudden explosion and a flash of flame. Dayni saw the burning body of a man who lived on his street, a middle-aged retiree like himself. Dayni moved to help the man, but it was pointless. He was dead. There was not much left of him.

Dayni stayed down. Thirty minutes later, it was over. The Americans had moved on into the city center. The Fedayeen and Syrians climbed out to collect their dead. There was talk of reinforcing the interchange, of moving in behind the Americans and cutting off Highway 8. Dayni thought it was futile. Now that the Americans were inside the city, he thought, the regime could not survive. And when it fell, there would be chaos. He thought about his home. He had evacuated his family, and the house was unprotected. As one of the few residents still living in his neighborhood, Dayni had taken it upon himself to watch over his neighbors' abandoned homes. As the fighters around him geared up for another confrontation with the Americans, he debated whether to stay in the bunker or walk back to check on his house. After a while, he got up and walked home.

In the city center, civilian cars were blundering into the fight. Many residents were not yet aware that American tanks had penetrated downtown districts, and they went about their normal business. Government-run radio was announcing that American forces had been defeated outside the capital. Traffic was lighter than usual, but some shops and gasoline stations remained open, even as Fedayeen and Baath Party militiamen surged through the streets.

Salah Mehdi Baqir al-Muosawi, a translator and driver for the *Daily Telegraph* newspaper of London, listened to the radio reports inside an office building in the well-to-do Mansour district on the western edge of the city center. He was debating whether to try to reach the Palestine Hotel, where the British reporters who had hired him were staying. Muosawi had heard that American forces were attacking the capital, but the government radio reports persuaded him that it was still safe to venture out. He took his job seriously, and he knew his services were needed on this important news day. Muosawi was proud of his impeccable English. He was fifty-two, a distinguished-looking man, a father of four with silver hair and a black mustache. He had been working for Western correspondents for more than a decade, and he considered himself a progressive. He often told his wife that he welcomed the American invasion and looked forward to the fall of the Baath regime.

Sometime after 8 a.m., Muosawi decided to drive into the city center. He got behind the wheel of his white Oldsmobile and headed east toward the Palestine, taking the same route he had used to reach the Palestine the day before. He made it as far as Zaidtoun Street near Zawra Park. There, coax rounds fired by an Abrams tank hidden beneath an overpass tore through the windshield, blowing off the driver's door and ripping into Muosawi. Witnesses who recovered his body told Muosawi's widow, Zubida Rida, that Muosawi had not appeared to notice the tank. His car, and two or three others behind it, had driven straight toward the tank and were fired upon, they told her. Several other civilians died along with Muosawi. Because of the chaos and danger, they told the widow, no one noticed whether the tank had first fired warning shots. But later, they said, the Americans dragged the cars across the road—with the bodies still inside—to create a barricade.

Half an hour later, Mohammed Hassan Jawad, sixty-two, a retired policeman, drove his blue Mercedes toward a gasoline station near the zoo at the edge of Zawra Park. Jawad had loaded his car with food and bottled water to deliver to his daughter, Mervet Jawad, who had been evacuated from the family's home to the northern city of Kirkuk. He was hoping to find gasoline at a station next the zoo, near a junction that connected to the main road to Kirkuk. As he approached the gas station, machine-gun rounds from an Abrams tank at the edge of the park shattered the car's windshield and collapsed the hood. Jawad was hit several times in the chest, and three fingers of his hand were blown off. Later, witnesses who led Jawad's relatives to his corpse told them that they had not seen the tank fire warning shots. It appeared to them, they said, that Jawad never noticed the tank and drove directly toward it. His car, too, was used by the Americans to create a barricade.

As Shawn Gibson's tank crashed through the metal gates of the Republican Palace complex at mid-morning, RPG teams opened fire from a series of bunkers dug into the woods on the left side of the palace roadway. Straight ahead, on the road in front of the palace, soldiers were unloading from troop trucks. A few fired automatic rifles toward Gibson's tank, but most of them tried to jump back onto the trucks. As Gibson surged forward, he could see that some of the soldiers in the bunker were climbing out of their holes and fleeing through the woods. Gibson had a name for soldiers who fired off a few rounds, then ran away. He called it "shittin' and gettin'." Gibson managed to kill quite a few of them, and his gunner got more of them with the coax.

Over the radio came Lieutenant Maurice Middleton's voice: "Hey, Sergeant Gibson, slow down! I need to get back up there with you." Gibson had pulled away from the rest of the column after blasting through the gates at the main archway, and now the other tanks were rushing to pull up behind him. He let Lieutenant Middleton swing ahead of him, then fell back into Assassin's regular formation, with Sergeant First Class Jonathan Lustig's tank directly behind him.

Farther back in the column was Captain Wolford, the company commander, whose tank had just rolled over the metal gate that had been smashed by Gibson. Wolford could see Iraqi soldiers scrambling out of the bunkers. They were poorly constructed fortifications—just holes in the woods covered by planks or metal sheeting topped with dirt and brush. The Iraqis' fighting positions were oriented to the northwest, with the soldiers' backs to the palace. It was obvious to Wolford that they had anticipated an attack from the north, through the woods. It seemed to him that the logical point of attack was the roadway from the west—the roadway Assassin had just taken. The miscalculation crystallized for Wolford the outlines of the entire battle for the city. Colonel Perkins's battle plan was designed to penetrate behind the Iraqi defenders, then to fight from the city center outward, attacking the enemy from the rear. That was precisely what was happening at the Republican Palace. The Iraqis had left their rear end exposed.

While many of the soldiers were fleeing, others were crawling out of the first sets of bunkers and turning around. They flopped on their bellies, facing the roadway, firing madly with RPGs and automatic rifles. The rate of fire was intense but inaccurate. They were completely exposed. Wolford ordered the tanks to open up with MPAT rounds and the Bradleys with coax. It was a slaughter. The soldiers pitched backward and died, and the bunkers exploded. Soldiers in the next set of bunkers leaped out and fled north through the woods, some of them toppling as the coax rounds tore into them. Dozens more escaped, running through the broad gap between Assassin Company and the Rogue companies to the north and west near the parade grounds and the park, or south across the palace ground to the riverbank. Butchering all those men left Wolford with a hollow feeling. It was his job to kill the enemy, but he got no satisfaction from mowing down soldiers who seemed so incompetent, so vulnerable, so poorly led. He didn't exactly feel sorry for them, but whatever he was feeling, it wasn't good.

The tanks moved on to the palace, past gardens and walkways and imposing stone mansions tucked behind walls draped with flowering vines. There were two entrances to the palace, each framed by guard shacks and wrought-iron gates that were left wide open. Wolford was amazed. It was like an invitation to walk right in. A couple of tanks rolled through the gates and stopped in the shadows of the four bronze busts of Saddam on the roof. The rest of the column set up in defensive positions on the main roadway; some of the crews were still killing a small group of Special Republican Guard soldiers who were firing from a small bunker complex directly across from the road.

In front of the sprawling palace was an expanse of manicured lawn that surrounded a circular fountain and beds of roses. The two main entryways led past stone porticos and towering palm trees into the palace itself. The complex was deserted. There were no bunkers, no gun emplacements, not a single soldier. It looked like a museum that was closed for the day. The palace walls rose up against the hazy morning sky, an expanse of pale tan stone and polished marble, silent and implacable. On the rooftop at each of the palace's four corners stood the huge bronze busts of Saddam. They depicted the dictator wearing a pith helmet over an Arab headdress, with a plume of feathers at the peak. Shawn Gibson wanted to put a tank round through one of them, but it was forbidden. The palace was a protected site.

Wolford sent a platoon of infantry to the back of the palace to clear an expanse of sandy ground that led down to the Tigris River. The palace was built on a sharp bend in the river, where the Tigris flowed west toward the spaghetti junction. Access roads on either side led down to a ragged beach, where antiaircraft pits and bunkers had been dug into the sand.

First Lieutenant Jeff McFarland, a tall, rangy West Point graduate, rode in the commander's hatch of a Bradley, making his way down the access road on the east side. He could see the barrels of the antiaircraft guns jutting from the sandy bunkers. Other bunkers contained military trucks and at least one ambulance. All had been abandoned. There were two Russian-made military helicopters on the beach, both also abandoned. Farther down the shoreline were more bunkers, and McFarland could see the helmeted heads of Iraqi soldiers. Behind them were more soldiers, but these men were sprinting away from McFarland, tossing aside their weapons and running up the river road or diving into the thicket of weeds at the water's edge. It seemed ludicrous, but some of them were paddling madly, swimming out into the river toward the opposite bank. Now *that's* desperation, McFarland thought. The river had to be a quarter mile wide, and it was flowing swiftly.

The soldiers in the bunkers opened fire. McFarland had four Bradleys in his platoon, and each one sprayed the bunkers with coax. Instead of staying down, the Iraqis kept popping their heads up—only to have their skulls splattered by the heavy coax roads. It was brutal, but some of the gunners laughed about it. It was a huge joke—a slow-motion Nintendo game, they thought, and not a very challenging one. They wondered if the Iraqis had ever had a single day of training. They seemed so clueless. The bunkers were cleared in less than half an hour.

McFarland was struck by the differences between his men and the Iraqis. He and his soldiers had been through months of training—in the States and in Kuwait. They trained for every conceivable situation, including clearing bunkers on a beach. There was a rigidly prescribed method, and it was ingrained into each man. The soldiers fell instinctively into their roles. They didn't have to think about it. Their movements were choreographed and effortless. The Iraqis, on the other hand, weren't an army— they were an unwieldy collection of individuals, none of them disciplined. They didn't know how to coordinate or maneuver. Each man acted independently of the others. McFarland was just twenty-five, with only three years of service, but he felt that he or any other American infantry lieutenant was better trained than any of the generals directing the Iraqi defenses of the capital.

After the bunkers had been cleared, McFarland ordered his infantrymen out of the Bradleys. They moved forward on foot, methodically searching each bunker, firing M-16 rifles or shotguns down into the dark holes and blowing each one with grenades. They fired into the weeds along the shoreline, hitting some of the swimmers. They dragged soldiers out of the water, some of them badly wounded, and turned them over to the medics for treatment. They gathered up huge piles of weapons and ammunition for the tanks, which lit them up with HEAT rounds. They searched the helicopters, finding leather executive seats and tray tables set with English china and crystal goblets.

At the front of the palace, Wolford finished setting up the perimeter and brought his tank down the access road to check on McFarland's progress. At the corner of the palace, where the road came to a T-intersection and turned right, a wounded Iraqi soldier crawled out onto the roadway. Wolford, in the commander's hatch, never saw him. He was focused on the beachfront. He felt the tank hit something and swung his head to the rear. He saw a man's head and neck, flattened and oozing.

He yelled at his driver, Sergeant Carlos Johnson. "Johnson! Did you see that?"

"No, sir. I didn't"

"Johnson, you didn't see that fucking guy right in the middle of the road?"

"No, sir, I really didn't."

Wolford felt ill. He didn't blame Johnson. It was just one of those things that happen in combat. There was nothing he could do for the poor bastard now. He continued rolling down to the beach to watch the infantrymen finish off the bunkers.

After the waterfront had been cleared, Wolford brought McFarland's platoon back up to clear the palace itself. They had not taken a single round from inside the huge structure. It was probably deserted, but Wolford wanted it carefully searched and secured nonetheless. The palace had been designated as the operations center for the Tusker battalion and, much later, as the postwar headquarters for an American-led occupation authority.

The infantrymen were in awe as they went from room to room inside the darkened palace. They had never even seen a photograph of the place. Few Iraqis had ever seen it, either; the palace had been sealed off as part of a restricted government zone reserved for top-ranking Baath Party and Republican Guard officials. It took fifteen minutes to walk from one end to the other, down marble hallways and through archways of polished stone. The infantrymen were like tourists, staring up at chandeliers and poking their heads into the marble-tiled bathrooms. There was a wrapped bar of scented Lux soap at every sink, and a fresh box of pink tissues next to each gleaming brass faucet. The toilets and sinks had not been used in a while. There was no electricity or running water.

The entire palace and grounds had been evacuated. The beds in the upstairs bedroom were made up, and blotters and telephones were neatly arranged on the desks in the offices downstairs. There were rotting eggs and vegetables in the stainless steel refrigerators in the various kitchens, and china and silverware in the cupboards. Each main hallway opened into a rotunda, the vaulted ceilings decorated in brilliant mosaic tiles. Doors leading into the high-ceilinged offices and drawing rooms were made of polished wood with inlaid mahogany. There were chandeliers in every room, small ones in the offices and massive fixtures and gilded mirrors in the grand ballrooms. In the main rotunda was a scale model of the palace, across from a huge mural depicting Saddam himself handing a brick to workers during palace construction.

It was a massive facility. Later, Lieutenant Colonel deCamp had his men count the palace rooms. He kept the tally on index cards tucked into his pocket: 142 offices, sixty-four bathrooms, twenty-two kitchens, nineteen meeting rooms, a movie theater, five ballrooms, and one "monster ballroom." The soldiers figured the palace was a good four football fields long.

After McFarland's men had finished clearing the building, everyone else in the company wanted to have a look. Wolford gave them ten minutes each for a quick tour, a handful of men at a time. They rushed through the halls, snapping photographs and posing under paintings and murals of a smiling, benevolent Saddam. It was only later, when the soldiers had more time to poke around, that they realized that some of what had seemed elegant and classic was actually fraudulent and almost vulgar. A few of the larger chandeliers were made of crystal, but most were made of ordinary glass and many were plastic. Some of the gilded furniture was made not of hardwood but cheap pine painted gold. The marble was expensive, but it was crudely cut and lumpish. The four massive Saddam heads on the roof, it turned out, were plated with bronze that was barely a quarter inch thick. The Republican Palace wasn't exactly Versailles. It was more like Las Vegas, with touches of Graceland.

Out back, the infantrymen found a garish swimming pool and ornate patio area decorated with brightly colored tiles. There was a recreation area with Ping-Pong tables, tennis courts, and exercise bicycles. Down a slope toward the shoreline was a ragged animal pen containing five feeble lions, a malnourished leopard, and an emaciated bear—apparently Saddam's private zoo. Later, some of the scouts dragged a sheep into the pen and watched the lions and leopard struggle weakly with the terrified animal before finally killing it and feasting on the bloody carcass.

Wolford set up a command post in the front driveway and arranged his tanks in a defensive perimeter. The battalion mortar teams set up on the lawn. There had been no enemy contact since the Special Republican Guard soldiers dug into a thick stand of trees across the main road had been killed or driven off shortly after the company's arrival. Wolford could hear explosions in the distance, but the immediate palace complex was quiet. Soldiers sat and smoked cigarettes or posed for photographs in front of the tanks, with the palace as a backdrop.

Wolford turned to his first sergeant and said, "You know, if this is all there is, I think this war is over in a couple of days. I really think this is it." But after considering the situation for a few more minutes, Wolford had second thoughts. It just didn't seem possible that the Iraqis would surrender the entire palace complex so easily. He was worried about the gap between his battalion and Rogue. He feared the Iraqis would counter-attack through the eastern edge of the gap, or down the river road behind the palace, to his rear. He told his tankers to stay alert. This thing wasn't over yet.

T E N

GOD WILL BURN THEIR BODIES IN HELL

Captain Jason Conroy had finally set up a secure perimeter around Saddam Hussein's parade grounds and the tomb of the unknown soldier by mid-morning on April 7. He was beginning to believe that things in his little world—his company's stretch of flat terrain between the VIP reviewing stand and the concrete tomb—were very much under control. He eyed the equestrian statue of Saddam and thought about how satisfying it would feel to put a tank round through it.

And then the mortars hit. They kept coming, one after the other, slamming down all around Conroy's positions. One round landed between two of the engineers' armored personnel carriers, exploding with a metallic rattle that peppered the vehicles with shrapnel and shook up the crews. Conroy was amazed that no one was hurt. Then another round splattered shrapnel within twenty meters of one of his tanks. Conroy had to reposition several tanks to move them out of the line of fire. He felt a rising sense of frustration and anger. Mortars always pissed him off—they were light and mobile, and it was hard to return fire. And in this case, Conroy didn't know *where* to return fire. The mortar rounds seemed to be falling out of the sky. People were asking one another over the radio net: "Where the hell are they coming from?"

As the morning wore on, the mortars began to slam down closer to the battalion command post. It had been set up hastily, and under fire, by backing up four command and medical tracks into a tight little circle a short distance from the tomb of the unknown soldier. The vehicles had been positioned around a concrete pavilion with a corrugated metal roof—what turned out to be a public toilet. The stench was overpowering, but the concrete walls afforded some protection from shrapnel.

Now, with the mortars inching closer, the command and control center for the entire Rogue battalion was under threat. It was a crowded place. Wounded American soldiers were being treated inside, and four or five enemy prisoners were under guard. Outside, the bodies of dead civilians had been collected for burial. Normally, the brigade's counterbattery radar would pinpoint the location of enemy mortars and relay grid coordinates for artillery or aircraft to run counterfire on them. But on this morning, the radar was not functioning properly. The Rogue battalion was on its own. Lieutenant Colonel Schwartz arrived on his tank and made it clear to everyone that he wanted somebody to figure out another way to locate the mortars—and quickly. Already, three or four men had been wounded by mortar shrapnel, including a medic and Captain David Hibner, the engineer company commander.

Inside one of the personnel carriers that formed the command center was Gunnery Sergeant Daniel Brown, a U.S. Marine assigned to the battalion to help coordinate close air support. He had ridden up Highway 8 that morning in the carrier commanded by Major Rick Nussio, the battalion executive officer. Brown was thirty-three, a father of two young boys. He had joined the marines fifteen years earlier to avoid working on a car plant assembly line like everyone else in his hometown of Detroit. Brown was a jack-of-all-trades, a graduate of several Marine Corps specialty training schools. One of his skills happened to be crater analysis—the esoteric art of poking through mortar or artillery craters to determine the type and location of enemy fire. In fact, Brown had taken a refresher course in crater analysis aboard the ship that had brought his unit to Kuwait.

Now a round whistled down and smacked into the wall of the toilet, exploding with a loud crack and scattering everybody inside the command center. That was it for Brown. He was starting to get angry now. He had survived the thunder run into the city that morning, killing two Iraqi soldiers with his M-16, and was in no mood to take mortar fire. He decided he was going to personally find out where the hell the rounds were coming from.

With only his helmet and flak vest for protection, and with mortars still raining down, Brown hustled out to inspect the fresh craters outside the toilet walls. The first thing he noticed was how small they were, about twelve to fourteen inches in diameter, no bigger than a pizza pan. He figured the mortars couldn't be any bigger than 60mm—but they still packed enough punch to disrupt Rogue's operations and they were quite capable of blowing a man in half. Another round exploded nearby, and Brown checked that crater, too. From the angle of impact, Brown figured the mortars were being launched from the northwest, about the ten o'clock position as he stood facing north. He went back inside to find Major Rick Nussio, who had a good set of satellite imagery maps. He wanted to see what was to the northwest.

At that moment, another marine from Brown's unit rolled up in an armored personnel carrier. Gunnery Sergeant William "Butch" Deas was riding with a military intelligence team and its Arabic-speaking interpreter, delivering a load of captured Iraqi soldiers to the command center. Deas was just the man Brown needed—he was a bona fide expert at crater analysis. In fact, Deas had taught the crater analysis course aboard ship. He was an easygoing, good-humored thirty-eight-year-old, an eighteen-year Marine Corps veteran from Asheville, North Carolina. He had started out as a military meteorologist, gauging wind speed and direction to adjust artillery fire. He seemed to have an instinctive feel for the trajectory of flying projectiles.

Deas was feeling miserable that morning. Two days before, on Rogue's first thunder run, his personnel carrier had been rocked by RPG and machine-gun fire on Highway 8. Deas had been up in the hatch, working his laser range-finder to locate targets for air strikes on Iraqi positions. The impact knocked him down. He was back on his feet and checking on the vehicle's stunned driver when he realized that blood was gushing from his own face. A piece of shrapnel had sliced through his nose and lodged in the back of his sinus cavity. Bright red blood was gushing from the wound. A medic finally got the bleeding stopped, and that night a surgeon used five stitches to close the hole in Deas's nose. He didn't want to risk moving the metal fragment, so now shrapnel the size of a marble was still lodged in Deas's sinus. It looked like a big pimple on his cheek, right beside his nose.

Now Brown called Deas over and asked him to take a look at the craters. Mortars were still whistling overhead as Deas crouched down in the soft dirt. The Iraqi crews were "walking" the rounds in, each one falling a bit closer. Some were hitting on the pavement, virtually worthless for crater analysis, but some were leaving perfectly preserved little craters in the packed dirt. Deas was intrigued by the craters' signatures. The pattern of spikes from flying dirt and debris suggested low-angle rounds—artillery shells. But Deas also found sections of a mortar fin and bits of shell casing from small mortars, probably 60mm. Mortars are typically fired at high angles—seventy or eighty degrees. But these were flying in at low angles, about forty-five degrees, like artillery. It was an unorthodox way to launch a mortar, but it had the advantage of concentrating rounds in a tight area. Deas had never seen mortars fired that way. He figured the Iraqis were either desperate or woefully trained, or both.

Deas talked it over with Brown. Deas told him he was convinced that the mortars were coming at a very low angle from the southwest, at about seven o'clock. He and Brown both knew the maximum range for a 60mm mortar was thirty-eight hundred meters, but Deas estimated the range of these rounds at about two thousand meters, factoring in the reduced distance due to the low angle. Brown took that as gospel. He had absolute faith in Deas's judgment. Deas couldn't offer anything more; his vehicle was pulling out, and he rushed off, leaving Brown to finish the analysis.

A minute later, a mortar round tore into a clump of trees outside the toilet. Brown went out to have a look and saw that the round had left a perfect hole in one of the trees. It was like an exit wound. Brown stood in the crater and looked up through the hole. He pointed his compass through the opening and shot an azimuth through it. He got a reading, then went back inside to plot the azimuth on Major Nussio's 1:25,000 scale map.

Brown ran a back azimuth, based on his readings from the hole in the tree, drawing a straight line using a coordinate scale and a straight edge. The line ended at an Iraqi military compound two kilometers away—a compound that was already programmed into the brigade's computerized target list. It had not yet been hit by coalition warplanes.

An air force officer attached to the battalion pulled out imagery photos taken during recent overflights by unmanned spy planes. Brown studied the imagery and noticed two rows of palm trees along the edge of the compound, just beyond a tall fence encircling the site. He was certain the mortar tubes were hidden in the palms; the Iraqis had put mortars and artillery in palm groves down south. And besides, the mortars could not have been fired from inside the compound because of the low angle and the height of the surrounding fence. He wrote down the map coordinates for the rows of palm trees.

It was a clean target. It was a clearly defined military compound. There were no civilian structures nearby, and there were no U.S. forces between the command center and the compound. Brown was radioing for approval to bring in an air strike when Schwartz arrived at the command center. He showed Schwartz the compound and palm trees on the satellite maps. "Yeah, go ahead. Go for it," Schwartz told him. Rounds were still flying overhead. "This is getting tiresome."

Brown called an immediate request for aircraft and was told that planes were already "on station"—up in the air over Baghdad. Because the mortars were hitting U.S. positions, the request for close air support got top priority. Within five minutes, two American F-18 fighters screamed overhead. Each one launched a pair of two-thousand-pound bombs known as JDAMs—joint direct attack munitions—on the palm trees next to the compound. Everybody inside the toilet building could hear the impact. Minutes later, the artillery unit unleashed a volley that echoed across the parade field.

The mortars ceased.

At the foot of the reviewing stand, Jason Conroy was up in the cupola of his tank, facing the statue of Saddam on horseback. With his perimeter now fairly well secured, he felt it was time to make a statement. The embedded Fox TV crew had arrived at the parade grounds, along with Colonel Perkins and the two battalion commanders, Schwartz and deCamp. Conroy had heard that they were getting ready for some kind of big powwow to determine where the mission was going from here. He thought it was an opportune moment to take down the statue.

He radioed Schwartz. "I got this beautiful statue here," he said. "Can I blow it up?" Schwartz told him to stand by. He wanted to talk to Perkins, who was busy talking on the radio to division headquarters at the airport.

Perkins had spent the previous half hour trying to persuade General Blount and his assistant division commander for maneuver, Brigadier General Lloyd Austin, that the strategically sound plan was to stay in the city center rather than pull back out. Perkins explained that he had taken a great risk and expended significant combat power to take every single strategic objective the brigade had targeted inside the palace and government complexes. He didn't want to have to fight his way back out. Nor did he want to surrender territory he had just seized. He was convinced that he could collapse the regime from within now that he was literally standing on Saddam's center of power.

The senior commanders at V Corps and, higher up, at U.S. Central Command forward headquarters in Doha, Qatar, were still envisioning the mission as another thunder run—one of several being planned to slowly chip away at Baghdad's defenses. If any of Perkins's units ended up spending the night, they thought, it would be the companies now setting up at the three main interchanges on Highway 8. V Corps expected Perkins's tank columns to punch to the edge of the city center, then pull out and return to the brigade TOC at the edge of Highway 8 south of the capital.

Inside the international passenger terminal at the Baghdad airport, V Corps had set up its ACP—its assault command post. The day's battle was playing out on military computer screens inside the terminal, where blue icons on digital maps depicted the tank battalions inside the palace complex. The computers were linked to a satellite-transmission system called FBCB2, for Force XXI Battle Command Brigade and Below. The system was maintained by civilian technicians working for the FBCB2 contractor, Northrop Grumman.

That morning, one of the contractors, Ron Legros, was summoned by a V Corps officer who was staring intently at his computer screen. The officer complained to Legros that the system was malfunctioning. Its icons were showing Second Brigade tanks and Bradleys set up in defensive positions inside the downtown palace complex. That wasn't possible, he said, because he had been told that no American forces would be setting up inside the capital. The officer was tapping on the computer screen, trying to dislodge the blue icons, like someone tapping a stuck speedometer needle.

Legros ran a diagnostic test of the system. It was working perfectly. The officer wasn't convinced. He continued to insist that there were no American tanks inside the city. Legros repeated that the system was in good working order. The officer did not seem inclined to accept the diagnosis, but Legros didn't want to get into a protracted argument. He walked away, leaving the officer still tapping at his screen.

From the airport, General Austin had radioed Perkins about a half hour after Phil Wolford's Assassin Company seized control of the Republican Palace. "Marne Six"—General Blount—"doesn't want to stay," Austin told Perkins. "The LOCs are too difficult to hold." Blount was also concerned that the First Marine Division was still south of the city and not yet in position to secure the Second Brigade's eastern flank on the east bank of the Tigris. And Blount wasn't certain he had enough combat power to hold the airport *and* send a quick reaction force to rescue Perkins if he happened to get overrun in the city center.

Perkins continued to press his case. "I am more secure on the palace grounds than I am at Saints," he told Austin, referring to Objective Saints, the code name for the tactical operations center at the junction of Highways 1 and 8 eighteen kilometers south of the city center. "We have a significant strategic opportunity that we wouldn't want to miss." He added, "Have spoken with my battalion commanders. If we hold the LOCs, stay the night, this war will be over."

A few minutes later, Austin radioed back. "I'm concerned about the fuel situation and our ability to hold the LOC" on Highway 8, he said. "It'll require significant combat power to do so." Even so, he said, Perkins's request to stay was being passed up the chain of command. "I'm working on it," Austin told him.

Then Austin abruptly changed the subject. He asked Perkins if he had located a monument or statue suitable for a public display of destruction. Blount, Austin, and Perkins had discussed beforehand the need to demonstrate in a very public and dramatic way that American forces had penetrated the heart of the city. Perkins asked Schwartz and deCamp to find a statue or monument of Saddam.

Schwartz radioed Captain Conroy and told him that higher command was "looking for a real good monument."

Conroy said, "This is a great monument—Saddam on a horse."

Schwartz cleared it with Perkins, and Conroy was finally given permission to take the statue down. He already had an MPAT round in the tube. Perkins radioed Conroy. "Don't miss," Perkins told him.

Perkins then radioed Austin on the division net. "We've found a statue of Saddam at the review stand—with key vantage points."

Austin asked Perkins, "Method of destruction?"

"One-twenty millimeter," Perkins said.

"Feel free to use as many rounds as it takes," Austin told him.

Blount's voice came over the net. "If you make any speeches, keep it short," he told Perkins. He didn't want American forces acting like occupiers—or worse, gloating before the Fox News camera.

"There will be no speeches," Perkins assured him.

From his commander's hatch across from the reviewing stand, Conroy told his gunner to let the round fly. An MPAT round is designed to punch a hole through the thick steel armor of a tank or personnel carrier before detonating a high-explosive shape charge in its warhead. The round pierced the statue's thin bronze shell and exploded in an eruption of brown smoke, shattering the horse and blowing Saddam's head from its torso. Conroy's crewmen retrieved the head later and hauled it around on the bustle racks, a singular war trophy.

Conroy had never experienced such euphoria—not during the sprint up from Kuwait, and not even on the momentous thunder run to the airport. He felt a sense of achievement and finality, a conviction that all his soldiers' training and sacrifice had built to this moment of triumph. He believed that this very moment, preserved for history by the Fox crew, would define the American defeat of the Iraqi regime. For the first time since leaving Kuwait, Conroy let himself believe that the end of the war was close at hand. His company had now secured optimum positions in and around Saddam's parade grounds and reviewing stand, a perfect 360 degrees of control, with clean, overlapping sectors of fire. There was no doubt in his mind that they were spending the night—and many more nights after that.

Just across from the reviewing stand, Schwartz and deCamp were interviewed live on Fox TV by correspondent Kelly. The two lieutenant colonels played off each other like a stand-up team—deCamp the energized and frenetic front man, Schwartz the restrained and confiding straight man. The overall effect was of two men thrust suddenly into unfamiliar surroundings, still getting their bearings but somehow persuaded that they stood at the crest of an irreversible tide. For TV viewers, it was a jarring and disorienting tableau. The split screen showed Information Minister Sahaf on the left, jaunty and boastful in his beret and gold-rimmed spectacles, describing Americans dying at the gates of Baghdad and vowing, "God will burn their bodies in hell!" On the right screen were deCamp and Schwartz, helmeted little men grimy with dust and sweat, squinting through the smoke, their voices straining over the steady pounding of Rogue's tank cannons at the far end of the parade field.

Schwartz mentioned that his tanks were parked outside Iraq's Ministry of Information about one and a half kilometers to the northeast. He had hoped that Sahaf would be addressing the media from the building, though the minister was actually just across the Tigris, at the Palestine

Hotel overlooking the river's east bank. The ministry building had been abandoned.

"He's just across the street from us," Schwartz said, deadpan. "We'll go over and talk to him. They can look right outside their window. They can see us."

DeCamp was asked whether the brigade's thrust into Baghdad was significant tactically or symbolically. His face lit up.

"Today is symbolic in the sense that we already had it," deCamp said, speaking rapidly in a hoarse voice. "The victory was won a long time ago. Now, today, we're just securing the symbol of the victory. About five days ago, his [Saddam's] regime was done. He was just continuing his propaganda. Today we just ended his propaganda campaign—because he can continue to show his lies on TV, but we're showing the American public where we are."

A tank cannon erupted somewhere behind them and Schwartz said, "There are a lot of bad guys still out there. There's not a lot of celebration going on yet, but we're feeling very good about being here. We've still got a lot of work to do."

Perkins felt his own confidence surge. Standing next to his personnel carrier, looking out over the blanket of smoke and haze that draped the parade grounds, he asked deCamp and Schwartz for situation reports. Both commanders assured him that their positions were secured, and both said they felt just as strongly as Perkins about staying the night. They didn't want to have to fight their way back out of the city. They were certain they could defend and hold their ground.

Perkins thought he was close to persuading Blount to let him set up for the night, and he was confident that the brass was flexible enough to let the commander on the ground make the call. Already, the senior command seemed to be focused on how to manage any American tactical victories inside Baghdad. Even before the Saddam statue fell, Perkins had received word from higher headquarters, through Austin, not to fly the American flag. Someone at the higher command, watching the Fox feed, had seen Major Rick Nussio hold up a three-by-five-foot American flag on the parade grounds. An order came down: there would be no overt displays of triumph, no lording it over the Iraqis. Perkins radioed Nussio and told him to put the flag away. But he later suggested that his men turn their right shoulders— the shoulders with the Stars and Stripes patch—toward the Fox camera.

Perkins confirmed for Blount that the Rogue and Tusker crews had shut down their tanks to conserve fuel. It was standard operating procedure; the brigade had shut off the tank engines down south after seizing terrain and securing their positions. The turbine engines burned fifty-six gallons of fuel an hour while rolling at full clip, about thirty gallons an hour when maneuvering in battle. They had left on the mission that morning carrying eight to ten hours of fuel—conservatively, four hours to get into the city and four hours to get back. The mission was now approaching Hour Four—the hour Perkins had set for himself for reaching the decision to stay or retreat. The crews could still fire their weapons systems, but each hour the tanks were turned off bought Perkins another hour. He wanted to make sure he had enough fuel to get out of the city if it came to that, although he was confident Steph Twitty's China battalion would hold the Highway 8 interchanges that the tank battalions had just blasted through.

At the Spartan Brigade TOC—eighteen kilometers south of the city center—Lieutenant Colonel Eric Wesley was feeling vindicated. The battle plan he and Perkins had been discussing for months was playing out almost flawlessly. The tank battalions had penetrated to the heart of Saddam's regime without losing a single man—a remarkable achievement considering the number of forces arrayed against them and the size of Baghdad itself, a sprawling metropolis of more than 5 million people.

Wesley was in charge of the TOC, which was running smoothly and efficiently that morning. The TOC was the brigade's computerized brain. It was a portable command center created by parking armored communications vehicles back to back, like covered wagons in a circle. The TOC had been set up inside the abandoned agricultural warehouse complex, in an open courtyard framed by two-story buildings. Officers monitored battles on laptops and radar screens, and via secure FM and satellite radio networks. They stood at map boards and sat at terminals arranged on folding tables. Olive drab canvas had been stretched over metal frames to provide walls and a roof. All information and data were routed through the TOC—division headquarters at the airport, Perkins and the tank battalion commanders in the city, warplanes circling the city and spy planes high overhead, and the artillery and mortar teams and scout platoons. Wesley and his crew of battle captains and NCOs inside the command tent were monitoring the battle, receiving and relaying updates and situation reports.

Wesley had guided Perkins up Highway 8 that morning, relaying feeds from 150-foot-long E-8C surveillance planes equipped with JSTARS radar—the joint surveillance and targeting aperture radar system. The radar system's MTI—moving target indicator—provided real-time warnings of approaching vehicles by transmitting data to radar screens inside the TOC. Wesley was able to see blinking lights on a screen, superimposed with a map depicting Highway 8, and then warn Perkins by radio of any approaching enemy vehicles. Commanders in tanks and Bradleys kept track of other American vehicles by watching blue icons on digital maps displayed via the FBCB2 system. Through on-board GPS systems, each command vehicle constantly relayed its changing location to other vehicles equipped with FBCB2.

Through the system, also known as Blue Force Tracker, Wesley was able to communicate by text with Perkins if Perkins's vehicle was out of FM radio range. The TOC also relayed reports from air force pilots scanning the highway. Lieutenant Colonel Gantt's artillery was under TOC control, as were the mortar crews, the multiple rocket launchers, and the fighter planes providing close air support. The entire battlefield—from the tank crews at the Republican Palace and parade grounds to the infantry now setting up on the Highway 8 interchanges—was being choreographed at the TOC that morning.

Wesley had also been mindful of the propaganda war. He had been monitoring the intelligence radio frequency, listening for word of any media reports of American tanks in the city so that he could keep Perkins updated. The BBC was particularly significant because of its global reach and because the network had failed to report the presence of Rogue's tanks in the city during the April 5 thunder run. When Wesley told Perkins that the BBC was reporting American tanks inside the palace complex, cheers went up over the radio net.

At the same time, Wesley had been holding two embedded reporters at bay. Julio Anguita Parrado, a Spanish reporter, and Christian Liebig, a German journalist, had been pestering Wesley for permission to alert their home offices about the American incursion into central Baghdad. The two young men had decided not to ride in on the thunder run, judging it too dangerous, and now they were desperate to keep up with competitors embedded with units inside Baghdad. Wesley did not want Parrado and Liebig filing too early and revealing the brigade's battle plan prematurely.

But when Wesley heard from Perkins that the tank battalions had secured the palace area, he nodded to the two reporters and said, "Go!" Cheers rose up inside the TOC as the reporters bolted from the TOC to call their offices on their satellite phones.

It was an emotional moment for Wesley. He and Perkins had been preparing for this mission for months, and now the brigade had taken over Saddam's government complex in a matter of hours. Things had moved more swiftly and dramatically than Wesley had ever imagined. He wanted to talk to Perkins privately, away from the monitored radio net, to congratulate him and share his own sense of elation. He walked out of the TOC to retrieve his iridium satellite phone from his Humvee, which was parked just inside the front gate of the compound. He took off his helmet and set it down on the hood, then stripped off his flak vest and tossed it inside the vehicle. He punched in Perkins's satellite phone number and wandered through the compound in the aimless way that people pace while talking on a mobile phone.

Perkins sounded upbeat and invigorated. He was standing inside Saddam's government complex now, and he tried to explain to Wesley how surreal it felt to be in control of a place that had been at the heart of the regime's command and control apparatus just days earlier. Wesley congratulated his boss, and the two men reflected on their planning sessions back in Kuwait and their preliminary bull sessions back at Fort Stewart.

"Eric, you wouldn't believe it," Perkins said. "It's everything we would've hoped for."

Wesley said, "Congratulations, sir, I—" and at that moment he heard what sounded like the whine of a low-flying airplane. For an instant Wesley wondered why close air support would be flying over the TOC, and so low. Then an orange fireball blew past him and a thunderclap slammed him to the ground. He was in the dirt now, struggling to catch his breath. All the oxygen seemed to have been sucked from the air. The sky had turned black. He felt an intense heat.

Wesley heard Perkins's voice: "What's up?"

He realized he still had the satellite phone in his hand. His head cleared. Now he realized what had happened. It wasn't an airplane he had heard. It was a surface-to-surface missile. The entire TOC compound was engulfed in flames.

Still on the ground, Wesley spoke into the phone. "Sir, we just got hammered."

"What?"

"Sir, the TOC just got hit."

Wesley heard Perkins shout to someone near him: "The TOC just got hit!"

Wesley couldn't see the TOC anymore. It seemed to have evaporated behind a curtain of smoke. He couldn't see his Humvee. He saw only a wall of flames. It was 10:24 a.m., just over four hours into the mission.

"Sir," he said wearily. "I'll have to call you back. It doesn't look good."

E L E V E N
GOING AMBER

The man in charge of putting the tactical operations center together and tearing it down was Captain William Glaser, the headquarters company commander. Glaser was thirty-three, a genial veteran from Tennessee, a state high school pole vault champion who had been recruited to West Point by the track and field team. Shortly after 10 a.m. on April 7, Glaser was sitting next to the battle board, with its magnetic icons depicting the tank battalions in downtown Baghdad. The icons showed a tight ring of American armor strung like a noose around Saddam's palace and government complex along the Tigris. Like everyone else inside the TOC, Glaser was in a buoyant mood. Some of the guys were high-fiving, celebrating the brigade's remarkable armored thrust into the capital.

Amid the tumult, one of the air force officers was busy arranging CAS—close air support—for the tank battalions inside the city. Glaser heard him shout out: "We have CAS on station!" At that moment, Glaser heard what sounded like the roar of an airplane, very low, just above the tree line. He thought: "Damn, that's *fast*."

Then he was tumbling across the TOC, blown from his chair by a tremendous blast of hot dirt and sand that collapsed the canvas roof and buckled the flimsy canvas walls. Computers and radios crashed to the ground, their cables snapping. The battle map was buried under debris. The light supports toppled and everything went black. Acrid smoke seemed to rise up from the ground and smother the dull light of morning.

A surface-to-surface missile—most likely an ANABIL-100 or a FROG-7—had just ripped into the courtyard, detonating next to a line of parked Humvees. Glaser struggled to his feet and saw that the entire walled compound had been swallowed by a fireball. The Humvees belonging to the brigade's top officers, parked in a neat row along the north side of the courtyard, were burning out of control. So were the signal vehicles parked along the southern wall. Men were writhing in the gravel, their skin and uniforms seared and smoking. Bundles of red plastic rice sacks, used to store fertilizer or agricultural products, had exploded and were now scattered across the courtyard, draping everything with a coat of melting red plastic.

Inside one of the Humvees, Specialist George Mitchell had been sitting behind the wheel, drinking coffee. Mitchell was the driver for the brigade's operations officer and a veteran of the first Gulf War. A father of three, he was thirty-five, much older than most specialists because he had spent time in the Army Reserves and had reenlisted after September 11 to, as he put it, "finish this thing off." Mitchell was a neat freak. His bunk area back in Kuwait was a model of crisp army perfection. On his bedside table was a photo of his grandparents and another of his wife and children. In the middle was a small American flag. Captain Glaser had been so impressed that he e-mailed a photo of Mitchell's bunk area to the Family Readiness Group Web site back at Fort Stewart.

Earlier that morning, Mitchell had managed to get a quick satellite telephone call through to his wife, Brenda, in the United States to assure her that he was fine. Now he was dead, killed instantly by a direct hit from the missile, his coffee thermos still in his lap and his dog tags around his neck.

The two embedded journalists, the Spanish reporter Julio Anguita Parrado and the German journalist Christian Liebig, had been standing next to Mitchell's Humvee. They were setting up their satellite phones to report to their home offices in Europe that the brigade's combat teams had seized Saddam's palace and government complex. They had decided against riding into the city on the thunder run, for it seemed too risky, and now they had their story. They had just grabbed their phones when the missile detonated next to the Humvee, digging out a ten-foot-deep crater. Both young men were incinerated in an instant, their bodies reduced to gray ash in the gravel.

Standing next to Perkins's command Humvee—he had left the soft-skinned vehicle behind—was the colonel's driver, Corporal Henry Brown, twenty-two, a devout young man who taught Sunday school back home in Natchez, Mississippi. Brown had married a fellow soldier just before shipping out to Kuwait, and she, too, was serving in Iraq. The fireball from the missile enveloped the Humvee and everything nearby. Brown was horribly burned, but he remained conscious and even managed to joke with the medics—"Hey, get that thing in there"—as they worked furiously to put an IV into his arm. Brown survived long enough to be evacuated, but he died later of his burns on a military hospital ship.

Across the courtyard from the Humvees, next to a low cement wall, stood Private First Class Anthony Miller, one of the brigade's mechanics. Miller was just a kid; he had turned nineteen in September. He had joined the army to help support his mother. He had been walking across the courtyard when the missile hit. Something—a piece of shrapnel or a shard of metal from one of the Humvees or a piece of flying equipment—tore into Miller. He was slammed into the wall, mutilating his body and killing him on the spot.

Eric Wesley was a few feet from Miller, flat on the ground, still holding the satellite phone. He got up and tried to clear his head. Soldiers were already running over to comfort the wounded and attend to the dead. Some of them grabbed fire extinguishers and bottles of water from parked vehicles and were trying, futilely, to put out the roaring fire. Wesley decided right away to try to triage the casualties until the medics arrived—and also triage the communications vehicles in an effort to determine which equipment could be salvaged and reused. He made sure the wounded were treated, gathered up, and moved to the forward surgical team, which, fortunately, had been set up just across the highway, only a few hundred meters away. Wesley arranged for intact vehicles to be moved away from the flames and for all working communications equipment to be retrieved to help fashion a new, makeshift TOC.

In the row of Humvees, next to a flaming ten-foot-deep crater left by the missile, Wesley's Humvee had incinerated. He had lost his helmet, his flak vest, all his personal gear—and the Humvee's radio. Later that day, Wesley sifted through the smoking debris and fished out a small pocket Bible his father-in-law had given to him. He found it under the only piece of the Humvee that still existed—the charred engine block. The book was singed around the edges, but its pages were intact. It was the only item Wesley owned that survived the explosion, and he considered it a special blessing at a terrible moment.

Near the Humvee, sitting upright on the ground, was Sergeant Major Alexander Gongora. Several soldiers were trying to comfort him. Wesley could see that Gongora was badly burned and in shock. Glaser saw him, too, but he couldn't tell who it was. Gongora's face had been disfigured by the burns. Gongora was the operations sergeant major, and Glaser had known him for a year. But Glaser didn't recognize him, and this moment of confusion at a time of crisis troubled him for a long while afterward.

Wesley came up to Glaser. He wanted his help in organizing the rescue and recovery operation. Wesley was the senior officer at the TOC and Glaser was the commander of the brigade's headquarters company. The two men had a quick, urgent conversation. Glaser was struck by how calm and focused Wesley seemed, even amid the flames and smoke and the cries of the wounded. Wesley told Glaser to take charge of treating and evacuating the wounded. Wesley would handle the recovery of communications vehicles and equipment and the cobbling together of a new TOC, which he intended to set up in a clearing about three hundred meters to the south. Wesley had no radio communications with the men who worked in the TOC, so as he ran into each of them amid the tumult of the rescue effort, he issued the same clear, simple instructions. He told them they had four primary missions: triage and evacuate the wounded, recover serviceable equipment, set up the new command post, and reestablish perimeter security.

It was essential to get the TOC up and running again as quickly as possible. The tank battalions—not to mention the brigade commander— were now operating nearly blind inside the city. Without the TOC, they were cut off from direct communications for command and control, close air support, spot intelligence, artillery, mortars—all the so-called combat multipliers that support men in battle. At the palace complex downtown, Perkins had as a matter of procedure established a TAC, a tactical command post, which consisted of his command personnel carrier and several other armored vehicles loaded with communications equipment. Now Perkins huddled with Kenneth Gantt, the artillery commander, and with the brigade's air liaison officer. He told them: "We're going to take over the whole fight. We're going to control the whole fight right here from the TAC." Perkins's small TAC now had to serve as an emergency TOC, coordinating the combat multipliers under duress until Wesley could build a new TOC using equipment salvaged from the fires that were still raging.

The battery in Wesley's satellite phone had gone dead, so he ordered one of his officers to follow him around the compound in a Humvee with a working radio. He managed to reach Perkins to keep him updated on the chaotic situation around the TOC. Perkins had assumed at first that the TOC had merely been hit by mortar rounds; the area had been receiving mortar fire off and on for the previous two days. But when Wesley finally called Perkins back and told him that the compound had taken a devastating hit from an Iraqi missile, Perkins thought: *Holy shit, I never anticipated anything this big.* A mission that had played out nearly perfectly for the first four hours was now in danger of unraveling. Perkins would now not only have to command and control the fight on the ground, but also coordinate all the air support, artillery, and communications.

Wesley told Perkins that the brigade had taken KIAs at the TOC. "Do you need to know who we lost?" he asked. Perkins paused. He hesitated to put these sort of personal losses out over the air. The radio net was still functioning, and now it fell silent. The entire brigade was listening in. "Yeah," Perkins said finally. "Go ahead and tell me."

Wesley listed the names: Corporal Mitchell, Specialist Miller, the two embedded reporters. Perkins asked who had been evacuated. Wesley mentioned Perkins's driver, Corporal Brown. He tried to describe the extent of Brown's burns. Wesley and Perkins had often discussed the need to remain in control of their emotions in times of crisis, to focus on the mission at hand no matter how callous it might seem. They were doing that now, and their voices were direct and clinical over the net. It had to be that way. When Wesley had finished, Perkins said flatly, "Roger," and signed off.

Inside the compound, Glaser could feel the heat of the flaming vehicles on his face. He ran over to a group of soldiers to order them to set up a casualty collection point—a protected area where the combat lifesavers could perform buddy aid while the wounded waited to be medevaced. He was surprised to see that a collection point had already been set up inside a concrete vehicle bay. The enlisted men had not waited for an officer to tell them what to do, and it seemed to Glaser that the initial rescue and recovery operation had sprung up instantly and was now running on its own. With the collection point established, he went in search of his first sergeant to check on the ambulance exchange point and to send soldiers with stretchers back to carry the wounded out to the ambulances.

Glaser tried to run out the front gate, but he ran into a wall of flames. He had to make his way to the rear of the compound, where a gate led past the burning signal vehicles to the two-story building where Perkins had delivered the mission operation order the night before. Normally, the white sand and the light tan buildings reflected the brilliant desert sunlight, and everybody wore sunglasses to see through the glare. But now the dark smoke and haze obscured everything, and Glaser struggled to find his way to the front entryway and the first sergeant's post.

As he jogged through the smoke, Glaser ran across one of his favorite soldiers, a thirty-two-year-old private first class named Conrad Camp, a gung ho soldier who had signed up right after September 11. Camp was only a private, but he was considered a wise old head, and younger men looked to him for guidance. But now Camp was acting like a lunatic. He was stumbling around bare-chested, wearing only one boot. His chest and back were smeared with blood. A young woman—a sergeant whom Glaser recognized as one of the military intelligence specialists—was pulling on Camp's arm, trying to persuade him to go to a casualty collection point. Camp would have nothing to do with her.

The woman shouted at Glaser, "I'm trying to get him to a medic. He just won't listen to me!"

Camp had been peppered with shrapnel. It was obvious to Glaser that the missile blast had disoriented him. "Camp!" he yelled. "Camp! Where you going?"

"Sir, I'm going to pull security!" Camp said. He didn't have a weapon, and the TOC had a permanent security perimeter that was manned twenty-four hours a day.

Glaser stopped Camp and made him look at him. "Camp, do you know who I am?" he asked.

Camp stared hard at his commander, as though he had just asked an impossibly stupid question. "Yeah, you're the CO," he said casually.

"Good," Glaser said. "Now this is your commander ordering you to go with this young lady and do what she says. Do you understand me?"

"Okay, yeah, I knew that," Camp said, and the sergeant led him away to be treated. Camp returned to duty two days later, but only after his wife had been told, mistakenly, that he had suffered serious shrapnel wounds to the spine and was being evacuated for surgery in the United States.

Glaser moved on, still searching for the first sergeant. Outside the front entrance, he could see a mushroom cloud of black smoke twisting into the hazy morning sky, drifting past the thick stand of date palms behind the compound. Most of the Humvees parked outside the compound had been shielded from the blast wave by a four-meter-high brick wall, but they were splattered with debris and with flaming bits of the red plastic bags. Scraps of the plastic hung like used-car-lot flags from defunct telephone lines stretched above the compound.

Glaser stumbled across his first sergeant, Rodric Dalton, and told him, "We need to set up an ambulance exchange point." Dalton gave him a quizzical look. "Sir," he said, "it's already being done." Glaser looked over the sergeant's shoulder and saw a sergeant guiding a medical vehicle into one of the concrete bays. *Damn,* Glaser thought, *these soldiers and NCOs must have this stuff hardwired into their brains.* They were taking care of every last detail.

Near the front wall, several soldiers were using water bottles to try to extinguish small vehicle fires triggered by the burning red plastic. Glaser ordered them to drive the vehicles away from the flames inside the compound, and then put out the fires. He jumped into the driver's seat of one of the Humvees and flipped the starter switch halfway to warm the engine. The glow plug light flashed WAIT while Glaser felt a burning sensation on his arms and neck. Melting plastic was dripping down on him, searing his skin. He stared at the yellow light, cursing in pain, and finally the light went out. He gunned the engine, peeling the hot plastic off his skin as he drove the Humvee to safety.

Glaser had not seen any of the wounded from the casualty collection point inside the compound at the ambulance exchange point. He grabbed a private and two stretchers and navigated his way through the smoky compound back to the vehicle bays. He saw that the combat lifesavers had done everything they could and were now talking softly to the wounded men. In a low sound, almost like cooing, they were whispering, "Hey, it's gonna be okay. You'll be fine. We're gonna take care of you."

It was time to move. The rounds were cooking off at increasing intervals. Glaser climbed up on a pile of pallets and yelled, "All eyes on me!" He issued a quick set of orders, assigning tasks to everyone. The casualties were evacuated through a maze of smashed walls and burning vehicles to medical vehicles outside.

In the dusty field outside the compound, a soldier ran up to Glaser and told him that someone was on the radio net, delivering alarming reports of the carnage inside the compound. He thought they were making it sound worse than it really was. Men in combat can be paralyzed by bad news, particularly bad news involving the brutal, violent deaths of their comrades. Glaser wanted desperately to find a working radio so that he could get on the net and clarify the situation, to assure the combat teams in the city that the TOC would be back up and functioning soon.

He ran to find his Humvee, which was outfitted with a radio. He saw a Humvee speed past him and thought he recognized the vehicle. It was clean and polished. It looked like Specialist Mitchell's Humvee. Mitchell was always cleaning his vehicle, even when all the other Humvees were caked with dust and grit. His radio was always spotless and in perfect working order.

"Mitchell!" Glaser hollered, trying to flag him down. "Mitchell! Mitchell!"

The Humvee sped past him. Glaser cursed. "Dammit, Mitchell! Stop! I need your radio!"

Glaser finally found his own Humvee. As he grabbed the hand mike to send out an accurate situation report, he heard Wesley gain control of the radio net and put out a calm and restrained assessment. Glaser went back to accounting for his soldiers. It was crucial to take a head count, to make sure the NCOs had a good handle on where everybody was. Sergeant First Class Stanley Griffin was taking charge of accountability, and he mentioned to Glaser that Specialist Mitchell was among the KIAs. No, Glaser said, Mitchell was fine. He had just seen him.

Griffin shook his head. "Sir," he said quietly, "I don't think you saw Mitchell." He walked Glaser over to Mitchell's burning Humvee. And there Glaser saw Mitchell's charred remains. He was shocked. He was certain he had seen Mitchell alive and well—and now this. Poor Mitchell, he thought—he was such a fine soldier.

Glaser tried now to focus on the big picture, to make sure soldiers weren't working at cross purposes. In any calamity, especially one involving trained soldiers, people have a tendency to want to help right away. They focus on the first task they encounter, not necessarily the most important. Often people get in one another's way, with everyone trying to do the same thing while other needs are overlooked. Now Glaser saw a sea of tan uniforms flowing toward him—a whole fresh crop of volunteers who had rushed to the flaming TOC compound to offer their help.

Captain Robert Steinhoff and First Sergeant Joseph Rasmussen ran over to Glaser and said, "We have assets. How can we help?" They were from the battalion maintenance section. Glaser knew there were serviceable vehicles trapped inside the compound not yet consumed by the flames. He told them to figure out a way to get the serviceable vehicles out before they caught fire.

Within minutes, the maintenance soldiers had rammed one of its huge M-88 recovery vehicles through the compound wall, using its plow blade to create a pathway big enough to drive vehicles through. By now, explosions were erupting from the vehicles that had caught fire. They were packed with small-arms ammunition and antitank weapons, and now the heat was cooking off the rounds, which ripped through the smoky air, hissing and crackling, the antitank projectiles exploding on impact. Soldiers ran through the flames, staying low to avoid the cooked-off rounds. They climbed into the vehicles and drove them through the hole to the safety of the field beyond the compound. Sergeant First Class Griffin sprinted past the fire to recover people and equipment, vomited from smoke inhalation, then ran back into the compound.

By this time, Wesley had supervised the hasty construction of an emerging new TOC. The vehicles that had formed the core of the TOC were all armored with steel plating, and they had survived the concussion and flames. The communications equipment inside was still in good working order, but all the external wiring and cables and antennae had been destroyed. Wesley had to find a way to cannibalize equipment from damaged vehicles and take backup equipment from others.

One of the singular attributes of the U.S. military is redundancy. The army goes to war with a healthy supply of spare parts and equipment. The mantra among soldiers assigned to Operation Iraqi Freedom was, "God will curse those who only bring one." Resupply convoys were notoriously slow and unreliable; they had lagged far behind the tanks and Bradleys on the long march up from Kuwait. There was no Home Depot in the combat zone. Everybody crammed their vehicles with extra supplies—from antennae and generators and radios to toilet paper and motor oil. Soldiers hauled out extra communications equipment from their vehicles and delivered it to the new TOC site.

Wesley and his team from the old TOC cobbled together a new secure tactical satellite communications network and a new FM radio net.

As Wesley came up on the net, the first thing he did was request close air support for Perkins in the palace complex. He heard General Austin's soothing voice: "Spartan Five. Hey, first I want you to know, it's good to hear your voice."

Now, barely an hour after the rocket attack, the brigade had a functioning TOC. It wasn't a green TOC—the fully equipped operations center that had been working so efficiently earlier that morning—but it was at least an amber TOC, a serviceable alternative. Wesley assembled the battle captains and the rest of the TOC staff. It was 11:30 a.m. They were back in the fight.

At Fort Stewart that morning, Wesley's wife, Cindy, was getting her two oldest children ready for school when the phone rang just before 8 a.m. It was a friend whose husband was in the air force. She had just received a call about an attack on the Second Brigade TOC outside Baghdad. Cindy had been worried about her husband's safety the entire war, and now her fears intensified. She tried to stay composed as she got her sons Tyler, eleven, and Austin, seven, ready for school. She knew that Tyler, as the oldest, understood the dangers his father faced; he realized when the war began that his dad might never come home again.

With her two boys off to school, Cindy switched on the television. She had recently arranged to have cable installed so that she could monitor war coverage. The news crawl across the bottom of the Fox News program described a missile attack on the TOC, with an estimated seven or eight dead. Cindy felt nauseous. She was afraid that at any moment someone in uniform would be knocking on her front door with bad news. She had memorized the casualty notification hours and knew that the only "safe" periods were after 11 p.m. and before 6 a.m. She was in the danger zone. She struggled to hold back her tears. She feared the worst—Eric was always at the TOC, at the center of things. She got down on her knees and began to pray.

Also at Fort Stewart, Ginger Perkins woke up that morning with the usual assortment of accessories at her bedside—her cell phone, her cordless phone, a notebook, and a pen. She sometimes got calls in the middle of the night, occasionally from her husband, David, and more often from the garrison commander of the brigade's rear detachment at Fort Stewart. She got up and woke her son and daughter for school, then turned on the television in the breakfast nook. She kept a videotape in overnight to record news reports while she slept. As the children got ready for school, she read the day's *Our Daily Bread* devotional aloud. Cassandra, seventeen, and Chad, thirteen, huddled with their mother in the hallway between the bedrooms. They locked hands and repeated prayers for David, for everyone in the brigade, and for all American soldiers deployed in the Middle East. Then the children left for school and Ginger Perkins sat down at the computer.

She checked first for "Velvet Rock" messages—an alert to the spouses of the division's brigade commanders of any casualty notification within the division. As she read her e-mails, she heard a Fox News announcer mention that correspondent Greg Kelly was broadcasting from Baghdad. She swung around in her chair and saw David standing next to Kelly in front of a palace. She felt elated. The brigade was in downtown Baghdad and her husband was fine, if a bit haggard and dirty.

When the segment ended, Ginger turned back to her e-mail and saw a message about a missile attack on the brigade TOC. It mentioned casualties: two soldiers and two reporters. She began to doubt what she had just seen on TV. She thought the segment showing her husband's interview had been live, but now she wasn't sure. She wasn't even certain now that David was even in Baghdad. And she didn't know exactly where the TOC was located. She called Captain Mike Enos, the brigade's rear detachment commander, who said he was on his way over. Then she called Cindy Wesley, who also decided to head over to the Perkins home.

Ginger Perkins, Enos, and Cindy Wesley decided that Ginger's home would be open to anyone throughout the day. They knew it would be hours, and almost certainly the next day, before casualties were confirmed and families were notified. They arranged for a chaplain to conduct an evening prayer meeting. Later, Captain Enos went to his headquarters to seek an update from the post casualty notification office.

Cindy Wesley still had no news about Eric. She had tried to prepare herself for the war, and for the worst, but there was really no way to prepare for something like this. She knew she had to stay home, by the phone. She had arranged for a friend to come over and watch her youngest child, Meredith, four, while she went to a doctor's appointment. She canceled it, but asked the friend to stay, not knowing what the day would hold.

The phone kept ringing. Friends and family members of brigade members were calling from around the country and around the world, seeking information and offering support. Around 11 a.m., Cindy's father, a retired army colonel and a Vietnam veteran, called her on her cell phone. His voice was cracking. He told his daughter that he had just seen on TV that Lieutenant Colonel Eric Wesley had described a missile attack on the Second Brigade TOC. He had survived. Cindy cried, and her father broke down, too. Then she got off the line so that she could call Eric's parents to let them know their son was alive.

As everyone continued to watch TV, awaiting updated news reports, Ginger Perkins's phone rang. It was her husband, calling on a satellite phone. Ginger cried at the sound of his voice. It was a brief conversation. David wasn't at the TOC—he was in downtown Baghdad. He told his wife that things were bad at the TOC, with multiple casualties. Through her tears, Ginger told him how sorry she was about his soldiers. She assured him that she would do everything she could on the home front.

The phones continued to ring throughout the afternoon and into the evening. Ginger Perkins spoke with Anita Blount, the wife of Major General Buford Blount, the division commander. More wives of Second Brigade soldiers dropped by. Everyone knew that most of them would be going out the next day to comfort the families of the soldiers who had died, so they baked bread to take along. By the end of the day, Ginger Perkins was feeling weak and unsteady. She had not eaten all day. A neighbor brought over a chicken dinner, and she felt better after eating. She said a prayer for the strength and courage to face the families of the dead men the next day.

That evening, about fifty spouses attended a prayer meeting, where the chaplain spoke and Captain Enos shared the latest updates from the rear detachment. Many of the women hugged one another, then sat and wrung their hands in silence. Some of them asked Ginger Perkins if she knew whether their husbands had been killed or injured. There was not much she could tell them; it was a painful evening.

Late that night, Ginger spoke on the phone with Charlene Austin, the wife of General Lloyd Austin, the assistant division commander, and gave her an update on the spouses. Then Ginger fell into bed with her cell phone, cordless phone, notebook, and pen beside her. She knew there would be Velvet Rock messages overnight, and she knew, too, that the next day would be even more difficult than the one that was ending.

On the military parade grounds downtown, Colonel Perkins had set up his command post roughly halfway between the towering pairs of crossed sabers. The curving blades gave off a dull silver glow in the murky haze, dwarfing the tanks and Bradleys arrayed across from the VIP reviewing stand. The air reeked of cordite and burning fuel. Perkins stood, map in hand, flanked by Schwartz and deCamp. He had just received an updated casualty report from the attack on the TOC: two dead enlisted men; two dead reporters; eighteen wounded soldiers, some with hideous burns; and twenty-two destroyed vehicles.

Over the radio net came more distressing news. Lieutenant Colonel Stephen Twitty, the commander of Task Force 3-15, the China battalion, was under siege on Highway 8. Twitty had set up his three companies on the three main interchanges leading north into the city center, code-named Objectives Moe, Larry, and Curly. Twitty had expected some resistance at all three objectives, but what he encountered was full-scale, close-quarters, balls-out firefights. His men were being pounded—by RPGs, small arms, mortars, technicals, suicide vehicles, armored troop carriers, and antiaircraft artillery. Gunmen were firing from rooftops, mosques, and primary schools. They were being delivered to the battle by buses and taxis and police cars.

Twitty had anticipated that the Rogue and Tusker battalions, backed by the early morning artillery and mortar barrages, would have cleared out most of the Iraqi positions at the interchanges. But it seemed to him now that the thunder run had somehow jarred the enemy awake. The Iraqis were fighting like madmen—they were fanatical. Twitty had never seen anything so intense—not in the first Gulf War, and not during all the firefights his men had endured in southern Iraq. His own gunner had just killed a suicide driver who had tried to ram his Bradley—in a taxicab.

Perkins sensed the urgency in Twitty's voice. He knew the man very well; he had worked closely with Twitty for months. He knew Twitty was not a man to panic. Nor was he a man given to soft-pedaling a situation. Twitty delivered situation reports straight up, unvarnished, no bullshit.

So when he told Perkins that things were bad on Highway 8, Perkins knew the situation was growing desperate.

"Sir, there is one hell of a fight here," Twitty told Perkins. Twitty was in the hatch of his Bradley, on the cloverleaf at Objective Larry, two and a half kilometers south of Moe and three and a half kilometers north of Curly. "I'll be honest with you. I don't know how long I can hold it here. I can't at this time confirm that I can keep Route Eight open."

Then Twitty told Perkins something that changed the dynamics of the entire mission—a mission that, even with the devastating hit on the TOC, had moved with surprising speed and success. Twitty reported that his company at Moe, at the huge spaghetti interchange that controlled access into the city center, was amber on ammunition. In the military's color-coded supply ratings system, amber meant that ammunition supplies were approaching dangerously low levels. Worse, Twitty said, the company was perhaps an hour or two away from going black, the level at which it would be unable to sustain the fight.

Now, for the first time that morning, Perkins began to fear that he would not be able to keep his two tank battalions in the city overnight. If the Iraqis punched through the company at Moe, they would be able to pour in Perkins's back door and attack the tank battalions from the rear. The tanks had already been shut down to conserve fuel, but if the company at Moe were overrun, they would be cut off from fuel and ammunition. Perkins briefly considered sending one of his tank battalions to reinforce the company at Moe and to try to keep the highway open between Moe and the city center.

But then Twitty told Perkins about Objective Curly, the interchange three and a half kilometers north of the brigade operations center. Twitty's men at Curly had no tanks—and they were absorbing a tremendous barrage of fire.

"I don't know how long they can hold it there," Twitty said. "I've got to get reinforcements."

"If you need it, you've got it," Perkins said. He had promised Twitty the day before that he would send any help he requested.

"I need it. I can't hold it any longer," Twitty said.

"Whatever you need, you'll get it," Perkins promised.

Perkins had spoken earlier with General Blount about sending a battalion from the division's First Brigade at the airport to reinforce positions on Highway 8. Now the battalion was launched down Highway 1, south of the airport. It would turn east to secure the Second Brigade's TOC at the intersection of Highways 1 and 8, then send a company north to reinforce the interchange at Curly. That would allow Twitty's beleaguered company at Curly to pull out and head north up Highway 8 to reinforce the company at the spaghetti interchange while also securing the mile-long roadway into the city center.

At the same time, Perkins passed Twitty's request for immediate reinforcements to Eric Wesley at the newly formed TOC. Twitty wanted one of two platoons from China battalion that had been left behind to protect the TOC. Wesley had listened over the reconstituted radio net to Twitty's increasingly desperate situation along Highway 8. He knew that securing the highway was crucial to getting fuel and ammunition to the tank battalions inside the city. Wesley told Twitty to take both platoons. That would leave the new TOC virtually undefended, but Wesley thought Twitty needed them more than he did. Wesley would have to send men from the TOC itself to secure the perimeter, armed only with M-16s. Soon the two platoons were pulling out. Wesley didn't tell anyone, but the thought of what he had just done scared him to death.

T W E L V E
CURLY

Even before he reached the highway interchange known as Objective Curly earlier that morning, Captain Harry "Zan" Hornbuckle knew he had problems. Lieutenant Colonel Twitty, the China battalion commander, came over the net and warned Hornbuckle about enemy gunmen dug into the cloverleaf, where the four-lane Ad Dawrah Highway rose up and over Highway 8. The Iraqi fighters had survived the thunder run by Rogue and Tusker earlier that morning—or perhaps they had moved up afterward from the dense neighborhoods flanking the highway. Twitty wasn't sure. All he knew was that there was still a lot of enemy firepower left at Curly.

Twitty had just sped through the interchange in the commander's hatch of a Bradley, under fire, on his way to set up his battalion command post at Objective Larry three and a half kilometers up the highway. Hornbuckle was somewhere behind him on Highway 8, bearing down on Curly with a combat team that had been ordered to seize and hold the interchange. Twitty tried to warn the captain. "Zan, you've got trenches on your right!" Twitty paused, trying to think of the best way to stress the severity of the threat. "They know we're coming," he said finally.

Hornbuckle felt challenged by the mission he had been given. Unlike the captains in charge of the interchanges north of him at Objectives Larry and Moe, Hornbuckle did not have a full combat company. The two northern interchanges were considered more dangerous than Curly, which was only six kilometers north of the brigade tactical operations center. Two platoons from the company now assigned to Hornbuckle had been left behind to provide security for the vulnerable brigade TOC. That left Hornbuckle with just the battalion's headquarters section, plus a mechanized infantry platoon and a mortar team. He had only eighty soldiers— and no tanks. He had just five Bradleys, a couple of armored Humvees with

.50-caliber machine guns, some scout and mortar vehicles, and an armored personnel carrier loaded with engineers.

It was an unwieldy combat team, and an unfamiliar one. Hornbuckle had not previously worked closely with most of the men assigned to him. He wasn't the company commander—he was the assistant battalion S-3, from the planning and operations shop. The CO was Captain Ronny Johnson, who was back with the two platoons at the brigade TOC. Worse, Hornbuckle had been given just six hours to assemble his men and pull together a battle plan with an unfamiliar team thrown together at the last minute—what the brigade planners called a company minus, or Team Zan. He felt rushed and undermanned, but he was determined to make the best of the situation. Lieutenant Colonel Twitty regarded Hornbuckle as a capable and resolute officer. He was twenty-nine, a soft-spoken southerner who had grown up in a small town in Georgia. He didn't come from a military family; his father was a mechanic and his mother was a music teacher. After graduating from high school, Hornbuckle enrolled at the Citadel, a military school in South Carolina, earning his commission in 1996. He was married to his high school girlfriend and had a young son at home. He had never before been in combat.

Hornbuckle's column of vehicles reached Curly early in the morning, not long after Tusker and Rogue had blasted through the interchange. Smoke was still wafting up from vehicles that had been lit up by the tank battalions. Visibility was terrible; a blustery sandstorm had kicked up swirls of dirt and sand that gave everything a dull tan patina. Hornbuckle saw that there were clear fields of fire in all directions, except for a long support wall that ran beneath the curving access ramps to the right of the main highway and blocked the view to the east. On both sides of the divided roadway were stretches of flat, sandy ground dotted with weeds and blowing garbage. Beyond the fields were tan stucco homes and multistory apartment buildings. An access road ran parallel to Highway 8 on the east side, leading to dusty streets and tight warrens of alleyways that disappeared into cramped residential neighborhoods.

Hornbuckle rolled up in his Bradley, tense and expectant, trying to get a good read on the trench network Twitty had described. The broad, curving access ramps were cloaked in a yellow haze. He sent four Bradleys up to the overpass, two facing east and two facing west. He wanted to deny the enemy access to the east-west highway, which disappeared into the neighborhoods on either side. Hornbuckle kept his own Bradley in the northbound lanes, just beneath the overpass. He sent his mortar crews south of the overpass, right on the highway, where they began setting up in the northbound lanes.

Everybody was still moving in and getting situated when a barrage of RPG and small-arms fire erupted from all directions. Gunmen were firing from trenches and bunkers on both sides of the highway, and from alleyways and windows and rooftops in the neighborhoods. It was a complete circle of fire. The rounds were pinging off the Bradleys on the overpass as they opened up with their 25mm cannons and coax. The .50-caliber gunners on the Humvees worked the butterfly triggers, trying to suppress gunmen hidden in the trenches and bunkers. As RPGs exploded across the interchange, Hornbuckle managed to get all his vehicles set up in a tight circle, with 360-degree fields of fire.

He had just positioned his own Bradley in the northbound lanes when the first suicide vehicle sped toward him. It was a pickup truck, bearing down on him from the north. Hornbuckle picked it up on his sight and hit it with several rounds from the 25mm cannon. The car exploded, followed by a much bigger explosion as ammunition stored inside cooked off. Minutes later, a technical with a machine gun mounted on the back suddenly appeared on the exit ramp. Hornbuckle couldn't figure out how it had penetrated the perimeter. The vehicle sped to within two hundred meters of his Bradley before everybody opened up on it—a grenade launcher, a .50-caliber machine gun, coax from a nearby Bradley, the main cannon from the captain's Bradley. The vehicle crumpled and burned.

The enemy tactics puzzled Hornbuckle. It was like they had no tactics at all. They kept sending in suicide vehicles to be destroyed—at least a dozen of them in the first couple of hours. And instead of concentrating their fire, the gunmen shot off bursts haphazardly, almost casually. Hornbuckle figured there were several hundred of them scattered around the interchange, supplied by caches of weapons and ammunition they had prepositioned in tiny caverns dug into the rubble beneath the on-ramps.

If they managed to coordinate and attack all at once, Hornbuckle thought, they might be able to overwhelm his undermanned combat team just by force of sheer numbers. But they fired from one direction for a while, then shut down and let other gunmen open fire from another direction. Hornbuckle was able to get the Bradley crews to swing from side to side, concentrating their weapons on the sector that happened to be mounting the biggest challenge at the moment. But he wasn't sure how long his guys could keep it up, or whether the enemy would shift tactics. For the moment, the gunmen in the distance seemed to be content with what Hornbuckle considered Somali tactics—move, harass, circle, and close. He knew he had to expand his perimeter, to push them back and keep them off balance before they closed in. He was badly outnumbered.

The rate of enemy fire was escalating when the man Hornbuckle had personally selected as his team first sergeant, Sergeant First Class Vincent Phillips, ran up to the captain's Bradley. Phillips was a savvy thirty-seven-year-old veteran, eight years older than Hornbuckle, and a man the captain trusted. Phillips looked like an NCO from a recruiting poster—square head, blocky torso, flattop haircut. He was one of those guys who loved action; he planned to get out of the service in another year or so to take a job as a cop.

Phillips had just arrived at Curly in an armored Humvee, pulling up near the wall that blocked the view to the east side of the highway. He got close enough to see that there was actually a series of support walls under the on-ramp, each one separated by narrow gaps. The walls provided ideal cover for RPG teams, which were almost certainly dug into the trenches Twitty had described. Phillips asked Hornbuckle for permission to start clearing beneath the on-ramp.

"Sir, we've got to get some guys down in there," he said. "I don't know what's down in there, but we've got to clear it before it gets hostile."

The captain quickly agreed. "Roger—you really need to go do that," he said.

Phillips ran back to the Humvee and grabbed the driver, Private First Class Adam Gregory. They would be a two-man clearing team.

Gregory was a tall kid, just twenty, with unruly short brown hair, prominent ears, a wispy mustache, and a flat California accent. He had been busted in rank back at Fort Stewart for failing to undergo the required tear-gas test. Everybody was required to enter a closed chamber as it filled with tear gas. Soldiers were to take off their gas masks for a few seconds, then put them back on. The idea was to test the masks and build soldiers' confidence in them. But Gregory had left without permission that day to visit his girlfriend, who he had just learned was pregnant. He missed physical training the next morning, too, and the NCOs got a key to his room and found him hiding in the closet. His commander, Captain Anthony Butler, had busted him and had also telephoned Gregory's father to tell him what had happened. Gregory had been humiliated, but he had resolved afterward to transform himself into the perfect combat soldier. He had come to realize that shaping up would help him survive combat and get him back home, where his girlfriend was expecting twins the very next month. And now, two weeks into the war, both Sergeant First Class Phillips and Captain Butler had been impressed with Gregory's newly honed dedication and professionalism.

Before heading to the on-ramp, Phillips ordered the Humvee gunner, Specialist Benjamin Agee, to swing his mounted machine gun toward the wall to cover them. Agee was surprised that just the two of them were going in, but he was pleased to be part of an actual combat operation. He had not seen much action on the way up from Kuwait, and had felt a stab of disappointment when he found out the night before that he was being sent to Curly. He had been under the impression that he would be sitting on the highway all day, bored, providing security, waiting for the fuel and ammo vehicles to pass through. The real fight, he had been told, would be at the palaces in the city. He was afraid he wouldn't even get a chance to fire his weapon. He wanted to get a taste of combat before his tour of duty was up. He had a political science degree from American University and planned to seek a job in Washington as a congressional committee staffer. But now, after four years in the army, he still hadn't seen any serious combat.

Agee swung the machine gun around and watched Phillips and Gregory creep down toward the wall. There were dark shadows beneath the ramp, and Gregory couldn't see much because of the cement support walls. The air was dank and stale. There was garbage and construction debris scattered everywhere. Gregory felt exposed, but also gratified that Phillips trusted him enough to include him on a combat mission. He was still trying to redeem himself.

Phillips was on Gregory's right as they made their way to a meter-wide gap in the first support wall. Phillips told Gregory to poke his head around the wall and see what was on the other side. Gregory peered into the shadows and saw a boot next to the wall. As his eyes adjusted to the dark, he saw the boot move. Somebody was down in the dirt on the other side of the wall, next to several RPG rounds.

Gregory leaped back and said to Phillips, "RPG team!"

"Prep your grenade," Phillips told him.

Gregory withdrew a hand grenade from his combat vest and removed the pin. As Phillips covered him, he leaned forward and tossed the grenade through the gap. The explosion reverberated off the cement support walls and the underside of the ramp. Phillips poked his head through the gap. Two shots rang out from the other side of the wall.

From his gun position on the Humvee, Agee saw Phillips duck just as the rounds tore into the wall where Phillips's head had been. It looked to Agee like a scene from an action movie, right down to the little spray of concrete chips from the impact of the bullets. Phillips dropped and rolled. Neither shot had struck him, but his eyes were filled with flying grit and his vision was blurred. He and Gregory stumbled back to the Humvee, covered by Agee, who fired into the opening with the machine gun.

Phillips had no idea how many RPG teams were behind the walls, but he knew it would take more than two soldiers to clear the dark expanse underneath the ramp. He had been joking around earlier that morning, telling everybody that April 7 was his wedding anniversary—"not a good day to die." Now, as he wiped the grit from his eyes, he was deadly serious. He told Agee to take his machine gun off the Humvee mount and follow him and Gregory. They were going back under the ramp, this time joined by a sniper Phillips had called over.

Agee's M-240 machine gun was a crew-served weapon, meaning it was designed as a two-man gun—the gunner and the loader. But Agee had served in a weapons squad, and he had trained to fire the heavy gun on his own. He felt comfortable with it. He was tall and big-boned, with huge hands and powerful shoulders. He was strong enough to fire the gun from the hip. He slung a belt of ammunition across his back and hauled the big machine gun toward the underbelly of the ramp.

The four-man team moved back to the opening in the wall, Phillips and Gregory in the lead with Agee and the sniper covering them. Their helmet liners were soaked with sweat now, and their heavy flak vests jostled as they crept along, the stiff Kevlar collars digging into their damp necks. They could hear the pounding of the Bradleys up on the overpass and the hiss of RPGs flying somewhere across the highway above them.

Phillips and Gregory stood on either side of the opening. Each man withdrew a grenade, pulled the pin, and flipped the grenade through the opening. All four men followed the sound of the explosion, darting through the narrow passageway. At least six men armed with RPGs and AK-47s were on their bellies in a shallow trench, stunned and bleeding. Gregory opened up with his M-16, killing some of them, and the sniper and Phillips got the rest. Agee came in behind them, the low groan of the M-240 echoing off the support walls. He was shooting from the hip, the big 7.62 rounds tearing into the gunmen's bodies. Even in the dark, with all the smoke and noise, Agee noticed that one of the men had lost both his legs. They were lying next to his torso, like two burned sticks. Agee kept firing.

The team moved from one support wall to the next, tossing grenades through the openings, killing everybody they saw. Beyond each wall was a network of trenches littered with RPG tubes and AK-47s. A few of the gunmen wore green uniforms, but most wore civilian clothes—jeans and sport shirts, mostly, topped by green army-issue web belts and ammunition pouches. They seemed startled by the sight of American soldiers on foot, and the few who managed to fire their weapons shot wildly, with no effect. Phillips kept wondering: Did these guys have any training, any tactics, any common sense? They seemed to be the very opposite of his soldiers, who had trained endlessly on how to move and clear an area.

As Gregory took cover behind one support wall, Phillips was able to see a gunman lying on the opposite side, waiting for Gregory to come through the opening. "Hey, there's a guy behind your wall!" Phillips yelled. Gregory backed up, ran around to the next opening, and shot the gunman from behind with his M-16.

The Iraqis were easy to kill. They didn't wear helmets or flak vests, so just one round through the head or torso put them down. Most of them didn't even get a chance to raise their weapons. They seemed to have no sense of cover and maneuver tactics. Agee didn't feel anything for them. He had never killed a man before, but the deaths of these strangers in the dark had no effect on him. He didn't even think about it. He just kept hosing down targets with the big M-240, hitting everything he saw. It did not occur to him to be afraid—in fact, it was an invigorating experience, almost thrilling. Combat was different than he had anticipated. It was . . . *interesting*. That was the only way to describe it—and, in fact, it was the word Agee used later when people asked him about the war. He made a point of soaking up every detail beneath the on-ramp, and everything was sharp and brilliant. He was intrigued by the way he was able to subsume himself to his training, and how straightforward it all was. It was just like his NCOs had always told him: pay attention, do it like you were trained, and things will take care of themselves. Agee glanced over at one point and made eye contact with Gregory. He could tell from the transfixed look on Gregory's face that he felt the same thing. He was enjoying himself, too.

As they cleared and moved, Phillips spotted a recoilless rifle beyond one of the support walls. It was mounted on a tripod, with a two-man crew crouched down beside it. Phillips motioned for Gregory, Agee, and the sniper to hold back and take cover. He wanted to get a clean shot at the weapon and its crew. He had mounted a scope on his M-16, and it gave him a clean view of the target. He squeezed off a few tracer rounds. The effect was astonishing. The recoilless rifle exploded in a shower of red sparks. It flipped up and cartwheeled through the air, the twelve-foot cannon spinning wildly. Phillips figured he must have somehow hit the priming charge.

The big gun came flying toward Agee, a huge, tumbling tube of metal. For an instant he thought it was going to crash down on him, but it landed about twenty meters short and tumbled away in a flash of smoke and flame. At the spot where the recoilless rifle had been mounted, the two crewmen were on fire. They were being burned alive. Phillips was shocked. He hadn't expected to take out an entire recoilless rifle and crew with just an M-16.

Phillips heard American voices behind him. Somebody was yelling, "We're moving up! We're moving up!" He turned to Gregory and said, "Oh, good, we're getting some more help."

The four of them had been fighting on their own for a good while, and Phillips was eager for backup. He glanced back and saw that several Special Forces soldiers were moving up just beyond the first support wall. Phillips had been briefed on the Special Forces A team that had been attached to the China battalion, but he wasn't quite sure what they were supposed to be doing. He didn't know any of them by name, but from chatting to them briefly the night before he and his men had sensed that the Special Forces guys thought they would be strolling out and talking to Iraqi civilians and imams, collecting intelligence. The A team had driven up to Curly with the rest of the convoy in two Toyota pickup trucks—one black and one silver—that looked a lot like Iraqi technical vehicles except for the bright orange fluorescent VS-17 panels that identified them as American vehicles. At the command briefing the night before, Colonel Perkins had ordered everybody to take a good look at the SF vehicles so that they didn't shoot them by mistake.

Now, in the tangle of debris and garbage below the on-ramp, Phillips saw the Special Forces team creeping up behind him. He said to Gregory, "The SF is coming up. We're good now."

One of the Special Forces medics had just run up to within a few feet of Agee when Agee heard him grunt—a low, involuntary grunt of pain and surprise. Agee looked around and saw the man go down, shot through the leg. Suddenly automatic rifle rounds were kicking up bits of sand and gouging holes in the cement support walls. A Special Forces soldier ran over to help the wounded medic. Agee shouted at him, "Hey, where's the fire coming from?" The soldier pointed south, to a trench system beyond the support wall.

Agee swung his machine gun around and started working the whole trench system, laying down a good seventy-five to a hundred of the big 7.62mm rounds. He could see gunmen crawling in the trenches, their boots sticking up. He heard the Special Forces soldier ask him if he was a medic. Agee thought it was an odd question. He yelled back, "No!" and hollered that he had his own job to do right then—to suppress enemy fire from the trenches. For the first time, it occurred to him that combat cut two ways, that he could get killed at any moment. If an SF guy was down, with all his high-speed training and skills, then a regular infantryman like Agee was liable to take a hit, too. And just then he heard another Special Forces soldier yelp and drop down, his knee and thigh ripped open in a huge scarlet wound.

Phillips saw it, too, and he grabbed Gregory and ran back to help. One of the wounded Special Forces soldiers was incoherent and bellowing in pain. The other was limping with a bloody ankle and foot, but still able to walk. Phillips realized that both soldiers were medics. He had a strange thought: What were the odds that two medics would get hit and need treatment?

The wounded men needed to be taken right away to the medical aid station, which had been set up on Highway 8, under the main overpass. Phillips, Gregory, and a Special Forces soldier lifted the badly wounded man out of the dirt and started hauling him back. One of the Special Forces men had already wrapped a thick field dressing around the medic's knee and thigh. The second wounded man limped after them, supported on one arm by a fellow Special Forces soldier. Agee kept up a steady rate of fire at the trenches, trying to cover their retreat.

They all ran back toward the highway, under fire, ducking under the narrow entryways through the support walls. Agee ran backward, still firing the machine gun. They made it to the highway and hustled north to the protected area beneath the overpass, where they found the medical aid station, protected by a semicircle of parked armored vehicles.

The battalion surgeon was Captain Erik Schobitz, a doctor from Fairfax, Virginia. Schobitz was thirty, but he looked younger, with his boyish features and his dark blond hair swept straight back under his helmet. He had no combat experience. In fact, he had never learned to fire an M-16 until a month earlier, when infantrymen in Kuwait gave him a quick lesson. He had spent his entire military career treating army dependents at military hospitals in the States. He was a pediatrician, a family man with a psychologist wife—today was her birthday—and three-year-old twins. In addition to his helmet and flak vest, Schobitz wore his pediatrician's stethoscope with a yellow plastic bunny attached.

The doctor had not found out until the night before that he would be sent into battle somewhere near Baghdad. He had planned to ride up in an ordinary Humvee until someone told him it was a sure way to get killed, and he was transferred to an armored vehicle. He had been stunned by the intensity of enemy fire when he arrived at the interchange, which he knew was somewhere on Highway 8. He did not learn until several days later that it was known as Objective Curly. The flat, dusty cloverleaf reminded him of the bleak futuristic landscape of the Mel Gibson movie *Mad Max*.

Schobitz told Phillips to take the wounded Special Forces soldiers into one of the armored medical vehicles. He knew instantly that one of them was in shock. He was pale and incoherent, his leg soaked through with blood. He was muttering, "I just been shot in the leg. Leave me alone!" He seemed to know he was being treated because he yelled at Schobitz, "Doc, it's just my damn leg!"

The back part of the man's knee had been blown out and the main artery shredded. Half his knee was gone, all the way into the thigh. It was a horrible wound. Schobitz removed the bloody dressing and bound the wound with pressure dressing to ease the bleeding. He was trying to quickly stabilize the man. In a few minutes, the soldier would be taken by armored vehicle to the forward surgical team. Schobitz decided not to put on a tourniquet, which would slow the bleeding but also increase the risk that the leg would have to be amputated. He wanted to give the man every chance to save his leg.

The medics evacuated the soldier and Schobitz turned to the second wounded SF soldier. His ankle was bloody and broken, but it was not a life-threatening wound. He was a medic, and he joked about treating himself as Schobitz dressed the wound and prepared him for medical evacuation to the forward surgical team.

At that moment, it dawned on Schobitz that they were now in a vicious firefight and might be pinned down at the interchange for a long time. The dust and explosions and smoke were disorienting. His face was flushed and streaked with sweat. He had no concept of the battle tactics being pursued, or what role the combat team at the interchange was playing in the larger battle for control of Baghdad. One of the captains looked at Schobitz and grinned. "Get used to it," he said. "We're going to be here for a while."

There was a brief lull of about twenty minutes—and then waves of casualties began to flow into the aid station. Soldiers suddenly began appearing with ragged pink shrapnel wounds—to the hands, the arms, the feet, the neck. A sergeant came in cradling his elbow with his free hand. The bone had been shattered by an AK-47 round. Schobitz told him he had to be medevaced right away for treatment, but the sergeant argued with him, saying he couldn't leave his men. He was near tears when the doctor handed him off to the medics for evacuation.

The sergeant was the last wounded man the medics were able to transport to the forward surgical team. Enemy fire was at murderous levels now. Rounds were penetrating the protected little cove they had set up beneath the overpass. Bullets were pinging off the support pillars and the underside of the expressway. It was worse out on the highway. The medics couldn't risk the lives of the crews to send the wounded through the gauntlet on Highway 8. Schobitz would have to stabilize them under the overpass until the combat team was able to get control of the interchange.

A private was brought in with a back injury and Schobitz strapped him to a backboard. A specialist came in with a piece of his finger shot off. There were leg wounds, shoulder wounds, neck wounds. Schobitz's surgical gloves were slick with blood, and he kept changing them. A soldier arrived with his leg impaled by a jagged strip of shrapnel. The shard had shot straight through the thick muscle and was protruding from either side. Schobitz left the piece in place; he feared he would tear the man's arteries if he tried to pull it out. He wrapped it tightly with a field dressing and administered antibiotics. The surgeons would have to cut the shrapnel out.

The wounded men kept coming. By mid-morning, the count had reached twenty. Remarkably, there were no head wounds, no sucking chest wounds, no wounds to vital organs. Schobitz was impressed by how thoroughly the soldiers' body armor and helmets had protected them. He had never fully appreciated their value, but he did now—especially after getting a good look at the ghastly wounds suffered by one of the poorly outfitted enemy soldiers dragged in for treatment.

The battalion chaplain had hauled him in. Captain Steve Hommel, a Baptist minister, had been out near the perimeter, trying to calm some of the infantrymen, when one of them motioned him over. "Sir, there's this *hajji* who's wounded real bad," the soldier said. "He's over there next to some dead guys. What do we do?"

Hommel saw a bloodied man in civilian clothes, badly burned and lying next to three dead enemy fighters. The chaplain made his way over to the man and managed to make eye contact. The fighter gestured to his forehead and spoke in broken English. It was clear to Hommel that the man wanted him either to help him or to put him out of his misery with a shot to the temple. Hommel ran back to find a litter and returned with two soldiers to help him. They carried the wounded fighter back to the aid station.

Schobitz examined him. He was badly burned over most of his body. He had shrapnel wounds in his arms and leg. His chin had been gashed and there was a hole through his cheek. He was delirious. The doctor sedated him with Demoral and gave him the muscle relaxant succinylcholine to temporarily paralyze him so that he could insert a breathing tube down his throat.

The vocal cords of a healthy adult male are pearly white. The fighter's vocal cords were stained black. He coughed up black, carbonaceous sputum. Schobitz tried twice to insert a breathing tube, but the man's vocal cords were nearly swollen shut. The doctor tried the smallest tube he carried in his bag—the size for an eight-year-old child—but that attempt also failed.

As he withdrew the tube, Schobitz heard a loud crack. Machine-gun rounds raked the ground next to the fighter's feet and tore through the aid station.

One of the medics yanked the doctor to the ground. "Sir, it's not worth dying for this guy . . . it's not worth it. He's dead," the medic said.

The medics treated another enemy casualty, a Syrian fighter in his late thirties, dressed in civilian clothes and sporting a bushy beard streaked with gray. The man was not critically injured. In pidgin English, he told the medics that he was a mercenary. He pulled a wad of blue Iraqi 250-dinar notes from his pocket and offered to pay for his release. The mustachioed portrait of a young Saddam Hussein was printed on the currency. The medics ignored him and treated his wounds.

Afterward, the Syrian lay in the dirt and methodically tore each dinar note in half, right across Saddam's face, and let them flutter away in the wind. "Bye bye, Saddam!" he chirped. "Bye bye, Saddam!"

They were taking more enemy fire now. Unlike Schobitz, Hommel had been in combat. He had fought in the first Gulf War as a combat infantryman, but he had never seen an Iraqi attack as terrifying as this one. From his vantage point beneath the overpass at the center of the interchange, it was obvious that the combat team was taking fire from all directions. They were surrounded. Hommel began to think that, even with their Bradleys and their superior equipment and training, they were in danger of being overrun. He felt a sense of alarm, though he hid it from the young infantrymen around him as he patted their backs and tried to joke with them.

Hommel was forty-one years old and a man of the cloth, but he had not fully forsaken his soldier's responsibilities. Later, when the interchange came under heavy attack, he decided that he was not going to give up without a fight, and he certainly was not going to surrender. Rounds were hitting all around the aid station, and some of the medics picked up their M-16s and returned fire. Hommel spotted an M-16 that had belonged to a wounded soldier. The chaplain was a noncombatant, but he believed he had the right to defend his own life and the lives of his fellow soldiers. He picked up the rifle and asked one of the medics for some ammunition. He squeezed off several bursts at muzzle flashes in the distance. He didn't know whether he hit anyone, and he didn't want to know.

* * *

Command Sergeant Major Robert Gallagher had set up his big M88 recovery vehicle directly beneath the overpass, next to the aid station. As the highest-ranking NCO in the entire battalion, Gallagher was helping Captain Hornbuckle direct the fight at Curly. He was caustic and forthright, a leathery-faced forty-year-old with a world-weary air. Some of the men called him Black Hawk Bob. Gallagher was a legendary figure in the battalion, a veteran of the disastrous Ranger raid in Mogadishu ten years earlier. He had been wounded several times during that fight, and his hand, arm, and back were dotted with gray bumps from where bits of shrapnel were still embedded. He sometimes joked about being one of those guys who set off alarms at airport metal detectors.

Even at the height of the battle at Curly, Gallagher paused during brief lulls to have a cup of coffee. He kept a coffeemaker in his armored vehicle, brewing grounds supplied by his wife. It was a tradition with him, just a little something to provide a sense of normality during times of stress and chaos, and to help everybody stay alert after several days without a decent night's sleep. He and Hornbuckle and some of the other soldiers around the C2 vehicle—the command and control vehicle—would gulp down hot coffee as they discussed the ongoing battle.

But now, with enemy fire penetrating the little cocoon formed by Gallagher's vehicle and the command and medical tracks, Gallagher was getting concerned. He did not believe they were in immediate danger of being overrun, but he did have his doubts about how long they could hold off the enemy with just eighty men and five Bradleys. Casualties were mounting, almost by the minute. The enemy had clearly prepared for a battle at the intersection. Gallagher could see that the trenches extended in all directions, connecting the interchange to the buildings a few hundreds meters away. Fighters were able to hustle back and forth to collect weapons and ammunition—and a seemingly inexhaustible supply of reinforcements from the crowded neighborhoods.

Gallagher was struck by a chilling thought: *Shit, we're doing it again— another Mogadishu.* There were unsettling similarities—a guerrilla force dressed in civilian clothes and attacking from civilian areas, a dense urban neighborhood where civilians blundered into the fight, suicide attacks by Muslim fanatics, and an outnumbered and surrounded American unit. Gallagher's team at Curly had armored vehicles and mortars and considerably more firepower than the lightly armed American teams Gallagher had fought alongside in Mogadishu, but they faced the same sort of withering attack by undisciplined gunmen fed by stockpiles of RPGs. Gallagher didn't like the way things were going. He thought they needed reinforcements—not later, but now.

Hornbuckle was concentrating on four- and five-story buildings to the northeast and the northwest, where RPG teams were able to fire straight down on his men dug into the cloverleaf. They were civilian buildings in a residential neighborhood, but under the rules of engagement they were now legitimate targets because they were being used by the enemy to attack American forces. Hornbuckle had first ordered his Bradley crews to fire high-explosive Twenty-five Mike Mike straight through the windows, where he could see the RPG teams firing and moving. The rounds reduced the rate of fire from the buildings but did not silence it. The captain had his mortar team fire "direct lay" into the buildings; they were close enough to see the target, so they didn't have to adjust their high-angle fire with the help of spotters. Instead, they lowered the mortar tubes and shot the rounds directly into the buildings, making their own sight adjustments and lateral shifts. The mortars chopped the buildings down, floor by floor.

Then Hornbuckle called in the Paladins, the 155mm artillery batteries set up south of the brigade command center. Their ninety-five-pound shells tore into two of the buildings, leveling both structures. But one round fell short, detonating on top of the overpass with a thunderous concussion that rocked the men in the armored vehicles parked directly below. No one was hurt, but Hornbuckle had to bring some of his infantrymen in under the overpass, constricting his perimeter. Then another short round exploded near the overpass, slightly wounding two soldiers. The artillery was shut off.

Hornbuckle climbed out of his Bradley from time to time to check on his men, to encourage them and tell them they were doing just fine. At one point, as he hustled between positions, an enemy gunman rose up from a trench and aimed his rifle at Hornbuckle. The captain raised his own rifle and fired. The man went down.

Under the overpass, Gallagher shared his concerns with Hornbuckle. He told the captain that he thought their position was tenuous. If they were going to hold the interchange, and thus the highway, they might not be able do it with the men and firepower now at hand. They needed reinforcements.

Hornbuckle didn't like the situation, either, but he thought they were getting on top of it.

From Objective Larry, three and a half kilometers to the north, Lieutenant Colonel Twitty radioed Hornbuckle for a situation report. Twitty was in the middle of his own fierce firefight, and he had just received an urgent request for more ammunition from his company commander at Objective Moe, who was trying to repulse a ferocious attack by Iraqi armored vehicles and RPG teams. Now Twitty wanted to know whether things were just as bad at Curly.

Hornbuckle described the situation, trying to be as specific as possible but also trying to project an air of confidence. He told Twitty he thought he had the situation under control. Twitty could hear the rattle of the firefight over the radio. He thought the captain was trying too hard to be the good soldier, to put a positive spin on things. He told him, "Zan, if you're having problems, let me know." Hornbuckle tried again to describe his predicament, but Twitty wasn't satisfied.

"Put Command Sergeant Major Gallagher on," he told the captain.

Twitty respected Gallagher's combat experience and savvy. He knew, too, that Gallagher would be blunt. He had survived Mogadishu. If the sergeant major thought he needed help, Twitty thought, he would not hesitate to ask for it.

"All right, Sergeant Major, I want to know the truth," Twitty told Gallagher. "Do you need reinforcements?"

Gallagher did not hesitate. "Sir, we need reinforcements."

It was at this point that Twitty radioed Perkins downtown, mindful of their discussion the night before, when Perkins had assured him that his shorthanded company at Curly would get help if it needed it. Now Perkins told Twitty he would get his reinforcements. He passed the request on to the reconstituted tactical operations center, where Eric Wesley offered Twitty both platoons.

Twitty radioed Captain Ronny Johnson, the company commander in charge of the two platoons protecting the area around Wesley's TOC. He wanted both platoons, even though taking them would leave the TOC undefended and also mean that the vulnerable fuel and ammunition convoy would lose the protection of Johnson's Bradleys.

"Captain Johnson," he said, "how fast can you get here?"

Johnson was in the hatch of his command Bradley, parked in the northbound lanes of Highway 8 less than a kilometer north of the TOC. With him on the highway was one of the two reserve platoons, which was providing security for the long line of fuel and ammunition vehicles awaiting the order to push north. It was this fuel and ammunition that the company at Objective Moe so desperately needed. Johnson knew he could lead his platoon the short distance to Curly in a matter of minutes. But it would probably take him fifteen to twenty minutes to round up his other platoon, which was more than a kilometer south, posted around the new TOC.

"Sir, I can be there in fifteen, twenty minutes," Johnson told Twitty.

"That's not fast enough," Twitty said. "You get here now."

"I can only get a platoon right now."

"I don't care," Twitty said. "Just get me some combat power up here right now."

It sounded dire. Johnson had been monitoring the increasingly desperate situation at Curly on the net, but his brief discussion with Twitty persuaded him that it was worse than he had envisioned. He ordered his platoon to move out.

Johnson was not a newcomer to combat. He had parachuted into Panama in 1989 and he had fought as an army Ranger in the first Gulf War. At age thirty-eight, he had a richer military background than most officers, having served half his seventeen-year career as an enlisted man before graduating from Officers Candidate School in 1995. He had seen combat from two perspectives—from the grunt on the ground who did as he was told, to the company commander who led younger men into the fight. A tall, powerfully built man, he inspired confidence in his men with his sure, quiet demeanor.

Several of Johnson's soldiers had complained to him the night before about the mission the company had been assigned. It sounded to them like a routine security detail. They were anxious to get into the fight, especially because three of their buddies had been wounded in a mortar attack that night at their base near the TOC. Now they feared they had been relegated to guarding fuel trucks and ambulances at the rear while the Tusker and Rogue battalions were being dispatched to the center of Baghdad, into the heart of the fight. Johnson had felt his company's morale sag that night. The men seemed to almost literally deflate, the wind going right out of them in little puffs of resignation and disappointment. Johnson tried to convince them that they might still get into a good fight, for Highway 8 was not likely to be secured—even after the thunder run by Tusker and Rogue. He also warned his men. "You may *think* you want to get into a big fight but, believe me, you really don't."

Now, on Highway 8, Johnson's platoon came under fire less than a minute after pulling out and heading north. RPGs whistled in from bunkers and rooftops, and small-arms fire rattled off the Bradleys. Johnson spotted two men with RPGs poking their heads up from a roadside bunker. He shouted at his gunner, Sergeant Joseph Conley, who killed both men with a quick burst of coax. But the rate of enemy fire actually intensified—a steady, metallic thump against the hull of the Bradley.

Conley got on the intercom to the captain and asked, "Hey, sir, are we getting hit?" He was new to combat.

"Yeah, we're getting hit," Johnson told him. "We're getting hit a lot."

THIRTEEN
BIG TIME

Lieutenant Colonel Stephen Twitty is right-handed, but on the morning of April 7 he found himself drawing diagrams with his left hand. He was crouched in the commander's hatch of his Bradley, clutching a radio with his right hand and awkwardly drawing with his left on a scrap of paper. He was trying to diagram an emergency battle plan. The fight was not playing out the way Twitty had anticipated. He had expected to seize the advantage, push out from all three interchanges, and take control of not only Highway 8 but also the access roads and the streets at the edge of the outlying commercial and residential districts. But now the enemy was taking the fight to his men, who were surrounded and under withering fire at all three interchanges.

Twitty had fought in the first Gulf War, but he had never seen anything like this. In the first war, he had watched Iraqi soldiers surrender by the thousands. If you put the slightest pressure on them, they folded. But here, along Highway 8, the Iraqi and Syrian fighters, and even some of the Republican Guards, were fanatic. The tanks and Bradleys were killing them by the dozens, but they kept coming. Twitty suspected they were high on drugs. Nothing else, he thought, could account for their fanaticism. They seemed determined to die. And they were reckless—absolutely reckless, with no sense of planning or tactics.

All sorts of civilian vehicles—taxis, police cars, buses, clumsy old Chevy Caprices—were dropping off gunmen at all four corners of the cloverleaf at Larry. But instead of dropping them off out of view of the tanks and Bradleys, the drivers pulled right up into the kill zone. Twitty got on the radio and shouted at his tank crews, "Don't mess with letting them get out. Just kill them right where they are." Many of the fighters died inside the vehicles, incinerated by HEAT rounds from the tanks. Twitty watched one bus burst into a fireball, burning alive two dozen fighters inside. He could see their RPGs poking out the windows. A second bus appeared, and it was clear to Twitty that the driver had just seen the bus in front of him go up in flames. Yet he sped forward, into the kill zone, and a HEAT round lit up his bus, too. In just two hours, the combat team at Larry had destroyed more than twenty vehicles.

And yet . . . they kept coming. Twitty was the battalion commander, responsible for commanding and controlling the battles at all three intersections, but now he was drawn into the fight. His Bradley was parked on Highway 8, just south of the overpass, where sniper fire from buildings to the southwest was tearing up chunks of asphalt from the roadway. Twitty squinted through his periscope and spotted a sniper firing from a window in a three-story building. He told his gunner to launch a TOW missile into the building. The TOW was a remarkably accurate weapon—designed to penetrate tank armor at distances of up to four kilometers. An optical sight in the launcher is connected to a computer inside the missile by a fine wire that unspools as the missile is launched. By tracking the target through his sight, the gunner can guide the warhead by keeping the sight's crosshairs trained on the target. Twitty's gunner guided the missile right through the window, pulverizing the whole side of the building. The sniper fire ceased.

Twitty was still drawing on the paper, scratching out a new battle plan, when he happened to look up and notice an orange-and-white taxi speeding north on Highway 8. The taxi had somehow penetrated his southern perimeter and was bearing down on the Bradleys and tanks arrayed across the highway. It was weaving through the burning wrecks of shot-up vehicles, and around the barriers the engineers had built from crushed guardrails and highway light towers. A man in the backseat was firing an AK-47 out the window.

Twitty heard himself yell, "Shit!" Then he shouted into the radio: "Taxi! Taxi coming!" Instantly, he realized how absurd he sounded, yelling about a taxi in the middle of a firefight. He screamed at his gunner, "Slew the turret and fire! No matter what you do, you'd better hit this fucker!" The gunner swung the main cannon around and unleashed a torrent of high-explosive 25mm rounds. Twitty saw the taxi erupt in flames. The smoking hulk of the vehicle remained there for the rest of the day, and every time Twitty looked at it he thought, *This guy would've killed us all.*

The fight was in full swing now. Uniformed Iraqi soldiers were firing from a dense thicket of date palms to the west of the highway. On the east side, RPG teams were launching grenades from the roofs and upper-story windows of an apartment complex. To the southeast, Republican Guards were advancing from a tree line, down a railroad track that ran parallel to Highway 8. And from the south came more technicals and more suicide vehicles and, from time to time, the preposterous sight of gunmen on motorcycles, swerving madly down the highway, sidecars swaying. The Iraqi and Syrian fighters and Fedayeen had regrouped after Tusker and Rogue had punched through, Twitty realized, and now they had mounted counterattacks—not only at Larry, but north at Moe and south at Curly. It was the first time he sensed that the enemy had devised an actual tactical plan, despite the haphazard and self-destructive way it was being carried out. The combat teams were fighting back hard. One of Twitty's company commanders had radioed a couple of times seeking permission to fire mortars into neighborhoods. Finally Twitty told him, "Don't ask me—just do it! Just level it. Take it down. Call artillery. Put mortars right on those buildings."

Over the brigade net came descriptions of the tank crews in the city. They were celebrating, relaying accounts of the crass opulence of the two palaces seized by Tusker. Twitty realized that while Colonel Perkins and the rest of the brigade command certainly were aware of his predicament, the tank battalions had only a limited understanding of what he was up against. Twitty found it difficult to comprehend that American troops were celebrating just a few miles away while he was in the fight of his life, and he felt a twinge of annoyance and even resentment.

Now there were more radio reports, these from the nearby crews at Larry. They had expended so much ammunition that they had reloaded several times and were now starting to run low. Twitty himself had reloaded once, and now his Bradley was at the amber level. If the battalion commander was going amber, he thought, things were getting serious. He could hear the crewmen around him screaming to their loaders, "More ammo! More ammo!" At the same time, Twitty heard over the net that one of his battalion's Bradleys was on fire nearby. But even with the radio chatter in his ear and the steady rumble of the battle, he tried to concentrate on his revised battle plan.

From Objective Curly to the south, Twitty heard reports of ongoing enemy counterattacks. The arrival of Captain Johnson's platoon, followed within a half hour by the platoon that had been guarding the TOC, had helped stabilize the perimeter. The reinforcements added at least eighty soldiers and ten Bradleys to Captain Hornbuckle's depleted company-minus. But wounded men were continuing to come into Captain Schobitz's aid station, and all medevacs had been put on hold because of the precarious situation on the open highway.

One of the wounded men was a staff sergeant who had just arrived with Johnson's platoon. Sergeant First Class Phillips was briefing him on the situation near the trench line when a bullet tore into the staff sergeant's arm. Private First Class Gregory was hit, too. Chunks of concrete blasted from the support walls by automatic-weapons fire under the on-ramp tore holes in Gregory's elbow and leg. He stayed in the fight. Only later, when he found an M-16 round that had penetrated his ammunition pouch, did he realize that he had come under friendly fire from infantrymen clearing the trenches behind him.

But enemy fire was also pouring through the openings in the support columns. Private Christopher Nauman, one of the infantrymen beside Gregory, went down with a wound to the leg. Nauman held on to his shotgun as two medics loaded him on a litter and hauled him back to the aid station beneath the main overpass. Along the way, Nauman spotted a wounded Iraqi fighter reaching for an AK-47. "That guy's still alive!" he yelled. Some of the infantrymen saw Nauman suddenly rise up on the litter and fire a shotgun blast. The story of Nauman and his shotgun later grew to legendary proportions. All you had to do was mention Nauman's name and guys who hadn't even been at Curly would start telling the shotgun story.

By now, the arrival of Captain Johnson's reinforcements had freed up several Bradleys to help the infantrymen clear the trenches. Backed by the Bradleys, Gregory, Phillips, and Specialist Agee were able to move past the on-ramp to an access road that ran parallel to Highway 8. Technicals and suicide vehicles had been using the road to break through the perimeter, so Agee got down on his belly and trained his M-240 machine gun on the roadway.

From time to time a civilian motorist would creep down the road, spot Agee and his machine gun, and back up and speed away. But then a small white sedan appeared. It didn't slow down—it actually picked up speed and headed straight for Agee. He opened up with the machine gun, trying to hold it steady enough to pump a few of the heavy 7.62mm rounds into the windshield. The entire car erupted in a ball of orange flame and black smoke. Agee was amazed that the M-240 had caused such a violent explosion. It was a big machine gun, certainly, but he had never imagined that it was capable of destroying a car. Then he heard the clanking of treads behind him. It was one of the Bradleys—it had fired several high-explosive 25mm Bushmaster chain-gun rounds into the sedan.

Agee saw the sedan's front doors pop open. Two men inside were on fire, trying to escape. Agee fired the M-240 and knocked both men to the pavement. He felt no guilt for killing them like that. They had come speeding straight into the fight, asking to be shot. At this point, after seeing the arms and legs of so many Americans ripped open by shrapnel, Agee was beyond worrying about who he shot. He thought those two guys in the sedan deserved to die. And anyway, he was growing accustomed to the level of violence and brutality required to do his job. He embraced it. Between him and Phillips and Gregory and the sniper, their little ad hoc team had killed more than twenty people.

After a while, Agee and Gregory and Phillips pulled back and let the Bradleys finish clearing the trench system. The way the coax and the Twenty-five Mike Mike ripped into the trenches was remarkable. Agee had never stood so close to a Bradley at work. He kept muttering under his breath, *Goddam, Goddam.* It was astonishing. It was like the whole underground system was turned inside out, with ammo belts and RPG tubes disgorged into the air and the gunmen's bodies disappearing in the smoke as the soft mounds of earth shuddered with each impact.

Beyond the trenches, in the flat sandy expanse that led to the little warren of houses, Phillips saw an Iraqi soldier walk out of a tent. The man looked as though he had just decided to step out for a breath of fresh air, apparently oblivious to the firefight raging all around him. Phillips was baffled by the soldier's detached attitude. He attributed it to poor Iraqi training and discipline. He watched the man tumble into the dirt, his torso ripped open by a blast of coax from one of the Bradleys.

From one of the smoking trenches, Agee saw a man wearing a red-and-white kaffiyeh rise up and fire an AK-47 from the hip and then duck down again. One of the Bradleys unleashed a spray of coax, and Agee didn't see the man again. Another fighter rose up halfway, with a tentative look.

He appeared to be trying to surrender. While Agee debated whether to shoot him or gesture for him to come out, one of the infantrymen behind him shot the man dead. Agee made a mental note: don't be the first guy to surrender.

More heads popped up from the trenches, and the Bradleys held their fire. Enemy fighters were tossing aside their weapons and raising their hands. The infantrymen shouted and gestured for the men to strip off their clothes. That was standard procedure with EPWs, enemy prisoners of war. They were forced to strip naked to make sure they weren't hiding grenades or explosives. The infantrymen had heard about guys down south getting suckered by phony surrenders. The fighters tore off their clothing. They looked small and pale, their bellies soft and hairy and their genitals tight and shriveled by the howling winds.

One of the engineers drove up with an ACE, an armored combat earthmover, a huge excavating machine equipped with an enormous shovel-like bowl with collapsing jaws. The infantrymen herded half a dozen prisoners into the bowl—a perfect little mobile holding cell. A couple of them were wailing and crying as the jaws closed on them. It wasn't exactly humane, but it was the most efficient way to corral the prisoners until a pen could be fashioned from concertina wire. Later, the battalion intelligence officer and some of the Special Forces soldiers interrogated the prisoners, most of whom wore long beards—unlike most Iraqis, who invariably sported standard Saddam-style black mustaches but were otherwise clean-shaven. The interrogators found Syrian passports in the prisoners' abandoned clothing, along with wads of Iraqi currency, confirming them as foreign mercenaries.

For all the enemy fighters who were dying or surrendering at Curly, there seemed to be no shortage of willing replacements. They kept coming, and the tanks and Bradleys and infantrymen kept killing them. This effort required prodigious amounts of ammunition, and by late morning supplies were running low. The radio reports from Curly reaching Lieutenant Colonel Twitty at Objective Larry now included urgent requests for an ammunition resupply. It was one more piece of information that filled out Twitty's mental picture of the situation at Curly, and one more factor to be considered as he continued to sketch out his battle diagram.

The reports from Objective Moe, two and a half kilometers north of Twitty, were more disturbing. There, at the spaghetti intersection, the company commanded by Captain Josh Wright was struggling to keep its perimeter intact. Wright was an aggressive young officer who had grown up in a small town in Illinois, watching old war movies like *Sands of Iwo Jima* and *The Green Berets*. Intrigued by the military's emphasis on duty and patriotism, Wright had signed up for ROTC at Eastern Illinois University, earning his commission as an infantry officer in 1995. He had trained for desert combat, and even for urban combat, but he had never trained to fight on a highway cloverleaf. It was an alien landscape. He had to adapt his whole combat thought process on the fly.

Wright was in the commanders' hatch of his Bradley, parked atop the overpass, with the enemy on all four sides. From the north, gunmen were firing from a mosque, supplied with weapons and ammunition from outbuildings inside the mosque compound. From the south, RPG teams were unleashing grenades from three-story buildings. From the east, soldiers were shooting from a forest of palm trees. And from the southwest, a mob of fighters backed by a heavy machine gun mounted on a pickup was advancing on the interchange. Suicide vehicles were speeding down the access roads, trying to penetrate the perimeter.

Two of Wright's three platoon sergeants had been wounded, and two engineers had gone down with shrapnel wounds. A gunner was hit with a ricochet. An infantryman dragging a wounded enemy soldier to safety was hit in the wrist and stomach. Every tank and Bradley was tattooed with small arms and shrapnel. The TOW missile launcher on one Bradley was destroyed by an RPG. Two more Bradleys had their coax guns go down, ruptured by shrapnel. One of the tanks lost the use of its main gun.

With the help of mortars fired by the crews at Curly, Wright was holding his own. But Wright's tank and Bradley crews were beginning to run low on rounds. They had already "cross-leveled" ammunition—trading coax, tank rounds, and .50-caliber ammunition back and forth. From the perimeter, the track commanders radioed Wright to tell him they were now going amber on both ammunition and fuel.

Then the mortars stopped. Wright got an urgent call from Lieutenant Josh Woodruff, the mortar platoon commander at Curly. Woodruff sounded apologetic. He felt terrible, he said, but he could no longer provide mortar support. He hand-fired every last round—his entire allotment of 240 mortar shells. He was black—completely dry.

Wright radioed Twitty. He tried to give a precise and nuanced report, neither overstating nor understating his predicament. Wright and Twitty were comfortable working together, and Twitty felt he knew how to read the captain. When Wright mentioned that he was considering collapsing his perimeter as a way to help the tanks conserve fuel, Twitty knew the situation was serious. He asked Wright how long he could continue to fight without fresh supplies of fuel and ammunition. Wright answered quickly: a few more hours.

Twitty realized that the time had come for him to make a decision on fuel and ammunition. It would take a while to get the supplies all the way up to Captain Wright at Moe. Twitty had expected his combat teams to fight to keep Highway 8 open for the resupply convoy. He had not expected that they would also be fighting just to survive. The brigade could not afford to lose any of the three interchanges, but Moe was particularly crucial. If Captain Wright were overrun, the enemy would pour through the spaghetti interchange and hammer Rogue and Tusker from the rear—and the two tank battalions would be cut off from the fuel and ammunition supply.

Twitty called Captain Ronny Johnson at Curly. Johnson had just fought his way up the highway to Curly from the brigade operations center. He was now in charge of the entire combined combat team. Twitty wanted to get his sense of the threat level along that stretch of Highway 8. Johnson gave him an honest answer. It was hot, he told him—extremely hot.

Twitty also requested a fresh update on the fighting at Curly.

"Sir," Johnson said, "what I can tell you is, it's not as intense a fight as it was an hour ago but we're still in a pretty good fight here."

Twitty asked to hear from Command Sergeant Major Gallagher. He asked Gallagher whether he thought the fuel and ammunition trucks could survive the gauntlet of RPG and recoilless rifle fire on the highway.

"Boss," Gallagher said, "we can get 'em through. I'm not going to tell you we can get 'em through without risk, but we can get 'em through."

Twitty signed off and put the radio down. He lowered his head. He had to make a decision. And whatever he decided, American soldiers were going to die. He knew it. They would die at one of the interchanges, where they would be overrun if they weren't resupplied. Or they would die on the resupply convoy trying to fight its way up Highway 8.

Twitty picked up the radio and called his executive officer. "All right," he said. "We're going to execute."

Just before the missile exploded inside the TOC compound, Captain Aaron Polsgrove had been sitting on top of his Humvee with his helmet off. He was relaxing, enjoying the warm weather after a long cold night, and marveling at the fact that American soldiers were bearing down on Baghdad just two weeks after leaving Kuwait. His Humvee was parked on the dusty shoulder of Highway 8, a few hundred meters west of the TOC compound, a complex of dull beige buildings set against a swaying backdrop of tall green date palms.

Polsgrove was twenty-six, a native of Louisville, a cheerful and engaging young officer, and a devout Christian. He had joined a Christian officers' group at West Point, and he served along with Lieutenant Colonel Wesley in the Officers' Christian Fellowship. He carried a Bible with him at all times. Every day, he tried to find a few minutes of privacy in his Humvee to read the "Daily Bread" devotionals his chaplain had given him. Polsgrove was the support platoon leader, in charge of keeping the fuel and ammunition trucks intact and moving as a unit. They were lined up behind him now on the highway shoulder, engines idling. The convoy was awaiting the order to move up and resupply the China battalion combat teams at the three interchanges.

Polsgrove had not seen a lot of action on the march up from Kuwait. (His wife was videotaping hours of TV news coverage for him.) The supply convoys tended to stay to the rear, behind the combat teams. In fact, Polsgrove's support platoon had not yet conducted a resupply under fire in Iraq. But now battles were raging up Highway 8, and he wasn't sure what to expect. He had only two radios, and neither could pick up transmissions from the men in the firefights at Moe, Larry, and Curly. The radio reception was so bad, in fact, that Polsgrove's boss, Captain J. O. Bailey, had taken three vehicles from the supply convoy and moved a few kilometers north so that he could talk to the commanders at Curly and get a feel for the situation there.

Polsgrove heard what he thought was a low-flying aircraft. The sound puzzled him. He thought the plane either was on an extremely low bombing run or was about to crash, and neither possibility made sense. Then the TOC exploded. Polsgrove saw a fireball erupt from inside the TOC compound, just over his right shoulder. He felt a blast of heat. Shards of flaming metal were raining down on the convoy. He thought they were under an artillery attack. He dove into his Humvee, put on his helmet, and reached for the radio. He had to move the convoy out of harm's way. The twenty-five-hundred-gallon fuel tankers were mobile bombs. The ammunition trucks were portable fireworks factories. A single shard of hot shrapnel could trigger a conflagration.

There were twenty-one vehicles in Polsgrove's convoy. With only two radios on hand, communicating with the driver of each vehicle was a maddening endeavor. Polsgrove had devised a series of hand signals to alert the drivers behind him to his orders. The only other radio was in his platoon sergeant's vehicle, the last one in the convoy. Polsgrove called him.

"Support Seven, this is Support Six, we're rolling," he said. He gave a circular wave of his arm to signal the drivers behind him.

The convoy sped north on Highway 8, past the flaming TOC and its funnels of black smoke. Polsgrove radioed Captain Bailey up ahead. Bailey was unaware of the missile strike. "The brigade TOC just got hit!" Polsgrove told Bailey. "I'm moving out. It's too dangerous here." Bailey told him to get up to his position as quickly as possible.

Bailey had managed to make radio contact with some of the officers and NCOs at the three interchanges, but he had not been able to get a clear picture of their fuel and ammunition needs. Most people were telling him they were amber. Others were red, and a couple said they were close to going black—not enough to sustain the fight. And now his support platoon was fleeing a missile hit.

Just as Polsgrove and the main body of the convoy pulled up, several mortar rounds whistled down and exploded in the barren fields at the edge of the highway. It was a nuisance, mostly, but it reinforced the sense of vulnerability that both Bailey and Polsgrove had felt all morning. They were hauling 110 tons of tank, Bradley, mortar, and small-arms ammunition and twenty thousand gallons of highly combustible JP8 fuel. One of their trailers was loaded with the engineers' mine-breaching device, a twisted sausagelike link of powerful C-4 explosive charges. And they had no armor to protect them—no tanks, no Bradleys.

The Humvee with Bailey's little group was mounted with a .50-caliber machine gun and the armored personnel carrier with him had another .50-caliber in the turret. But Bailey's own armored track had no crew-served weapon; he had only his M-16 automatic rifle. Polsgrove's twenty-one vehicles had just six crew-served guns—three .50-caliber machine guns and one MK-19 grenade launcher on four ammunition trucks, an M-240 medium machine gun on the platoon sergeant's Humvee, and a grenade launcher mounted on Polsgrove's Humvee.

Polsgrove was firing his M-16 from his Humvee, trying to hit a couple of men who appeared to be enemy mortar spotters, when three armored Humvees pulled up. They were scouts assigned to bolster security for the convoy; two of the Humvees were armed with .50-caliber machine guns and the other had a grenade launcher mounted in the turret ring on top. Polsgrove was relieved to see them. It wasn't as good as getting tanks or Bradleys, but the scouts afforded the convoy a reassuring extra dose of combat power.

Polsgrove knew one of the scouts, Sergeant First Class John Marshall. Marshall was fifty, ancient by combat standards, where many infantrymen were teenagers and most of the company commanders were still in their late twenties. Polsgrove figured Marshall was probably the oldest guy in the whole battalion. Hell, he was eleven years older than the battalion commander, Lieutenant Colonel Twitty. Marshall had volunteered for combat duty after the September 11 terrorist attacks, even though he had a wife and children. He told people that he felt a responsibility to get involved, though seemingly he had done enough already—he had fought in the first Gulf War.

Polsgrove welcomed Marshall's combat expertise; he was a good man to have around. Marshall took enormous pride in being a scout. He was unflappable, with an even disposition. He was always smiling and pleasant, and he rarely cursed or even raised his voice. Polsgrove knew Marshall would keep his cool under fire.

Marshall joined Polsgrove in firing on the mortar spotters, squeezing off bursts from his M-16. Then Marshall called his two scout Humvees over and had the gunners open up with their .50-caliber machine guns. Polsgrove couldn't tell if they hit anything, but the mortars soon stopped. Things had calmed down considerably by the time Captain Bailey got the radio call ordering him to launch the convoy north up Highway 8.

Bailey had serious misgivings about taking a convoy of soft-skin vehicles on an exposed highway in the middle of a firefight. He knew from the radio traffic that the combat team at Curly was being pounded with RPGs and small-arms fire. He had no idea where he was going to park nearly two dozen vulnerable tankers, ammo trucks, and other vehicles at a highway interchange with ordnance flying all around. He had gotten on the radio and asked the battalion executive officer, Major Denton Knapp, to send down Bradleys to escort him. Not possible, Knapp told him. Knapp was in the middle of a ferocious firefight. The combat teams couldn't afford to give up their Bradleys at this crucial interlude, he told Bailey. Holding Curly was paramount. The resupply convoy would have to fight its way up with the help of the scout vehicles and the crew-served weapons.

Bailey didn't think he had enough firepower. His soft-skinned vehicles were easy targets. He needed Bradleys to suppress enemy fire. Bailey repeated his request, this time with a sharp edge in his voice. The answer came back from Knapp: no Bradleys. They couldn't be spared from the fight.

Frustrated and angry, and fearing the worst, Bailey reluctantly gave the order to move out.

Sergeant Marshall assigned one of his Humvees to the rear of Captain Polsgrove's column and another to the middle. He yelled at Polsgrove, asking him where the captain wanted Marhall's own Humvee. Polsgrove was an officer, but he didn't have Marshall's combat experience. He felt awkward telling a guy like Marshall how to situate himself.

"Hell, Sergeant Marshall," he said, "you know what you're doing. You tell me where you think you need to be."

Marshall thought for a moment and said, "Sir, scouts lead the way. I'll take the front."

It was the first time since Polsgrove's unit crossed into Iraq more than two weeks earlier that the captain was not in the lead vehicle. But he deferred to Marshall. The sergeant knew what he was doing. Polsgrove pulled his Humvee behind Marshall's.

There was a brief moment of confusion just before they pulled out, right as Marshall was telling his scouts to mount up. There was nobody in the gunner's mount of Marshall's vehicle.

Earlier that morning, Marshall had pulled the regular gunner, Specialist Kenneth Krofta, because Krofta was worn out. He had been up all night escorting medical vehicles that were transporting the three soldiers wounded during the mortar attack on China battalion near the TOC. Marshall had said to Krofta, "Hey, Big Time"—he called everybody Big Time—"get in the back and get some rest." Krofta had protested. His birthday was on the sixth, and he told Marshall he wanted to celebrate by firing the grenade launcher as they rode into Baghdad on the seventh.

"That's right, Big Time, hog all the glory," Marshall had said, and he insisted that Krofta stay off the weapon and rest. Krofta and Marshall had a special kinship because both men loved the grenade launcher, and both were quite accomplished on the weapon. Krofta was just twenty-two, a short, thin scout with a wispy blond mustache. He thought of Marshall as a grandfather figure, though he didn't dare tell him that.

As the convoy prepared to pull out on Highway 8, the scout who was supposed to be in the gunner's mount had disappeared. He had hustled over to the side of the highway to urinate. Marshall was furious—this was no time to take a leak. Krofta had never seen Marshall so annoyed. Marshall climbed into the gunner's mount, took over the grenade launcher, and told the wayward scout to zip up and get into the back. Krofta hopped into Marshall's customary spot in the front passenger seat, where he could monitor the radio and the combat computer.

They rolled north, Captain Bailey and his three vehicles at the front, followed by Polsgrove's extended convoy, which was led by Marshall's Humvee. Marshall focused on staying close on the tail of the last of the three vehicles in Bailey's group, an armored personnel carrier with a .50-caliber machine gun mounted in the top hatch. Marshall was manning the grenade launcher on his Humvee, working the radio, scanning both sides of the highway for signs of the enemy. He wanted to be able to radio back quickly and warn Polsgrove and the rear of the column the instant they came under fire.

Manning the .50-caliber on an armored personnel carrier behind Marshall was a thirty-six-year-old mechanic, Staff Sergeant Robert Stever, whom everyone called Catfish because of his mustache and a pair of thick spectacles that magnified the size of his eyes. Stever was known as a guy who could fix anything, mechanical or otherwise. Once, he figured out a way to tie a cargo strap to repair a dented cargo hatch that had prevented Polsgrove from traversing his grenade launcher. He was well known in the battalion for using ether to get balky engines to turn over, and some of the mechanics had nicknamed him Ether Queen. He was a coffee hound, too, and everybody knew to go find Catfish when they needed a caffeine jolt.

And even though Stever was a mechanic, not a combat infantryman, he loved firing the big .50-caliber. He was a fine shot.

Lieutenant Colonel Twitty considered Stever the hardest-working mechanic in the battalion. He had known Stever since their days posted together in Germany, and the two men often had sat and chatted in Twitty's office back at Fort Stewart or in the motor-pool bays. Some nights, Twitty would walk to the motor pool late at night and find Stever working alone, covered in grease, and he would have to order him to go home. When the unit was sent to Kuwait to train for the war, Twitty and Stever continued their regular chats. Just before they rolled into Iraq, Stever thanked his commander for the rigorous training sessions Twitty had imposed on the battalion. Stever said he felt prepared for war, and prepared to die. "Sir," he told Twitty, "I'll take a bullet for you any day."

The head of the convoy passed beneath a tall archway across Highway 8. Krofta thought it looked like the St. Louis arch. He yelled up at Marshall in the turret. "Hey, sergeant, we just passed into St. Louis!" Marshall let out a little laugh. "Right, Big Time!" he shouted.

The convoy had been rolling for less than five minutes when Polsgrove noticed several knots of men in civilian clothes gathered in front of a complex of two-story and three-story buildings about two hundred meters to the east, across a set of railroad tracks that ran parallel to the highway. There was something odd about them—about the expectant looks on their faces. Bailey noticed it, too. He wondered why so many men would be congregating just as an American convoy was approaching. He radioed Polsgrove and said, "This doesn't look right."

Polsgrove was about to reply when gunfire erupted from somewhere across the railroad tracks. He could see muzzle flashes just in front of the low buildings and from the rooftops. Directly in front of him, Marshall opened up with the MK-19, launching grenades in a high arc over the railroad tracks and into the buildings.

Polsgrove looked over his right shoulder and saw the blazing red fireball of an RPG, trailed by thick white smoke. It was head-high, about three meters off the ground. He thought it was going to hit him in the head. The fireball streaked in front of him and exploded on top of Marshall.

Polsgrove watched Marshall's body fly out of the turret. It was like he had been launched. The grenade had struck the sergeant squarely in the torso, ripping out his midsection. Polsgrove saw Marshall hit the roadway with an awful thump. There was a gaping cavity where his chest had been. Polsgrove had never seen a man killed in combat, and the sight of Marshall's body smacking down on the pavement was shocking. Until that moment Polsgrove had been a confident and gung ho young commander, fired up about leading men into combat. Now he was overwhelmed by a sudden, tight terror. He had always envisioned himself as the kind of soldier who would charge a machine-gun nest or jump on a live grenade. But now he knew he wasn't that man, and he felt a terrible disappointment. He was afraid and confused, and not as fearless as he wanted to be.

The terror was something that would paralyze him if he did not get it under control. He knew he had to take charge—of himself and his men. He had to get the convoy out of the kill zone. He couldn't stop his vehicle to recover Marshall's body. If he stopped, every vehicle behind him would stop. That was the way they had trained. Polsgrove screamed at his driver to speed up, knowing the vehicles behind him would follow his lead and accelerate. He was focused now—focused on getting his men out of the ambush alive. He had overcome his fear, and he had taken charge, trying to will himself into the combat leader he had always longed to be.

In the front passenger seat of Marshall's Humvee, Krofta had seen a flash of light and had felt a tremendous thump that flung him against the radio mount. He heard somebody scream. The Humvee pitched and rocked. Krofta thought they had crashed into something. The Humvee was filling with black smoke. He looked up into the turret to ask Marshall what had happened. He couldn't see him. Sergeant Marshall had disappeared.

Next to Krofta, in the driver's seat, Private First Class Angel Cruz was stunned and disoriented. The smoke was burning his eyes. He didn't know what to do. Normally, Sergeant Marshall would issue orders, but Cruz couldn't see him anymore. Nor could he see well enough to drive. He pulled over and stopped at the edge of the highway. It had just begun to dawn on him that Marshall had been hit and blown out of the vehicle.

Cruz and Krofta got out onto the highway to look for their sergeant. They couldn't leave him there. That was the code—you left no man behind, dead or alive. It would be a devastating thing for them to let Sergeant Marshall—or his remains—fall into enemy hands. The two men checked the turret. It was still smoking, and it gave off a pungent odor, like the smell of burning flesh. Marshall's two hand mikes, which had connected him to the radio, had been blown off. The stripped wires were dangling over the edge of the turret. On the handle of the grenade launcher were scraps of flesh and fatigues, and dark smears of fresh blood.

Cruz and Krofta looked up and down the highway. There was no sign of Marshall. They could see gunmen moving toward them, and they heard rifle rounds ricocheting off the highway and off the frame of the Humvee. Cruz fired his M-16 across the road. Captain Polsgrove pulled up in his Humvee, slowing down, yelling something at them.

"Sir!" Cruz said. "Sergeant Marshall's gone! He's not in the vehicle! We don't know where he's at!"

Polsgrove's heart was racing. He didn't want to have to stop and explain that he had seen Marshall's body, because then the whole convoy would stop behind him. He just wanted Marshall's Humvee out of the kill zone.

"I saw him! He's dead!" Polsgrove shouted. There was no other way to say it. "Let's go! Keep fucking moving!"

It pained the captain to leave Marshall like that. He hated doing it—it violated every instinct in him. But he feared more men would die if they stopped to try to recover the remains. As soon as possible—as soon as they got to safety and could mount a sizable search party—they would come back for the sergeant. Polsgrove would not rest until Sergeant Marshall was found and sent home for burial. But right now he was forced to make a snap decision, and he decided to save the living, not the dead.

Polsgrove's driver was speeding away as the captain shouted over his shoulder to Krofta and Cruz, two small, forlorn figures in the roadway: "We'll come back and get him later!"

FOURTEEN
CATFISH

When the fuel and ammunition convoy was ambushed, everyone manning a weapon in the lead vehicles opened fire. Staff Sergeant Stever worked the butterfly triggers on his .50-caliber, trying to aim the big rounds at the gunmen massed across the railroad tracks. He fired off several hundred rounds toward the muzzle flashes. Inside Stever's armored personnel carrier, Chief Warrant Officer Three Angel Acevedo was up in the crew hatch, firing his M-16 across the right side. Beside Acevedo was Sergeant Eric Gubler, pumping away on his M-4 carbine. And behind them, in what was now the lead Humvee because of the death of Sergeant Marshall, Captain Polsgrove was launching grenades from his MK-19, trying to detonate them on the rooftops, where he could see muzzle flashes from automatic rifles.

But the enemy fire only escalated, a sustained volley of automatic rifle rounds and hissing RPGs. The bright flaming grenades whooshed between the vehicles and exploded on the pavement. It was remarkable that the RPGs kept missing, Polsgrove thought, given the accuracy of the direct hit on Sergeant Marshall just a minute earlier. He was afraid another vehicle would get hit—perhaps a fuel truck, which would ignite in a massive fireball and explosion that would almost certainly block and trap the vehicles to the rear.

Polsgrove was firing the grenade launcher when he caught a glimpse of an RPG streaking in from the right side. He saw it skip across the top of the armored personnel carrier directly in front of him and rip into Sergeant Stever's head. There was a sickening explosion. Pieces of something flew out onto the highway. What was left of Stever collapsed down into the hatch.

The explosion blew the driver, Private First Class Jarred Metz, out of his seat. Metz couldn't feel his legs. He thought his body had been blown in half. He looked down and saw streaks of blood. Shrapnel had torn through his lower back and buttocks. His legs were tingling. He scrambled to his feet and realized the vehicle was careening off the highway. He tried to get the big carrier under control but it crashed into the guardrail on the left side of Highway 8.

Metz heard Chief Warrant Officer Acevedo's voice over the radio. "You all right?" Acevedo had been up in a hatch next to Stever.

Metz wasn't sure. He told Acevedo he thought he was okay. He was bleeding, but he could move his legs—and he thought he was in good enough shape to drive.

Acevedo was bleeding, too. His back had been lacerated by shrapnel from the RPG, soaking his uniform with blood. He got on the radio to tell Captain Bailey that Stever was down, but he couldn't get it to work. He gave up and took command of the carrier, trying to direct Metz through the ambush. He wasn't able to fire Stever's .50-caliber. The RPG had smashed the handle. He opened up with his M-16.

Inside the crew hatch, something had hit Sergeant Gubler in the leg and knocked him down, but he was able to get back up. He heard Acevedo asking if he was okay, and he said, "Yeah." He found his weapon. He got back up in the hatch and fired at the muzzle flashes coming from the buildings on the right side. Stever's corpse was crumpled on the floor of the turret. Gubler knew he was dead; he had practically been decapitated. It was horrifying to see his friend like that. He and Acevedo wanted to treat their sergeant with dignity, but they were under fire and fighting for their lives, so they just left his body where it had fallen.

With Acevedo yelling instructions from up above, Metz managed to get the carrier back on the highway. He steered it into the column, where Captain Polsgrove was desperately trying to keep the vehicles together and lead them out of the kill zone. The captain was screaming at his driver to speed up. The Humvee was probably going forty-eight kilometers an hour, but it seemed to Polsgrove that they were barely moving. RPGs were raining down, and small-arms rounds were hissing and cracking overhead. Polsgrove got Captain Bailey on the radio and told him that both Marshall and Stever were dead. Bailey already knew. From the hatch of his armored vehicle at the head of the convoy, he had seen both men go down.

Polsgrove was feeling guilty about abandoning Marshall's corpse and about having let Marshall take the lead. He fought with himself to maintain his focus, to keep the rest of his men alive. He was still launching grenades from his MK-19 to suppress the RPG teams across the highway in order to protect the fuel and ammunition, still screaming at his driver to speed up. It was less than one and a half kilometers to Curly. The convoy sped on, the drivers gunning the engines on the lumbering fuel tankers and ammunition trucks, willing the vehicles forward. Some of them were driving with one hand and firing their automatic rifles on full burst out the driver's window with the other.

Through the thick haze, Polsgrove could make out the outlines of the cloverleaf at Curly. The gunfire from the ambush was fading, but now he heard the thunderous racket of the ongoing firefight at the interchange. They were driving straight into a battle—with no safe place to park the vulnerable fuel and ammunition trucks. Polsgrove could see that the command and medical vehicles from the combat team at Curly were occupying the only protected space—the part of the highway beneath the overpass.

Polsgrove and Bailey decided to pull the vehicles over on the right shoulder, just south of the overpass, where the raised entry ramp afforded some protection. As soon as Polsgrove's Humvee rolled in, the Bravo Company first sergeant ran over, screaming and cursing. He couldn't believe the support platoon was bringing fuel tankers and ammo trucks to a firefight. No one had told him that the resupply convoy had been dispatched to Curly.

"Sir!" he screamed. "What the fuck are you doing here? What are you doing, bringing fuel and ammo trucks to my objective? You're gonna get us all killed!"

Polsgrove told the sergeant he didn't have any choice—and he didn't have time to argue about it. He ran back to check on the convoy and was astonished to discover that every last vehicle was still intact. He and Bailey had a hectic discussion about how to arrange the vehicles. It was hard to hear over the roar of the battle. They decided, finally, to just park the trucks motor pool–style, side by side, until they figured out a better way to protect them. They didn't want to leave them that way for very long; if one of the tankers or ammunition trucks were to be hit, it would become a huge exploding grenade, spewing hot shards of metal that would ignite the adjacent trucks.

The enormous relief Polsgrove had felt upon escaping the ambush was now draining away. The tankers and ammunition trucks were even more vulnerable and exposed now because they were stationary targets.

While on the move, they at least had had a fighting chance. Now Polsgrove felt helpless to protect them from the RPGs exploding up and down the highway. It didn't help his frame of mind when he noticed the blackened remains of Charlie One Two, the Rogue tank that had burned on the highway just north of the interchange two days earlier. If the enemy could burn an Abrams, Polsgrove thought, imagine what they could do to a soft-skin fueler.

Within minutes, RPGs were sailing over the tops of the trucks. Polsgrove and Bailey realized that the RPG teams firing from the buildings east of the highway were targeting the trucks, trying to ignite them. One truck was hit by an RPG that failed to explode. The dud grenade bounced off and rattled down the highway. Bailey rounded up one of the engineers and asked him to try to clear rubble from the west shoulder of the highway so that some of the trucks could be moved to a spot partially protected by the raised curve of the western on-ramp. The rate of enemy fire from the west was less intense than from the east now that the mortar teams had demolished the troublesome building there.

At the same time, Polsgrove ordered the gunners on crew-served weapons to stay in the vehicles and lay down suppressive fire to the east, where RPG teams were in the windows and on rooftops. He ordered the rest of his men out of the trucks and into the trench system that had been cleared by the infantrymen. They were needed to help hold the perimeter. The men ran, ducking and weaving, and crawled into the trenches with their automatic rifles. Some of them had to shove aside enemy corpses to make room.

Dr. Schobitz's medics treated the wounded men from Stever's personnel carrier. They bagged up Stever's remains and lay him behind the aid station, next to one of the concrete support beams beneath the overpass. It was a protected spot, as safe as any other place around the aid station, given the fact that occasional rounds were smacking into the support columns, spraying the medics with flying bits of concrete. It seemed somehow disrespectful to just stick Sergeant Stever off in the corner, but the firefight was in full throttle and there was no time to think of a better way.

The arrival of the supply convoy triggered a surge of confidence for the commanders leading the fight at the interchange. For Captain Hornbuckle and Command Sergeant Major Gallagher—and for Captain Johnson, who was now in charge of the entire combined combat team at

Curly—the fresh fuel and ammunition eased their fears. Separately, each man had harbored a dread that the situation was deteriorating into another Mogadishu. They had envisioned being overrun, short on combat power and ammunition, with no way for reinforcements to get through. Now their men were unloading ammunition for the Bradleys and the infantrymen, and Lieutenant Woodruff's mortar crews were getting fresh loads of the high-explosive, 120mm mortars that had been so effective in demolishing the buildings housing RPG teams. Hornbuckle, Gallagher, and Johnson knew they were now in a position not only to hold the interchange, but also to eventually kill, capture, or drive off the gunmen surrounding them. Johnson figured his men had killed at least 130 enemy fighters and destroyed two dozen vehicles. Hornbuckle thought his men had probably killed another 150 fighters and destroyed perhaps a dozen vehicles.

They were now superior in every respect—armor, infantry, ammunition, and fuel. They thought they had seized control of the fight.

Beneath the overpass, hunched over the radio inside his command vehicle, Major Denton Knapp had been monitoring the radio nets, keeping abreast of developments up and down Highway 8 and inside the palace complex. As the executive officer for Task Force 3-15—China battalion and its assets—Knapp was the number two man below Twitty. More than anyone at Curly, he had absorbed the full scope of the Spartan Brigade's battle for Baghdad that morning. Knapp had monitored Twitty's conversations with Colonel Perkins on the brigade command net and, on the task force net, the discussions between Twitty and his commanders at the three interchanges. He had also monitored the Rogue and Tusker thrusts into the city. It was Knapp, in fact, who passed on to Twitty the reports that Tusker had seized the palace.

Knapp hated being stuck inside his command vehicle while the battle raged outside. He wanted to be part of the fight. It was hot and stuffy in the hull, and he felt trapped and claustrophobic. He could hear the RPGs exploding outside, and the vehicle had pitched and rocked when the short 155mm artillery round detonated next to the overpass.

At one point, Knapp's driver came tumbling down into the hull from the upper hatch of his M577 armored command vehicle. The driver had been firing a .50-caliber machine gun north up Highway 8, trying to subdue the gunmen in the trenches and inside the buildings. Knapp's vehicle didn't have a gun mount, but he had rigged one up by tying the .50-caliber tripod to the top of the vehicle with green parachute cord. Now his driver was crashing down beside him, his arm bleeding. It had been torn open by shrapnel. Knapp took a look at the wound, but before he could do anything about it the driver yanked his arm away and said he was okay. He climbed back up top and resumed firing.

Knapp had not anticipated a fight of such intensity. On the march up from the Kuwaiti border, the battalion had always taken the fight to the enemy. He and his men were the aggressors, seeking out enemy positions and surprising them and killing them. Curly was different. The Iraqi soldiers and the Syrian mercenaries had surprised the battalion with their tenacity and their ability to attack from all sides. Knapp had never imagined that they would deliver fighters to the front in civilian buses and taxis and even motorcycles. Nor had he anticipated the sophisticated trench system or the prepositioned weapons caches dug into both sides of the highway.

Knapp was not a man who was easily cowed, but there were moments, especially early in the fight before Ronny Johnson arrived with reinforcements, that he feared being overrun. Knapp was a veteran officer, thirty-eight years old, with nearly seventeen years in the army. He was a West Point man, commissioned in 1987. He had grown up in Gillette, Wyoming, the son of a surveyor and part-time country-and-western musician. He played army with the kids in his neighborhood, where his next-door neighbor went off to attend the Air Force Academy. Knapp decided in high school that he, too, would be a military officer.

Until he crossed the border into Iraq, Knapp had never been in combat. Even after several firefights down south, he had been edgy and apprehensive as he sat through Lieutenant Colonel Twitty's impassioned briefing the night of the sixth. He sensed that the fight on Highway 8 would be like nothing he had experienced before. He lay down in the middle of the night, still wearing his helmet and flak vest, and tried to get a couple hours' sleep. It was impossible. He was too agitated.

Now, with the fight raging in all directions, Knapp couldn't stand it inside the vehicle any longer. He had to see what was going on. He climbed out and stood beneath the overpass in the command and control area framed by armored vehicles backed up butt to butt, their rear hatches touching. He couldn't see much because the air was a milky yellow, with swirling dust and pungent black smoke from the massive loads of ammunition being expended. From time to time, Sergeant Major Gallagher and Captain Hornbuckle ran over to discuss the progress of the fight. By this time, late in the morning, they all agreed that the situation had stabilized. The infantrymen and Bradleys were slowly extending the perimeter. In military terms, Knapp felt, they had established "positive control" of Objective Curly.

Then, over the brigade command net, Knapp got a FRAGO—a fragmentary order—just before noon. Colonel Perkins, determined to set conditions that would allow the tank battalions to spend the night in the city center, had decided to move the combat team from Curly. He was worried about the mile-long stretch of the Kindi Highway that connected the spaghetti interchange at Moe to Perkins's command center at the Sujud Palace. General Blount had already designated a battalion from the division's First Brigade at the airport as a backup force. Blount and Perkins had decided to send that force, the Second Battalion, Seventh Infantry—known as 2-7—to relieve the combat teams at Curly and provide security for Lieutenant Colonel Wesley's vulnerable new TOC. Knapp was ordered to round up everyone now at Curly—Captain Hornbuckle's team, Captain Johnson's team, and the resupply convoy—and roll north on Highway 8 after coordinating a handoff to the 2-7 battalion.

The move would allow Perkins to meet two of his primary goals that morning. The supply convoy would be able to drop off ammunition and fuel designated for the combat teams at the three interchanges, bolstering them in their fight to keep Highway 8 open. Johnson's combat teams would then secure the unsecured stretch of the Kindi Highway, shoring up Perkins's exposed rear. There was also the added benefit of having more combat power inside the city.

For Knapp and the other commanders at Curly, the order created a tactical and logistical nightmare. It was difficult enough to hand off positions from one unit to another in secured areas. But now they had to accomplish the handoff under the battalion's heaviest firefight of the war, with the enemy dug in across a 360-degree perimeter. There was also the issue of the fuel tankers and ammunition trucks. Bailey and Polsgrove were still trying to move as many of the vehicles as possible out of the line of fire on the east side of the highway to a more protected site on the west side. Now they had to get them arranged back in convoy formation while under fire.

As Knapp huddled with the battle captains to coordinate the pull-out, an advance team from 2-7 sped into the intersection on Highway 8 from the south. Major Rod Coffey, the 2-7 battalion S-3, or operations officer, had fought his way up from Lieutenant Colonel Wesley's rebuilt brigade TOC in a Bradley, accompanied by a Humvee. Knapp was relieved to see him. The two majors had already spoken on the radio, but face-to-face coordination was essential amid the chaos of a battlefield handoff, where friendly fire was a very real possibility. Two of Knapp's men had already been winged by friendly fire—the two soldiers hit by the 155mm short round. Now, instead of trying to talk by radio to strangers in a battalion from another brigade, Knapp had Coffey right next to him, talking directly to his own men. Even with the barrage of enemy fire, Knapp felt confident about the handoff.

After climbing down from his Bradley, Major Coffey made his way toward the command post under the overpass at Curly. He wanted to get briefed right away on the situation at the interchange. His battalion had been given just two hours to prepare for a dangerous and complex mission—to take over for another unit in the middle of a furious firefight. Coffey was forty-one, a confident, experienced fifteen-year army veteran, but this was a unique challenge. Coffey had spoken briefly at the Second Brigade command center with Lieutenant Colonel Eric Wesley, the brigade executive officer, but now he needed an on-the-ground description of the enemy as well as the plan for the handoff. He recognized Sergeant Major Gallagher, who described the enemy tactics and mentioned that many of the fighters were Syrian mercenaries. Coffey spoke briefly with Captain Ronny Johnson, then made his way to the command post to huddle with Major Knapp. He realized the interchange had been under fire for hours, and he thought the soldiers there looked fatigued. He ducked inside the rear hatch of Knapp's command armored personnel carrier and the two majors discussed details of the handoff. Knapp said he wanted to begin the transition with one company from 2-7 at the southern perimeter, gradually moving north until all units had been replaced. He wanted a step-by-step boundary change.

As Coffey made his way back to his Bradley parked at the northern edge of the overpass, it seemed to him that not all the soldiers at the interchange were returning fire effectively as they took cover. The soldiers were not under his command, but the situation angered him. He started screaming at some of the men, "Move forward and engage the enemy!"

Coffey also realized that the combat teams now at the interchange were loading up and preparing to move north. He had assumed that the handoff would be a "relief in place"—a step-by-step transition, with soldiers pulling out of fighting positions as the new unit's soldiers moved in. But now, Coffey feared, the relief in place wasn't going to happen. He decided to go back to confer with Knapp. Rounds were pinging off vehicles now, gouging out hunks off asphalt from the roadway and chips of concrete from the overpass. Coffey thought the safest route back to Knapp's command vehicle was through the front of the Humvee that had accompanied him to the interchange. As he crawled through the vehicle, he saw the flaming head of an RPG flash to his left. The round exploded against the Humvee, sending shrapnel ripping through Coffey's leg and ankle. His lower left leg bone was shattered. A second RPG thundered in, setting the Humvee on fire.

Coffey had an uplifting thought: *I'm not dead yet.* He crawled out of the Humvee and limped across the asphalt to Knapp's command vehicle, dragging his bleeding leg. An RPG whizzed in behind him and slammed into the left side of his Bradley, which was parked near Knapp's vehicle. Two rucksacks hanging on the side erupted in flames, but Coffey could see that the grenade had not penetrated the Bradley's armor. He reached Knapp's vehicle and hobbled inside. As Knapp tried to get a look at Coffey's leg wounds, the two men quickly discussed the handoff. They agreed that the lead company from 2-7 should move up right away. Knapp wanted a controlled handoff.

Coffey limped over to his Bradley, only to discover that his driver had disappeared. The two soldiers who had been in the Humvee that was now burning were also gone. Coffey yelled for his driver, who sprinted up from the south, where he had taken cover behind a concrete abutment after the Bradley was hit. One of the two infantrymen who had ridden up Highway 8 in the back of the Bradley was now in the Bradley commander's hatch. Coffey told the soldier to move aside, but the crew insisted that he get his leg bandaged first. Specialist Nicholas Cochrane, an infantryman from the two-man team, managed to get a pressure bandage on the major's leg to stop the bleeding.

Coffey was focused at this point on helping Johnson's combat team keep suppressive fire on the Iraqis so that the handoff could take place. He crawled up into the commander's hatch and ordered Cochrane and the other infantrymen to get out and lay down suppressive fire with their M-16s. He yelled at his driver to pull forward and told his gunner to fire. The Bradley plunged into the fight.

Sergeant Shawn Kemmer had been disappointed the night before, when his squad got the order to pull security at Objective Curly. Kemmer was a squad leader on a China mortar platoon, an aggressive young NCO from Hampton, Virginia, who was eager to prove himself in combat. He had envisioned an uneventful day on security duty, sitting around and swatting flies while the real fight played out in the city center. He had come all the way to the edge of Baghdad, he felt, only to be reduced to guarding a highway. He joked about being the water boy when everybody else was out on the field, playing in the big game.

Now Kemmer was in the middle of the brigade's biggest firefight of the war, and things were not going smoothly. Within minutes of pulling out on Highway 8, in command of the tail vehicle on Captain Johnson's first reinforcement platoon, he had immediately encountered a problem. He had spotted a wounded Iraqi soldier at the side of the highway, crawling to retrieve his weapon, and he had ordered one of his soldiers to kill the man with his M-16. Kemmer was in the hatch of his armored personnel carrier, manning a .50-caliber machine gun, which he thought was too much weapon for killing just one man. But his own soldier hesitated; he didn't want to shoot a wounded man. Finally Kemmer cursed and swung the machine gun around to fire—only to have his soldier, belatedly, kill the man with a burst from his M-16. Kemmer had no regrets about killing a wounded man, but he was troubled by the soldier's hesitancy. It was a bad sign.

Once Kemmer's team arrived at Curly, he set up his personnel carrier on the southern perimeter, right on Highway 8, completely exposed. Kemmer was firing the .50-caliber into a building on the west side of the highway when bullets began ringing off the sides of the vehicle. He was ordering everybody to get down and close the hatches when something smashed into the handle of his machine gun. Kemmer felt a burning sensation in his arm. He hollered, "I'm hit! I'm hit!" He looked down and realized that a flaming piece of the handle had burned his arm. He felt foolish. "I'm fine! I'm fine!" he yelled.

Kemmer radioed for permission to fire direct lay into the building to the west—to fire his 120mm mortars straight into the structure. He didn't need spotters. He would just aim the tubes and adjust by sight. The building was only a few hundred meters away, and he could see it clearly. He had his crews fire four rounds from mortars mounted on the armored vehicles. The first two rounds landed behind the building. Kemmer had the crews adjust their fire, and the next two rounds crashed down on the top of the building, caving in the roof and top floor. The enemy fire ceased from that direction, and Kemmer felt a small sense of accomplishment and vindication.

But then one of his men screwed up one of the mortars. The soldier was cleaning the mortar tube with a swab—like a huge Q-tip cleaning out an ear—but he had neglected to oil the swab first. It got jammed in the tube. The soldier was crouched on top of an armored vehicle, under fire, yanking madly on the swab.

"Didn't I tell you to put fucking oil on the swab before you put it in?" Kemmer screamed.

"Sorry, sorry, I tried," the soldier said.

Kemmer cursed him and told him to get down before he got killed. The soldier took cover, but not before he completely jammed the mortar by forcing the swab out of the tube. Kemmer had to jury-rig the weapon to get it to fire properly. He felt his frustration mounting. The middle of a firefight wasn't the time or place to teach a guy how clean a mortar tube.

The next threat came from the south—a sedan that was speeding north up Highway 8, directly at Kemmer's personnel carrier. There were two men inside. Kemmer couldn't tell whether they had weapons, so he followed the rules of engagement. He fired his machine gun into the pavement, but the sedan kept coming. He fired into the hood, but the car did not slow down. Then he shot out the windshield and saw the passenger go down. The car burst into flames and slowly rolled to a stop about fifty meters away. The left front door flew open. The driver raced to the right side of the highway and climbed down into a bunker. He was dressed in civilian clothes. Kemmer couldn't tell if he had a weapon, but he was in an enemy bunker that had fired on his squad earlier. In Kemmer's mind, that made the driver an enemy combatant.

Kemmer laced the bunker with machine-gun fire. Some of the other gunners opened fire, too, and the driver went down and stayed down. It was the first time Kemmer had killed anyone, and he was struck by how impersonal it seemed. He felt no anger or hatred. He saw the target and he hit it. He had nothing against the guy. In fact, he figured the man probably had a wife and kids at home, just like him. So it was nothing personal.

Later, there was yet another threat from the south, and Kemmer braced for another suicide car. Bright tracers began whizzing past his vehicle—big rounds. He could hear them smacking into vehicles behind him. Whoever was firing at them was a long way down the highway, perhaps fifteen hundred meters. A couple of his gunners fired a few shots in that direction. A sergeant grabbed his binoculars and looked down the highway.

"Shit!" he yelled. "They're Bradleys!"

The lead platoon of 2-7 had opened fire on Objective Curly.

Major Knapp was conferring outside his command vehicle with Gallagher, Johnson, and Hornbuckle. Knapp had tried to complete his handoff discussion with Major Coffey, but he had not been able to get Coffey's attention inside the Bradley. Now Knapp and the others were trying to coordinate the battlefield handoff when the overpass was suddenly pounded with heavy white tracer rounds. Ronny Johnson started grabbing people and shoving them inside Knapp's command vehicle. Knapp clambered inside behind them, pushed in by Johnson. He could hear explosions on top of the overpass. Rounds were thumping against the roof of his vehicle.

A lead Bradley from 2-7's Alpha Company had opened up by mistake with its 25mm Bushmaster chain gun. At least one round tore into one of the Special Forces Toyota pickups. The truck was mounted with an M-240 machine gun and from a distance had the same profile as an Iraqi technical vehicle. The pickup exploded in an orange fireball that sprayed shards of hot metal across the highway. A Bradley from Captain Johnson's Bravo Company on the southern perimeter also was rocked by Twenty-five Mike Mike. The fire support officer's M577 armored personnel carrier was hammered by a 25mm round that exploded against the commander's hatch. The soldiers on the highway, screaming in confusion and panic, managed to take accountability. Miraculously, no one had been hit by the friendly fire.

At the southern edge of the perimeter, First Sergeant Chris French had his driver pull his armored personnel carrier out onto the highway, racing south toward the advancing 2-7 Bradleys. French was up in his hatch, waving an orange VS-17 panel, trying to get the Bradley crewmen to see that they were firing on friendly vehicles. Sergeant Kemmer's mortar crews were up in their hatches, too, waving and screaming. The Bradleys were bearing down on the interchange, less than two kilometers away. The men from the China battalion waved the orange panel and flapped their arms. The friendly fire ceased.

But at the same moment that the 2-7 Bradley had accidentally opened fire, Iraqi fighters had concentrated a volley of RPGs on the fuel and ammunition trucks and at the tight cluster of command vehicles beneath the overpass. The interchange was rocked by a series of rapid explosions. Shrapnel from an RPG sliced into Sergeant Major Gallagher's lower left leg. He hopped around, cursing. He grabbed his automatic rifle and leaned against his armored recovery vehicle, squeezing off several bursts. Captain Hornbuckle bent down and tried to get a bandage on Gallagher's wound. Gallagher kept shooting.

Across the highway, an RPG tore into one of Captain Polsgrove's ammunition trucks. The flatbed vehicle was loaded with several tons of ordnance—120mm tank rounds, 25mm Bradley rounds, 7.62mm coax and M-240 belts, 5.56 ammunition for M-16s and M-4s, hand grenades, antitank rockets, and claymore mines. It had been packed specifically to meet the needs of Captain Wright's tanks, Bradleys, and infantrymen at Objective Moe. The fireball at the head of the streaking grenade punched through one of the ammunition pallets, igniting a honeycombed load of tank rounds. The explosion released an enormous fireball and a cascading blast wave. Knapp felt the heat and the concussion inside the hull of his command carrier—a tremendous release of energy that reverberated beneath the overpass. Something slammed into a storage box on top of the hatch, tearing it to shreds. Knapp had been eager to be part of the fight, but now, amid the chaos and the pounding explosions, he wished he were somewhere else, anywhere but at Objective Curly.

The exploding ammunition on the supply truck sent bullets and flaming chunks of shrapnel in all directions. The truck was now a weapons platform, firing off tank and Bradley and small-arms ammunition in a fusillade even more intense than the enemy fire that had been pelting the interchange for several hours. Something shot straight through the thin metal skin of a fuel tanker, igniting another massive fireball and blast wave. The southeastern corner of the interchange was consumed now by flames and billowing smoke. The fireballs expanded up and out, engulfing the supply vehicles parked along the edge of the highway. Polsgrove and Bailey had managed to move only one of the trucks to the west side of the highway. Now two more ammunition trucks and another fuel tanker exploded, spraying the interchange with more cooked-off ammunition and more hot shards of metal.

At the aid station beneath the overpass, Dr. Schobitz was trying to get a look at Sergeant Major Gallagher's leg wound. He gave him an injection of antibiotics, and Gallagher complained bitterly that the doctor was slowing him down. He wanted to get back into the fight. The intelligence officer, Captain Felix Almaguer, limped over with a spray of shrapnel in his leg, and Schobitz's medics got him bandaged. It was deafening and confusing under the overpass, with soldiers hobbling around with shrapnel wounds, the wounded enemy prisoners moaning and yelping, and the heat from the fireballs washing over the aid station.

Schobitz saw one of the intelligence officers point to the ammunition trucks and yell, "Hey, you know there's rockets on there!" Suddenly the doctor realized that they might all be ripped apart by their own exploding ammunition or burned to death by the expanding fireballs. Then he was knocked to the roadway. He thought somebody had sucker punched him. He looked up and saw that one of the medics had gone down, too, hit by shrapnel. Schobitz realized that he had been struck in the face by something. He looked at the medic and saw that the man wasn't badly hurt. Schobitz asked him, "Hey, am I good?" The medic told Schobitz that he had been cut in the cheek by a tiny sliver of shrapnel. "You're good, sir," he told the doctor.

Schobitz got up and went to check on the badly burned fighter he had treated earlier. It was obvious that the man had died—painlessly, Schobitz believed. The doctor and the medics wrapped the corpse in a blanket and laid him on a litter behind a highway support column.

Schobitz couldn't find the Syrian fighter he had bandaged earlier. He had apparently taken advantage of the confusion to flee, his hands still bound by plastic cuffs.

As the supply trucks exploded, Captain Polsgrove tried to gather as many of the men as possible from his support platoon and herd them to cover beneath the overpass. He was afraid, and he could tell from the looks on the faces of some of his men that they were scared, too. They were drivers and quartermaster specialists. Many of them were trying to return fire, but they hadn't expected to be caught up in a firefight—and certainly not a firefight that included an attack by their own Bradleys. Polsgrove feared that the situation would spiral out of control, and he worked to stay calm and restore order. He spoke firmly to his men, trying not to betray his own fears. He even tried to smile, though he realized he wasn't fooling anybody. He said a little prayer, asking God to get him and his men through the day alive.

Polsgrove led a group of soldiers to cover next to a cement support wall beneath the overpass, where they could take cover and return fire. They all tried to press up against the wall, but they stumbled over something on the highway. Polsgrove looked down and saw the bloodied corpses of Syrian fighters. He told his men to shove the bodies out of the way. One of the wounded men was still breathing. Polsgrove saw his chest heave and fall. His midsection was wrapped in an American field dressing that was soaked through with blood. He was dying. Polsgrove's men pushed him aside. They needed the cover.

Polsgrove noticed that several of the supply trucks were now moving. Some of the support platoon soldiers had sprinted across the highway and jumped into the truck cabs to get the vehicles away from the approaching fire. Polsgrove hadn't ordered them to do it; he couldn't have because he didn't know where everyone was. They had acted on their own. One of the men had run over and pulled out the .50-caliber gunner of the first ammunition truck that had been hit. The concussion had knocked the gunner unconscious, and his fellow soldier had dragged him to safety.

The first man to run for the trucks was Staff Sergeant Joe Todd, the gunner on Gallagher's armored vehicle. Todd was a dark-haired, stocky thirty-six-year-old NCO, a Gulf War veteran with a wife and two children. He was feeling distraught that afternoon, for he had just learned of the death of Sergeant Stever. Todd and Stever had been close friends, and the news stunned him. Todd had poured his grief and his despair into his .50-caliber machine gun, keeping up a steady stream of fire at gunmen in the trenches and on the rooftops. He had provided cover for Sergeant Phillips's four-man clearing team and had helped destroy a cement truck that had tried to crash through the perimeter. In all, Todd had fired more than eight hundred rounds. Now, just as the supply trucks burst into flames, he had run out of ammunition. He climbed down off his vehicle, dashed across the highway, and jumped behind the wheel of a burning truck. He couldn't get the engine started, but his failed attempt had prompted other men in the support platoon to run over and move at least a dozen trucks to safety. They managed to salvage the bulk of the fuel and ammunition resupply for the combat team at all three interchanges.

Sergeant Andrew Johnson ran over to Polsgrove and asked for permission to try to rescue his fuel truck. Polsgrove could see that exploding ammunition was ripping into the tanker. "No, I'm not going to make you do that," he said.

Johnson argued with him. He was angry. "Sir, all my stuff is on that truck. I've got to get my stuff."

Polsgrove relented. "All right, go ahead," he said. "But I'm not going to order you to do that." He didn't know what else to say.

Johnson half-ran and half-crawled to his truck and climbed into the cab. He tried several times to start the engine. Bright yellow flames were shooting out of the truck next to him, just a meter away, and finally Johnson gave up and ran back to cover.

Polsgrove had regretted allowing Johnson to leave in the first place, and now he was relieved to have him back safely. Johnson was bent over, catching his breath, saying something to Polsgrove. The captain didn't understand him, but then he heard Johnson say, "Sir, I couldn't get it started, but now I think I know what it was. I think I can get it started."

Johnson started to run back across the highway. Polsgrove grabbed him by the strap of his flak vest and yanked him back. "No way you're going back out there," he said, and he ordered Johnson to stay put.

By now, there was pandemonium beneath the overpass. Men were bleeding from shrapnel wounds; Polsgrove saw something take off part of a soldier's hand. Officers and NCOs were screaming out orders. Soldiers were firing and scrambling for cover. Exploding ammunition was splattering the command vehicles and the support walls. RPGs were exploding on the roadway, and small-arms fire was chipping holes in the underside of the overpass. The conflagration of burning fuel and cooking ammunition sent up plumes of black smoke that blotted out the hazy midday sun.

Officers and senior NCOs are conditioned to bring order to chaos. Soldiers look to them in moments of fear and confusion for some marker of stability, of decisiveness. If the leaders hesitate, they sow panic in the ranks. Now, beneath the overpass at Curly, the commanders quickly found one another and huddled. They gathered in the tight space between the command carriers—Major Knapp, Captain Johnson, Captain Bailey, Captain Hornbuckle, Command Sergeant Major Gallagher, and a few others. They worked to bring the situation under control, shouting and gesturing to make themselves understood amid the gunshots and explosions. It was a pivotal moment: they were under fire, and they were returning fire. An advancing unit had just opened up on friendly positions. Ammunition was cooking off. Fires were raging around the five burning trucks. The surviving fuel and ammunition trucks were still exposed to enemy fire. And in the middle of all this, the combat teams at the interchange still had to hand off their positions to the 2-7 forces, and then prepare to fight their way up Highway 8. At the same time, the supply convoy had to be reorganized in preparation to roll north under fire. Prisoners had to be transferred and the wounded had to be evacuated. Knapp, Johnson, Gallagher, Bailey, and Hornbuckle moved their soldiers off their positions and into formation as the lead company from 2-7 pulled into the southern perimeter. China's Bradleys continued to fire and hold the perimeter. Given the chaotic circumstances, it was a remarkably controlled handoff.

Major Coffey was just north of the overpass, firing from his Bradley at a building to the northwest where gunmen were firing on the interchange with RPGs and small-arms fire. Coffey was still angry, still shouting at soldiers to lay down suppressive fire. It appeared to him that not all the .50-caliber machine guns mounted on the surviving supply trucks were being manned. Then he saw a Special Forces soldier climb up on one of the trucks and open up with the .50-caliber at targets to the south and west.

As Coffey directed his gunner from the Bradley turret, three Iraqi fighters closed in on the vehicle from behind. One of the Bradley infantrymen, Specialist Cochrane, saw them and opened fire with his M-16. All three went down. They were more than 150 meters away. Cochrane continued to lay down suppressive fire, and the Bradley kept pounding the building as Coffey spoke by radio with the commander of the lead 2-7 company on the highway to the south. He tried to guide him in as the China battalion units pulled out.

Coffey was worried that the remaining Special Forces pickup would be targeted by the advancing Bradleys, even with the bright orange panels designating it as a friendly vehicle. He yelled at one of the Special Forces soldiers to pull his pickup behind the Bradley for safety. The soldier looked relieved. "Roger that," he said. "Got it."

Near the overpass, Bailey and Polsgrove got the support platoon drivers and gunners back into the surviving vehicles and lined up in convoy formation. There were hectic discussions regarding security for the unwieldy formation of armored and soft-skinned vehicles. It was decided that the sixteen surviving fuel and ammunition trucks would be protected at the front and rear by Bradleys. There were plenty of Bradleys by now—Johnson had ten and Hornbuckle had five. There were also several Humvees mounted with .50-caliber machine guns and grenade launchers. It was the first time that day that the resupply convoy would travel with adequate firepower.

Along the highway, Specialist Agee and Private First Class Gregory were guarding more than two dozen naked prisoners huddled inside the pen of concertina wire when they got the order to load up and move out. The medic teams next to the prisoners' pen were loading up, too, and Agee feared that all the running around was disrupting the prisoner exchange. They were supposed to be handing the prisoners off to incoming teams from 2-7, but Special Forces soldiers were still interrogating some of the captives. Then one of the medics, followed by a captain, ran up to Agee and yelled, "They forgot Sergeant Stever! Come on!"

In the noise and confusion, the medical teams had forgotten all about Stever's bagged corpse, which had been set down next to a support wall protected by the overpass. Agee and Gregory were ordered to run up the highway to the overpass to retrieve him. Agee could see the black outlines of the burning trucks framed against the brilliant red of the flames and the billowing mushroom clouds of black smoke. He could hear the steady pop of the ammunition cooking off, and the hiss of the spraying rounds. He could feel the heat, damp and insistent, against his cheek.

They found Stever in the gloom under the overpass, still in the green body bag. Agee and Gregory picked up either end. It suddenly struck Agee, just as he felt the stiffness of Stever's lifeless form tucked inside the body bag, that Stever was gone and wasn't coming back. Until the medic told him that Stever's body had been left behind, Agee hadn't known that Stever was one of the two soldiers who had died in the ambush. He knew Stever. He used to wrestle with him in competitions between the mechanics and the guys from the TOC. Stever was strong and agile, and Agee admired his sneaky wrestling moves. Now, as he hustled across the pavement, lugging Stever's corpse with Gregory and the captain providing cover fire, Agee thought how surreal it was, getting shot at and nearly burned alive while carrying a dead American.

They made it back to where the medical vehicles had been, but now they couldn't find the medics. It was getting late in the afternoon, and smoke was drifting across the intersection. The convoy was lining up and getting ready to pull out. Agee and Gregory were growing anxious. They still had to find their Humvee and load up, and they feared being left behind.

Gregory spotted one of the big ammunition trucks. There was an empty cargo well on the side, about halfway up, big enough to accommodate a man's body.

"Put him in there—right there!" he said.

They didn't know what else to do. It seemed logical. They gently lay Sergeant Stever across the well and tied him securely with cargo straps.

Agee and Gregory ran back to their Humvee, where Sergeant Phillips was waiting for them. As they climbed aboard, a soldier pushed a prisoner toward them. Gregory realized that the concertina pen had been opened and that the prisoners were being handed over to the teams from 2-7. But now, for some reason, they found themselves stuck with a loose prisoner.

He was a middle-aged man with a beard and a tiny bald spot on the back of his head. He was whimpering and crying and making gestures, cringing at the sounds of the ammunition cooking off. He was naked and his hands were bound by plastic cuffs; someone had tied a shirt around his plump midsection.

They didn't know what to do with him. The column was pulling out now. Agee, looking down from the gunner's turret, felt sorry for the

man. He pointed at him and yelled the only thing he could think of:
"Go! Go!"

The prisoner trotted away, disappearing in the smoke. The Humvee
pulled away, headed north on Highway 8.

Next to the overpass, Polsgrove and Bailey had finally managed to
get their supply trucks and escort vehicles in convoy formation. Polsgrove
was struggling with accountability. He thought he had all his men ac-
counted for, but some of them had taken up positions in the trenches with
his platoon sergeant. He was counting on the sergeant to get all those men
back into the vehicles.

Because he had lost five trucks, Polsgrove now had to find rides for
almost a dozen men. The Bradley crews took some of them, and a few more
were jammed into the escort Humvees, along with the two men from
Coffey's detail whose Humvee had burned to the ground. Polsgrove's own
Humvee was filling up with soldiers as the captain noticed a naked prisoner sitting on the highway, his hands bound behind him. He may have
been the man abandoned by Agee's group. Polsgrove didn't know what he
was supposed to do with him. He thought 2-7 was supposed to take control of all prisoners.

The man was weeping and blubbering, mumbling in English, "I help
you! I help you!" Polsgrove didn't want to leave him there on the pavement. He lifted him up and sat him down in the front passenger seat of his
Humvee. The man was still crying, the tears soaking his beard. Polsgrove
got the impression the prisoner thought he was going to be executed. To
shut him up, he tossed an MRE into the man's lap. He quickly realized
how foolish that was—the guy's hands were bound.

The order came to move out. Two more support platoon drivers ran
up, looking for a ride. Polsgrove motioned for them to jump inside. Now
he was overloaded; he had to get rid of the prisoner. From his perch in the
turret behind the grenade launcher, Polsgrove yelled over to some of the
other Humvees. "Can anybody give this guy a ride?" He didn't want to
just dump the prisoner. He might have valuable information for American interrogators.

Nobody wanted to get stuck hauling a prisoner. Polsgrove's own
Humvee now had seven soldiers in a vehicle designed to carry five at the
most. Polsgrove had to make a snap decision. He ordered his men to jetti-
son the prisoner. They left him there on the roadway and rolled north
toward Objective Larry.

FIFTEEN
MOE, LARRY

American combat commanders are trained to develop a decision support matrix, an analytical breakdown of alternatives based on a rapidly unfolding chain of circumstances. For David Perkins, the matrix was telling him: cut your losses, retreat, come back another day. Perkins was still in the parade grounds late in the morning, under the crossed sabers, standing beside his command vehicle with deCamp and Schwartz. The time had come for Perkins to make the call on spending the night in the city, and the logical move was to pull back and regroup. His brigade command center had burned. He had just spent his reserve force, leaving the rebuilt TOC vulnerable to another attack. His resupply convoy for the combat teams on Highway 8 had been ambushed, and now five of his fuel and ammunition trucks were burning on the highway. The surviving trucks were preparing to move up the highway, with no guarantee that they wouldn't be ambushed again. His combat team at the crucial spaghetti interchange—the force Perkins was counting on to protect his exposed rear—was running low on ammunition and fuel.

Rationally, Perkins knew the prudent move was to pull out of the city. That was the safe call. But instinctively, he felt compelled to hold his ground. His men had fought furiously to break through to the palace complex. Two of his men had died trying to bring up fuel and ammunition. It seemed somehow obscene to ask his men to fight their way back out now and to surrender terrain infused with surpassing psychological and strategic value.

And Perkins had risked his own personal capital—his very integrity as a combat commander—persuading General Blount and General Austin to press his case with V Corps and the U.S. Central Command (CENTCOM). Blount and Austin believed in Perkins, and they had put their own credibility on the line while attempting to persuade their superiors to let the commander on the ground make the call. Now Blount came back to Perkins over the radio from the airport with the decision from the higher command: the brass had put the most crucial decision of the war in the hands of a forty-four-year-old bird colonel who had never been in combat prior to the invasion. "It's your call, Dave," Blount said.

For all the setbacks his commanders and soldiers had endured that morning, Perkins had confidence in them—in their training, their professionalism, their determination to complete the mission. He trusted them to hold Highway 8 and to get the fuel and ammunition into the palace complex, even at the risk of more casualties. Both deCamp and Schwartz wanted to stay, and Perkins trusted their judgment. Like Perkins, they wanted to make a bold statement—to their own men, to the higher command, to the world at large, and especially to Sahaf, the information minister. Perkins thought about Sahaf's rants, and how a retreat now would only validate his outrageous propaganda. It would undermine in the eyes of the world the brigade's singular achievement, which had put American soldiers inside Saddam's two main palaces and American boots on Saddam's personal reviewing stand.

Perkins stood under the sabers, map in hand, flanked by his two tank battalion commanders. The air was heavy with smoke and swirling sand and grit. Black plumes of oily smoke rose from burning vehicles and bunkers. The big guns on Rogue's tanks and Bradleys were pounding Iraqis still dug into the park, the concussions rocking the reviewing stand. Perkins turned to deCamp and Schwartz. "We're staying," he said.

It was the suicide vehicles that worried Dan Hubbard. They were relentless. They kept speeding north up Highway 8, swerving past the barricades the combat engineers had erected just south of the interchange at Objective Larry, trying to ram Hubbard's tanks and Bradleys. Hubbard could understand the enemy's desire to breach the perimeter, but he couldn't comprehend the repeated, futile forays—each one ending in an eruption of flames and flying metal as one vehicle after another was destroyed by high-explosive rounds. The hulks of at least twenty cars and trucks and motorcycles were still smoking on the highway. The drivers were fanatics—they were burned alive. Hubbard chalked it up to some sort of Islamic desire to die a spectacular death.

Hubbard was a captain, the commander of the combat team at Larry, where Lieutenant Colonel Twitty had set up his task force command post.

He was thirty-four, with prematurely steel gray hair—a stocky, green-eyed, snuff-dipping Tennessean with a soft drawl. He had spent the morning at Larry under constant fire from all directions. His tank, which he had situated on the east-west overpass, had been hit five times by RPGs. He had counted at least a hundred RPGs exploding across the interchange that morning. RPG teams were launching grenades from buildings to the east. From the west, gunmen in civilian clothes were emerging from palm groves and opening fire. To the southeast, across a set of railroad tracks, Republican Guards in uniform were attacking through another grove of date palms. And to the southwest was a dense urban area that worried Hubbard because it seemed to be an ammunition supply depot.

At one point, shortly after Hubbard's team had set up on the interchange just after first light, he actually had to fight off enemy dismounts who were trying to close in on his tank on foot from the west. He had never expected them to get so close. Hubbard opened up with his .50-caliber machine gun while his gunner worked the coax, but the dismounts kept coming. Finally his loader had to toss grenades from the hatch to drive them back.

Just after Hubbard's tank was smacked by an exploding RPG for the fourth time, he heard one of the tank commanders on the northern ramp scream for help over the radio. Something had exploded on his bustle racks, and gear and ammunition stored on them were burning and popping.

"I been hit! I been hit!" the commander screamed.

Hubbard could hear panic in the man's voice. He radioed the commander's platoon leader, who was in the next tank, and told him to try to put out the fire. But the ammunition in the bustle racks began to explode and the platoon leader yelled, "I can't! His rounds are cooking off!"

Hubbard told him to back off. "Let it burn!" he said. He knew the Abrams was designed to withstand explosions from its ammunition.

The commander of the stricken tank was still panicking. He radioed and said, "I'm on fire!"

Hubbard dropped down on the commander's radio net and tried to speak calmly to him. "Hey, you're doing all right," he told him. "Just continue fighting these guys. Don't worry about the fire—it's not going to hurt you. It's the way the tank's designed."

The commander recovered his composure as the fire of the bustle racks smoldered and eventually burned itself out. He lost personal gear and ammunition, but his tank got back into the fight. It was the second tank to burn after being hit by an RPG. Two of Hubbard's Bradleys were also hit. They suffered structural damage, but both stayed in the fight with the RPG projectiles still embedded in their armored plates.

As the firefight intensified, Hubbard climbed down off his tank several times and made his way to the perimeter. He had sent thirty infantrymen from the Bradleys to dig in along the perimeter next to the on-ramps, and now they were absorbing a barrage of small-arms fire. Hubbard had been a marine machine gunner in the Gulf War, a ground pounder, and he had drawn great inspiration from commanders who joined their men on the lines. Now he had sent his own men into harm's way, and he felt an obligation to expose himself to the same risk. He wasn't a West Point guy. He was an ROTC officer, from East Tennessee State University, and in many ways still an enlisted man at heart. He thought it was a chickenshit move to stay safely buttoned up in a tank while his infantrymen were putting their lives on the line. So he moved from man to man along the perimeter, slapping backs, telling each one he was doing a hell of a job, that he was an American hero. The little forays also gave Hubbard a chance to speak face-to-face with his platoon leaders and platoon sergeants. That was more satisfying, and more productive, than trying to communicate by radio.

Despite the intensity of fire, Hubbard was confident he could hold the interchange. He had eight tanks, versus four tanks at Moe and none at Curly. He had fought the first part of the battle with just six tanks because one had been dispatched to help rescue the burning tank from Rogue's thunder run at dawn and another had been sent later as backup. But now all eight tanks were firing, and they were killing people with a stunning efficiency, hour after hour, like an assembly line. And the artillery was just as destructive, collapsing roofs and walls onto enemy fighters and pulverizing the flimsy sandbagged bunkers. Hubbard had called in nine artillery and mortar missions, seven of them danger close, or within a few hundred meters of his own men. He could feel the concussions and hear the whiz of flying shrapnel, even inside his tank. He had to temporarily move his infantrymen off the perimeter to protect them from short rounds.

Hubbard was concerned about how some of his young enlisted men were reacting to the brutality required to destroy the suicide vehicles. Some of the passengers in the exploding cars had somehow survived the tank blasts and climbed out of the flaming wreckage. They had reached down and grabbed AK-47s from the arms caches that had been stored in holes dug into the highway shoulder. They had opened fire, and the tank gunners had torn them apart with coax. By the end of the day, more than forty vehicles would be incinerated. It was such an awful waste of human life.

Private First Class Jacob McLaughlin, an infantryman, was assigned to guard prisoners. One of them was a very young man—a boy, really—in a Special Republican Guard uniform. Something had blown his leg apart, and now it hung by a few flaps of gray tissue. The young man was grinning and flashing McLaughlin a thumbs-up sign. Another prisoner had been shot in the face. He was dressed in an Iraqi police uniform and seemed well fed and prosperous. He was in his mid-thirties, slightly paunchy, with wavy black hair. He had been at the wheel of a black Honda Civic that was fired on by the combat team as it sped toward the tanks and Bradleys. His face was burned and his entire cheek was blown off. McLaughlin could see inside the man's head, all the way to the bone. A round had entered behind his ear and exploded out through his cheek, leaving an oozing red cavity. Now the man was sitting cross-legged on the pavement, letting a medic apply gauze strips to his blackened face. He was staring at McLaughlin. McLaughlin waited for the man to look away, but he wouldn't stop staring. McLaughlin wanted to say something, anything, to get the man to turn away. It was a horrible wound, and he couldn't bear to see it. It was McLaughlin who finally looked away.

At one point Hubbard's loader, Private Charles Francis, who had just turned nineteen, suddenly looked up at Hubbard and said, "Damn, we're killing a lot of people here."

Hubbard nodded and said, "Yeah, that's our job."

"Yeah, but you act like it doesn't affect you," Francis said.

Hubbard had to admit that he did not show his emotions in battle. He had learned to put them aside, to deal with them later. He was a religious man, and he did not enjoy killing anyone. But his focus was on getting his men out alive—he had only one soldier wounded that day, which he attributed to God's good grace—and on appearing strong and resolute in front of his men. The killing and the violence were disturbing, but that was a very private thing for Hubbard, and something he would reconcile later. Right now, he was a man with a wife and two children and two dogs, and he was determined to see them again.

The loader in the executive officer's tank, Private Chad Ortz, had never seen a man killed in battle. Ortz saw one of the first suicide vehicles get hammered—he got a good look at it through his binoculars. He saw the car explode, and he saw human beings explode, too. It was a shocking thing, and he asked the executive officer, Lieutenant Mike Martin, "Hey, sir, like, are we doing the right thing?"

Martin told him, "Yeah, it's them or you. They're coming to kill us."

So the tank kept killing, and after a while Ortz just learned to get used to it. It almost seemed routine, and that would have been disturbing if Ortz had had time to really think about it. He was glad to be busy, holding back the enemy soldiers who were trying to kill him.

Just south of the intersection, next to two south-facing tanks on Highway 8, Lieutenant Colonel Twitty was still in the middle of the fight. His Bradley crew was still firing south down the highway, backing up the two tanks. They had already reloaded once, and ammunition was running short. Twitty was worried about getting the resupply convoy safely up to Larry from Curly—and then north to Captain Wright at Moe, who was in the worst shape on ammunition and fuel among the three combat teams.

Twitty got on the radio to Captain Bailey at Curly and asked for an update on his losses. Bailey was trying to reorganize his supply convoy for the move north, and he still wasn't certain how much fuel and ammunition had been destroyed in the explosions and fires. He told Twitty he thought he still had at least two of the trucks designated for Larry. He thought most of the lost fuel and ammunition had been designated for Moe.

Twitty radioed Captain Hubbard on the overpass and warned him that he might have to give up some of his diminishing ammunition reserves to be sent to Moe. They would have to wait to decide how to reallocate supplies until Bailey arrived with the convoy. Twitty envisioned losing even more fuel and ammunition on the highway between Curly and Larry. It wasn't secure. The convoy had been ambushed on the way to Curly, so it stood to reason that it might also be ambushed on the way to Larry.

Twitty radioed Captain Johnson to make sure Johnson was putting every last one of his Bradleys on the resupply convoy. Johnson assured him that he was positioning Bradleys at the front, middle, and rear of the column. They would lay down a wall of fire.

As the convoy pulled out of Curly, every vehicle in the column was firing—even the fuel and ammunition trucks. The .50-caliber machine gunners opened up on top of the trucks, and from each passenger window the soldiers riding in the front seats pumped away on their automatic rifles. Even the drivers were firing, steering with their left hands and firing on full burst out the window with their right hands. The tracers lit up the dull afternoon sky. It looked as though bright-colored streamers had been hung on both sides of the flat, drab highway.

Twitty told Johnson to make sure the entire convoy stayed in the right-hand lanes. The Bradleys at Larry would clear the way by firing in the left-hand lanes, eliminating any threat from the western side of the highway. The roadway itself was now clear. Twitty had sent his engineers out earlier to shove aside the smoking wrecks of the suicide vehicles littering the highway. There were so many of them—technicals and taxis and buses—that they had completely blocked the roadway from the south.

It was only three and a half kilometers from Curly to Larry, and the convoy was moving briskly, probably forty-five kilometers an hour. Captain Polsgrove, in one of the lead Humvees, was surprised by how quickly the interchange at Larry came into view through the haze. He was pumping grenades from his launcher into upper-story windows along the highway when he suddenly realized they were already approaching Larry.

From his tank hatch up on the overpass, Captain Hubbard saw rounds smack into the sides of the support beams and kick up dirt next to the curving on-ramps, where his infantry was dug in. He realized that the gunfire was coming from the advancing resupply convoy. He got on the task force radio net and started screaming for the gunners to shut down, to stop firing at friendlies. He managed to get them to stop shooting before any of his men was hit. Hubbard was delighted to see the fuel and ammunition, but he would have preferred that it had arrived in a less dramatic fashion.

On his Bradley, Twitty felt a rush of relief. For hours, he had been agonizing over his tenuous hold on all three interchanges and his combat teams' steadily dwindling supplies of fuel and ammunition. Now two of Polsgrove's ammunition trucks and two of his fuel tankers were pulling in under the overpass with enough supplies to last Twitty and Hubbard through the night and well into the next day. Even with the loss of the five trucks in the conflagration at Curly, there was still enough fuel and ammunition left over to resupply Captain Wright at Moe. For the first time that day, Twitty felt confident not only about holding the interchange at Larry, but also about securing the entire resupply route all the way up Highway 8. He thought to himself, "I've got this now. It's mine."

Twitty told Johnson to escort the rest of the convoy to Moe, then continue on, as Perkins had ordered, to secure the highway that ran east from Moe to Perkins's command post at the Sujud Palace. It was an opportune time to launch the convoy. For the first time that day, there was a lull in the fighting. Twitty sank back in the hatch of his Bradley, overcome by a sudden sense of weariness bordering on exhaustion. He felt overwhelmed. For nearly eight hours straight, he had been fighting and screaming into the radio and drawing up a battle plan and worrying about the resupply. Now he felt his body starting to shut down. He had not had a decent night's sleep for more than a week. He had not slept at all the previous two nights. He was filthy with dust and soaked with sweat. He lay back and shut his eyes. For fifteen blissful minutes, even with his gunner still firing below him, he sank into a fitful sleep.

First Sergeant Jeff Moser was surprised to find himself out on the perimeter and under fire at Objective Moe. He was in charge of the company trains—two medical tracks, a maintenance vehicle, the operations officer's command Bradley, and Moser's own M113 armored personnel carrier. Moser had expected the company trains to be in a more protected spot, perhaps under the overpass, where the medics could work in relative safety. That was the way it usually worked, and he assumed that's the way it was laid out in the mission brief. But, in truth, Moser had missed most of the mission brief the night before. He and his men had come under RPG fire as they were preparing for the mission, so things were a bit disjointed. He barely got a chance to glance at the map imagery to see where they were supposed to go. He ended up having to tell his driver just to stay on the tail of the Bradley in front of them all the way up Highway 8 that morning. The next thing he knew, they were setting up just past the northwest on-ramp at the big spaghetti intersection—at Moe—with RPGs zooming over their heads.

Moser was thirty-seven, an experienced NCO, a seventeen-year lifer. He had joined the army right out of high school in Dearborn, Michigan, where his father worked the assembly line for the Ford Motor Company, putting together Mustangs. Moser had grown up with Arab neighbors, and he had learned a few Arabic phrases, which he thought he might put to good use in Iraq. He had combat experience, too, in Panama, but that was nothing like what was confronting him now, at Moe.

Their little group out on the northwest perimeter was getting pounded. Moser saw exploding RPGs and small-arms tracers, plus antiaircraft guns lowered to direct-fire mode and an occasional mortar round. He figured there were several hundred gunmen unloading on them. Moser's men were protected from the rear by the elevated concrete on-ramp, but they were exposed to their front, where a field and a park led to an enormous mosque with twin minarets. It was the Um al-Tabul Mosque, one of the biggest in Baghdad, a towering pale yellow structure where hundreds of Baghdad's middle-class Sunnis worshipped. It seemed to Moser that some of the enemy fire was originating from the direction of the mosque.

On the edge of the mosque compound closest to the interchange was a stout fence anchored by concrete pillars. Moser could see gunmen ducking and running next to the fence, and he opened up with an M-240 from the open hatch of his personnel carrier. He was still firing when word came over the radio of the first casualty of the morning. It was Specialist Steven Atkinson, one of the infantrymen. He had run into the open to grab a wounded enemy fighter who was bellowing in pain on the western edge of the company perimeter. Atkinson was trying to drag the man in for medical care when an AK-47 round tore into his abdomen, just under his combat vest.

One of Moser's responsibilities as first sergeant was casualty evacuation. He tried to get one of the medical tracks over to Atkinson, but enemy fire was too heavy. The infantrymen in Atkinson's platoon put him into an armored vehicle that delivered him to Moser's group. One of the medics treated Atkinson, but the wound was serious enough to require evacuation to the forward aid station three kilometers to the south, just north of Objective Larry. Moser put Atkinson in his personnel carrier and got one of the Bradleys to escort him. They took heavy fire all the way down the highway; an RPG destroyed an M-240 machine gun mounted on the Bradley, which got everyone's attention.

Moser made it back to Moe just in time to deal with another casualty. It was Sergeant William Staun, the gunner in a tank that had set up on Highway 8 just south of the interchange. His tank commander, Sergeant

First Class Robert Ford, had been up in the commander's hatch when he heard Staun scream. Ford couldn't figure out how Staun had been hurt; he was down in the turret, protected by several inches of steel. He looked down and saw that Staun's coax gun had jammed. Somehow, one of the rounds had cooked off and ripped through Staun's left bicep. Ford put on a pressure dressing and got him to the medics. Moser evacuated Staun, too.

The casualties kept coming. Two engineers were hit with shrapnel as they tried to tear down light poles and palm trees to build barriers to fend off suicide vehicles. Then a Bradley on the southern perimeter was rocked by an RPG that tore straight through a TOW missile launcher and exploded against the commander's hatch. A piece of shrapnel ripped a hole in the right shoulder of the Bradley commander, Sergeant First Class John Morales, while he was looking through his integrated sight unit. The medics treated Morales on the spot and got him returned to action, but it was the second time someone presumedly safe inside a tank or Bradley had been wounded. Moser thought things were starting to get out of control.

The fire from the mosque was getting heavier. Moser was certain now that fighters were taking advantage of the structure's protected status, using it for cover in the belief that the Americans would not fire back. From what Moser could see, the fighters were being supplied with ammunition and weapons stored in the mosque compound. He was worried that the Iraqis would fire on the trailer the engineers had parked at the edge of the perimeter. It was loaded with mine-clearing charges—the sausagelike links of powerful C-4 explosives. If gunfire detonated the charges, the explosion would probably level the mosque—and kill every American on the perimeter.

Moser radioed Captain Wright in his command Bradley to the east. "We're taking fire from the mosque," he told him.

Wright was busy fielding radio reports from all his track commanders, but he was aware of fire coming from the direction of the mosque. He scanned the compound through his sights and spotted an RPG team on the roof and one team on each minaret. He was not eager to destroy a huge mosque in the middle of Baghdad, but he wasn't about to just stand by and let his men get pounded.

"Roger," he told Moser. "Let me clear it up and see what's going on."

From his command and control Bradley next to Moser, Major Roger Shuck had also radioed Wright to report fire from the mosque. Shuck was the battalion S-3, or operations officer, in charge of monitoring the battle at Moe and keeping Wright appraised of events up and down the highway. At first, Shuck thought the enemy fire was coming from the park and gardens in front of the mosque. But then he scanned the mosque through the Bradley's sights and saw a two-man RPG team standing on a railing midway up one of the minarets. He described it to Wright. He was dying to take them out.

Wright radioed Twitty and described the RPG teams firing from the mosque, and the ammunition and weapons cache within the mosque compound. Opening fire on a mosque was a sensitive subject. The rules of engagement clearly listed mosques as protected targets. Along with schools and hospitals, the houses of worship were the sites most often discussed by combat commanders. But the rules of engagement also permitted American forces to return fire from the enemy—even if the enemy was firing from a mosque. Twitty and Wright had a brief discussion. Twitty knew Wright's team was getting hammered. He gave the captain permission to return fire from the mosque.

Shuck was a senior officer, but he didn't mind being in the middle of a firefight. Eight days earlier, near Karbala, his Bradley had been ambushed by an RPG team. A grenade had torn through the back of his turret, severing the heater hose and punching through to the ammunition rack inside the turret. Two high-explosive Twenty-five Mike Mike rounds exploded, slamming Shuck into the turret. The concussion had ruptured his eardrum, and now he couldn't hear anything out of his left ear. He could monitor only one radio net at a time, so he had to have his gunner monitor the brigade net while Shuck listened to the task force net with his good ear.

But Shuck was still able to fire a weapon, and he thought of himself as a pretty fair shot. On the way up Highway 8 that morning, he had shot and killed two enemy fighters with his M-16. One had been lying on the right shoulder of the highway, playing dead, and Shuck got him from about seventy-five meters. Later, as he passed under an overpass, Shuck noticed an orange-and-white taxi parked on the elevated roadway. He thought it was odd that a taxi would just be sitting there in the middle of a firefight. He had his gunner traverse the turret to the rear. As he looked back, Shuck saw two men get out of the taxi and lean across the vehicle with an RPG launcher. He braced himself against the turret, aimed his M-16, and shot one of the men through the head. His gunner chopped down the second man with a burst of Twenty-five Mike Mike.

Now, staring at the mosque, Shuck was trying to point out the RPG team on the minaret to a .50-caliber gunner on the personnel carrier next to him. The minaret was about 250 meters away. Shuck aimed his M-16 and fired. One of the men on the minaret went down. The .50-caliber gunner saw where the M-16 rounds had hit and opened up with the big gun, sending the second man toppling from the minaret. Then Shuck's gunner let loose with the 25mm main gun, blowing up two ammunition and communications trucks parked in the mosque compound. Moser followed up with his AT-4, the antitank rocket launcher. He hit a small trailer in the courtyard, unleashing a tremendous explosion as the ammunition stored inside cooked off.

The fire from the mosque stopped, but gunmen were still moving up and down the fence in front of the mosque compound. Moser sprayed them again with his mounted M-240 medium machine gun. The gunmen were dressed in black, and Moser assumed they were Fedayeen. They were poorly organized. They didn't coordinate their fire. One man would pop his head up and shoot off a few rounds or an RPG, then hunker down and let somebody else fire. But several of them stayed up too long, and Moser was able to kill each man as he rose up. The others would try to recover the dead men's bodies and weapons, only to expose themselves to Moser's M-240.

Some of Moser's soldiers started laughing and making cracks like, "How stupid *are* these guys?" Moser thought he should reprimand them, because it really wasn't funny. They were killing people. But he had to admit that his men were right. These people were inept. Moser had been harping on his men to be smart, to stay alert, to remember their training. They had all seen dead Republican Guard soldiers hauled off the battlefield down south, their boots poking from the trunks of cars. Moser often told his men, "Don't be the guy with his boots sticking out of the trunk." Now it was the enemy doing stupid things, and it struck everybody as comical.

Moser did not enjoy killing these men. He hated the carnage. Earlier that morning, along Highway 8, he had seen a dog feasting on the spilled entrails of a dead Iraqi soldier, and that image poisoned the fight for him. He couldn't get it out of his mind.

*   *   *

The interchange at Moe was more complex than the simple figure-eight intersections at Larry and Curly. Several highways merged at Moe into a tangle of on-ramps and overpasses that took motorists in all directions— north toward the exclusive neighborhood of Yarmouk, east to the palace complex, west to the airport, and south down Highway 8, the desert route to the city of Hillah. The overpasses were stacked on top of one another, their concrete support pillars overlapping in a maze of light and shadows. Below them were neighborhoods and shops and markets. Objective Moe wasn't part of a clear open highway. It was a dense urban cluster, and a nightmare to defend.

One of Josh Wright's military instructors had once told him to analyze the countryside anytime he was driving his car, just to practice thinking about how he would defend the terrain. Wright had trained to maneuver in open desert, and his battalion had even trained briefly in Kuwait for urban combat. But he had never expected to be fighting at a highway interchange. It wasn't something he had ever thought about. And only after the battle was raging did he realize that combat wasn't like the fights he had seen in Hollywood movies. It was chaotic. Everything overlapped. It wasn't linear and confined. It was three-dimensional, with threats beating down from all directions.

Wright thought his most effective weapon at Moe was mortar fire. Thick stands of date palms blocked some of the fields of fire for the tanks and Bradleys, but the high arc of the mortars brought the rounds over the trees and straight down on the targets. A volley of 120mm mortars destroyed a technical mounted with a heavy machine gun to the southwest and killed several fighters using the vehicle for cover. In the wood line north and east of the interchange, groups of soldiers were advancing on Wright's infantrymen. He walked in seven "danger close" mortar missions, some to within a hundred meters of his infantrymen, and the mortars drove back the enemy with no harm to Wright's men. Wright was planning to bring in mortars on gunmen firing from buildings to his west, but then he got the apologetic radio call from the mortar platoon lieutenant at Curly, saying that he had used up all his rounds.

Wright had managed to get his snipers and infantrymen on the rooftops and upper stories of buildings to his north and south—though one infantryman was stabbed in the leg with a bayonet while clearing one structure. That not only gave Wright the high ground to fire down on the enemy, but it also gave him more pairs of eyes—and thermal scopes—up high so that he had a better understanding of the battlefield. His fire support officer was also feeding Wright reports from air force pilots overhead of enemy armored vehicles approaching the interchange. Wright's tanks had already destroyed two BMPs, the Russian-made armored personnel carriers, and Wright warned the tank commanders to prepare for more.

By mid-afternoon, the losses had begun to pile up. Eight men had been wounded, including two of Wright's three platoon sergeants. Every vehicle had been struck at least once by an RPG. Staff Sergeant Jamus Patrick lost the coax gun on his Bradley to an RPG that punched through the front and sent a fireball streaking between Patrick's legs. A second Bradley coax was also knocked out, along with the main gun tube of a tank, which had a hole ripped straight through it by antiaircraft fire.

From the west and north came suicide cars and trucks, nearly twenty of them by mid-afternoon. One sedan was speeding at nearly one hundred kilometers an hour before a tank HEAT round blew it off the highway. The driver somehow survived and emerged firing an AK-47 until a burst of coax cut him down. From the west, a blue Chevrolet Caprice roared up to two Bradleys and was stopped by a blast of 25mm fire. The driver crawled out, holding a grenade. It detonated, blowing the man in half. Sergeant First Class Ford blew up a taxi that sped toward his tank carrying a crude bomb in the trunk fashioned from a propane cooking canister.

For Wright, the low point of the day came when an enemy team breached the perimeter. Somehow, a team of Iraqis rolled a 90mm recoilless rifle right under one of the main overpasses, behind Wright's tanks and Bradleys. A team of engineers was preparing to build barricades on the west side of the highway when the recoilless rifle team fired on their armored vehicle. The engineers responded with their mounted .50-caliber machine gun, killing the crew. Then they destroyed the gun with thermite grenades.

The incident alarmed Wright. The infantry had somehow missed the big gun when they cleared the interchange that morning. Wright started wondering how many more enemy teams had penetrated behind his lines. He pulled infantry platoons off the perimeter, one by one, and had them clear their quadrants again. They didn't find any other enemy soldiers, but they did uncover huge caches of RPGs, AK-47s, and Italian-made land mines. Only then did Wright realize just how carefully the Iraqis had prepared for a fight at Moe.

By about 3 p.m., Wright began to get urgent radio calls from his platoon leaders, warning him that they were amber on ammunition for both tanks and Bradleys, and amber on fuel for the tanks. They had already cross-leveled ammunition, trading off from crew to crew. Some of the crews were black—too low to sustain the fight—on .50-caliber and coax ammunition. Wright decided to consolidate his perimeter, to give up some of his gains in order to reduce the stress on men and machines trying to defend a bigger chunk of terrain. It was at that moment, and only at that moment, that Wright feared he might be overrun.

Wright radioed Twitty and laid out his fuel and ammunition situation, including the fact that some of his tanks were on their last fuel cells. They could still fight while shut down, but they would not be able to maneuver—and Wright did not want to be in that predicament with nightfall only a few hours away. He felt more confident after discussing the situation with Twitty, who assured him he would not let Wright go black.

Over the next hour or so, Wright's spirits soared and plunged. First he heard over the net that the resupply convoy had been launched. Then he heard it was ambushed. Then he heard the convoy had reached Curly and had resupplied the mortar crews, which meant Wright could now request mortars again. Then he heard that several ammunition trucks and fuelers had exploded at Curly—*his* fuel and ammo. Then he was told he had priority for any requests for artillery. And finally, he heard that the resupply convoy had reached Larry, where it was reconfigured in order to move farther north to supply Wright's team at Moe.

The firefight at Objective Larry had eased by the time Johnson, Bailey, and Polsgrove led the remainder of the resupply convoy north toward Objective Moe. But the fight at Moe was still in full swing, and the convoy rolled straight into it. Johnson and Wright talked over the net, with Johnson explaining that his men would hold their fire to avoid hitting friendly positions. Johnson trusted Wright, who knew the situation on the ground, to cover his convoy from enemy fire.

Johnson, under fire, led the convoy into the interchange. He paused long enough to allow the reconfigured fuel and ammunition trucks now designated for Wright's team to peel off. That was Johnson's understanding of what was supposed to happen; it was the way they had done it at Larry. But in the chaos and confusion of the handoff at Curly and, now, in the midst of the firefight at Moe, the lines of communication broke down.

Word had not reached the supply convoy, and the trucks were not peeling off at Moe. They were waiting to pull out behind Johnson. It was too dark and smoky at the interchange for Johnson to see what was happening behind him, but he assumed the supply trucks had peeled off to resupply Wright's combat team. But as Johnson pulled out to lead his men to secure the Kindi Highway, as ordered by Colonel Perkins, the resupply vehicles followed them.

From the commander's hatch on his Bradley, Wright watched them go. His heart sank. He had waited all afternoon for his fuel and ammunition, and now it was rolling up the highway and disappearing down the exit ramp to the Kindi Highway.

In the hatch of his armored personnel carrier, First Sergeant Moser could see the first hints of fear in the eyes of some of his men. They were all running low on ammunition. Moser had earlier discussed his ammunition needs over the net with Captain Bailey when Bailey was with the resupply convoy at Curly. Now Moser's M113 crew was completely out of 7.62mm ammunition, which meant they could fire neither of their big M-240 machine guns. He thought about borrowing some 7.62mm ammunition from the Bradley crews but, as the first sergeant in charge of tracking fuel and ammunition, he knew the Bradleys were running low, too. Then Moser saw the resupply convoy roll past the interchange and speed toward the city. That was *his* fuel and ammo. "What the hell are we supposed to do now?" he said.

S I X T E E N
PLAYING
THE GAME

Somewhere in the jumble of supply trucks and Humvees lined up on Highway 8, somebody was playing a George Strait CD. Lieutenant Philip Xuan Luu usually let his guys listen to music during downtime, and this was certainly downtime. Luu's support platoon had been stacked up on the highway, just west of the brigade command post, for several hours on the morning of April 7. There wasn't much else to do except listen to music and talk. Luu was in charge of the fuel and ammunition support platoon for the Desert Rogues battalion, whose combat teams were now firmly established in the palace complex downtown. Since topping off the Rogue tanks with JP8 fuel just before they launched the thunder run at dawn, Luu's men had been sitting and waiting for the call to roll north to bring up the battalion's fuel and ammunition—the R2 package, for rearm and refuel. Each of these battalions had its own resupply package.

Luu had no idea what was going on in the city. He had lost radio contact with his superior, Captain Anderson Puckett, the battalion S-4, or supply officer, who had gone into the city on Rogue's armored column. Luu had only two radios, so every time he wanted to communicate with the rest of the vehicles, he had to walk up and down the column, speaking to his men one at a time. He liked to keep his people informed. They were nervous about pushing all the way up into Baghdad in soft-skinned vehicles, and Luu wanted to reassure anyone who might need a little bucking up.

Luu was twenty-five, the son of Vietnamese immigrants. His father had been a lieutenant in the South Vietnamese navy and had seen action in the Vietnam War. As Saigon was falling, he fled as a political refugee, passing through refugee camps in the Philippines and Guam before a Lions Club in Arkansas sponsored his entry into the United States in 1975. Philip Luu grew up in Fort Worth, Texas, where his father had found work as a car mechanic. In part because his father had attended a military academy in Vietnam, Luu decided to attend West Point. He was commissioned in May 2000, and had been in the army less than three years by the time he was put in charge of Rogue's support platoon.

Hauling fuel and ammo wasn't the most glamorous job of the war, but Luu knew it was essential—every bit as essential as commanding a tank or Bradley platoon. He knew the combat teams depended on his platoon to keep them supplied with the matériel they needed to sustain a fight, and that the armored crews appreciated their efforts. And in this case, in the pivotal battle of the war, Luu and his men absolutely had to reach the city center in order for Rogue to fight through the night.

The George Strait music was still playing when Luu heard what sounded like a jet fighter flying overhead. He was in his Humvee with his helmet off, chatting with his former roommate from Fort Stewart. Luu's driver, Private First Class James Lundquist, yelled out, "Hey, LT, there's one of our jets getting ready to hit some targets. That's cool!"

Then somebody hollered "Incoming!" and the TOC went up in flames in the compound across the highway. Luu thought the convoy was being bracketed by artillery. He had always told his soldiers to move out immediately if they ever came under artillery fire. Now, even before he could pull on his helmet and give the circular arm signal to move out, his drivers were in their truck cabs and cranking the engines. Luu saw the support platoons for Tusker and China start to move, but he had no idea where they were going. He didn't know where he was going, either, but he knew he had to get his vehicles out of the impact zone.

His convoy was in the southbound lanes of Highway 8 because the other two support platoons were jammed into the northbound lanes. Luu ordered Lundquist to speed north. He knew the lanes had been blocked up ahead because the engineers had not yet cleared mines from the southbound lanes, but he was hoping to find a way to turn off before he reached the minefield.

Luu spotted a dirt road to the left and yelled at Lundquist to take it. Lundquist was screaming at him, "LT, where we going? Where we going?" Luu told him to shut up and make the left turn. The road took them west, then turned sharply to the south, back toward the burning TOC.

"We're headed back to the impact area!" Lundquist screamed.

"Don't worry about it," Luu said. "Just keep driving."

Luu braced for another artillery barrage and began thinking about which way he would go if they got bracketed. The road turned again, leading them around the TOC and then to the south. Luu led the convoy down, speeding for nearly four kilometers before signaling everybody to pull over and park in a herringbone pattern for security. They were now well south of the TOC. Some of the drivers were pretty shaken up, and Luu walked back and tried to calm them. It didn't help matters when word came over the radio that the TOC had been incinerated by a missile, with several KIAs.

They waited for a good while on the highway until Luu heard from Captain Puckett, who had located a radio that allowed him to get through over the battalion net from his position downtown.

"Be careful," Puckett told Luu. "The brigade TOC got hit."

"Yes, sir, I know that," Luu said.

"And Three-Fifteen just got ambushed."

Luu hadn't realized that China's resupply convoy had moved north, much less that it had been hit.

"Damn, I didn't know that," he said.

"Highway Eight is still hot," Puckett said. "Sit tight down there and wait a couple more hours."

Luu was relieved. His men were professionals and would follow orders, but few of them were eager to drive their soft-skin vehicles through a free-fire zone. In part because of the ambush of the China convoy, four Bradleys were being dispatched now from the city center to escort the convoy. Each of the five ammunition trucks was mounted with a .50-caliber machine gun, and both Luu's Humvee and his platoon sergeant's Humvee also had .50-calibers. Even so, it was eighteen long kilometers into the palace complex.

Two hours passed, and Luu and his men began to assume that they would be spending the night on the highway. It was mid-afternoon, and they knew that commanders did not want the resupply convoy trying to negotiate Highway 8 in the dark. They figured they would go in at first light. That was okay with most of the crews, who preferred to give the combat teams at the interchanges more time to secure the highway.

Then Luu got a radio call from Captain Puckett. "We're going to spend the night in Baghdad," he said. "We need you to come up, bring all your fuel trucks, all your ammo trucks."

Luu wasn't expecting the order at this late juncture. "Are you kidding?" he asked.

"No, I'm not," Puckett said flatly. He paused and added, "By the way, the highway is still hot."

Luu and Puckett had a sort of running joke going between them, involving Luu's pleas during earlier thunder runs to have his guys included. Several times down south, Puckett had refused to include the support vehicles during combat missions. Some of Luu's guys were action junkies, and they wanted a taste of combat. Luu had thought he did, too. But now, with Puckett ordering them into the middle of the brigade's biggest fight of the war, he wasn't so sure.

"Hey," Puckett reminded Luu, "you wanted to play the game."

Luu laughed and said, right over the radio net, "Yeah, but I didn't want to play *this* game."

Luu walked down the convoy line, breaking the news to the drivers and gunners on the fuel and ammunition trucks. They seemed more surprised than afraid. Luu reviewed the rules of engagement—all the details about firing warning shots into the roadway and then into engine blocks if vehicles approached the convoy. Luu didn't expect his men to waste a lot of time on warning shots, given what had happened to the 3-15 resupply convoy. He told them not to be afraid to shoot at anything that seemed to be a threat. "If it looks suspicious," he said, "go ahead and light it up."

When Luu got back to his Humvee at the head of the convoy, he had a sudden worrying thought: What would happen to his bike if he got killed? He had a beautiful Harley-Davidson motorcycle back home. It was his prized possession. He didn't want to go into the fight without clearing up that little piece of business. He sat down with the guys inside his Humvee and gave them specific instructions. If he didn't make it, they were to make sure the bike was handed over to his best friend back in Fort Worth.

At the palace complex that afternoon, Lieutenant Colonel Flip deCamp had discussed his resupply needs with Colonel Perkins. DeCamp's tanks had been shut down for several hours, saving significant amounts of JP8 fuel. But with nightfall approaching, deCamp wanted his tanks to be able to maneuver if the Iraqis launched a counterattack in the dark. The tank battalions would not risk staying the night without the resupply convoys.

The only question now was when to launch them—and how to protect them. By mid-afternoon, deCamp thought the time had come to order his battalion's convoy up Highway 8. Perkins agreed, and he told deCamp to launch the package.

DeCamp decided that speed, not armor, was the convoy's best defense. He thought it was safer to go with wheeled vehicles, which could move faster than the tracked vehicles. For security, he would dispatch a scout platoon in armored Humvees mounted with .50-caliber machine guns. With just Humvees and trucks, the convoy could probably maintain a forty-five-mile-per-hour clip, fast enough to speed through the enemy gauntlet, with the .50-calibers laying down suppressive fire.

The officer in charge of coordinating the resupply run was Major Kent Rideout, the battalion's executive officer and deCamp's number two man. Rideout was posted in the driveway outside the Republican Palace, where Assassin Company had set up its tanks and Bradleys in a defensive perimeter. He radioed Captain Ed Ballanco, the S-4, or supply officer, who was now with the Task Force 4-64—the Tusker battalion—resupply convoy parked along Highway 8 just north of the new brigade TOC. Rideout told Ballanco that deCamp had decided to launch the convoy in order to get it to the palace before dark. "You're going with wheels only," he said.

Ballanco didn't like hearing that. He wanted to take armor along. There was a tank available—in fact, it was deCamp's command tank, HQ Six Six, nicknamed *Hannibal*. The mechanics had worked on it all night, trying to get a broken track repaired, and now it was finally ready to go. DeCamp had been forced to ride into Baghdad in a tank commanded by one of the company executive officers, which meant the battalion commander had been loading ammo and firing an M-240 while trying to direct the battle over the radio. Now, with deCamp's tank repaired and ready, Ballanco wanted to use it as a security escort.

Over the net, Ballanco asked Rideout: "You *do* know what happened to Three-Fifteen's LOGPAC?"—the logistical resupply package for Task Force 3-15, the China battalion. Ballanco had heard, incorrectly, that five men had been killed in the highway ambush of China's resupply convoy, not two.

"Just wanted to make sure you knew about that because we're going to go in and it's going to be hot all the way through," he told Rideout.

"Roger, I know that," Rideout said. "But we need that LOGPAC in here right away."

Ballanco considered just saying the hell with it, he'd take the tank anyway. It could keep up with the wheeled vehicles. Ballanco had argued with Rideout on previous occasions, and a couple of times he had just gone ahead and done things his way, regardless of what Rideout wanted. He and Rideout usually worked it out later. But now Ballanco decided to do it Rideout's way, to forget about the tank and do what he was told.

Ballanco had a long discussion with the captain in charge of the scout escorts about how to stagger the vehicles in the convoy. They decided to put scout Humvees at the front and rear, then blend the other scout Humvees into the convoy, each one protecting a pair of fuel and ammunition trucks. They made sure to separate the fuel trucks so that if one fueler was hit, it wouldn't trigger the explosion of another fueler. Ballanco would ride in the middle of the convoy, in his Humvee. It was a soft-skinned Humvee, but it had a .50-caliber mounted on top.

Then Ballanco was reminded that Rideout had told him earlier to leave his Humvee and ride in the engineer company commander's M113 armored personnel carrier. The carrier had three radios, versus just one radio in Ballanco's Humvee. Going in the M113 would give Ballanco better communications. The engineers, along with the mortar teams and other tracked vehicles, would be coming up separately from the main convoy, about twenty minutes behind.

Ballanco didn't like the idea. He was asking his drivers to go up Highway 8 in soft-skin fuel and ammo trucks. He'd look like a coward in front of his own men if he suddenly opted for the relative safety of an M113. And if he left his Humvee behind, he would be stuck inside the city without his own means of transportation and without all his gear. He would also have to leave behind his Humvee driver and gunner. Both men were begging Ballanco not to leave them. They were young and eager to get into the fight. Ballanco's gunner, Private Justin Morey, was eighteen. His driver, Specialist Christopher Wood, was twenty-one. To Ballanco, a ripe old twenty-nine, they seemed like kids. They hadn't seen much combat, and they didn't want to miss the pivotal battle of the war. They were hounding Ballanco: "Come on, sir, come on! Take us in!"

Finally Ballanco made the call. He was taking the Humvee. He tried to amuse himself with a morbid thought: if he ended up getting killed in a soft-skin vehicle after being ordered to ride in a personnel carrier, he'd have some explaining to do.

Ballanco was an independent type, a bit of a risk-taker. He had grown up as an air force brat, the son of a fighter pilot, and he had always wanted to be a fighter pilot himself. But in college, at Florida State, he decided to join the army ROTC, mainly because he thought the army offered more leadership possibilities. He was commissioned after graduating in 1996, and he welcomed the opportunity to serve in Iraq after his father had served in the first Gulf War.

Ballanco loved adventure—skiing, mountain climbing, orienteering. He was drawn to dangerous situations where men relied on one another for survival. He had felt a thrill that morning when he awoke at dawn to the sound of the Rogue and Tusker tanks and Bradleys thundering up the highway to Baghdad.

"It's an amazing thing to see men headed to fight a major battle," he wrote to his wife, Jeannette. "It sounds like training, and the guys do the same things they do in training, but they're on their way to fight and risk their lives. A wave of emotion overcame me. It's hard to describe. I felt proud for them and scared for them. I hoped that they all got through it OK.

"I think it's a strange thing to think to yourself, 'This is the day I could be killed,' and to know how dangerous your mission is. And yet they all still drove forward to Baghdad. I thought all these things in an instant— like I said, it's hard to explain. But there we were, invading the city of Baghdad. We knew the world was watching us."

Now Ballanco himself was headed into the city, jammed into the front seat of his Humvee, working the radio and pointing the barrel of his M-16 out the window. He was ready for whatever awaited him up the highway, but he couldn't stop wishing that he had brought the tank along with him.

Philip Luu's convoy had been rolling up Highway 8 for only a matter of minutes when the first small-arms rounds starting pinging off the asphalt. Green tracers were skipping off the roadway, little arcs of light streaking off into the milky haze. Gunmen were up on rooftops, firing down at the convoy from both sides of the highway. Almost every vehicle on the convoy returned fire—the Bradleys with coax, the .50-caliber gunners on top of the ammunition trucks and the Humvees, the front-seat passengers in the trucks and Humvees, and even the drivers, their automatic rifles braced in the crooks of their left arms. One of the drivers got so carried away that he accidentally shot out his side view mirror.

They were lighting up the rooftops and windows of any building where the gunners saw people with weapons. The big .50-caliber rounds went right through the walls, and Luu hoped that any families in the neighborhoods had had the good sense to flee.

With just two radios, there was no way for Luu to control the .50-caliber gunners. He had to trust them to maintain their assigned orientations and to avoid friendly fire. He was worried, too, about how he would handle a casualty or a debilitating hit on one of the vehicles. He had given very specific orders: keep the convoy moving. That was paramount. They would not stop to try to save a stricken vehicle. The rear vehicles would evacuate the crews and the wounded and leave the vehicle to burn. "Remember the cargo," Luu had told the drivers. "People in the city need that fuel and ammo."

The enemy fire was steady, but not as heavy as Luu had anticipated. And each time they sped into one of the interchanges held by the American combat teams, a strange thing happened. The firing stopped, like it had been turned off with a switch. It seemed to Luu that the combat teams were finally beginning to seize control of the interchanges.

At Objective Curly, the firefight had raged for more than eight hours straight, but there was a lull when the resupply convoy rolled through. The engineers had cleared the northbound lanes of wrecked suicide vehicles and other detritus. Luu could see that the fighting had been intense. There were dead Iraqis everywhere, their weapons flung to the side. He got a good look at China's five burning fuel and ammo trucks. They were still smoking. Luu thought, *Good God, this is worse than anything we've seen. This is serious.*

Just north of Curly, the convoy came under heavy fire. An RPG streaked in from the left side of the highway. Another one bounced off the asphalt between Luu's Humvee and the ammunition truck directly behind him. Luu kept thinking about the fuel trucks, and how a single RPG would create a raging bonfire—like the burning vehicles he had just passed at Curly.

Luu was up in the turret, manning the .50-caliber. To his left, he caught a glimpse of a man lying on his stomach next to a low building about 150 meters away. He saw a puff of white smoke, and then the glowing red nose of an RPG sailing past the Humvee. Luu pressed the butterfly triggers. As the officer in charge of putting together the ammunition for the support platoon, he had made sure that his guys got armor-piercing incendiary rounds, just like the tankers used. But instead of a tracer every fourth or fifth round, Luu made sure every single round was a tracer. That made it easier to walk the rounds to the target. These were bright red tracers, and Luu guided them straight into the man who had fired the RPG. It was like a straight line connecting him to the target.

"Hey, LT, you hit the guy!" his driver yelled.

"No shit," Luu said, and everybody inside the Humvee laughed. It wasn't funny, really, but they laughed, stoked up on adrenaline and fear. Luu had no particular feeling about killing the man. The Iraqi had tried to kill them. He was the enemy—a mortal threat, and Luu had eliminated him. It wasn't something that bothered him, even later, after he had time to reflect.

They kept firing until they reached the big spaghetti intersection where, again, the enemy fire ceased. And here, too, Luu saw evidence of a fierce firefight—enemy corpses, weapons, thousands of expended brass casings. It was a confusing interchange, and at one point the lead Bradley commander got lost. Luu got him on the radio, and the commander asked Luu to stand by for a minute while he checked his grid. The elevated ramp put the convoy at rooftop level, and Luu sat for what seemed like an eternity, waiting for someone to fire at them from the rooftops.

He was trying to get a reading on a commercial GPS device he carried—he preferred it to the military GPS Pluggers—when the Bradley commander radioed to say he was backing up. All the truck and Humvee drivers had to get into reverse and go back down the ramp. Luu got on the radio to his section sergeant in the last vehicle and told him to back up. The entire convoy inched back down the ramp. After a brief delay, the Bradley commander found the right ramp, and everybody rolled forward and down onto the Kindi Highway.

Suddenly Luu saw the silver arc of the twin sabers at the military reviewing stand, and he realized they were home free. They were pulling into the government complex, where the main roadways had been secured by tanks and Bradleys from Rogue and Tusker. Luu was surprised by how quickly they had made the trip. He had expected it to take forever.

When the convoy turned onto the parade field, just beyond the tomb of the unknown soldier, the Rogue tank crews rushed over to greet the support platoon. They were desperate for fuel and ammunition. Some of them were surprised to see the soft-skin Humvees and trucks. They had been told that no soft-skin vehicles were coming into the city. "You guys are crazy," one of the tankers told Luu.

The drivers got out and whooped and high-fived and punched one another's arms. They ran from truck to truck, inspecting the vehicles for battle damage. Every fuel and ammunition truck had arrived intact. Luu joked around with his driver, Private First Class Lundquist. The private was an antitobacco zealot. He delivered an antismoking lecture every time somebody lit up inside the Humvee. Now Luu offered him a pack of cigarettes. Lundquist took two and lit up.

As Ed Ballanco's convoy sped up Highway 8, trying to keep the column moving as fast as possible, he suddenly had to slow down. They had gone so fast that the lead scout Humvee had caught up with the tail end of Philip Luu's resupply convoy. Ballanco could hear the scouts cursing and bitching over the radio net. He didn't blame Rogue—he had good friends in the unit—but Rogue's tracked escort vehicles were slowing down Ballanco's wheeled vehicles.

Ballanco had to keep slowing down his convoy to let Luu's vehicles get ahead of them. He didn't want both convoys pulling into the friendly interchanges at the same time. But slowing down defeated the whole purpose of using only wheeled vehicles, and Ballanco kept wishing he had brought along the tank.

Ballanco was in the front passenger seat of his Humvee, talking over the radio to the scout captain and keeping the barrel of his M-16 aimed out the window. Shortly after passing through the interchange at Curly, RPG teams opened fire on the rear of the convoy. Several RPGs sailed past the last vehicle, one of the scouts' armored Humvees, and several small-arms rounds pinged off the Humvee frame. Farther up the column, one of the ammunition-truck drivers spotted an Iraqi gunman on the right side of the road. The driver couldn't fire on the man from the driver's window, so he pulled his automatic rifle inside and pointed it at the windshield. He fired a burst at the gunman, peppering the windshield with bullet holes.

Toward the front of the column, an Iraqi soldier ran up behind Ballanco's Humvee from the left flank and opened fire with an AK-47.

Ballanco didn't realize he was being shot at until he heard the driver of the truck behind him open fire with an M-4 carbine. The Iraqi went down in a spray of dust and dirt.

A few minutes later, Ballanco spotted a machine-gun nest on the left side. A machine gun opened fire on one of the fuelers ahead of his Humvee. Ballanco's gunner, Private Morey, saw it, too. Morey was in the turret, firing the .50-caliber at bunkers on the right side of the highway, thrilled to be in a firefight. The turret was broken. It couldn't be traversed, and the .50-caliber was locked into position over the right side. Morey was determined to fire at the machine-gun nest to the left, so he crawled up on the Humvee's roof. He grabbed the .50-caliber and twisted the gun mount so that the weapon swung over to the left side. Even with the gun now aimed properly, it was still a difficult shot because Morey had to fire between the fueler and a concrete support pillar, with the Humvee rolling at a fast clip. But he shot straight through the narrow gap and laced the machine-gun nest with several bursts of tracer fire. The enemy machine gun fell silent.

"Hee-yah!" Morey screamed. "I shot that motherfucker!"

Ballanco had to admit it: it was an impressive piece of shooting.

The convoy was now approaching Objective Larry, where Ballanco's buddy, Lieutenant Mike Martin, was posted. Martin was the executive officer for Captain Hubbard's Bravo Company. There was no enemy gunfire as Ballanco's Humvee and the rest of the convoy made its way through the interchange, but some of the gunners behind Ballanco were still shooting. Later, Martin told Ballanco that one of the convoy gunners had accidentally fired at one of the tanks posted at Larry. The tank wasn't hit, but Martin took the opportunity to chide the Tusker crews. For a long time afterward, Martin would joke with the guys from Tusker every time he saw them, performing a mock radio report: "Here comes a LOGPAC. Holy shit! It's Four–Sixty-four! Everybody get down!"

Ballanco didn't mind. He was glad to be alive. After passing Larry, the convoy came under fire only once more, from the right side. One of the Bradleys stationed on the roadway returned fire with its 25mm main gun, and the enemy guns stopped firing. The convoy threaded its way through the maze of ramps at Objective Moe and swung over a ramp and down into the city center, to their final destination at the four-head palace to resupply Tusker. Ballanco saw two Abrams tanks guarding the roadway and let out a sigh of relief. *We're good*, he thought. *We finally made it.*

For the first time that day, he let himself relax, and he felt the adrenaline drain from him.

There were cheers from the Cyclone Company crews at the Fourteen of July circle when the convoy rolled through at dusk. And when they finally pulled up in front of the Republican Palace, Ballanco was struck by the sheer size of the structure and the deep green of the grass and the brilliance of the blooming red roses. He had seen nothing but dust and desert for weeks. The tank crews came over to greet them, and Captain Phil Wolford, the Assassin Company commander, sought out Ballanco and shook his hand. The drivers and gunners climbed down from the trucks, whooping and cheering. They gave one another bear hugs and high fives. Ballanco thought it looked like an end-zone celebration at the Super Bowl. It was the support platoon's own little Super Bowl, and they all felt that they had achieved something special. They had delivered the goods, and every last man was still alive.

Wolford showed Ballanco the Iraqi machine-gun nests that had been blasted by Assassin's tanks that morning. The stiff corpses of Iraqi soldiers were still inside, caked with dark dried blood. Wolford gave Ballanco a quick tour of the palace, where a couple of soldiers had stumbled across crates of bottled Pepsis. Ballanco hauled the drinks over to his guys, and they sucked them down. These were their first sodas since leaving Kuwait. They went down like champagne.

By the time the Rogue and Tusker resupply convoys reached the palace complex, the remnants of China's resupply convoy had already been escorted to its destination along the Kindi Highway. The trucks set up a fuel and ammunition supply point in front of the Baath Party headquarters, which had been seized that morning by the Attack Company attached to Tusker. The headquarters was across the highway from the Sujud Palace, where Colonel Perkins had set up his tactical command post.

Captain Polsgrove worked on getting the fuel and ammunition ready for Captain Wright at Objective Moe. He felt badly that the supplies had not been delivered at Moe during the chaos of the firefight, and he made sure someone radioed the GPS grid for their position to First Sergeant Moser at Moe. The guys at Moe would have to figure out a way to come pick up their fuel and ammo. They had missed out on the "tailgate resupply," where the trucks came to them. Now they would have to pull off a "service station resupply" and go to the trucks and fuelers.

At the interchange, Moser still wasn't sure exactly what was left of his original resupply package because some of the trucks that had burned at Objective Curly had been designated for his combat team. He discussed it with Captain Wright. It was dusk now, and the fighting had eased considerably. The Iraqis didn't like to fight at night. They seemed to realize that the Americans held a distinct advantage with their night-vision goggles and thermal imaging systems. The Iraqis usually stopped shooting at nightfall to eat and rest and drink tea.

Just before dark, two suicide vehicles tried to breach the perimeter, but the bombs inside both cars exploded prematurely when hit with tank fire. After that, the Iraqis fired several RPGs straight into the air, dropping them down inside the perimeter like mortars. Then it was quiet.

Wright decided to send two tanks to the Baath Party headquarters to grab all the ammunition they could carry, and also to get a better understanding of how much fuel and ammunition was available. Sergeant First Class Ford was red on ammunition; he had fired almost nine hundred rounds from the .50-caliber machine gun. Ford's tank and a second tank from his platoon were dispatched for the two-and-a-half-kilometer ride down the highway. They drove through small-arms fire most of the way down.

At the resupply point, Ford discovered that there was enough fuel and ammunition for the entire combat team. He radioed Moser and asked him what he wanted. It was like calling home on a supply run to the hardware store.

"Yeah, Twenty-five Mike Mike ammo!" Moser told him. The Bradleys were low on main gun ammunition. "Grab as many cases of Twenty-five Mike Mike as you can carry."

Ford and his wingman filled up on fuel and stacked their turrets and bustle racks with ammunition boxes. There was no way to take back more fuel. The other two tanks would have to make their own trip.

When Ford and his wingman returned to Moe, Moser unloaded the Bradley ammunition onto his armored personnel carrier and delivered it to the Bradley platoons. Then he sent the remaining pair of tanks down the highway to the Baath Party headquarters to refuel and load up on ammunition.

Later that night, after the enemy fire had virtually ended, Moser rode his personnel carrier down to the resupply point, escorted by a Bradley and another M113. Their little convoy rounded up the remaining fuel and ammunition trucks and escorted them back to Objective Moe, where the Bradleys were refueled and the rest of the ammunition was unloaded.

Wright now believed his position was the strongest it had been since he pulled into the interchange that morning. His perimeter had held, and now he would be able to expand it. He had enough fuel and ammunition to last at least another day. He had mortars if he needed them, plus artillery. He owned Objective Moe now, and he knew the Iraqis would never get it back.

For Colonel Perkins, the delivery of the fuel and ammunition to Wright's combat team secured his hold on the city center and Highway 8. He had run a race against the night, and he had finally won it. All three combat teams on the highway were now resupplied and in control of their interchanges, where the firefights had eased for the night. Inside the city, the tank battalions were dug in with a fresh supply of fuel and ammunition. Perkins had been deeply worried all day, fearful that he would be trapped inside the city. Now the battle was playing out the way he had envisioned it over the past several months. His men were in for the night, and Perkins wasn't planning on ever sending them back out. If the Iraqis wanted their city back, they would have to come and fight for it.

S E V E N T E E N
COUNTERATTACK

Outside the Republican Palace, Major Kent Rideout helped set up the Tusker battalion command post in the main driveway, just off the building's towering northeast portico and beneath one of the bronze Saddam busts. Rideout had fought his way up Highway 8 inside a Bradley, and now its rear ramp had been lowered to serve as his makeshift communications center. As the executive officer, Rideout was responsible for coordinating what the military calls combat multipliers—artillery and mortars, fighter planes and helicopter gunships. He ran the command post.

Although it was surprisingly quiet around the palace on the afternoon of the seventh, Rideout was worried about the exposed seam between the Tusker and Rogue battalions. He feared the Iraqi soldiers and militiamen who had fled Assassin's charge into the palace compound would infiltrate back through the seam. Tusker now held the expanse of palace and government buildings from the Republican Palace west, past the bend in the Tigris, to the Sujud Palace and Baath Party headquarters—a stretch about four kilometers long. Rogue was securing the military parade grounds and reviewing stand, the tomb of the unknown soldier, the Rashid Hotel, the information ministry, Zawra Park, the Baghdad zoo, and the amusement park. But in between was a gap that ran east to the river, where a series of five bridges over the Tigris were not yet secured. Rogue's easternmost blocking positions were at least a couple of blocks from the bridges, and those units couldn't see whether enemy fighters were stealing across the river.

Rideout and Flip deCamp, the Tusker commander, thought Rogue should push all the way to the bridges to seal them. They feared the Iraqis would pour across to mount a counterattack. Both men relayed their concerns over the brigade net to Major Rick Nussio, Rogue's executive officer. Nussio understood their dilemma, but he couldn't spare any units to push to the bridges. Rogue was in a hell of a fight near the zoo—a bigger fight than anyone had anticipated. They were fighting off dismounts and suicide vehicles. If Nussio shifted units to the east, it would open a new, bigger seam to the west, where Rogue was now linked near the Baath Party headquarters with the China battalion. So he told deCamp and Rideout he was sorry, but he couldn't help with the bridges.

In addition to the bridges, Rideout was also worried about occasional enemy fire from the east bank of the Tigris. He had no idea what was over there. He had satellite imagery maps of only the west bank—the palace and government complex. The east bank had been designated as the area of operations for the U.S. Marines, who were still fighting their way north through the southeast corner of the city. Behind the palace, Tusker's scouts used their thermal sights to identify gunmen popping up out of fighting holes to fire across the river. Rideout had the scouts fire grenade launchers at the opposite bank. He wanted to suppress the enemy fire, but he didn't want to fire .50-caliber machine guns because the muzzle flashes and tracers would clearly identify the battalion's positions. The grenades managed to keep enemy fire to a minimum.

Rideout had a lot on his mind. He was an intense, driven officer. He could be brusque and short-tempered, and he had a reputation as a no-nonsense commander. But he was respected within the battalion as a soldier who knew his stuff, and one who demanded top performance from himself and others. That week, in particular, Rideout was a deeply troubled and conflicted man. He was haunted by a friendly fire incident, an accident three days earlier that had cost the battalion its first death in Iraq.

On April 4, on a narrow road about fifteen miles southeast of Baghdad, Rideout had been at the tail of an armored column attacking Iraqi positions. A Russian-made T-72 tank had just been destroyed, and the crews were watching it burn. Without telling anyone, a captain on the convoy, Ed Korn, climbed out of his armored vehicle and headed into a forest of date palms. Korn was not well known within the battalion; he had joined the unit just six days earlier. He was thirty-one, an energetic and enthusiastic Gulf War veteran who had volunteered for the Iraqi war in March and had rushed north to join the battalion in the southern Iraqi desert. Known to his friends as Jason, not Ed, Korn had told fellow soldiers on the ride up through the southern Iraqi desert that he was not going to let the fear of death hold him back, or paralyze him, once he got into combat.

It was hot on the fourth, and Korn was wearing just his flak vest over a brown T-shirt as he disappeared into the palms. He hadn't told anyone where he was going, or why—he may have been trying to scout enemy positions—but a sergeant got out and followed him. When Korn stumbled across a second T-72 camouflaged by palm fronds, he sent the sergeant back to the column to retrieve an antitank weapon.

From his vehicle, Rideout noticed a campfire just beyond the burning tank, well over two hundred meters away. A teapot was on the fire, and there were sleeping bags on the ground and chickens wandering around. Rideout assumed it was a campsite for Iraqi tank crews. Suddenly he saw someone near the campfire drop down, then stand up and hide behind the second T-72 tank. Rideout's driver, Specialist John Durst, saw him, too. Durst asked Rideout for permission to fire. Both men were convinced the man was an Iraqi tank crewman. "Engage," Rideout said.

Durst took aim and fired a single round from his M-16. The man went down. It was an incredible shot—the most amazing shot Rideout had ever seen. He slapped Durst on his helmet. "Great fucking shot!" he told him.

Next to Rideout's vehicle, a captain commanding a Bradley was scanning the area through thermal sights and spotted the second tank, just beyond the burning tank. He also saw the man Durst had hit. He was on the ground, his hand raised in the air. The captain ordered his gunner to destroy the tank to prevent it from firing on the column. Rounds from the 25mm main gun tore into the T-72, setting it aflame and sending ricochets tearing into the wounded man on the ground.

At that moment the sergeant who had accompanied Korn emerged from the tree line behind Rideout and yelled to the major: "Captain Korn is in the woods, sir!" He pointed to the trees.

Rideout couldn't believe it. "You have got to be fucking kidding me!" he said. He radioed a cease-fire order to get the attention of the Bradley commander, then raised his fist, the signal to the Bradley crew to stop firing.

Rideout's heart was pounding. He gathered up a few men and walked through the woods to the campsite. He hoped desperately that he would stumble across Korn along the way—that he would see the captain grinning and bullshitting about finding an enemy tank. But when they reached the campsite Rideout could tell that the dead man on the ground, his torso blown in half by the Bradley, was Ed Korn. His glasses were still on his face. It was the worst day of Rideout's long military career, and it weighed on him terribly. He knew he would have to live with it for the rest of his life.

Three days later, Korn's death was still a crushing weight as Rideout worked to solidify the battalion's positions around the Republican Palace. He had not slept in three days, and he was exhausted. Around 11 p.m., when things seemed at least somewhat under control, Rideout realized he needed to sleep for a couple of hours. He would be no good to anybody if he didn't get some rest. He went inside the palace and dragged a mattress from one of the bedrooms. He flopped it on the driveway outside, next to his Bradley, and fell into a light slumber.

Just before midnight, Rideout bolted upright. There was a huge explosion that reverberated off the palace walls. As Rideout leaped to his feet, still in his underwear, some of the officers who were awake started laughing at him. The engineers had just blown up a cache of enemy weapons and ammunition, but nobody had told Rideout. Now ammunition was cooking off and some of the palm trees were on fire. The whole city was probably awake. And if the enemy had been wondering where the Americans were, they certainly knew now.

Rideout was furious. "You guys are a bunch of idiots," he said. "You just gave our fucking position away. That's just super." He gave an order to stop blowing up weapons caches, then tried to go back to sleep.

It was the first chance in several days for members of the battalion to sleep. Lieutenant Colonel deCamp went inside the palace to catch a quick nap. He hadn't slept much over the past few days. Captain Ed Ballanco, who had brought up the fuel and ammunition convoy, also went inside the palace to try to get a couple of hours of sleep. He foraged through one of the bedrooms and found a bed and plopped down. He kept thinking how strange it was—how no one would ever believe it—that he was sleeping in Saddam Hussein's palace.

Phil Wolford's tank crews were beat, too. After nightfall, Wolford put four tanks on Ready Condition One—up and ready to fire, with all crewmen at their battle stations. He put the other tank crews on Ready Condition Two—ready to fight in fifteen minutes. Two crewmen on each tank would be able to catch quick naps, then switch with the other two crewmen assigned to scan through the thermals and monitor the radio. They had turned off their engines early that afternoon to conserve fuel.

Staff Sergeant Shawn Gibson had stood so long in his tank turret that his legs and feet had swollen grotesquely, and they throbbed with a searing pain. He was glad to get off his feet. He climbed up on the turret and lay flat on his back. He put his M-4 carbine next to him and lay his 9mm pistol across his chest. He didn't expect to fall asleep—he was notorious in the platoon for never sleeping. He always told his crew, "I'll sleep when I get home." Gibson was voluble and easygoing, a thirty-eight-year-old NCO who had spent almost seventeen years—nearly half his life—in the army. He was born in Philadelphia, but his mother had packed up the family and moved to Virginia when Gibson was seven to get away from drug gangs in North Philadelphia. A veteran of the first Gulf War, Gibson had a wife and three children anxiously awaiting his safe return from Iraq.

On this dark night, outside the palace, Gibson kept bolting upright every time he heard noises in the dark, but he was at least able to take the pressure off his swollen legs and feet. After stretching out for a while, the swelling subsided and the pain eased. Later on, unable to sleep, he crawled down next to the tank to relieve himself.

On the command tank, Wolford managed to get a radio call through to his good friend Captain Steve Barry from Cyclone Company. Barry was holding the Fourteenth of July traffic circle and bridge, just a kilometer west of the palace. The two commanders discussed the seam between their positions and Rogue's and the fact that neither of them had a clear picture of exactly where Rogue's guys were set up. Barry told Wolford it was fairly quiet at the circle, but he expected a counterattack at some point. Wolford agreed. "This can't be all there is," he said. "There's got to be a lot more."

When the time came for Wolford and his loader to take a break, they switched with the driver and gunner on Wolford's tank. Wolford hadn't taken his boots off for days. His feet were foul, and he wanted to air them out. He and his loader both took off their boots and stretched out on top of the tank. They fell asleep almost instantly.

Just beyond the northeast corner of the palace, Sergeant First Class Lustig had been posted on the perimeter with three other tanks from his platoon. The crews were watching the main palace road, known as Haifa Street, which broke sharply to the north and led through the palace complex to the foot of the Jumhuriya Bridge about one and a half kilometers away. Straight up the roadway, a few hundred meters away, Lustig could see a small stone archway that separated the main palace grounds from the rest of the palace complex.

By 3:20 a.m., Lustig had been down in the turret for about half an hour, scanning the roadway through the thermal imaging system while two of his crewmen dozed atop the tank. It was hot and stuffy inside, so Lustig climbed up through the hatch to get some fresh air. When he came back down and squinted again through the thermals, he saw the glowing green forms of two men several hundred meters away. They were casually strolling down the road toward the arch. Lustig thought they might be from the company's infantry platoon. The infantry was supposed to be posted on the beachfront behind the palace but, he thought, perhaps they had sent a patrol down the road without telling anyone.

Lustig looked again through the magnified thermals. The two men weren't wearing Kevlar helmets. He shook his head to clear his vision. He was afraid he had dozed off and was seeing things in his sleep. He looked again. He had the sights set on ten-power magnification, and now he could see that the two men were dressed in civilian clothes. They wore backpacks, with satchels strapped to their chests. They were carrying automatic rifles—and suddenly at least twenty more men came into view behind them, all of them carrying weapons.

Lustig told the two crewmen atop the tank to wake up and get to their positions inside the turret. "We've got enemy dismounts coming up the road," he whispered. The crewmen were slow to respond, so Lustig started cursing to get them to move. He got on the radio, trying to alert Captain Wolford back at the palace driveway. The captain was asleep on top of his tank, but his gunner was on the radio. The gunner heard Lustig whisper that dismounts were approaching. Lustig sounded angry with his crew. "There's gonna be a fuck load of trouble if these guys don't start getting down inside," he whispered over the radio.

Lustig looked through the thermals again. The men on the road had split into two groups, with a dozen or so moving through the trees on the left side of the road and another ten to fifteen advancing next to a two-meter wall on the right side. Lustig charged the .50-caliber machine gun, preparing it to fire. He saw one of the men handing out RPG grenades from a backpack. He got back on the radio.

By this time, Wolford had been shaken awake by his gunner. He leaped up in his stocking feet and put on his communications helmet. Lustig was still whispering, trying not to give away his position.

"I have about thirty to thirty-five dismounts walking down the road straight toward you," Lustig said.

"How far out are they—are they in RPG range?" Wolford asked.

"About five hundred meters."

"Okay, don't fire till I get the company ready," Wolford said. It would take a few minutes for the crews to get into position and start up the tank engines.

Wolford reached down to put on his boots—and he couldn't find them. He would have to command his company in his stocking feet. He got on the radio and issued orders to his platoon leaders. He wanted them to start their tanks all at once as soon as their crews were up and ready. Wolford knew the RPG teams would be able to identify the tanks the instant they turned over their big turbine engines, so it made sense to crank them all at once. The crews scrambled into position and Wolford gave a short countdown.

The tank engines roared to life. The gunmen on the roadway were only a couple hundred meters from Lustig's tank on the northeast perimeter when his driver, Private First Class Donte Pirl, cranked the engine. Pirl had just slammed his hatch shut when the tank was rocked by a thunderous explosion. An RPG had rocketed in from the front, exploding against the steel frame where the gun tube is attached to the turret.

Lustig heard Pirl scream. *Oh Christ,* he thought, *Pirl didn't get the hatch closed in time.* Then Pirl yelled that he was okay. He wanted to know how to position the tank. The turret was still locked up from a previous battle and would not traverse, so Pirl and Lustig had worked out a way to pivot the tank from side to side in order to position the main gun.

Lustig was climbing up to fire the .50-caliber machine gun from the cupola when another explosion jolted the tank. He ducked down. Something had slammed into the main gun tube. Lustig looked to see if any hydraulic fluid was leaking. There was nothing. The main cannon seemed fine. It was locked in the forward position, a multipurpose MPAT shell loaded in the breech. The RPG teams were moving closer. Lustig decided to fire the main gun, hoping to at least knock the gunmen off their feet with the concussion. He squeezed the cadillac triggers. The round exploded into the roadway, scattering some of the men.

But other fighters had managed to launch antitank rockets and more RPGs. One RPG slammed into the palace, just below one of the Saddam busts. The explosion jolted Kent Rideout awake. He leaped up from his mattress thinking, *That's no frigging engineer explosion.* Still in his underwear, he ran inside the hull of his Bradley to get on the radio. Then he realized he wasn't in uniform, so he hustled back and got dressed before getting back on the radio to help direct the fight.

Inside the palace, the exploding RPGs awakened Captain Ballanco in his darkened bedroom. He got dressed and rounded up two soldiers from the support platoon who had also taken refuge in the palace. Ballanco, fearing the palace had been overrun by Iraqis, told the soldiers to have their M-16s ready to fire. He slung his own M-16 across his back and took out his 9mm pistol so that he could hold the pistol in one hand and a flashlight in the other. He cursed his own stupidity for leaving his helmet outside.

The palace hallways were pitch black. The three men tiptoed down the marble hallways toward the northeast portico, one of two main palace entryways. But once they found the portico, they decided not to go outside for fear their own men would mistake them for infiltrating Iraqis and open fire. They backtracked, trying to find the southwest portico. Their footsteps echoed off the marble walls. They kept wandering down the wrong hallways, getting lost in the maze of corridors. It took ten minutes to find the portico. Ballanco peeked outside and caught a glimpse of Captain Rich Blenz, the support platoon leader, crouching down behind the fuel and ammunition trucks. He ran over and grabbed Blenz, followed by the other two soldiers.

Blenz was worried about friendly fire—that the support platoon drivers and mechanics would mistakenly fire on the tankers. Ballanco started to tell the support platoon guys to keep weapons tight, meaning not to fire unless a target has been clearly identified. But then he realized that they might not be familiar with the term, so he just told them: "Don't fire a round unless you know he's an enemy soldier." Ballanco wanted them to be wary, but also ready to open fire in order to keep the RPG teams away from the tankers. A single grenade fired into the fuel trucks might torch the whole line of vehicles clustered in the main palace driveway. The support platoon soldiers held their fire and let the tanks do the fighting. Rideout called on the radio and told Ballanco to make sure he protected the fuelers. Ballanco assured the major that he was on top of it.

At the opposite end of the palace, along the main roadway at the building's southwest corner, Shawn Gibson was down on the pavement next to his tank, squatting on the roadway. His pants were down and his rear was, literally, exposed.

From inside the tank, Gibson's loader yelled out, "Sergeant Gibson! Where you at?" He had just heard Lustig's whispered warning over the radio.

"I'm using the bathroom!" Gibson hollered.

"Hurry up! Here they come! They're coming!"

"What?"

An RPG flashed through the night, punching straight through a blue metal road sign on the palace road. It shot directly over Gibson's head and exploded against the side of his tank, just above the left front fuel cell. Gibson dove to the pavement and crawled under the tank. He could hear bullets pinging off the steel skirts. He hid behind the road wheels, hitching up his pants, and pulled out his 9mm pistol. He didn't know who was firing at him or where they were. He could hear his gunner firing the tank's coax. He screamed up at him, "Keep shooting at those guys! I'm going to come up there as soon as I hear a break in the fire!"

Gibson waited a few moments until the enemy fire seemed to wane. He climbed into the commander's hatch and got on the radio to Lieutenant Maurice Middleton, the platoon leader who had led the company's charge up Highway 8. Gibson was worried about a road that ran down the southwest side of the palace to the riverbank. He was afraid enemy soldiers had infiltrated the roadway. His tank was exposed from that direction. Gibson knew the company's infantry platoon had been posted somewhere along the shoreline behind the road, but he wasn't sure they were still back there. He didn't want to fire on them by mistake.

"Let me know where those guys are at, because if I see somebody coming down that road, I'm going to take them out," Gibson said.

Middleton wasn't sure, either, so he radioed Wolford and found out that the infantry was still behind the palace. "They're still down there," Middleton told Gibson. "If you see somebody running across that road, it's them. So don't shoot."

Gibson was still worried about his rear flank, and still disoriented. He focused his .50-caliber machine gun on what he assumed were RPG teams on the far roadway, and he had his gunner lay down suppressive fire with the coax. He didn't want to use the main gun with the tanks from Lustig's platoon so close by.

Just down the roadway, Middleton was still getting his crew together. When the RPG slammed into Gibson's tank nearby, Middleton had been in the commander's hatch of his tank. His loader had been jarred awake, and was still half asleep as he leaped into his hatch. Something on his Nomex jumpsuit caught on the hatch and he was left dangling in the turret, screaming for help. Middleton thought he had been shot. The gunner reached up and yanked the loader inside, ripping his entire jumpsuit right off him. The loader fought for the next several hours wearing just his boxer shorts, tanker's vest, a T-shirt, and combat boots.

The platoon commanded by Lieutenant Jason Redmon had all four tanks on Readiness Condition Two, with two men up and two down. The crews were scrambling now. Redmon was young and enthusiastic, a 2001 graduate of Middle Tennessee State University with short-cropped blond hair and a slight gap between his front teeth that gave him a wholesome, boy-next-door look. He heard the first two RPGs slam into Lustig's tank on the far end of the perimeter and tried to get Captain Wolford on the radio. He couldn't make contact. He tried Middleton. No luck. Then he heard Lustig say he'd been hit. Redmon wasn't sure if Lustig meant himself or just his tank. For an instant he thought, *Oh, my God, they're coming down and killing us all.*

Wolford wasn't available on the radio because he and his crew were trying to get his tank to start. They had been having problems with bad batteries for several days, but they had been unable to locate replacements. The slow and spotty supply lines had been a chronic problem the entire war. The crews had learned to either bring their own replacement parts or horse-trade with other crews.

Wolford's gunner and driver were yelling at each other, trying to get the tank started. They were under fire. Lustig's tank had just been hit twice, and RPGs were exploding into the roadway and up against the palace walls. Wolford had just been on the radio to Lustig, trying to get a read on the enemy, and now his tank was stalled and his crew was bickering. His feet were hurting. He had finally found a pair of boots to put on, but they belonged to his loader.

"Listen!" he screamed. "Shut the fuck up! Let's go!"

The company executive officer pulled up in his tank and tossed out his slave cables. They were like jumper cables—they connected one tank battery to another. The two crews managed to hook up the cables under fire and get the company commander's tank started.

Now Wolford was able to function properly. He realized the RPG teams had seized control of the fight. He had never seen the Iraqis lay down such an effective volume of fire. They were really taking it to his men, and at the moment Wolford had only two tanks in the fight—Lustig's and the tank of Lustig's wingman, Staff Sergeant Kennith Leverette.

But then Gibson opened up, followed by Redmon. Wolford radioed Lieutenant Middleton and told him to pull up to support Lustig and Leverette. He also called Lieutenant Jeff McFarland, whose Bradley infantry platoon was still manning the riverbank behind the palace. Wolford ordered McFarland to bring his Bradleys to the front of the palace. He knew he would need the infantry to clear the woods across the road. Some of the RPG teams had fled into the woods to escape fire from the tanks.

Lustig and his driver had managed to position their tank so that the main gun tube was pointed down the roadway. The RPG teams on the right side of the road had moved so close that they were now trapped between the tanks and the two-meter wall that ran down the right side. Lustig's gunner fired several main gun rounds and Lustig worked the .50-caliber. Several gunmen went down, and the others scattered.

Lustig thought they were retreating back to the small stone arch about three hundred meters up the road. He wasn't certain. He had spent so much time squinting through the bright thermals that he had become night-blind. When he tried to look out from the top of the cupola, everything was black. There was no moon, no streetlights. He had to keep ducking back down and looking through the thermals.

Wolford radioed Lustig and told him to push forward toward the small arch to get a better idea of how many fighters they were up against. He told him that the infantrymen were now on the ground, moving through the wood line to the left of the roadway. Wolford had ordered them to clear the woods on foot, and he wanted to make sure Lustig didn't fire in their direction.

At the arch, Lustig was able to see through an opening in the wall along the right side of the road. Men carrying AK-47s and RPGs were moving around, slowly and deliberately, apparently unaware that an American tank was moving up behind them. Lustig's gunner asked for permission to fire on them, but Lustig told him, "No, wait. These guys are going to walk right into us." He put the targeting reticle on the sidewalk and roadway just in front of the opening in the wall. Moments later, four of the men walked through the opening and onto the roadway. Lustig squeezed the triggers and all four men went down, torn apart by a blast of coax.

Wolford and Lustig had some of the crewmen toss grenades over the wall to kill or maim anyone hiding behind it. They didn't want RPG teams sneaking out from behind the wall later to fire at the tanks' rear ends. Wolford believed in using every weapon available to keep dismounts away from tank crews. He had often fired his automatic rifle and even his pistol from the commander's hatch. He had lobbed so many grenades into trees and shrubbery down south that Kent Rideout had nicknamed him Hedgerow Phil.

Wolford brought up more tanks from the palace. He swung his gun tube over the left side and told McFarland, the infantry commander, to clear everything behind the tube. The tank would roll slowly up the road, guiding McFarland and his men as they cleared the woods. The infantrymen went at it with methodical precision, pumping automatic-rifle rounds into each flimsy bunker and fighting hole, then finishing things off with grenades. It took them at least forty-five minutes to clear the wood line, killing some of the gunmen who sought refuge there and sending the others fleeing north toward the Jumhuriya Bridge.

One of the gunmen crawled out of a bunker on the left side of the road, ahead of the advancing infantry. He was holding an RPG launcher. The company executive officer, Lieutenant Mark Tomlinson, spotted him from the commander's hatch of his tank. He radioed Wolford and asked, "What do you want me to do?"

"Kill him," Wolford said.

Tomlinson opened up with coax, killing the man where he lay.

Wolford came to a stop. He believed he had now eliminated the immediate threat to the battalion command post at the palace by securing the roadway and woods between his position and the front of the palace. He called Lieutenant Redmon and told him to push forward past the small arch with his platoon of four tanks.

As Redmon rolled up the roadway, he could see that the infantry-men were flushing more gunmen out of the woods and onto the road. His gunner, Sergeant John Heath, saw the outline of two men through his thermal sights. They were about a hundred meters away.

"Sir," he said to Redmon, "do you see this shit?"

"Oh, yeah," Redmon said. He told Heath to wait until the two men moved closer together. Heath was feeling anxious. He had survived the thunder run up Highway 8 the previous morning, and now he had been thrown straight into another firefight. He had just blown a man apart with his coax, and he was ready to kill more of them. He had to. He had promised his wife that he wouldn't get killed. She had pleaded with him, saying, "You better be careful. I don't want you to get your ass blown up. I don't want to have to explain to our children what happened to you." Heath was determined to keep his promise, to eliminate any threat as quickly as possible.

Redmon waited a few moments, then gave the order to fire. Heath launched a HEAT round that incinerated the two men. He couldn't see them through the thermals anymore. They had evaporated.

They pushed forward, unleashing HEAT rounds into every bunker they saw. There were government buildings on the sides of this section of Haifa Street, and snipers were firing down from some of the rooftops and windows. All four tanks in Redmon's platoon were firing—coax, .50-caliber, main gun rounds, through the windows and into the rooftops. Heath put an IMPAT round into a concrete bunker where he had seen a gunman crouching. He was shocked to see the man crawl out from the spray of white smoke and pulverized concrete, blood oozing from his mouth and ears. Heath left him there. An infantryman came up from behind, strapped plastic handcuffs on the wounded man, and put him in a Bradley to be transported for medical treatment.

The platoon came to an intersection about six hundred meters north of the small arch. Redmon saw a small blue guard booth in the median. Two men were crouched behind it. He saw a puff of white smoke and heard a loud screech. An RPG slammed into the tank's left front ballistic skirt, rocking the crew inside. Heath tried to put the targeting reticle on the booth; it was too close to get a range. He squeezed the trigger anyway, and an IMPAT blew out the bottom of the booth. Redmon couldn't see either man, but he assumed they were dead.

At least a dozen more fighters appeared at the intersection, trying to set up to fire RPGs. Sergeant First Class Phillip Cornell, a tank commander and platoon sergeant in Redmon's platoon, saw a young man wearing a red flannel shirt and work boots emerge from the shrubbery and launch an RPG. The round flew over the back of Redmon's tank and exploded against a second guard booth. Heath fired a main gun round that sent the man flying. Cornell looked back and saw that the gunman had survived—he had been bowled over and bloodied by the concussion.

Redmon radioed Wolford to let him know about the heavy contact. The captain decided to push forward to the intersection with more tanks. Every tank that arrived opened fire, but it still took another twenty minutes to clear the intersection and the bunkers and buildings around it. The intensity of the fire set some of the date palms ablaze.

It was nearly dawn now. Assassin Company had been fighting, off and on, almost three hours. Wolford suspected that the fighters he was seeing were just an advance guard. He was afraid there were many more up near the Jumhuriya Bridge, which lay at the far eastern end of the unsecured gap between the Rogue and Tusker battalions. He radioed Lieutenant Middleton and told him to take his platoon farther north to get a look at the big intersection where Yafa Street rose up to meet the foot of the bridge. The company was now back in regular formation, with Middleton in the lead.

Middleton moved to within less than a kilometer of the towering stone arch that separated the palace and government complex from the intersection. Through his magnified sights, he could tell that the arch was very similar to the arch that Staff Sergeant Gibson had smashed through the previous morning at the western entrance to the complex. And, like the western arch, the top of this arch was defended by what appeared to be either antiaircraft guns or heavy machine guns.

On the far side of the arch, a remarkable scene was unfolding. Middleton had never seen anything like it. The entire intersection was filling up with vehicles and soldiers and equipment. Vehicles were speeding across the bridge—sedans, SUVs, taxis, buses, motorcycles, military trucks—and dropping off soldiers and gunmen in civilian clothes. There was a network of bunkers in two city parks north and west of the intersection. The bridge ramp and intersection appeared to be part of an elaborate set of military fortifications.

Middleton got on the radio to Wolford. "Assassin Six, this is Red One. Sir, I've identified—" he said, and then he paused. Wolford thought he'd been hit.

"Red One, Assassin Six? Red One, Assassin Six," Wolford said, trying to raise Middleton.

The lieutenant's voice came back over the net. "Sir, I have a shitload of vehicles up here dropping dismounts all over that intersection to the north. They're all over the place," he said.

At that moment, Wolford realized that a massive Iraqi counterattack was being mounted. His and Flip deCamp's fears that the Iraqis would capitalize on the unsecured gap leading to the bridge had been realized. Wolford radioed deCamp back at the palace command post and described the situation.

"Sir, we've got to seal that bridge right now," he said. "I've got to make it to that bridge, through that intersection, because if we don't, they're just going to keep loading up and coming at us all day long."

DeCamp agreed. He was concerned that the Iraqis would move west and then south to try to outflank Wolford's tank company by exploiting the seam. He told Wolford to move forward and try to take control of the intersection and the western end of the bridge. Wolford wanted to soften up the intersection before he attacked. He requested a mortar suppression-fire mission from the mortar platoon set up on the palace lawn, then radioed Middleton to warn him to have his crews button up. The mortar rounds exploded on the southeast corner of the intersection, next to a ten-story redbrick building that housed the Ministry of Planning. Wolford could hear the explosions and could see gray smoke drifting skyward. He called for an adjustment, sending a second volley of mortar rounds exploding north of the intersection, into the bunker complex in the park.

At about 6:45 a.m., with the sun rising up over the Tigris, Wolford ordered Middleton's platoon to lead the company into the intersection. The mortar mission had just ended. Middleton's gunner fired a HEAT round into the metal gates attached to the arch, blasting them open. The tank crashed through the wreckage, followed by the rest of his platoon, with Captain Wolford right behind them.

The tankers of Assassin Company did not know—they could not have known—all that awaited them at the foot of the Jumhuriya Bridge.

E I G H T E E N
THE BRIDGE

As Maurice Middleton's lead tank crashed through the ruined metal gates of the palace complex and into the Yafa Street intersection, the first thing he saw was a recoilless rifle, aimed right at him. He happened to have an MPAT round in the tube, and he let it fly. The big truck-mounted recoilless rifle exploded and burned as the multipurpose round penetrated its steel armor and detonated. It was like some sort of trip wire that set off what sounded like a series of thunderclaps. Gunfire and grenades and rockets erupted from all directions—from the park bunkers straight in front of Middleton, from street-side bunkers to his far left, from a three-story building to the northwest, from the foot of the bridge to his right, and from the looming red Ministry of Planning building to his far right. It was like driving into a hailstorm. Middleton realized that he was surrounded—and he hadn't even set up his platoon yet.

On the second Assassin tank through, Shawn Gibson rolled up over a high median strip in the middle of the intersection. Machine-gun fire was ricocheting off his turret, an insistent metallic hammering. His driver swung the tank hard to the right, trying to get it into position facing east toward the bridge to form a tight arc, with Middleton to his left rear. Gibson heard the loud kick of a recoilless rifle somewhere nearby, and he was afraid one of the cannon blasts would hit his rear grille and disable his tank right in the middle of the intersection.

On the third tank, Jonathan Lustig punched through the arch and swung his tank to the west, where his locked-up turret could fire down Yafa Street. He set up to form a tight circle next to the two lead tanks, with Kennith Leverette's trail tank completing the ring behind him, to the southwest corner of the intersection. It crossed Lustig's mind that they were circling up like Custer's last stand, surrounded and under assault. He had never seen the Iraqis produce such a withering volume of fire—not during the desert firefights down south, and not on the thunder run the previous morning. It seemed well coordinated, and nothing like the wild, scattershot attacks on the highway or the desperate volleys from the bunkers during Assassin's charge to the palace. The Iraqis were bringing in artillery and mortars. Mortar rounds were crashing down onto the pavement in front of him. Some of them were duds, and Lustig saw one round cartwheel past his turret, bounce off a light pole, and go spinning down the roadway.

Lustig felt disoriented. He had been up all night, scanning the thermals, fighting his way up Haifa Street, killing and killing. Now he was surrounded, taking fire from ground level, from bunkers belowground, and from snipers and RPG teams on the rooftops. It was a three-dimensional attack, the kind of lethal urban trap that traditional army doctrine often cited as a reason not to bring tanks into a city. Lustig dropped down in the turret to talk face-to-face with his gunner and loader. "Men, I hope this gets over with quick because it's starting to get dark and I damned sure don't want to be sitting at this intersection at night," he told them. They stared back at him. It wasn't getting dark. It was just past daybreak. Lustig thought he had been fighting all day. Now he realized he had been at it for only a few hours, and that the real fight was just beginning.

As the platoon got into position, Captain Wolford pulled his tank into the center of the intersection. He was shocked by the rate of enemy fire and by the way the Iraqis were able to concentrate it on his tanks. They were pouring so much fire on the tight little circle that some of the rounds were flying past the tanks and hitting Iraqi soldiers in the bunkers dug into the parks. But the rounds were also banging against the tanks, gouging out holes in the thick steel armor and blowing out some of the vision blocks. The tank crews could hear the hollow pop of streetlights exploding above them.

On the northwest corner was a multistory apartment building where RPG teams and snipers were running from window to window. Each time they fired, the windows were marked by flashes and swirls of gray smoke. Wolford radioed Lustig and said, "You better give that building some love."

Lustig had his driver pivot-steer—holding one side of the driver's handle to lock up one track in order to pivot on it—so that the gun tube was pointed at the building. He elevated and fired five quick main gun rounds, the loader shoving fresh shells into the breech after each recoil. The building shuddered, but the fire from the northwest didn't stop. Lustig was impressed, despite his fear and anxiety. The Iraqis were relentless. They were standing and fighting.

The crews were expending huge loads of ammunition—.50-caliber, coax, M-240, machine-gun, and main gun rounds. They were setting vehicles and buildings on fire, and spirals of black smoke were now obscuring the intersection. Wolford had intended to try to seal all four roads and then expand his perimeter, but that wasn't possible now. It was all he could do to hold his position in the middle of the intersection.

Wolford called up the infantry platoon, which pushed through the intersection and set up on the north end, facing the park. Then Wolford got on the radio to Lieutenant Redmon, who was still south of the main arch with his platoon. "I need you up here right now!" he told him. "Haul ass, get up here!"

Redmon led the platoon into the intersection, the incoming rounds skittering off all four tanks. He saw the four Bradleys from the infantry platoon in a tight half-moon formation at the edge of the two parks, just north of Middleton's tank. Redmon swung hard to the right and set up past Gibson, toward the foot of the bridge, with the Ministry of Planning on his right.

The entire planning building was infested with snipers and RPG teams. Redmon could see them firing from windows and the rooftop. In the commander's hatch of the tank next to him, Staff Sergeant Michael Lucas saw a sniper in an upper window firing down on Redmon. Lucas, twenty-nine, had been in firefights down south, but nothing as intense as this. He had a wife and two young sons. His wife was so worried about him that she couldn't bring herself to watch TV newscasts about the war. Lucas was worried, too, and terrified, though he didn't tell his wife until much later.

When he saw the sniper, Lucas reacted without conscious thought. His training overcame his fear. He traversed the turret over and up. He fired a main gun round that tore into the window in a flash of flame and smoke. The sniper's legs were blown back into the room. His torso toppled out the window and landed somewhere on the pavement below.

To the west, Wolford was trying to mount an effective volume of fire. He believed volume of fire was the key to winning any firefight. The side that builds effective fire the quickest will prevail. But in this case, the enemy had the upper hand. The Iraqis had mounted their volume of fire faster, and it was just as effective as Wolford's tanks. Two bunkers at the edge of the park were putting down a particularly heavy flow of fire, and Wolford was trying to get his tanks to focus on them.

He radioed back to the battalion command post at the palace with a situation report. "I'm getting hammered up here," he said. Major Rideout heard the frustration and agitation in Wolford's voice, and that concerned him. Wolford was usually calm and even-tempered. If *he* was getting riled up, Rideout thought, the situation must be getting desperate. Rideout was worried that Wolford didn't have enough firepower and was in danger of being overrun. He radioed Colonel Perkins and asked for permission to blow up the Jumhuriya Bridge—and the two bridges north of it—to cut off the flow of enemy reinforcements. Perkins told him he would have to get clearance from higher command.

At the intersection, Wolford had already fired more than five hundred rounds of .50-caliber ammunition in just five minutes, and now he needed to reload. He screamed down at his loader to hand up another box of ammunition. The loader had a stricken look. "Sir, get down in the tank!" he yelled. He had just seen more than two dozen automatic-rifle rounds ricochet off the tank's skirts. The Iraqis were walking the rounds right up the pavement to the tank.

Wolford felt something slam into his neck. It was hard and heavy, like a blow from a metal baseball bat. His head snapped back and smacked against the hatch. He tumbled down into the turret, unconscious. The loader looked at the captain's slack face and got on the battalion net. "Assassin Six is down! He's been hit!" he said.

The report sent a shock wave through the company. When a commander goes down—especially a popular and dynamic commander like Wolford—there is a brief moment of paralysis and confusion as his soldiers try to come to grips with the loss. Wolford's crews kept firing, but in a suspended way, waiting and wondering, listening on the net for more information and for guidance. Wolford had been in charge of the entire fight, and now he was down.

Wolford's loader checked him for wounds. There was no blood— just a red welt on the captain's neck. Wolford was breathing and muttering, "Holy shit . . . holy shit." Finally he mumbled, "I'm all right, I'm all right." He was stunned and disoriented. He looked down in his lap and saw an expended .50-caliber brass ammunition jacket. Something had hit the brass as it lay on the turret, sending it whistling into Wolford's neck. The blow had briefly knocked him unconscious, but now he was coming out of it.

"I'm all right, I'm all right," he said again. "Let's go." He climbed up into the turret to get back on the .50-caliber. It was dented from the small-arms fire. Wolford tried to fire it but the gun was jammed.

To Wolford's east, closer to the foot of the bridge, Sergeant First Class Phillip Cornell had set up his tank behind Redmon, his platoon leader. Cornell was the platoon sergeant. He was thirty-four, a Gulf War veteran from Orlando, Florida, with a wife and eight-year-old son. He was garrulous and extroverted, with stiff red hair and a thin red mustache. His narrow face was often creased with a wry smile, as if he were about to relate a funny story.

Cornell had seen Wolford go down in the hatch and had ordered his driver to back up. He wanted to get over and help cover the captain's tank. He was up in the cupola, trying to direct the driver while struggling to get his .50-caliber elevated to fire into the planning ministry. As the tank turned, he saw muzzle flashes erupting from behind palm trees in the park to the north. He yelled to his gunner, "Come left! Come left!" trying to get him to fire into the trees.

In the middle of the intersection, Lustig saw Cornell standing up in his cupola, exposed to fire. He said to his crew, "Hey, that guy's going to get hit if he doesn't get his ass down inside." Cornell liked to be up and out of the hatch, where he could get a clear look at targets and help direct fire.

As Cornell was shouting instructions to his gunner, something exploded against the front of his tank. Hot shrapnel ripped through the machine-gun mount and tore into Cornell's chest. He was wearing a tanker's vest, which is smaller and lighter than the standard body armor worn by infantrymen. A shard sliced through the base of his throat, just above the top of the vest, and tunneled down through his chest. Another piece of shrapnel tore a hunk of flesh from his elbow. The blows slammed Cornell down into the turret. For an instant he thought something had smacked into his vest, and he started to say something. But then he saw blood spurt from his chest and splatter his gunner, Sergeant Paul Harris. Cornell thought, *Oh, damn, this is serious.*

Harris knew he had to get pressure on the wound right away. It was flowing like a geyser. He looked around and spotted a rag. He grabbed it and pressed it against Cornell's chest, hard. Even in his pain and terror, Cornell was mortified. The rag was filthy. It was smeared with grease and oil. What the hell kind of infection was *that* going to cause? Then he had another odd thought: *This tank is going to be hell to clean.* The crews had been told when they were issued their tanks in Kuwait that they would be required to turn them in as clean as they had found them. Cornell envisioned spending days trying to get all the blood out.

Harris rummaged around inside the turret and found the first-aid kit. He pulled out a compression bandage and replaced the dirty rag, stanching the surge of blood. Cornell's feet felt warm and wet. His boots had filled with blood.

Cornell's loader that day was Staff Sergeant Greg Samson. Normally, a tank's loader is the most inexperienced man on the four-man crew. But Samson was a veteran NCO who was normally a tank commander. He instantly took control of Cornell's tank, giving the crew a swift, seamless change of command. Samson got on the radio and said, "Sergeant Cornell is hit!"

Lieutenant Redmon asked how bad it was.

"It's pretty fucking bad," Samson said. Cornell was down and bleeding.

Redmon radioed Wolford and said, "White Four just got hit. Looks like it's in the chest. Looks pretty fucking bad."

Wolford was still groggy, but he was able to order Redmon to mount a medical evacuation back to the aid station near the palace. Redmon knew what to do. The company had trained over and over on medevac procedures. He had two tanks back up to form a protective wall, then ordered Samson to pull his tank back through the arch and on to the aid station. Under fire, escorted by a second tank, Samson directed the driver through the arch, sped down Haifa Street, and got Cornell loaded into an ambulance back near the palace. DeCamp rushed up from the palace to the ambulance exchange point, for he believed it was important for a wounded man to see his battalion commander. He was startled by Cornell's pale and bloodless look, though the sergeant was still conscious and talking.

At the intersection, Wolford was back up in the cupola, still unable to fire his .50-caliber. He was trying to get his gunner to fire the coax into the two troublesome bunkers to his left, at the edge of the park. The gunner was focused on a building where soldiers were running back and forth and firing. Wolford was getting irritated. He couldn't seem to get the gunner's full attention.

"Listen to me!" he screamed. "Left! Left! Left!"

"I'm right there, sir," the gunner said.

He still wasn't hitting the bunkers. "No, I said left! Left!"

Someone was firing into the bunkers, but it wasn't Wolford's tank. The captain looked over and saw Private First Class Synquoiry Smith, the loader on Sergeant Gibson's tank. Smith was firing his M-240 machine gun into the bunkers.

Wolford yelled at Smith. He didn't bother with the radio. Smith was close enough to hear him. "Keep firing! Stay on those bunkers! Stay on 'em!"

Gibson heard Wolford yell something and saw him pointing wildly. He assumed the captain wanted more fire directed at the bunkers, but Smith was already right on them. He was pounding away so hard on the M-240, in fact, that he fired off all his ammunition. Smith dropped down into the turret, grabbed more rounds, and popped back up to reload. Gibson heard Smith yelp and shout, "Sergeant Gibson, I'm hit!"

A bullet had ricocheted off the M-240 gun mount and sliced into Smith's upper arm. He dropped straight down into the turret. "Smitty!" Gibson screamed. He went down after him and saw that his face was smeared with blood. He wiped at it, trying to locate the wound.

"It's not my face—it's my arm," Smith said. He spoke calmly, as if he were giving someone traffic directions.

Gibson found the bright red wound in Smith's arm and grabbed the first-aid kit. He applied a pressure dressing, squeezing Smith's arm with his left hand while he reached up and fired the .50-caliber machine gun with his right hand, using the elevation handle. They were still taking fire from the bunkers.

As Gibson fired, Smith broke free from his grasp. He climbed back into the loader's hatch with a 9mm pistol in his hand and started pumping rounds toward the bunkers. He was cursing and screaming. He emptied the clip, then dropped back down to reload. The tank rocked and he lost his grip on the gun. It tumbled to the turret floor. Before Smith could retrieve it, the gun was crushed as Gibson traversed the turret. Smith cursed again.

To Gibson's left, Wolford had given up trying to get his gunner to locate the bunkers. He hit the override switch, giving himself control of the main gun and the coax. He laced the bunkers with coax, backed by

Gibson's spray from his .50-caliber. The return fire from the bunkers eased long enough for Wolford to fire an MPAT round into each of the bunkers, effectively destroying them.

Gibson stopped firing and got on the radio to tell Middleton that Smith had been hit. "I got to get him back to the palace," he said. Middleton radioed Wolford and said, "Red Two Lima has been hit."

"Dammit, holy shit!" Wolford yelled. They were getting pounded. He had taken two casualties. He had already lost two tanks to medevac Cornell, and now he was losing Gibson's tank as it pulled away through the arch to medevac Smith. The company had still not managed to mount an effective volume of fire. Even after the tanks had pounded buildings and bunkers with main gun rounds, and had expended thousands of rounds of .50-caliber and coax, the Iraqis were still returning effective fire. If anything, their rate of fire was intensifying as more reinforcements poured across the bridge. And Wolford's crews were running low on ammunition; they had been fighting since 3:30 a.m. Lustig's tank alone had fired eight thousand rounds of M-240 and coax ammunition, and nine hundred rounds of .50-caliber.

They were taking more and more enemy mortars now. Wolford had already called in seven mortar missions of his own from the crews on the palace lawn. The rounds had slammed down north of the intersection, in the grassy areas of both parks, where the bunkers were concentrated. Wolford couldn't tell how much damage the mortars had done, but it was obvious that they had not significantly reduced the rate of fire from the bunkers.

Wolford realized that the situation was getting out of control. If he stayed much longer, he was going to take more casualties—probably KIAs. He decided to pull out. He would call in mortars and artillery and close air support to pound the bunkers and take down the buildings. He radioed Lieutenant Colonel deCamp and told him that the situation was untenable. He could no longer hold the intersection.

DeCamp didn't try to second-guess him. He trusted Wolford's judgment. He told him to withdraw.

Wolford gave the order over the company net. He wanted the crews to retreat in an orderly fashion. Retreats can be dangerous and chaotic; sometimes the worst casualties come when units are desperately trying to withdraw from a fight. Wolford told Redmon's platoon to go first, because it was down to two tanks, followed by McFarland's infantry platoon and then Middleton's platoon.

The retreat went smoothly until only Wolford, Middleton, and Lustig were left in the middle of the intersection. As Wolford prepared to move out, an RPG exploded near the front of his tank. He saw an RPG team in the park, moving toward him. With his .50-caliber still jammed, he had to move his tank back so that his gunner could fire toward the park.

"Back up! Back up!" he yelled to his driver.

The driver backed straight into Lustig's tank with a heavy jolt. The two tanks locked tracks.

"Shit!" Wolford shouted. He asked his gunner what he thought; the gunner was quite knowledgeable about the M1A1 Abrams. He wasn't sure. "I don't know if we're going to get off of here without popping track," Wolford said. The gunner said he didn't think so, either.

Wolford asked Lustig what he could see. "I can see the whole bottom of your tank," Lustig told him. "You have to pull off."

They were taking heavy fire now. Every Iraqi soldier at the intersection seemed to be focusing on them, especially from the bunkers in the park. Middleton pulled his tank in front of Wolford and Lustig, directly in the line of fire from the park, and opened up on the bunkers.

Wolford ordered his driver to pull away from Lustig's tank. The tank lurched and groaned. There was a sharp noise as the number one and number two steel skirts on the front of Lustig's tanks were torn off. Now Lustig was not only fighting with a locked-up turret, but he had also lost much of the ballistic armor on the front of his tank. He rolled out of the intersection and through the arch, his gun tube locked and firing over the left side. Middleton and Wolford followed, their main guns booming, racing back toward the palace and safety.

For the first time, after nearly three weeks of fighting, a combat team from the Spartan Brigade had been forced to retreat under fire.

Back at the Republican Palace, Flip deCamp and his executive officer, Kent Rideout, were still trying to persuade the Rogue battalion to move east and secure the Jumhuriya Bridge and the five bridges directly to the north, at the edge of the Rogue sector. Based on the brigade boundary line, deCamp contacted Rogue to request that they push all the way to the bridges to seal them. Soldiers and vehicles were pouring across the bridges now, infiltrating Rogue's sector as well as Tusker's. Rick Nussio, the Rogue executive officer, understood the predicament, but he had his own battles to deal with. Again, he told deCamp and Rideout that he couldn't spare anyone to push to the bridges. To do so would create even worse gaps and vulnerabilities at the margins of his sector. He would keep his forces where they were in Rogue's sector, three or four blocks west of the bridges.

Meanwhile, Rideout's request to block the bridges by blowing them up had been denied. A central tenet of American military strategy was to leave intact as much infrastructure as possible in order to support the eventual postwar—and presumably pro-American—Iraqi government. If the bridges were to be shut down, they would have to be blocked with tanks and infantry, not by blowing them up.

DeCamp now had a seven-kilometer stretch of hostile territory to secure. He decided to pull forces from his other two companies and send them north and east to block the bridges. That required a difficult and complex shuffling and reallocation of platoons and sections within his task force. He did it on the fly, working the radio to hand off platoons and sections from one company to another—what he later called a task organization shell game.

He pulled Captain Steve Barry and most of his Cyclone Company off the Fourteenth of July Bridge and traffic circle and sent them to secure the first two bridges north of the Jumhuriya. He replaced Barry with an engineer company, leaving behind one of Barry's tank platoons for protection. Later, deCamp had Captain Chris Carter from Attack Company take a tank platoon and an infantry platoon from the Sujud Palace to secure the two bridges above Barry. Those moves, deCamp hoped, would take some of the pressure off Wolford's company at the Jumhuriya intersection. He intended to send Assassin Company back into the intersection after pounding the intersection with artillery and close air support.

At the Republican Palace, Wolford's tanks and Bradleys pulled in for more ammunition. DeCamp came over to have a look and to get a first-hand feel for the fight from some of the crews. The vehicles had taken a thumping, but they were still in fighting condition—even Lustig's battered tank, with its missing skirts and locked-up turret. Lieutenant Redmon was surprised at how generous the support platoon guys were with their ammunition supplies. Normally, they restricted the tank crews to prescribed amounts of ammunition. But now they were dumping boxes of ammunition onto the tanks, telling Redmon, "What else you need?" and "Take all you need—we got plenty!" They had all been listening over the net to the battle at the intersection.

At deCamp's order, Wolford requested mortars and air support. The battalion's fire support officer at the palace, Captain William Todd Smith, was in direct radio contact with air force officers. A-10 Thunderbolts—squat, ugly tank-killing planes nicknamed Warthogs—were already up in the air over Baghdad. Smith was told that they were "on station" and available. He radioed Wolford and told him, "Phil, I've got you air support for the rest of your life."

That brightened Wolford's mood. He loved the Warthogs. They were wicked little planes that pulverized bunkers—they just killed everything in sight. Each Warthog was armed with an enormous Avenger 30mm Gatling gun that was twenty-two feet long and weighed two tons. The seven-barrel guns were flying cannons. They fired thirty-nine hundred rounds a minute, either armor-piercing or high-explosive. The armor-piercing rounds contained a slug of depleted uranium so dense that it self-sharpened as it penetrated armor, burrowing and turning steel into hot molten metal that ignited and burned. The Warthogs also carried five-hundred-pound bombs, high-explosive rockets, and Maverick and Sidewinder missiles. Wolford was eager to see what the Warthogs would do to the bunkers and buildings at the Yafa Street intersection.

Earlier that morning, Major Jim Ewald had taken off in his Warthog from Jaber air base in Kuwait. He didn't know what his mission would be; his tasking assignment normally didn't arrive until he was on station, circling in the skies over Iraq. Ewald assumed he would be supporting the Third Infantry Division, which at the moment was the main show in Baghdad. He had flown in support of the Rogue thunder run on the morning of the fifth, hitting Iraqi antiaircraft artillery positions in the so-called Triple A Park just west of Highway 8, and his wingman, Major Don Henry, had made several formation attacks on the fifth, destroying the Triple A vehicles and infantry with eight five-hundred-pound bombs, a couple of Mavericks per pass, high-explosive rockets, and six hundred rounds from the Gatling gun.

The fifth had been a beautiful day, so sunny and clear that everything on the ground was sharp and brilliant. Ewald could see the tan tanks and Bradleys on the highway, the antiaircraft pieces dug into pits, and the sparkling muzzle flashes from the Iraqi roadside bunkers. He could see military trucks bearing down on the armored column, and he radioed warnings that were passed on to Rogue by forward air controllers on the ground. He saw white puffs of antiaircraft fire, like popcorn popping in the sky. He saw bright red secondary explosions and it was beautiful. It sounded strange, but *beautiful* was the word for it.

At thirty-seven, Ewald was a veteran pilot, and he loved flying. He had been an air force pilot for nine years before taking a job as a commercial pilot for United Airlines. That lasted fifteen months before he was laid off. As the military geared up for the Iraqi war, he was called up to the Michigan Air National Guard in January and sent to Kuwait. His call sign was *Chocks.*

Now, on the morning of the eighth, the weather was much worse. The skies were blotted by yellow haze and dirty brown smog. The cloud ceiling was below eight thousand feet, and visibility was terrible. Ewald had been on station for about thirty minutes when he and his wingman, also in a Warthog, got the call to support American ground forces at the foot of a bridge. Ewald had to drop down below eight thousand feet to see anything, and on his first pass he could make out the bridge and the shapes of American tanks and Bradleys toward the palace. But he couldn't clearly identify enemy targets, and he held his fire because the forward air controllers were concerned about friendly fire with the armored units so close. He got a good look at men and vehicles near the bridge, and he was certain they were enemy. He needed to make sure; the forward air controllers were also concerned about collateral damage—killing civilians.

Ewald pulled the Warthog back up to prepare for a second pass. This time, he dropped down very low. As he swung down over the bridge a second time, the men and vehicles were gone. Ewald assumed they had been alarmed by his first pass and had run for cover. He and his wingman pulled up and flew in a broad arc west toward the airport to await further instructions from the ground.

Ewald never saw the surface-to-air missile, but his wingman did. He saw it streak in from the left side and punch into Ewald's right engine. The

Warthog was jolted by the impact. The aircraft, in the vernacular of pilots, "departed control flight." Ewald was able to regain control. He wasn't hurt; a Warthog pilot is enclosed in a titanium armor "bathtub" that also protects the cockpit. In his control panel, Ewald could see the reflection of red flames from the missile's detonation.

He flew south, trying to reach American lines. He fought to keep the plane under control, straining his arm and leg muscles. He was losing oil pressure and hydraulics. The plane was shaking, and Ewald couldn't focus to read his emergency checklist. He had to radio his wingman and ask him to read the list to him, to walk him through it. Ewald went through the procedures on the list, watching pieces of the burning engine break off and tumble away behind him.

The engine was now lost. Ewald lost control as the Warthog veered into a right flat spin. Ewald pulled the ejection handles and was catapulted out of the canopy in the pilot's ejection seat. There was a blast of air. His chute popped open and he floated down, looking out at farms and canals and roadways.

He hit the ground with a jolt, landing in a farmer's field. From somewhere came the sound of gunfire. Ewald disconnected his parachute and began evasion maneuvers, as dictated by his training. He ran to a nearby irrigation canal and hid among tall green reeds. He was equipped with a handheld radio and he used it to call for help. Then he waited. He realized that what he had thought were gunshots was actually the Gatling gun's 30mm rounds cooking off inside the burning wreck of the Warthog somewhere in the distance.

For the next fifteen to twenty minutes, Ewald hid among the reeds and waited. He wasn't sure whether he had landed in enemy territory, where Fedayeen and Iraqi regulars were still posted, or in areas secured by the American military. He decided not to venture out.

He heard an approaching vehicle, and then voices. He debated whether to turn and sneak away down the dry bed of the canal. The voices drew closer and Ewald heard someone saying something in English. He didn't know what to do. He was worried that it was an Iraqi soldier who had gone to language school and was posing as an American soldier. Then he heard another voice call out, in distinctively American-accented English, "Hey, pilot dude! Come out! We're Americans!"

Ewald poked his head up and saw soldiers from an American army engineer battalion. They had seen him eject and had rushed to the canal. He stood up and saw young American soldiers grinning and running over to grab him.

Two days later, Ewald was back on duty with his unit, ready to fly again. He was able to find out the name of the National Guard ariman who had packed his ejection seat and parachute—a staff sergeant named Andrew Hansen in Boise, Idaho. When Ewald got back home, he made sure to send Hansen a bottle of single-malt Scotch.

Phil Wolford and his men had no idea that a Warthog had gone down— or that a second Warthog also had been hit and had limped back to base. The captain was in his tank on Haifa Road, a couple of hundred meters back from the archway leading into the intersection. He wanted to be close enough to direct mortar fire, which he had requested prior to the strikes by the Warthogs. The mortars had damaged the bunkers, softening them up for the air strikes.

When the Warthogs swooped down, Wolford was amazed at how low they flew. He had seen Warthogs in action in the Gulf War, but never this low. There were four of them, attacking in pairs. They were dropping flares to confuse and deflect surface-to-air missles. Their Gatling guns gave off a deep, low groan, a grinding noise like a chain saw tearing at a tree. It was a thrilling sound, and it had a visceral effect on Wolford and his tankers. They had been hammered hard at the intersection, and now they watched as the homely little planes tore into the bunkers in the parks.

When the Warthogs were finished, Wolford waited for the air strikes he and deCamp had requested. He wanted hits on the Ministry of Planning and on a three-story building at the northwest corner of the intersection where snipers and RPG teams had pounded his tanks. He couldn't see the planes, but he could hear them. An F-18 dropped a JDAM bomb— a joint direct-attack munition—that missed the ministry building and exploded on top of a pile of rubble in front of the building. A second JDAM slammed directly into the three-story building with a tremendous wallop that leveled the structure, collapsing all three floors.

Wolford was ready now to go back in, this time with four extra tanks that had been assigned to him by deCamp. He now had fourteen tanks and four Bradleys. Just before the company rolled back into the intersection, the infantry platoon destroyed the remaining gun positions on top of the arch with wire-guided TOW missiles fired from the Bradleys. That eliminated some of the threat from the south.

Just forty-five minutes had passed since the company had retreated from the intersection, but now the battlefield was a much different place. Wolford's tanks were peppered again by RPGs and small arms as they rolled through the archway and set up again in the intersection. But this time, the rate of fire was not as heavy or as concentrated. It appeared to Wolford that the Iraqis had dragged off their wounded and some of their dead, piling them into police cars and sedans and trucks and ferrying them east across the river. But he could also see that more vehicles were still speeding west across the bridge and into the intersection, bringing in reinforcements to replace the fighters killed by the air strikes.

This time, with more tanks and a weakened enemy, Wolford's company was quickly able to mount an effective volume of fire. The tanks and Bradleys poured fire on the bunkers and the buildings, and toward gunmen running back and forth beneath the bridge supports. Gibson fired coax at arriving trucks, and at RPG teams that were piling out of an ambulance near the bridge. Lustig had his gunner lay down fire in every window where he still saw people with weapons. He felt more confident now because he knew where most of the enemy soldiers were and how they were attacking. Even so, Lustig was still surprised by their dogged resistance. Even after the Warthogs and the JDAMs, they were still fighting, and fighting hard. He hated them but he had to admit that he also respected them, in a purely military sense.

Now that Wolford had mounted an effective volume of fire, he ordered Lieutenant McFarland to dismount his infantrymen from the Bradleys to clear the park. He set up Redmon's platoon facing southwest to cover the infantrymen.

"I want you to go up and down the road and fuck it up," Wolford told Redmon over the radio. "I want you to give equal love to both sides of it. Do you understand—equal love to both sides?"

"Roger," Redmon answered. He had all four tanks fire their main guns, clearing the way for the infantry.

McFarland's troops hustled from the rear hatches of the Bradleys and into the parks. The bunkers were burning. The park was littered with enemy corpses, many of them smoldering and giving off the sharp, sour smell of burning flesh. The infantrymen went from bunker to bunker, firing into the holes and clearing them with grenades. McFarland didn't bother trying to take prisoners. The few fighters who were still alive were in horrible shape. They were not going to live long. The Iraqis had not managed to remove all their dead. McFarland counted at least sixty corpses.

Wolford spotted several fighters running toward a bunker to the north. He radioed McFarland, "Scorpion on the Ground, this is Assassin Six. I want you to clear that bunker about two hundred meters north of you where a couple of guys just went. I'm going to soften it up for you, and you get ready right after. Stand by."

Wolford got back to Redmon. "You see that bunker I'm talking about? You see it? I want you to hit it with your coax for thirty seconds using a Z-pattern."

He returned to McFarland. "Scorpion on the Ground, you ready?"

And then he told Redmon, "Okay, White One, fire."

Redmon's gunner laced the bunker, ripping up everything and everyone inside. Wolford's adrenaline was pumping hard now, and he could sense the battle swinging his way.

"Yeah!" he screamed into the radio at McFarland. "Scorpion on the Ground, you like that? You like that, don't you. Okay, go in and kill 'em!"

At the southwest corner of the intersection, Redmon's platoon was fighting to protect the infantry's rear flank. The tanks were firing coax into buildings and rooftops. Then the first suicide cars appeared. They came from the west, speeding up the roadway toward the tanks. Redmon was astonished. A late-model Mercedes was bearing down on them—on a platoon of tanks in the middle of a firefight. Redmon thought, *Damn, that's a nice car.* Then he fired a warning burst from his .50-caliber machine gun. The Mercedes kept coming. He hit it with the .50-caliber and the car swerved and crashed.

Another car emerged and sped toward the tanks, and then a truck. Neither vehicle slowed down, even after warning bursts of .50-caliber fire. Redmon's platoon hit those vehicles, too, killing whoever was inside. The occupants were too far away for Redmon to see whether they were armed, but he didn't care. Anyone who threatened his men was going down.

After about thirty minutes of heavy fighting, Wolford felt he was in control of the intersection. The Iraqis were retreating toward the bridge and into the crowded neighborhoods north and west of the intersection. He heard over the battalion net that his friend Steve Barry—whose tanks and Bradleys were several blocks west—had pushed north and east to the next two bridges up the river, helping to stabilize Wolford's north flank. Barry's tanks and Bradleys were also driving Iraqi fighters back toward Wolford. At the same time, Wolford's company was forcing some of the fighters at the intersection north toward Barry's company. They had them squeezed, beginning to seal the gap between the two companies.

By now, the enemy fire from the buildings and bunkers around the intersection had eased significantly. Wolford ordered Middleton's platoon up to the base of the bridge in order to block it and stop the infiltration from the east bank. Middleton rolled forward, putting two tanks up on a side street just below the bridge and two more at the base, where Yafa Street rose up to meet the bridge. Almost immediately, the platoon came under fire—this time from across the river, and from a group of Fedayeen militiamen firing from a collection of houses on the west bank of the river, just below the Ministry of Planning.

Wolford moved up and directed several tanks to pound the Fedayeen, and the enemy fire from the ministry eased. But the rate of fire from across the river intensified—RPGs, small arms, and a few mortar rounds. Middleton and Gibson moved their tanks up onto the bridge itself to get a better look at the east bank. The Jumhuriya Bridge is crowned, with its highest point in the middle, so the tanks had to creep out to exposed positions on the bridge in order for Middleton and Gibson to see the opposite bank.

When they finally scanned through their sights, they saw the same frenzied movement of men and vehicles they had witnessed earlier in the intersection. Taxis, police cars, buses, and ambulances were dropping off soldiers and gunmen on the east bank, where Middleton could see fighting positions dug into the riverbank and muzzle flashes from behind walls and buildings. Snipers were firing from windows. Middleton thought it looked like an ant colony that had been disturbed.

Middleton and Gibson were both scanning the opposite bank when a series of mortar rounds whistled overhead. Several rounds exploded on the pavement, rocking the bridge. A few of the rounds were duds, and

Gibson watched them bounce across the bridge. Then an artillery shell screamed down and exploded next to Middleton's tank. The bridge shuddered. For an instant, Gibson was afraid his tank would plunge into the river and drown the crew.

The bridge stabilized and Gibson looked again across the river. A man and two little boys—it struck him as curious that two boys would be out in the middle of a firefight—were pointing underneath the bridge. Gibson could hear gunfire from under the bridge on his side of the river. He was afraid they were trying to set explosives to blow up the bridge.

He radioed Middleton. "Hey, sir, we've got some motherfuckers up under the bridge here shooting at us! We need to back the hell up."

The two tanks rolled part of the way back toward the intersection to get a better angle on the gunmen beneath the bridge. At that moment, Sergeant Leverette moved over from the intersection and opened fire on several RPG teams hiding under the bridge on the northern side. From his vantage point, Leverette could also see men with weapons squatting in small boats that were launching from the opposite bank. Middleton, still on the bridge, saw them, too. The lieutenant and Leverette sank the boats with blasts of coax and .50-caliber machine-gun fire.

Middleton and Gibson rolled back up the bridge, still trying to figure out what they were up against on the east bank of the Tigris.

On a balcony outside Room 1502 of the Palestine Hotel, across the Tigris, photographer Faleh Khaiber was trying to get shots of American aircraft in the skies over Baghdad that morning. Khaiber was an Iraqi, a Baghdad native who worked as a photographer for the Reuters news agency. He was staying in Room 935, but he had come up to the Reuters room because its two balconies faced north and slightly west, affording a view of the west bank of the Tigris. Khaiber was forty-seven, but he looked much younger. He was short and trim, with small features, his black hair tinged with silver and combed forward. He was nimble and quick, and good with a camera.

Khaiber was one of nearly a hundred reporters and photographers staying at the Palestine, a tan, seventeen-story high-rise on the east bank of the Tigris about a kilometer and a half southeast of the midspan of the Jumhuriya Bridge. Some of the journalists had moved in recent days from the Rashid Hotel across the river, which had been seized the morning before by the tanks and Bradleys of the Rogue battalion. All morning on the eighth, journalists had watched from the Palestine as Assassin Company fought off an Iraqi counterattack at the intersection at the foot of the bridge on the west bank. The hotel's balconies and rooftop afforded a fairly good view of the fight, while far enough away, seemingly, to keep journalists from getting caught up in it.

Outside room 1502, Khaiber was photographing the aircraft from the balcony to the east. On the adjacent balcony was one of the occupants of the room, Taras Protsyuk, a Ukrainian-born Reuters TV cameraman. Protsyuk's camera was set up on a tripod, but he wasn't filming at the moment. On the balcony directly below, Jose Couso, a Spanish cameraman for Spain's Telecinco, had set up his camera and was filming the battle across the river.

On his balcony, Khaiber wheeled around and tried to squeeze off a few frames of an aircraft roaring overhead. He wanted to get a few more shots before stepping over to Protsyuk's balcony to retrieve camera gear he had left there.

On the bridge, the tanks began taking fire from a high-rise building at the eastern end, at the northern foot of the bridge. It was a beige structure with a light brown center concrete facade that protruded the length of the building. The crews began returning firing toward the base of the structure, where men with RPGs were running and hiding along the riverbank. Wolford radioed a request for a jet fighter to drop a bomb on the building to eliminate whoever was firing at his tanks. He described the building to Major Rideout back at the palace. The request was passed up the chain of command to Colonel Perkins.

Then the battalion was presented with a piece of intelligence that seemed to promise a way to disrupt the Iraqi mortar fire. Earlier that morning, in the part of the governmental complex controlled by the Rogue battalion, a Bradley crew had destroyed a car loaded with armed men. From the wreckage, the crews had recovered a two-way Motorola radio that was turned on and still working. It was a small black radio, about eight inches long and two inches thick, like a handheld police radio. Hearing voices chattering in Arabic, the crewmen turned the radio over to the battalion's military intelligence team.

Chief Warrant Officer Two Willis Young, a fluent Arabic speaker who specialized in human intelligence, was intrigued as he listened to the conversations coming over the radio. He took the radio to Nussio, the battalion's executive officer, who was in the back of his armored personnel carrier next to the converted public toilet that was serving as a command post at the edge of the parade grounds. Young translated for Nussio: someone in a tall building was describing an American tank on the Jumhuriya Bridge. He mentioned that he was in a building that contained a Turkish restaurant.

Nussio radioed Major Rideout at the Republican Palace and warned him that one of Wolford's tanks was being observed by an Arabic-speaker in a building across the river. He was concerned that the speaker was a forward observer—a spotter—for Iraqi mortar and artillery crews.

Rideout radioed Wolford at the intersection: "Hey, you've got an FO across the river with eyes on you. You need to pay close attention. I'll get back to you with more later."

A minute later, Nussio radioed Rideout with an update. The voice on the radio was now describing more tanks across the river. He was telling someone that he wanted mortars fired to try to hit the tanks he saw on the bridge.

Rideout radioed back to Wolford and warned him to watch for mortars.

"We're getting mortars already!" Wolford told him. He described a garage across the river where RPG teams had taken cover behind construction equipment and were firing on his tanks. It was near the tan high-rise building. Rideout told Wolford to look for a building with a Turkish restaurant. That's where the forward observer was.

On the Jumhuriya Bridge, Staff Sergeant Gibson had been told by Lieutenant Middleton that a forward observer overheard on a two-way radio was in a high-rise building across the river, trying to direct mortar and artillery strikes. Middleton had relayed the report directly from Wolford, who had told him, "See if you can find a spotter."

Gibson and Middleton were alarmed. At least one artillery shell and several mortar rounds had already slammed down on or near the bridge.

If a forward observer now had a clear view of the bridge in order to direct mortar or artillery fire, he could easily bring it right down on their heads. American soldiers threatened by mortars or artillery are trained to locate the forward observer and kill him as quickly as possible. "We've got to find this guy," Middleton said.

The tanks were receiving RPG and small-arms fire not only from the tan high-rise directly across the river, but also from gunmen running up and down a stretch of the opposite riverbank that extended hundreds of meters south of the bridge. Some of the tanks returned fire with coax and .50-caliber at RPG and machine-gun positions along that section of the opposite bank. As Gibson searched the opposite bank for anyone in a high-rise building, his gunner yelled up to him, "Hey, Sergeant Gibson, I got a guy over here looking at us with binoculars." It was a man on the upper floor of a light-colored high-rise across the river, about a kilometer to the south.

Gibson dropped down and looked through the tank's magnified sights. The gunner had the sights on 3X magnification. Gibson punched it up to 10X. It was difficult to see through the haze and smoke, but when Gibson scanned the high-rise building the gunner had indicated, he saw a figure holding what appeared to be a pair of binoculars next to something on a tripod.

In his tank at the edge of the bridge, Lustig heard Gibson describe the tripod and "some kind of optics." Lustig thought it might be a GLLD, a ground/vehicular laser locater designator—a tripod-mounted laser targeting device used by forward observers to direct artillery fire.

Middleton relayed the information by radio to Wolford. Moments later, the captain radioed the lieutenant back for a more detailed description. "What do you have?" he asked.

Middleton described the figure on the balcony, the tripod, and what appeared to be binoculars. Wolford asked him for the range—the distance to the building. He knew the marines were moving up the opposite bank somewhere to the south, and he was worried about accidentally firing on them. Middleton said the range was 1,740 meters. The captain told him to stand by.

The radio nets were humming. Wolford was trying to keep Rideout and deCamp informed, while also fielding reports and requests from his platoon leaders and directing his gunner in the firefight. Lieutenant

McFarland radioed to ask about Captain Barry's position. Wolford gave McFarland the location, then turned his attention back to the situation across the river. He still wanted bombs dropped on the tan high-rise at the opposite end of the bridge, where gunmen were firing on his tanks. He was also worried about mortar fire, and in particular the forward observer Gibson and Middleton had just identified in the tall building across the river and farther south. The spotter had to be eliminated.

Wolford got back on the radio to Middleton. "Okay," he told him, "you've got permission to take the target out."

Middleton relayed the order to Gibson, who turned to his gunner and told him, "Fire a HEAT round at the target."

The round erupted from the gun tube with an orange flash and tore into the side of the building, just below and to the right of the balcony where Gibson had seen the figure standing. It exploded in a cloud of gray smoke and debris. Gibson was fairly certain he had finally taken out the forward observer.

Moments later, Major Nussio called Rideout with an update from the monitored Motorola conversations: "Whatever you're doing, keep it up. This guy is now calling his buddy and saying he's getting suppressed and has to move."

Rideout radioed Wolford and told him, "Whatever you're fucking doing right now, keep it up! You're starting to move the guy around. He has to find a new location." Rideout thought it was a hell of a coup, to drive out a forward observer using a captured radio.

Now there was more fire coming from directly across the bridge. Gibson had his gunner traverse the gun tube. He spotted four men with RPG launchers as they took up firing positions behind a wall in an alley at the far eastern end of the bridge. He fired another main gun round that collapsed the wall and, Gibson thought, killed all four men. He traversed the gun tube again and scanned up and down the riverbank, searching for more targets.

Consumed by the fight, Gibson had no idea that the HEAT round fired moments earlier had mortally wounded Taras Protsyuk, the Reuters cameraman who had set up his camera on the balcony. Protsyuk was thirty-five, with a wife and an eight-year-old son. The impact had also struck Jose Couso, the Spanish cameraman who had been filming on the balcony below, severely wounding him in the face and leg. Couso was thirty-seven, with a wife and two children, aged six and three. Couso and Protsyuk both died of their wounds at Baghdad hospitals.

On the second balcony outside Room 1502, Reuters photographer Faleh Khaiber was knocked unconscious by the force of the blast, his head cut by flying debris. He recovered, along with two other journalists who were also injured by the exploding tank round.

At some point just before the Palestine was hit, Major Mark Rasins, the operations officer for the Tusker battalion, had been frantically trying to help Rideout and Wolford locate the building with the Turkish restaurant—based on the intercepted Motorola conversations. Rasins was extroverted and hands-on—the type of officer who was quick to address problems. Riding in a Bradley at the end of Barry's Cyclone Company as it moved past Wolford's company, Rasins was listening to the discussions over the brigade radio net. He thought the battalion needed to get out into the streets with an Arabic-speaking interpreter to find someone who could locate the Turkish restaurant. Rasins had the Bradley driver rush back to Sujud Palace, where Rideout had told him he could find Abdulla, a university teacher from California who was one of the brigade's interpreters.

Rasins and Abdulla arrived in the Bradley a few minutes later at an intersection held by Barry's company just off the west bank of the river at a bridge north of the Jumhuriya Bridge. They found a cluster of men in civilian clothes near the river. The men were like tourists, craning their necks and trying to see the firefights raging up and down the riverbanks. Abdulla spoke to a neatly dressed middle-aged man who said he knew the building where the Turkish restaurant was—it was directly across the Jumhuriya Bridge. It was the beige high-rise. That suggested that the Iraqi spotter overheard on the Motorola had been in that building. The man added that the building housing the restaurant recently had been taken over as the headquarters for Iraqi military intelligence. Rasins grabbed the man, put him in the back of the Bradley, and rushed to the Jumhuriya Bridge. But by the time they reached the intersection, the Palestine already had been hit.

Meanwhile, Colonel Perkins had begun to act on the Tusker battalion's request for an air strike on the beige high-rise. As he discussed the air strike with Major Rideout over the radio, Perkins was overheard by Greg Kelly, the embedded Fox News correspondent. Kelly was standing next to Perkins on the raised front driveway of Sujud Palace, where the colonel's command vehicle was parked. When Kelly heard Perkins discussing a high-rise building across the Tigris, he told the colonel to make sure the building wasn't the Palestine Hotel. Kelly knew the hotel was somewhere across the river, filled with journalists.

Perkins had never heard of the Palestine. The east bank of the Tigris was not his area of operations. It had been assigned to the marines, who were still fighting their way up through the southeastern edge of the city. Kelly told Perkins that most of the foreign press were staying at the Palestine. He knew it was across the river, but he wasn't certain of its exact location.

Kelly offered to call his New York office on his Thuraya satellite phone to try to find someone who could describe the hotel. He was given the number in Amman, Jordan, of a Fox producer who had recently stayed at the Palestine. Kelly reached the producer and jotted down notes as the man described the hotel. Kelly was trying to relay the descriptions to Perkins, but finally he just handed the phone to the colonel and let him speak to the producer himself. Kelly had been with Perkins for the entire war, and he had never seen him so insistent and agitated.

Perkins wanted to make sure that the building being targeted for the air strike wasn't the Palestine. He sent a soldier down the ramp to get Chris Tomlinson, an Associated Press reporter embedded with the brigade's Attack Company. Tomlinson, who had served in the army, was wearing a tanker's CVC communications helmet and had been monitoring the brigade's radio traffic. He rushed up the ramp to find Perkins desperately asking about the Palestine. Did Tomlinson know what it looked like?

Tomlinson had never been to the hotel, but he offered to contact the AP reporter based at the Palestine. He sent an e-mail message on his laptop and also tried calling on his Thuraya satellite phone. There was no reply. Much later, Tomlinson realized that the hotel had already been hit and that all the journalists were either fleeing their rooms or helping evacuate the mortally wounded reporters.

Tomlinson called the AP office in Doha, Qatar and asked Danica Kirka, his editor there, for the map coordinates of the Palestine. She didn't know, so she tried calling the Palestine and sending a text message over the AP internal network to the AP reporter there. Again, there was no reply. Kirka told Tomlinson that AP reporter Nico Price, now in Amman, Jordan, had just stayed at the Palestine. She patched Tomlinson through to

Price, who gave him a detailed description of the building. Tomlinson took notes, then gave Perkins a description of a tall, pink-colored building with balconies jutting out at an angle. He told him it was located at the sharp bend in the Tigris River, right next to the Sheraton Hotel.

Perkins radioed Rideout at the palace with the description of the Palestine. He told the major that he wanted to be certain the high-rise directly across the bridge wasn't the Palestine Hotel before he approved dropping a bomb on it. Rideout said the high-rise wasn't pinkish in color, nor was it located next to any other tall building or the bend in the river, which was farther south. Based on the description he had been given by Wolford in preparation for the air strike, Rideout did not believe it was a hotel.

At this point, deCamp got on the net. Perkins told him to make sure his people didn't accidentally fire on the Palestine Hotel. DeCamp had never heard of the Palestine. It wasn't in his sector. The only hotel he knew about was the Rashid Hotel, which had been taken by the Rogue battalion the day before. But deCamp did know from Wolford, and from scouts posted behind the Republican Palace, that RPG teams and snipers were firing from positions up and down the opposite riverbank. He told Perkins that he'd find out about the Palestine.

Perkins still wasn't satisfied. He decided to go over to the bridge and personally have a look at the situation across the river.

Meanwhile, deCamp got on the radio to Wolford. In a loud voice that was unmistakable over the net, he asked the captain whether he had fired on the "Palestinian Hotel," as deCamp called it. DeCamp ordered Wolford to make absolutely sure his company didn't fire on the hotel. Neither man realized that the hotel had already been hit. Wolford, like deCamp, had never heard of the Palestine—or Palestinian—Hotel. He told deCamp that his men had been firing at the beige high-rise directly across the bridge. DeCamp had difficulty deciphering the captain's descriptions of a building with a "brown stripe" running down the side and "a pyramid" on top. He decided to get into his tank and go to the intersection to speak with Wolford directly—and to look across the river himself.

It did not take long for the news of an American attack on a Baghdad hotel filled with journalists to hit the international news wires. Between soldiers monitoring BBC radio and reporters embedded with the Second Brigade, the first reports of the deaths at the Palestine soon reached Colonel Perkins. It was not immediately clear to him whether the hotel had been hit by a bomb or a tank round. The reports confused Perkins. He hadn't been cleared for an air strike on any building across the river. He checked with the air force controllers, who told him that the bombing mission on the high-rise building had not taken place. Perkins hoped the reports were mistaken—perhaps, he thought, the Palestine had been hit by an RPG. Then deCamp, based on his discussions with Wolford, radioed that an Assassin Company tank had earlier fired a round at a building across the river that housed a suspected Iraqi forward observer. Perkins gave an order not to fire on any other buildings across the river until further notice. Soon he got a confirmed report that the Palestine had indeed been hit by an Assassin Company tank round and that two journalists were dead.

Perkins was dismayed by the realization that an American tank had killed two journalists. He didn't blame Wolford or Gibson. Assassin Company had been under heavy fire. The crews had been warned that a forward observer had spotted American tanks and was calling in mortars. Mortar rounds had already exploded near the tanks. Enemy fire was coming from the opposite bank. Cut off from news reports since leaving Kuwait almost three weeks earlier, the crews had never heard of the Palestine. Under attack in the heat of battle, Wolford was not required to seek higher approval to fire on a building with a suspected forward observer. Given the circumstances, Perkins thought, it was the right call—with tragic, unintended results.

Earlier, as he was trying to get a description of the Palestine, Chris Tomlinson had asked his editor in Doha to get word to the reporters inside the hotel to hang bedsheets from their windows as a way of identifying the building. By early afternoon, the bedsheets were out. (Iraqi soldiers later ordered the reporters to remove them.)

From the bridge, Wolford saw sheets fluttering from the building his men had hit, and his heart sank. He glanced over at Middleton, and he saw from the look on his face that the lieutenant knew it, too. It was a miserable feeling.

Shortly after Shawn Gibson hit the Palestine and fired on the RPG teams in the alley, enemy fire from the east bank began to taper off. Assassin Company had by now seized control of both the intersection and the bridge, and the rapid shift from full-scale war to relative calm was startling. The stream of vehicles delivering gunmen had dried up. There wasn't as much movement across the river—just whirls of smoke drifting past burning vehicles and clusters of debris. Many enemy fighters had fled north, where they were soon fired on by Captain Barry's Cyclone Company at the next two bridges.

From time to time near the Jumhuriya, sniper fire rang out and an occasional RPG sailed overhead. But the Iraqis on both riverbanks were beaten now, and the Assassin crews knew it. They came up out of the hatches, filthy and exhausted, but relieved to be done with it. Some of them lit up cigarettes. A knot of vehicles was gathering at the foot of the bridge, where Colonel Perkins was in his M113 command carrier, joined by deCamp and other officers from the Tusker battalion. Some of them were on the street, talking to the crews.

Behind them, in the two city parks, the stiff corpses of the Iraqi dead were splayed in awkward poses in the dirt next to their fighting holes. Some of the faces were smooth and young and almost peaceful. If viewed from a distance, where the congealed black blood and the half-burned uniforms and the torn pink flesh were not so apparent, some of them could have been men resting in the sun after a hard morning's work. It was past midday. The sun was fighting through the blanket of haze, and a warm breeze was beginning to disperse some of the smoke from the battle. It was developing into a fine April day in downtown Baghdad.

To the north, Barry's men moved to secure his two assigned bridges, and the sounds of the firefight echoed along the riverbank. The Iraqis were able to mount several intense volleys against Barry's company, but were unable to sustain their counterattack. It seemed to Wolford, who had fought them all night and all morning, that the Iraqis had such poor command and control that each group of men was essentially fighting on its own. The soldiers apparently had been told that holding the bridges was crucial, so they fought bitterly to keep them. When they were at last driven off the Jumhuriya Bridge, they fell back to the next bridge to the north. And when they encountered Cyclone Company there, they leapfrogged north to the next bridge, where they fought Cyclone all over again.

Barry called in two mortar missions of twelve rounds each that drove out Iraqi soldiers dug in along the riverbank between the bridges. His tanks fired HEAT rounds to destroy three Russian-made BMPs that had tried to maneuver and attack. His infantrymen spent the rest of the day chasing down and killing small groups of fighters moving through the streets. At one point, one of Barry's crews fired on a boat full of armed men trying to cross the river, sinking the vessel and killing everyone aboard. The firefights were infused with moments of intensity but they lacked the sustained ferocity of Assassin's battle at the bridge. Barry had seen the carnage at the Jumhuriya. When he pushed past Wolford's intersection, he had asked him over the radio, "Assassin Six, what the hell were you fighting up here—World War Three?"

At the Jumhuriya Bridge, Wolford's request for an air strike on the beige high-rise directly across the bridge had been held up following the deaths at the Palestine. Early in the afternoon, as Perkins was in his command vehicle at the foot of the bridge, two missiles fired from the building sailed over his head. At the same time, pilots overhead were reporting armed men moving in and out of the rear of the high-rise. Gunfire was starting to pick up again from across the river.

By this time, Major Rasins had arrived with the Iraqi civilian and his information that Iraqi military intelligence was in the building. Rasins got out of his Bradley to talk to Wolford, whose tank was at the base of the bridge. As he climbed up on Wolford's tank, Rasins realized that the captain was in "open protected" position, with only a six-inch opening in the hatch. The battle seemed to be over, so Rasins asked Wolford why he was still in open protected. "Because it's fucking dangerous out there," Wolford told him. "They're still shooting from across the river."

Rasins climbed down into the safety of the turret and told Wolford what the Iraqi civilian had said about the high-rise. As Rasins ran back to his Bradley, two Iraqi gunmen opened fire from a building just north of the bridge, on the near side of the river. Assassin Company returned the fire, and Rasins fired his 9mm pistol, killing one of the men.

Concerns about civilian casualties and possible friendly fire had delayed approval of the air strike. But now, with hostilities on the increase, the bombing of the high-rise was approved. Marine Major Mark Jewell and his mixed air liaison crew of marines and Third Infantry soldiers had been parked on the bridge inside their Bradley since shortly after noon, awaiting clearance to guide the fighter planes in. It was hot and airless inside the Bradley, and Jewell let the crewmen step outside for fresh air. But when an RPG screamed overhead and exploded against a wall next to the planning ministry, everybody hustled back inside and buttoned up. Then Jewell got word that the planes were tasked and ready.

"Three minutes, men!" Jewell yelled. "We're taking this building down."

Jewell was on the radio to pilots who had been pulled off the "stack," a sort of parking lot in the sky for pilots awaiting orders, and assigned to attack the high-rise. Jewell was having trouble understanding one of the pilots, a British officer flying a Tornado. The pilot was speaking English, but it was British English, and the accent was throwing Jewell off. But he worked through it, and finally the two found a common, military language.

It was Jewell's job to mark the targets for the pilots. His laser range finder had been destroyed in a battle against the Medina Division three days earlier, so he had to ask a lieutenant in a fire-support Bradley nearby to fire a laser at the high-rise and pass its GPS grid coordinates on to him.

In the rear of Jewell's Bradley, Marine Captain David Cooper had painstakingly converted the GPS grids to longitude and latitude coordinates used by the pilots to program their bombs. Cooper's face was dotted with red welts and cuts, and an ugly crimson bruise snaked across both eyes, which were badly bloodshot. The day before, shortly after Cyclone Company had taken the Fourteenth of July traffic circle, Cooper had been standing in the street, consulting with Captain Barry. Geoff Mohan, the embedded *Los Angeles Times* reporter, was standing beside them.

Cooper and Mohan heard someone shout "RPG! RPG!" A grenade exploded against either a street sign or a tank turret, and Cooper and Mohan went down hard. It felt like hot iron filings were being blasted into their faces. Mohan reached up and felt his face, but he was afraid to look at his hands because he thought he'd be holding pieces of his face. He asked Cooper, "Is my face okay?"

Cooper said, "You're fine."

Mohan looked at Cooper and told him, "You've got a cut on your cheek." Cooper smirked and wiped it away. He told Mohan they had to get back to their vehicles.

They ran back to Jewell's Bradley, Lightning 28, where Jewell washed out Cooper's eyes. A medic worked on Mohan's eyes, which were clogged with dirt and grit, and told him he'd live to die another day. Cooper escaped with a bad headache and two black eyes, but it had been a sobering experience. Now, on the bridge, he was glad to be inside the Bradley.

From the turret, Jewell fired a laser toward the top of the high-rise, indicating the target. The laser shot just over a portrait of Saddam Hussein mounted on a small arch stretched across the crest of the bridge. A British Tornado GR4 fighter-bomber roared over the city, somewhere high above. A pair of thousand-pound Mark-83 JDAMs swooshed down. Their inertial navigation systems, programmed with the three-dimensional location of the target, directed the bombs to the high-rise. They tore two black gashes into the tan face of the tower, unleashing a spiral of gray smoke. Jewell's voice came over the radio inside the Bradley: "Outstanding hits!" The Bradley crewmen scrambled out to watch the smoke pour from the building. One of them pulled out a disposable camera and snapped off a few photos.

For the next strike, U.S. Navy Lieutenant Commander Scott Toppel, known to his colleagues as Skweez, was piloting a Navy F/A-18 Super Hornet high over the Tigris. Toppel and his wingman, also in a Super Hornet, had taken off that morning from the USS *Nimitz*. They had their "kill box," the area designated for close air support. Ground controllers had told them to switch to a frequency that connected them to Lightning 28. Toppel heard Jewell's voice describe the target as a tall building on the east bank of the Tigris. Jewell also warned that an A-10 Warthog had been shot down in the area that morning.

Toppel's wingman went first, banking over the river. The gray form of the jet was barely visible from the bridge against the curtain of smoke. A bright flash burst from beneath a wing, and a black streak slammed into the building, unleashing a ball of orange flame framed by white smoke. A second laser-guided Maverick missile ripped another jagged hole in the tower. Toppel followed, his first missile locking on to the laser beam. He pressed the red PICKLE button on the control stick, heard the *whoosh* of the missile, and watched it shoot toward the building. He thought it was going to miss high, but then it pitched over and exploded against the top story. The second missile misfired and locked up on the rail. By the end of the mission, five missiles from three F-18s had scored direct hits on the high-rise.

Over the radio came Cooper's voice: "Good effects on entire building. Building still standing, but I guarantee you there's nothing left inside."

The bombing of the building was an oddly anticlimactic coda to the battle for the bridge, and for the city itself. The tank and Bradley crews cheered and slapped palms at the sight of the burning black holes ripped into the building, but they did not feel the same satisfaction they had experienced upon driving the enemy back across the bridge. It was beginning to dawn on them that the war was rapidly drawing to a close, and weeks earlier than anyone had anticipated. It was something they wanted, something they had risked their lives to achieve, but somehow they were not quite prepared for the finality of it. It was so sudden. They were sleep-deprived and stoked up on adrenaline and fear, almost giddy with relief at having survived. Now the thunder run was over. They knew what they were supposed to do next —to set up a perimeter behind new berms being built by the engineers from burned-out cars and toppled lampposts, to stay alert and hold their positions through the night, and to fight another pitched battle if it came to that. That much they knew. But they did not know what was coming next, in the half-light between war and what passed for peace, and this uncertainty weighed heavily on them for a long time.

No one in the Spartan Brigade was able to define with any certainty the moment when the balance tipped, when the second thunder run reached that point in any battle where men on both sides realize that the outcome has been ordained. It may have been when the first fuel and ammunition convoy reached Objective Curly at the height of the battle there. It may have been later, when the same convoy resupplied the beleaguered combat team at Objective Larry, or still later, when the tank battalions' relief convoys rolled into the palace complex. It may have been when tanks from Objective Moe stole into the city at night for fuel and ammunition. And if there was an emblem for what they had achieved, it was probably the American flag that Rick Nussio had waved in the parade grounds, or perhaps Jason Conroy's kill shot into the equestrian statue of Saddam Hussein.

They couldn't say. They knew only that their experience was bewildering and shattering and utterly unique, and something that no one who had not been with them could ever comprehend. It occurred to Staff Sergeant Tom Slago on the eighth, as he was eating an MRE of beef and mushrooms inside his Bradley in the downtown district, that all the killing he had accomplished had left an indelible mark on him. Through his sights, he caught a glimpse of an Iraqi soldier, armed with an AK-47, poking his head around a building. Slago watched and waited, certain that the Iraqi would draw closer. And the soldier did creep closer. At last Slago fired a burst of coax that tore the man in two, and with barely a pause he resumed his beef and mushrooms. Those same involuntary impulses also affected Specialist Benjamin Agee, the infantryman who had used his big M-240 machine gun to help his four-man team kill at least twenty men in the gloom beneath the overpass at Curly on the seventh. By April 8, Agee was deployed inside the downtown parade grounds complex. The firefights had eased considerably by then, and it was clear to him that the war was ending. Agee was uneasy, and he found himself actually wishing somebody would take a shot at him so that he could get back into the fight. He missed the wild intensity of it all, the purity of effort and will.

The next day, the ninth, the marines fought their way into the downtown neighborhoods of the east bank of the Tigris after a punishing two-and-a-half-week march of their own. At Firdos Square, just across from the Palestine Hotel, television news crews captured a scene of celebration and triumph. With the help of a marine armored recovery vehicle, the marines and a mob of Iraqis toppled a towering statue of Saddam Hussein that had dominated the square for years. The figure crashed to the pavement and shattered. Men and boys stomped the remains and pelted them with garbage. Some Iraqis swatted the statue's fallen head with their shoes, a grave insult among the Arabs. The images were relayed live around the world, symbolizing a startling and decisive military victory for millions of Americans watching back home. The men from the Spartan Brigade did not see the footage until much later, but it made no difference. For them, it wasn't the end of anything, only the beginning of something worse than war.

EPILOGUE

By the middle of the day on April 8, the firefight was over at Objective Moe. Captain Josh Wright's company had spent the morning responding to sustained enemy fire, but by early afternoon the combat team had managed to expand and secure its hold on the intersection. The Iraqi and Arab fighters who had been attacking the interchange for two days melted away, dragging away their dead but leaving those who still lay in the fields of fire. Wright did not conduct a BDA, a battle damage assessment, and thus he did not know how many fighters his men had killed. Major Roger Shuck, the battalion operations officer, figured they had killed as many as two hundred and had destroyed at least forty-five vehicles. The company had not lost a man, though eight soldiers had been wounded, all during the fierce battles the day before.

By late afternoon, civilians began to emerge from their homes in the poor, densely packed neighborhood of Ummal and from the middle-class district of Al Qadisiyah. They had the lost, dazed expressions of flood or hurricane survivors, for the battle had approached the scale of a natural disaster. Some of the residents were relatives of soldiers killed in the fight, and they scoured the sandy ground for their corpses. The English speakers among them, and there were many, told the Americans the names of Republican Guard or Fedayeen fighters they were seeking. The soldiers, of course, had no idea who they had fought, and they certainly did not know who among the enemy had lived or died.

A few of the residents led Wright's men to ammunition caches in their neighborhoods, and others complained bitterly that the Syrian mercenaries had turned their homes into fighting positions. Some families left with the bodies of relatives, but no one touched the corpses of the Syrians or other foreign mercenaries. Wright thought some of the dead Arabs looked like college students, with their jeans and sneakers and polo shirts, all accessorized with ammunition bandoliers and cloth combat vests with ammo pouches. Later the engineers dug graves and buried them.

Wright and his men were exhausted, but also euphoric at having survived and having held the interchange in the face of surprisingly robust resistance. Some of the men said they never, ever wanted to endure a battle like that again. Wright thought he would do it all over again if he had to, and he would fight just as hard. But he also knew that when he got back to the States and back behind the wheel of his car, he would never look at a highway interchange the same way again.

Down the highway, at Objective Larry, Lieutenant Colonel Twitty had been confident when the fighting eased around sundown on the seventh after a full day of fighting. He was convinced that the enemy had given up and would disappear overnight. But just after the sun came up on the eighth, the Republican Guards and Fedayeen and Syrians were right back at it, firing volleys of RPGs that were just as intense as the day before. Twitty radioed Colonel Perkins in the city and told him, "Sir, you're not going to believe this—we're back in contact!"

Much of the fire was coming from the southwest, from the neighborhood of Hay al Qtisadiyin. First Lieutenant Mark Brzozowski, a twenty-six-year-old West Point graduate from Hampton, Virginia, ended up leading two forays into the neighborhood to eliminate the threat. Brzozowksi hadn't expected to spend more than a few hours at the interchange. Like his commander, Captain Dan Hubbard, and most of the men in the company, he had assumed they would stay just long enough to hold the highway until the Tusker and Rogue battalions returned after a quick thunder run into the city on the seventh. Now Brzozowksi was gearing up for another day of fighting after having spent the seventh in full-scale combat, losing his CD and DVD players and a CD containing his fifty-page personal war journal when his rucksacks burned up on the outside of his Bradley.

On Brzozowski's first foray into the adjacent neighborhood, his team of two Bradleys and seven soldiers discovered three trucks packed with RPGs, AK-47 automatic rifles, and ammunition. They rigged up explosives, then had to jump back in the Bradleys and pull out under fire to escape secondary explosions as the weapons caches detonated. The ammunition cooked off for several more hours.

The second foray was more treacherous. The team stumbled across a mosque courtyard stacked knee-high with weapons and ammunition.

Brzozowski got out of his Bradley and went into the compound to set up demolition charges of C-4 explosives to destroy the cache. He needed both hands, so he put his automatic rifle down. As he added incendiary grenades to the cache, an Iraqi soldier stepped around the corner of the mosque and fired an AK-47. The shots missed Brzozowski but tore into an incendiary grenade and set it off. Brzozowski drew his 9mm pistol from his thigh holster and fired, killing the soldier.

As the grenade burned, Brzozowski ran back outside to the two Bradleys to get everyone loaded up and back to the interchange. Then he realized he hadn't initiated the timing fuses on the four C-4 charges he had set up. He had to run back inside, initiate the fuses, then race back outside and climb into his Bradley. The team had traveled most of the way back to the intersection when the C-4 charges went off, triggering an enormous explosion. Chunks of shrapnel and weapons and debris rained down on the southwest corner of the intersection in what Captain Hubbard later described as a "Nagasaki-Hiroshima black mushroom cloud–type explosion."

The detonation put an end to the threat from the neighborhood. By early afternoon, there was a lull in the fighting. Hubbard could feel his body shutting down; he hadn't slept in days. He was soaked through with sweat, and his legs and feet were swollen and aching from standing in the turret for two days straight. At one point he felt himself nodding off, so he handed off his duties to his executive officer and fell into a hard sleep. He woke up an hour later, refreshed and ready to get back into the fight.

Enemy gunfire picked up again late in the day. Hubbard had seen enough. He got permission from Twitty to call in three artillery missions of six big 155mm rounds each. The artillery exploded on top of enemy fighters dug into the date palms to the northwest and the southeast, and the ground shuddered each time the shells slammed down. Afterward, there were no more RPG volleys and only a smattering of small-arms fire by the time the sun went down. The battle for Objective Larry was over. Hubbard figured his men had killed up to four hundred enemy fighters and had destroyed perhaps eighty vehicles. A single American soldier had been injured—a minor shrapnel wound.

The highway was littered with corpses and with the burned-out hulks of vehicles. Piled among the trucks, cars, and motorcycles that had been packed with soldiers and armed men were the smoldering remains of a tan

2003 Toyota Camry. The car, driven by Bashar Hindi, had sped into the interchange on April 7, bound north to Baghdad. Hindi, twenty-eight, and his brother Waddah Hindi, thirty-four, who was in the passenger seat, apparently had not realized that they were driving into a firefight. They were leather dealers returning to the city from a trip to pay their employees, unaware that American forces had invaded. The Hindi brothers were partners in a leather business that exported skins to Italy and Spain—two wealthy, expensively dressed, educated men with an older brother who had attended George Washington University. Waddah Hindi, whose wife of three weeks was pregnant, apparently was struck in the head by fire from the combat team at Objective Larry and killed instantly. Bashar Hindi was severely wounded and bled to death on the highway. The brothers' relatives, who recovered their corpses on April 11, did not know whether warning shots had been fired at the two men, or whether the brothers simply had not realized they were supposed to stop and turn around. Captain Hubbard was certain that his men fired warning shots at every vehicle that approached the interchange, and he did not recall that any civilians had been killed in cars there.

Farther south, at Objective Curly, the men from 2-7 Infantry had come under sustained fire shortly after relieving the combat teams from the China battalion on the afternoon of April 7. Major Rod Coffey, the unit's operations officer, whose leg had been broken by a shrapnel blast, gave the arriving commanders an assessment of the enemy threat as the new combat team took up positions in place of the men from the China battalion. At sunset, thirty to forty fighters, backed by a BMP, began firing on the interchange from bunkers behind a wall about three hundred meters to the south. As engineers moved in to destroy the wall with a combat excavator, Staff Sergeant Lincoln Hollinsaid, twenty-seven, was killed by enemy fire. Later that evening, after the wall had been toppled and the bunkers cleared, the interchange was attacked by four BMPs and a group of soldiers. The men from 2-7 destroyed all four armored vehicles and killed or drove off the soldiers. The next day, the unit killed several more fighters who had attacked the forward aid station about eight hundred meters south of the interchange.

By the end of the day on the eighth, the battle was over. On the ninth, families began to emerge from their homes on either side of the highway. Some of them collected their dead from the tangle of corpses in the trench lines to the west. Others set upon the adjacent warehouses and businesses, dragging out supplies and office equipment. It seemed to Coffey a highly sophisticated form of looting, not at all frenzied or convulsive. The looters were orderly and intent, more opportunistic than predatory. Coffey watched old women and young children drag out bathtubs and office desks, and some of them waved gaily.

In addition to Hollinsaid, Sergeant First Class Marshall and Staff Sergeant Stever had died in the fight to hold Curly—Marshall and Stever during the ambush of the resupply convoy just south of the interchange. Nine American soldiers were wounded seriously enough at Curly to require medical evacuation, and thirty more were wounded but returned to the fight after treatment.

The friendly fire at Curly from the 2-7 Battalion became a contentious issue. Members of the China Battalion said it made the battlefield handoff even more complicated and dangerous. Lieutenant Colonel Scott E. Rutter, the 2-7 commander, later suggested that enemy fire—or fire from China itself—was actually responsible. Rutter said his battalion had rescued China, which he said had failed to fully clear Objective Curly.

On the morning of the eighth, Captain Anthony Butler, commander of the battalion's headquarters company, rode down Highway 8 with several other soldiers to try to find Marshall's body. Marshall had been left behind as the resupply convoy, under Captain Aaron Polsgrove, tried desperately to escape the ambush and avoid further casualties. Marshall's Humvee was still intact and still being used by his crewmen, Specialist Krofta and Private First Class Cruz. Across the roof of the vehicle, they had written in flowing black letters: "In memory of SFC Marshall—'Big Time' not forgotten."

Searching Highway 8, Captain Butler questioned American soldiers near the interchange at Curly. One told him that a local resident had claimed earlier in the day that he had seen the half-buried body of an American soldier nearby. But the soldier had not had the presence of mind to detain the resident so that he could lead the way to the body. Butler drove up and down the highway, searching north and south of the spot where Marshall had been blown out of his Humvee. His little search party came across an Iraqi civilian who said he had seen a dead American. He led Butler to a uniformed corpse that was swollen and overrun with flies. The body was dressed in an American uniform top with a US ARMY tag, but it also bore an Iraqi military web belt and Iraqi military boots. Butler looked closely. It wasn't Marshall—it was an Iraqi fighter.

The search party did not find Marshall that day, but they did find pieces of Stever, which one of the chaplains recovered and bagged for burial. The next day, Butler had flyers printed in both Arabic and English, offering a $100 reward for information leading to the recovery of the remains of Sergeant First Class John W. Marshall.

Four days later, on April 12, a young Iraqi boy approached soldiers from the 101st Airborne Division who were patrolling along Highway 8. He told them he had seen the remains of an American soldier in a shallow grave not far from the cloverleaf at Objective Curly. He led the soldiers to the grave, where they saw an arm and a leg protruding from the dirt. The corpse in the grave wore desert tan American combat fatigues. The rank—Sergeant First Class—was still on the sleeve, and over the right breast pocket was the name: MARSHALL. The remains of John Marshall were gently laid into a body bag and draped with an American flag to be shipped to the United States for burial with full military honors.

The recovery of Marshall's remains was a balm for Aaron Polsgrove, who had been consumed by guilt and regret for leaving Marshall behind during the ambush. He did not second-guess himself for his decision under fire; he believed it was the right call, and that it had almost certainly prevented further casualties. But he knew that if Marshall had not put himself at the head of the column—Polsgrove's usual position—it would have been Polsgrove's own corpse there on the highway. And even now, with Marshall's remains on their way back home to his family, there was still a troubling question for Polsgrove: Why hadn't God protected Sergeant Marshall, too? Polsgrove promised himself that when he reached heaven, he would ask God why.

The following winter, Polsgrove and his wife were told that she was pregnant with their first child. Polsgrove believed with all his heart that the small life growing inside her would not have been possible without the sacrifice of John Marshall.

In downtown Baghdad on April 9, the tanks and Bradleys of Captain Chris Carter's Attack Company were killing off the last holdouts among the soldiers and miltiamen who had infiltrated Rogue's sector from across the Tigris River. The company was hit by several volleys of RPGs and small-arms rounds during the day, returning fire each time until the volleys stopped. From across the river, RPG teams hiding behind a wall next to a mosque opened fire. Carter's Bradleys tore down the wall with several blasts of Twenty-five Mike Mike, and the fighters fled. By the end of the day, there was only sporadic contact, and the two northernmost bridges were secured.

The next day, April 10, Staff Sergeant Tom Slago, whose Bradley *Nocturnal* had been damaged twice in RPG attacks the previous week, was on duty on the west bank of the Tigris River, next to one of the northern bridges. His gunner, Specialist Gary Techur, was scanning through his sights across the river, where he could see people waving and celebrating on the balconies of their homes. The platoon commander motioned for Slago to move his Bradley toward an alley. Slago had his driver pull to the edge of the alley, where Techur could scan the buildings and Slago could keep an eye on a crowd of civilians gathering at the far end. Slago was watching the crowd when he noticed a white cloud of smoke. He was wondering what it was when something exploded against the Bradley and slammed him down to the floor of the turret. He yelled up at Techur, "Shoot! Shoot! Shoot!" and heard the other tanks and Bradleys open up. Then he realized that his face was burning and his eyes were swelling shut. Suddenly a sergeant from another vehicle was grabbing at him and yanking him up and out of the turret. He laid Slago down on the sidewalk, saying something to him in a low voice. Slago asked the sergeant to pat him down and check for wounds. The soldier looked at him and said, "I don't see no blood."

Slago heard a medical vehicle drive up and the sounds of the medics yelling something. The sergeant yelled back at them, "He's got really bad burns to his face—and shrapnel wounds to his stomach!" Someone lifted Slago and put him in the back of the medical vehicle. Slago lay there, afraid to touch his own belly because he feared that his intestines would spill out into his hands. He began to weep, not for his injuries, but because at that moment he believed he had let his family and his buddies down, and he worried about what they would think of him. Later, at the trauma center, he thought the medics had left him out in the hot sun. His face was burning and he screamed, "Kill the pain!" and then, "Roman Catholic—A positive!" A voice asked if he wanted morphine. "Oh, yeah," he heard himself reply. He felt a warm flow wash over him and the pain was gone.

Later that summer, Slago's face healed and his eyebrows and eyelashes grew back. The shrapnel to his belly had gone straight through him, a clean wound, and the scars soon healed. Slago felt blessed to be alive. When he returned to duty, he checked the ammo ready box on the Bradley, where he had stashed the Bible his wife's parents had sent him. It was still there, intact, with only the gold-leaf trim on the pages burned away.

Two more wounded men from the Tusker battalion also recovered— Private First Class Synquoiry Smith, the gunner wounded in the arm at the Jumhuriya Bridge intersection, and Sergeant First Class Phillip Cornell, the tank commander shot through the chest. As Cornell was being medevaced, he happened to look across at the next stretcher and saw the young Iraqi fighter in the red flannel shirt and work boots he had seen lying wounded on the palace roadway before the fight at the intersection. Even in his pain and confusion, this struck Cornell as an absurd coincidence. He thought about it for a long time, even as he was recuperating back home and joking about his wife treating him like a houseplant, dusting him off every few hours and turning him toward the sun. Cornell returned to duty at Fort Stewart later that year. A chunk of flesh was missing from his arm. Rough scars snaked across his chest and abdomen, and a piece of shrapnel the size of his pinkie was still lodged in his shoulder blade.

Beneath the crossed sabers on the military parade grounds, the Charlie Company crews from Rogue who had lost Charlie One Two to the tank fire on the fifth had survived the thunder run on the seventh while fighting from inside replacement tanks. Staff Sergeant Jason Diaz, the tank commander on Charlie One Two, served on the seventh as the gunner for Lieutenant Roger Gruneisen on a tank commanded by the lieutenant. Gruneisen's own tank, Charlie One One—*Creeping Death*—was still being repaired following the crash into the bridge abutment on Highway 8 on the fifth. Afterward, Sergeant Carlos Hernandez, the gunner on Charlie One One, had told the tank manufacturer's repair representative that the tank's gun tube had been bent. The rep insisted that an Abrams gun tube could not possibly be bent—until he got a good look at Charlie One One. The tank was later repaired and returned to service. Much later, Charlie One Two was recovered just north of Objective Curly and towed to Kuwait to be cannibalized for spare parts.

The Charlie Company crews fought battles downtown near the Baghdad train station and the national museum throughout the day on the seventh. On the eighth, their tanks were attacked by half a dozen suicide vehicles. The tank commanded by Gruneisen was actually rammed by one car, rocking the Abrams but causing no serious damage. Gruneisen's platoon destroyed at least two suicide cars that day. The lieutenant never found out who or what had been inside the vehicles, but he didn't care. He figured that if a driver kept charging a tank after taking warning shots to the pavement and through the grille, he was either an imbecile or intent on suicide. Either way, Gruneisen had no regrets about what he had done.

Private First Class Don Schafer and Private First Class Chris Shipley, the Charlie Company tank crewmen who had been wounded after transferring to an armored personnel carrier during the thunder run on April 5, were shipped to a U.S. Navy hospital in Spain and later to the States. The last thing Shipley remembered after an AK-47 round tore through his right eye was vomiting up blood. He did not know that Schafer had been wounded in the same incident until he awoke in his hospital bed in Spain and saw Schafer in the same ward, his arm wrapped with a huge bandage.

Later, Shipley had reconstructive surgery on his face and a prosthesis was created to replace his ruined right eye. His left arm healed reasonably well, but he did not have his previous range of movement. He turned twenty that autumn. He made plans to go back home to Arizona after his medical treatment was exhausted. He planned to leave the army. He wanted to go to a technical school and earn a computer science degree.

At the hospital in Spain, Schafer developed a bacterial infection, slowing his recovery. Back in the States, doctors pieced his upper right arm back together after drilling metal pins into his elbow and shoulder and connecting a reinforcing bar to help the bones regrow. Schafer could no longer lift his arm above his head or behind his back, and the doctors told him he probably never would. Schafer planned to get out of the army and go home to Baltimore to take criminal justice classes at a junior college. He intended to transfer to Florida State University. He had always wanted to be a police officer, but now that seemed unlikely, given his arm problems and the fact that he couldn't run very far without gasping for breath. He thought he might try something in the police field, perhaps forensics. He was ready to leave the army. It seemed to him that the military medical people, at least, didn't want much to do with him once they had him all patched up.

Between the train station and the Special Republican Guards head-quarters in downtown Baghdad, Captain Jason Conroy's company from Rogue fought a series of running street battles on the eighth with bands of Special Republican Guards, Fedayeen, and Syrians. RPG teams were on the rooftops, firing down on the tanks and Bradleys. Suicide vehicles attacked from the flanks, and on some streets antiaircraft guns were shooting in direct-fire mode. There were more antiaircraft guns on the roof of the train station. In front of the station was a series of bunkers infested with gunmen. The company killed dozens of soldiers and militiamen throughout the morning and afternoon, but more emerged from side streets and alleyways. On one street, the fighters used a long pole with a hook on the end—it reminded Conroy of the poles used in vaudeville to yank a struggling performer off the stage—to drag in their wounded and dead, and their weapons, too.

It took most of the day to secure the area, but the sniping and harassment from the enemy went on sporadically for another six days. Despite the intensity of the fighting in the city, Rogue did not lose another man. The loss of Staff Sergeant Stevon Booker on the fifth still weighed heavily on everyone, even months later, when U.S. Marines in south-central Iraq captured an Iraqi fighter and recovered an M-4 rifle. An investigation revealed that it was the M-4 Booker that had been firing when he was killed. The discovery didn't bring Booker back, but it seemed to bring a certain closure to his passing.

Talal Ahmed al-Doori, the Baath Party militia leader in downtown Baghdad, drove home during the thunder run on April 7 and later found a job driving a taxi. Colonel Raaed Faik, the Republican Guard officer who got off the bus to Baghdad on April 7, went home to his family in the Yarmouk district. Brigadier Baha Ali Nasr, the air force officer, stayed in his downtown office until April 9 and then went home. General Omar Adul Karim, the warehouse commander, drove home in his uniform on April 9, stubbornly ignoring the jeers of defecting soldiers, who yelled at him, "Take off your uniform! It's over!" And Nabeel al-Qaisy, the reluctant Baath Party militiaman on duty in the Baghdad bunker, walked home on April 7. Later he sold his AK-47, quit the party, and resumed his job as a fine arts teacher.

* * *

At the Ministry of Justice complex, two blocks west of the Tigris River bridge defended by Captain Steve Barry's Cyclone Company, an infantry patrol moved in just after dawn on April 9 to investigate scraping noises coming from the high-rise building that housed the ministry offices. As the infantrymen approached the main entry vestibule, they raised their rifles at the sound of footsteps. And there, emerging from the shadows, were two smiling Iraqi boys hauling plastic buckets brimming with stolen desk blotters, staplers, pens, and paper clips. The infantrymen shooed the boys away and entered the stairwells, only to discover that the entire building was infested with looters. Young men and boys were thundering down the stairs lugging computers and printers and telephones. One stairwell was blocked by a huge sofa that two bearded men had tried to force down the narrow passageway. In the offices upstairs, looters had stomped framed photos of Saddam Hussein and emptied out file cabinets. Thousands of files and papers from the ministry were floating down from the windows, landing in the courtyard below like a blanket of snow. One burly man had managed to drag a huge air-conditioning unit all the way to the ground floor, where he asked two young infantrymen—in English—for assistance. The soldiers laughed at him, but they had to admire his initiative.

The patrol leader radioed back for guidance. No one had ever briefed the infantrymen on what do about looters. The local commanders passed the query up the chain of command. They, too, were not quite certain how to respond. For months, their focus had been on defeating the Iraqi military and toppling Saddam Hussein's regime with a combination of speed and shock and firepower. There had been virtually no discussion of what do *after* Baghdad had fallen. Word came back from the higher command: secure the perimeter, disarm anyone with a weapon, but don't shoot at the looters. For the rest of the day, the men from Cyclone Company held their perimeter and watched the mobs systematically loot the Ministry of Justice and then move on to other government buildings in the downtown complex.

A mile to the south, at the Republican Palace, Captain Phil Wolford made his way up the palace roadway on the afternoon of the eighth to have a look at the battlefield in the calm light of day. At the small arch where the gunmen in the road had surprised Sergeant First Class Lustig with two quick RPG blasts into his tank, Wolford got his first close look at the fighters who had charged the palace in the middle of the night. If they hadn't been carrying weapons and ammunition belts, he would have thought they were college students. Most were dressed in jeans and sneakers and very stylish sport shirts. Many of them had backpacks. One of the corpses was wearing sunglasses, which struck Wolford as bizarre since they had attacked on the darkest night he had seen in Iraq. He could not understand what had possessed them to stroll down the palace road in the middle of the night to fight an American tank company. At one point that day, he counted the bodies on that section of the roadway and in the tree line. The total came to sixteen and a half.

At the intersection near the Jumhuriya Bridge, Wolford discovered an elaborate bunker at the southwest corner. It was made from a metal cargo container that had been buried underground. It was equipped with a thick wooden door, and inside were a desk, a nonworking military field phone, and piles of supplies—an entire command post.

Two weeks after the battle for the bridge, Wolford was on patrol when he noticed several Iraqi ambulances parked at the far northern end of the two city parks near the intersection. A group of men wearing surgeons' masks were extracting corpses from a series of bunkers. The men were from the city coroner's office. They had been summoned by residents complaining of an overpowering stench from the park. They recovered fifty-four bodies.

Afterward, Assassin Company spent several weeks manning a checkpoint in the ruins of the intersection, controlling access through the arch, which came to be known as Assassin's Gate. The arch was a flashpoint for trouble. One day Wolford's men had to put down a near-riot after a mob of former Iraqi soldiers demanding back pay rushed the checkpoint. Another day, an elderly woman approached the Americans while clutching a live Iraqi army hand grenade. After she pulled the pin, an Assassin Company sergeant managed to wrap both hands around the woman's hand and the grenade's spoon, or handle, then flung it over a wall just before it exploded. Later, an Iraqi man with a knife and another with a shard of broken glass attacked the men from Assassin, who wrestled the attackers to the ground and disarmed them.

Captain Ed Ballanco, who had led Tusker's resupply convoy up Highway 8 on the seventh, also went out to the palace roadway on the eighth. He saw one dead fighter who was probably eighteen years old, but he looked sixteen. He felt no pity; he was glad the kid was dead. Later, Ballanco took stock of the ammunition Assassin Company had fired on the eighth. At the battle in the intersection alone, the company fired twenty-four thousand rounds of coax, ten thousand rounds of .50-caliber machine-gun ammunition, and sixty-four main gun rounds. During its two days at the palace, it had fired seventy thousand rounds of coax and M-240 machine-gun ammunition. Some tank companies didn't fire off that many machine-gun rounds in a year of training.

Major Rideout also went out to have a look at the enemy corpses. He saw one young man with jeans and spectacles who gripped an AK-47 in one hand, with an RPG launcher slung over his shoulder. Rideout wondered if he was the knucklehead who had fired the RPG over his head while he was trying to sleep. The corpse, and most of the others, was already starting to swell and stink in the hot April sun. After another day or two, Rideout had the engineers start digging graves in the stand of trees across from the palace, where the Iraqi soldiers had been killed in their bunkers as Assassin Company burst through the arch on the morning of the seventh. The engineers and civil affairs teams saved whatever identification they could find on the corpses and marked the graves with eight-digit GPS grids. With the help of Iraqi volunteers, the bodies were washed and buried facing Mecca. The engineers spent the next several days pulling wet, oozing remains from burned-out cars and trucks, and peeling maggot-infested corpses off walls and bridge abutments.

Later that summer, after Rideout had rotated back to the States, he arranged to visit Annette Hale, the stepmother of Captain Ed "Jason" Korn, the officer killed by friendly fire. He wasn't sure how she would receive him, but it was something he felt compelled to do. He sat down around a coffee table with Korn's stepmother and the rest of Korn's immediate family in Savannah, Georgia. Rideout had recovered the captain's helmet, cleaning off the blood and affixing new Third Infantry patches on either side. He presented it to Korn's stepmother, along with Korn's wristwatch.

Rideout related Korn's entire Iraqi experience—how he had volunteered and rushed to catch up with the brigade in the desert, how eager he had been to get into the fight, and how he had walked away from the column in the palm forest without telling anyone. He drew maps showing the road and the trees and the two Iraqi tanks that Korn had gone to investigate. As he spoke, Hale interrupted and put her hand on Rideout's arm.

"Everything you have just told me is true," she told him.

Rideout was startled. He wanted to tell her that this was one of the hardest things he'd ever had to do. He wanted to ask her why she thought he would lie to her after all that had happened. He told her, "Ma'am, everything I've told you *is* true."

She handed Rideout a letter and told him to read it. It was from her stepson, written two days before he died. It had arrived just a week before Rideout's visit. Rideout read it and saw that Korn had told his stepmother some of the same things Rideout had just related. Rideout realized that the family bore no grudge against him, that they did not blame him for Ed Korn's death. As he poured out more details of the incident, describing how Korn had discovered the Iraqi tank in the trees and then sent a sergeant back to fetch an antitank weapon, the family members nodded and said, "Yeah, that was Jason."

Early in their conversation, an alarm had suddenly sounded on Korn's wristwatch on the coffee table. His stepmother had looked at it and told Rideout, "He's talking to us."

By April 9, the deaths of the two cameramen at the Palestine Hotel had triggered the beginnings of an international incident. Outraged journalist groups asked how an American combat unit, equipped with satellite technology and sophisticated computer equipment, could have fired on a building that was clearly marked as a hotel. It had been widely reported, they pointed out, that the Palestine was home to nearly one hundred journalists covering the war from inside Baghdad. They said the crews should have taken more care to identify their target before firing. The following month, the Committee to Protect Journalists published a detailed report on the incident, concluding that the attack on the hotel was not deliberate but was avoidable, in large part because the hotel was so well known and easily identifiable. The Second Brigade should have known not to fire on the hotel, the report concluded.

The U.S. military conducted a series of investigations, and Perkins, deCamp, Wolford, and others were interviewed several times. The commanders walked the investigators through the battlefield at the intersection and across the bridge. In August, the U.S. Central Command issued an investigative report concluding that the men from Assassin Company were justified in firing at what they reasonably believed was an enemy position. A CENTCOM statement said the unit's actions were "fully in accordance" with the rules of engagement because the soldiers believed they were firing on "a suspected enemy hunter/killer team."

The summary of the report did not address assertions by journalists that higher U.S. military commands in Kuwait and Qatar, which had direct access to TV news reports and to journalists, should have alerted commanders in Baghdad that the Palestine was in the area where American tanks were engaging Iraqi forces on April 8.

The soldiers and commanders involved, from Colonel Perkins down to Staff Sergeant Gibson, expressed sorrow and remorse at the deaths of the cameramen. But they also felt frustration and anger at what they perceived as unfair and uninformed criticism of their actions by people who had little understanding of the speed, chaos, and terror of modern combat. They believed press reports had portrayed their attempts to locate the Palestine while also clearing an air strike on the beige high-rise as a conspiracy to fire on the hotel. There were personal repercussions as well. Captain Wolford's wife in Georgia answered her home phone one day and heard a man's voice ask, "Do you and your family want to die tonight?" Lieutenant Colonel deCamp's wife also received a threatening phone call. DeCamp, Wolford, and Gibson were indicted in Spain, home of one of the dead cameramen.

Colonel David Perkins was left with a hollow feeling in the pit of his stomach. The Palestine incident had been one of the more tragic and painful episodes of the Iraqi campaign, and it was all the more difficult for him to endure given the efforts Perkins had expended to locate the hotel at the height of one of the most intense battles of the war. It was certainly unprecedented, Perkins thought, for a brigade commander in the middle of a firefight to enlist embedded reporters to help locate a building in an effort to avoid civilian casualties. That effort ultimately had fallen short, but Perkins believed in his heart that he and his men had acted with good intentions and honorable motives in a time of war.

As April passed into May, the American military focus shifted from combat missions to the vague and amorphous business of stabilization and rebuilding. The sudden and precipitous displacement was jarring and disorienting for soldiers and commanders who had trained for months to destroy the enemy and topple the regime. They felt adrift. The euphoria of taking Baghdad, of charging into the palaces and the ministries, had faded. They had achieved something remarkable and even historic—an armored charge by fewer than a thousand men into an enemy capital defended by thousands of soldiers and militiamen. The brigade's bold strike had forever altered established armor doctrine for urban warfare and had shortened the war by weeks. It had precluded the long, bloody siege anticipated by Pentagon planners, who had envisioned a drawn-out urban clearing operation by airborne infantry. At a memorial service on Saddam's former parade grounds, Perkins told his men, "Many different methods by many different countries have been tried to force the Saddam regime to collapse, but only one worked. The one that worked was putting the boots of American soldiers on the streets of Baghdad."

It was true that the brigade had fought a dispirited and outmatched enemy whose strength and capabilities had been drained by the decisive coalition victory in the first Gulf War and by years of economic sanctions. The American military was the best-trained and most technologically superior fighting force on the planet. The Iraqi military had no navy, no helicopter gunships, a grounded fleet of outdated fighter planes, and armored units debilitated by a U.S. and British bombing campaign. Thousands of Iraqi soldiers had thrown off their uniforms and gone home. Even so, thousands more Special Republican Guards, Fedayeen, Arab *jihadis,* and Baath Party militiamen had mounted a furious and fanatical resistance on Highway 8 and inside the city. If the battle of Baghdad seemed a cakewalk to American TV viewers and the armchair generals serving as commentators, the soldiers who had conquered the Iraqi regime knew the truth.

The battalions held the palace complex for several more weeks, until the brigade was transferred to Falloujah, a crowded Sunni town in the flat desert landscape sixty-five kilometers west of Baghdad. They would spend a difficult summer there before the brigade returned to Fort Stewart that fall. Falloujah was a notorious center of resistance, perhaps the most virulently anti-American urban center in the broad swath north and west of Baghdad known as the Sunni Triangle. Emerging "postcombat" responsibilities dictated that the battalions rely less on tanks and Bradleys and more on Humvees in order to more effectively patrol civilian areas. But the changeover exposed soldiers to greater threats from hit-and-run attacks mounted by a revitalized insurgency that was refining its tactics—an insurgency comprised of many of the same fighters who had survived the thunder runs. In addition to RPG, small-arms, and mortar attacks, the Iraqis and their Arab confederates turned to strategically placed suicide vehicles and to roadside bombs known as IEDs—improvised explosive devices. That July, an IED killed Specialist Joel Lynn Bertoldie, twenty, a driver for the Tusker battalion, as he drove a Humvee through a traffic circle overlooking the Euphrates River in Falloujah. The death of Bertoldie, the father of a ten-month-old baby boy, was a benchmark. He was the 148th member of the U.S. military to die in Operation Iraqi Freedom, surpassing the combat death toll of 147 from the 1991 Persian Gulf War.

Well before Bertoldie was killed—in fact, shortly after the April 7 thunder run was over—many of the soldiers of the brigade had begun to experience a fleeting sense of loss. They had spent months training for combat. They had survived three intense weeks of relentless desert and urban warfare. They had been honed and focused. They had had a clear mission and a defined goal that drove them and united them in a singular, shared purpose. For all the terror and confusion they had experienced in battle, and for all the misery of their living conditions, they had felt a re-markable sense of clarity and fulfillment.

After the adrenaline had drained away and they were suddenly at rest, some of them sought out the chaplains and poured out their emotions. They had been fighting and moving and killing for day after day, and sud-denly it had all been shut down. They wanted—they needed—to sort through it all. Some soldiers confessed that they had not comprehended precisely what would be asked of them while in pursuit of the enemy. They had not doubted that they would win the war, but they had not fully real-ized what it would take to prevail. It was not that they felt guilty; they felt overwhelmed and somehow incomplete. A few of them realized that they had embraced the thrill of the fight, and this discovery troubled them deeply. But most of all, the men from the Second Brigade felt an ineffable loss of purity. They had been part of a unique moment in modern mili-tary history. They had captured something seductive and elusive, and they did not know how to get it back.

AFTERWORD

Just three months after the Second Brigade returned to the United States in the fall of 2003, the unit was issued orders for a second deployment to Iraq. By early 2005, the brigade was on its way back to the combat zone.

It was a much different unit than the one that led the charge into Baghdad in April 2003. Many of the men who had fought during the invasion had transferred to other units, and some had left the service. The Spartan Brigade's entire top command had moved on.

Colonel David Perkins, the brigade commander, took a Pentagon job as executive assistant to the vice chairman of the Joint Chiefs of Staff. The brigade executive officer, Lieutenant Colonel Eric Wesley, took command of a tank battalion with the 1st Armored Division, a battalion that was ordered to Iraq in early 2005. Lieutenant Colonel Eric Schwartz, commander of the Desert Rogues, joined the U.S. Pacific Command in Hawaii. Lieutenant Colonel Philip deCamp, the Tusker commander, became a professor of military science at the College of William and Mary. Lieutenant Colonel Stephen Twitty, the China commander, entered studies at National Defense University. Lieutenant Colonel Kenneth Gantt, the Battle Kings artillery commander, was sent to the Pentagon to work for the chief of staff of the U.S. Army.

For many of the lower-ranking soldiers from the tank and Bradley crews, the battle for Baghdad was the most searing experience of their lives. It continued to dominate their psyches, long after they were back home with their friends and families. Young and emotionally unprepared for the scale of the killing on the thunder runs, they could not find the words to express what they had endured. Several wives and girlfriends complained that their men were incapable of openly sharing what had happened to them in Iraq. The soldiers seemed to crave normality, embracing mundane chores and daily routines that kept their emotions blanketed. Many found a curious comfort in training drills, which gave them a sense of purpose distinct from their fractured domestic existence.

The soldiers had not yet recovered from their first deployment when they learned that they were headed back to Iraq. They accepted the news with stoicism, though their families did not. They knew the situation in Iraq had changed dramatically, but no one could articulate their new mission with any certainty. During the thunder runs, they had been aggressors. They had closed on the enemy and killed him. But during their summer in Falloujah in 2003, they had been confronted with the new, postinvasion reality: They were no longer on the attack. They were on patrol. They were targets.

For the Second Brigade officers and men sent back to Iraq, the country was a more confusing and menacing place than the one they had left just a year earlier. The insurgency had spread and mutated into a lethal and largely unseen force. American soldiers were dying every day, but rarely in the face-to-face combat of the invasion. They were more likely to be killed in hit-and-run attacks by insurgents who melted back into the civilian population, or by remote-triggered roadside bombs. On the worst days, the number of attacks spiked past eighty. Iraqi civilians were dying, too, either killed by terrorist car bombs or when caught up in strikes by American forces. The effort to rebuild Iraq faltered so badly in the face of relentless attacks on infrastructure and against officials of the interim Iraqi government that Washington diverted huge sums of money from reconstruction to security.

Only in retrospect did it become apparent that the thunder runs in Baghdad in April 2003 were a prelude to an expanding insurgency. Many of the same fighters who had survived the battle for Baghdad had refined their tactics. They regrouped, transforming themselves into a classic guerrilla force relying on stealth, surprise, and terror. The Saddam Hussein regime had been driven from power, but many of the men who once helped maintain Saddam's brutal police state were still at large. With the help of some of the same jihadis who had fought in the thunder runs, they were directing a shadow terror-state-within-a-state.

The two thunder runs had shown that tanks and Bradleys could fight and prevail in cities, at least under certain conditions. Though it was not immediately apparent in April 2003, conditions in Baghdad proved to be nearly ideal for an armored strike into the capital. American armor was able to seize the initiative, moving with speed and daring. Iraqi forces, with a few notable exceptions, were disorganized and poorly led. The main battlefields—Highway 8 and the downtown government and palace complex—were largely devoid of high-rise buildings and dense civilian neighborhoods.

The capture of Baghdad has come to represent the pinnacle of American combat achievement in Iraq. After the fall of the capital, it appeared that the U.S. military had avoided the bloody, grinding, disheartening urban warfare that so many Americans had feared. But less than two years later, as the Second Brigade returned to a much different battlefield, that fight was now upon them.

ACKNOWLEDGMENTS

Any story of war is the story of men—of their performance in the face of stress and danger and fear. This book, a chronicle of men in modern combat, would not have been possible without the willingness of the officers and soldiers of the Spartan Brigade to share their stories with me. Each man's story was uniquely personal and, in many cases, painful. These soldiers were honest about their fears and their anxieties, and about the emotional toll inflicted on young lives by the killing of fellow human beings. As Major Mark Rasins remarked to me one day in Baghdad, "We're in the business of managing violence." No one I spoke with exulted in killing people. Some men expressed certain regrets, but all spoke of the pride they felt in what the brigade had accomplished under trying and often terrifying conditions. They had not asked to go to war, but when sent they responded with courage and sacrifice and, often, with valor. They were tested, and they prevailed. This book is for them.

Several members of the brigade spent many hours helping me to confirm various accounts and details of the battle. They helped me correct many of my own errors and misconceptions. I owe a special debt to Colonel David Perkins, Lieutenant Colonel Eric Wesley, Lieutenant Colonel Philip deCamp, Lieutenant Colonel Stephen Twitty, Lieutenant Colonel Kenneth Gantt, Major Mark Rasins, Major Kent Rideout, Major Denton Knapp, Major Rick Nussio, Major Michael Donovan, Captain Edward Ballanco, Captain Aaron Polsgrove, Captain William Glaser, and Captain Phillip Wolford.

I received considerable assistance from Major Dane Childs, a U.S. Army historian who during the war was attached to the Third Infantry Division (Mechanized) as commander of the 102nd Military History Detachment. His insights and comments were invaluable in ensuring the accuracy and authenticity of this book. I also thank Professor James O. Kievit of the Center for Strategic Leadership at the U.S. Army War College for his help in researching the origins of the military term *thunder run*. Several members of U.S. Army public affairs units in Iraq and at Fort Stewart,

Georgia—Sergeant First Class James M. Brantley, Specialist Mason Lowery, and Specialist Katherine Robinson—were particularly helpful in locating soldiers for interviews.

Many former members of the Iraqi military, along with numerous Iraqi civilians, took calculated risks in sharing their stories with me, and for that I am grateful.

Several people came to my assistance after I lost all my possessions in a troop truck plunge into a canal near Karbala. Colonel David Perkins allowed me to embed with his brigade combat team, and my colleagues Geoffrey Mohan of the *Los Angeles Times* and Gregg Zoroya of *USA Today* graciously offered the use of their satellite phones and laptop computers. Photographer Rick Loomis of the *Los Angeles Times* was an inspired and irrepressible traveling companion who shared with me an unforgettable adventure in Iraq.

This book began as an article published in the *Los Angeles Times Magazine,* and I relied heavily on my early reporting in Iraq as an embedded reporter for the *Times.* I thank editors John Carroll, Dean Baquet, Scott Kraft, and Marjorie Miller for their support, and the newspaper for granting me a leave of absence to write *Thunder Run.*

I also thank Brando Skyhorse and Morgan Entrekin at Atlantic Monthly Press for believing in this book and my agent, Flip Brophy, for her faith in me.

I am indebted to several friends for their careful reading of sections of the manuscript and for their suggestions and advice: Mark Bowden, Ed Hille, Rick Nichols, Dennis (Piano Legs) Rickman, and my brothers Larry and Vincent Zucchino. I am especially grateful for my favorite editor, my wife, Kacey, who guided me through the manuscript's many rough patches while also keeping our family together while I was preoccupied with this project. This is her book, too.

APPENDIX

COMBAT AWARDS
SPARTAN BRIGADE

SILVER STAR

RANK	NAME
CPT	BARRY, STEVEN
CPT	BENTON, LEROY D.
SSG	BOOKER, STEVON A.
CPT	BURRIS, LARRY Q.
CPT	CARTER, CHRISTOPHER
CPT	CONROY, JASON P.
LTC	DECAMP, PHILIP D.
SSG	DIAZ, JASON
SSG	EDGY, GANNON
SSG	FRANCO, KENNETH
SFC	GAINES, RONALD
CSM	GALLAGHER, ROBERT
CPT	HIBNER, DAVID
CPT	HILMES, ANDREW
SSG	HOBBS, CRAIG
CPT	HUBBARD, DANIEL
CPT	JOHNSON, RONNY
SFC	LUSTIG, JONATHAN M.
SFC	MARSHALL, JOHN
COL	PERKINS, DAVID G.
LTC	SCHWARTZ, ERIC. C
SSG	STEVER, ROBERT
LTC	TWITTY, STEPHEN
SSG	WILSON, OBERT
CPT	WOLFORD, PHILLIP
CPT	WRIGHT, JOSHUA

BRONZE STAR with "V" for Valor

RANK	NAME
CPT	AHEARN, JAMES A.
1SG	ALEN, SILAS JR.
SFC	ANSLINGER, MICHAEL
SSG	ARROYO-MERLO, ROBERTO
SSG	AUSTIN, DALE
1LT	BAKER, DOUGLAS
1LT	BALL, ROBERT
CSM	BARNELLO, WILLIAM
1SG	BAUGH, JAMES A.
SSG	BELL, JOE S.
1LT	BERRIMAN, MICHAEL
SSG	BIRTHISEL, JEFFERY W.
SSG	BORJA, DANIEL
SGT	BRISLEY, CHRISTOPHER
2LT	BURNS, MICHAEL
SSG	BYRD, ROBERT
1LT	CANADAY, ERIC

1LT	CASE, BRIAN	SSG	LEVESQUE, LEO A. III
1LT	CASTRO, FRANCIS	SGT	LUCAS, DUSTIN
SSG	CHANDLER, DON E.	SFC	LUJAN, JEFFREY
SFC	CHILDERS, DAVID	SFC	LUSTIG, JONATHAN M.
SGT	COUVERTIER, JOSE L.	SSG	MACPHAIL, DUNCAN C.
SGT	COX, BRADLEY	SSG	MAO, CHHAY
SFC	CURTIS, DAVID	CPT	MCFARLAND, STEFAN
MAJ	DONOVAN, MICHAEL	1LT	MCKENNA, MATTHEW
SFC	DUNFEE, MICHAEL	1LT	MCKNIGHT, LEE
MAJ	DUNLOP, KEVIN	SFC	MEADOWS, JOHNNY
SSG	EMPSON, JEFFERY	1SG	MERCADO, JOSE
LTC	FAIRCHILD, JAMES	1LT	MIDDLETON, MAURICE
1LT	FEW, JAMES	SSG	MILLS, CHRISTOPHER
SPC	FRANKS, TERRY	SFC	MORALES, JOHN N.
1SG	FRENCH, CHRISTOPHER	SGT	MORGAN, ADAM
LTC	GANTT, KENNETH	1SG	MOSER, JEFF D.
SSG	GASAWAY, KEITH A.	SSG	MURRAY, WALTER
SGT	GIBBONS, DAVID A.	MAJ	NUSSIO, RICKY
SGM	GONGORA, BARREIRO, A.	SFC	OLSON, ERIC
SSG	GRISHAM, CHRISTOPHER	SFC	PALMER, JEROD S.
1LT	GRUNEISEN, ROGER	1LT	PANETTA, EDWARD
SSG	HALL, JASON S.	SSG	PATRICK, JAMUS
2LT	HART, JEFFERY	SGT	PERDUE, JOHNNY
SFC	HAY, ROBERT A.	LTC	PRESNELL, MICHAEL
SGT	HERNANDEZ, CARLOS	MAJ	RASINS, MARK
SFC	HOLMAN, JASON	SSG	RICHARD, DAVID
SPC	HORTON, MATTHEW	PFC	RICHARDSON, MICHAEL
1LT	HOYT, DOUGLAS M.	MAJ	RIDEOUT, KENT
SGT	INGRAM, PAUL F.	CPL	ROBICHEAU
MAJ	KNAPP, EVERETT	SSG	RUSSELL, RODNEY
1LT	KUO, RYAN	SSG	SANDERS, CHARLES
CPT	LAWRENCE, HARRIS	1LT	SHELL, BRANDON
SFC	LEGRANT, ANDRE	PFC	SHIPLEY, CHRIS L.

SSG	SLAGO, THOMAS W.
SFC	STEFANSKI, JAMES E.
SGT	STRUNK, MARK E.
SPC	SULLIVAN, SHAWN B.
SFC	TERPAK, TIMOTHY
KOS	TERS, JAMES A.
SGT	THAYER, BRADLEY
PFC	TOPAHA, VIRGIL
1LT	VAN KIRK, DANIEL
SSG	VEGA, FELIPE
CW2	WALKER, STEVEN K. JR.
LTC	WESLEY, ERIC
SSG	WHELAN, DENNIS
SFC	WHITE, RAY
SSG	WITHERSPOON, EUGENE
SSG	WOLENS, JAMES C.
CPT	WOODWARD, SCOTT
SFC	WRIGHT, ERIC
PFC	YAZZIE, TERRANCE A.
CW2	YOUNG, WILLIS G.
SSG	ZUMEK, JASON

BRONZE STAR

RANK	NAME
CW3	ACEVEDO, ANGEL
CPT	AHEARN, JAMES
SSG	ALBRIGHT, CHRISTOPHER M.
SSG	ALEXANDER, LARRICCO
SFC	ALFIERI, ERIC J.
CPT	ALMAGUER, FELIX
1LT	AMARA, CHRISTOPHER
SFC	ARROWOOD, RODNEY

SSG	AUSTIN, KENNETH
CPT	BAILEY, JIMMY
SSG	BAKER, GORDON
SGT	BALDWIN, DON
CPT	BALLANCO, EDWARD J.
CSM	BARNELLO, WILLIAM
1LT	BARR, JASON
MAJ	BARREN, JAMES E.
CPT	BARRY, STEVEN T.
SPC	BAUMGARTE, CAMERON
SSG	BECK, JOHN J.
CPT	BEESON, PALMER R.
SFC	BERTRAND, ROBERT S.
CPT	BIAGIOTTI, WILLIAM T.
CW2	BISCHOFF, RAY M.
SFC	BLACK, RICHARD
CPT	BLENZ, RICHARD A.
1LT	BOGDA, DEREK R.
SSG	BOOKER, STEVON A.
1LT	BOOTH, THOMAS
SSG	BOUTON, DANNY
CPT	BOWEN, MAJOR
1LT	BOWERS, WILLIAM
SSG	BRIGHAM, DENNIS
CPT	BRODANY, WILLIAM
1LT	BROWNING, MICHAEL
SSG	BRYANT, LESTER
1LT	BRZOZOWSKI, MARK
CPT	BULLOCK, BRADLEY
MAJ	BURGESS, JOHN E.
1SG	BURNS, CEDRIC S.
CPT	BURRIS, LARRY Q.
CPT	BUTLER, ANTHONY L.

1SG	BUTLER, KENDRICK J.	1SG	EYNON, DONALD
CPT	CANNAN, FREDERICK	SGM	FALKNER, DOUGLAS A.
SSG	CAPAZ, CASEY S.	CPT	FAULK, DAVID M.
CPT	CAPRA, KEVIN S.	CPT	FERRILL, JASON B.
SSG	CARMON, TROY	1LT	FISHER, BRADFORD A.
CPT	CARTER, CHRISTOPHER	CW3	FORD, JOE W.
1LT	CASMAER, MONICA L.	1LT	FRASURE, JOHN P.
1LT	CHEN, DAVID H.	1LT	GACHERU, MIGWI M.
SGT	CHISLER, PATRICK E.	1LT	GARABATO, DAVIS
SGT	CHOAT, AARON B.	SSG	GARRETT, STEPHON
CPT	CHONG, STEVE C.	SSG	GIBSON, SHAWN L.
1LT	COFER, CHESTER W.	1LT	GIFFORD, STEPHEN
CPT	CONROY, JASON P.	SSG	GILES, JASON
CSM	COOK, VERNON A.	CPT	GLASER, WILLIAM
CPT	COOPER, RONALD	CPT	GLASS, GEORGE L.
CPT	CORREZ, RICK	CPT	GLASSCOCK, CHARLES G.
CPT	CORYELL, WILLIAM F.	1SG	GOODMAN, JEFFERY
SFC	COTTINGHAM, PATRICK L.	CPT	GOVAN, JOHN F. III
SSG	CRAWLEY, RICHARD	SFC	GRANT, HAROLD E.
SSG	CRESPO, MICHAEL	CPT	GREGG, CHESTER J.
SSG	CROSS, SHELBY D.	PFC	GREGORY, ADAM
1SG	DALTON, RODRIC V.	SFC	GROVER, MARK
SSG	DAVIS, WILBERT	CW2	GUILLEMETTE, ROGER U.
SSG	DELGADO, RAUL	SGT	HAIOLA, BLAYNE
SFC	DENMARK, ABRAHAM	SFC	HARKINS, WAYNE J.
1SG	DENNIS, MARK A.	CPT	HARRIS, CHRISTOPHER
SFC	DIEHL, MICHAEL	SFC	HARRISON, WILLIE W.
COL	DISALVO, JOSEPH	CPT	HAYTH, BENNETT E.
MAJ	DOVOVAN, MICHAEL P.	CPT	HENDERSON, MCKELLE L.
CPT	DOYLE, ANDREW	1SG	HERNANDEZ, ALFRED
MAJ	DUNLOP, KEVIN	1LT	HESS, ADAM A.
CPT	DYCHES, MICHAEL D.	CPT	HIBNER, DAVID
SGT	ELLIS, JEFFREY T.	CPT	HILMES, ANDREW

CPT	HOMMEL, STEPHEN	CPT	KOLINSKI, MICHAEL
1LT	HOOPER, MICHAEL E.	CPT	KORN, EDWARD
CPT	HORNBUCKLE, HARRY	1LT	KREMMERS, ERIC T.
W01	HOWELL, DWAYNE E.	SFC	KUZIEL, JOHN
CPT	HUBBARD, DANIEL	MSG	LAMDERTIS, ALVARO
SSG	HUDSON, TERODER L.	SGT	LAROCQUE, GEARY H.
1SG	HUELL, DAN JR.	SSG	LAWSON, JAMES
CW2	HUGHES, REGINALD	SSG	LEATH, AARON
CPT	HUME, SHANNON	SFC	LEE, JERRY D.
1SG	HUNT, HARRY	1LT	LEGGETTE, HERB
MSG	HUNTER, ANDREW	CW2	LEMIESZEK, RONALD
SSG	IVINGS, BRYCE E.	CPT	LETCHER, MICHELLE M. T.
SSG	JACOBSON, MELVIN E.	1LT	LEVAN, KEVIN M.
SSG	JENNINGS, CHARLES	2LT	LEVY, RUTHIE
CPT	JENSEN, JOHN F.	CPT	LINN, JOSEPH I.
SGT	JOCKISH, PATRICK J.	SSG	LITTLE, RICHARD A.
SSG	JOHNSON, MELDON	CPT	LOPEZ, ROBERT
CPT	JOHNSON, PETER	LTC	LUCK, GARY
SSG	JOHNSON, RICARDO F.	1LT	LUU, PHILIP
CPT	JOHNSON, RONNY	CPT	MAHAFFEY, CHRISTOPHER S.
SSG	JONES, ALECK	CPT	MARM, WILLIAM J.
SGT	JONES, MATTHEW	SSG	MARRERO, ADOLFO
SFC	JONES, MICHAEL C.	SFC	MARSHALL, JOHN
CPT	JUDGE, PAUL C.	SGT	MARTINEZ, DAVID
CPT	KADET, BRIAN	MAJ	MARX, GARY
CPT	KENNEDY, KEVIN	1LT	MATHENY, WILLIAM A.
CPL	KEOWN, MATTHEW	CPT	MAZUREK, JAMES L.
SFC	KESTER, RONALD J. JR.	SFC	MCCREA, DEREK D.
CPT	KINLAW, DAVID A.	1LT	MCFARLAND, JEFF
CPT	KINSEY, WILLIAM R.	1SG	MCKEEVER, CLARK
MAJ	KIRBY, HOMER E.	MSG	MCNEILL, MELVIN
SSG	KNAPP, TIMOTHY	CPT	MCNULTY, JASON S.
SSG	KNOX, MANSO	SGT	MCVAY, DANIEL L.

CPT	MEADOWS, ROBERT	CPT	POWELL, SHERMAN S.
1LT	MEYER, PAUL E.	1LT	PROSSER, ADAM
SFC	MICHEL, RONNY	CPT	PUCKETT, ANDERSON H.
SSG	MILES, TERRY B.	SGT	QUINONES, PEDRO J.
PV2	MILLER, ANTHONY	CPT	RANGARAM, JAY P.
SSG	MILTON, GERMELL	MAJ	RASINS, MARK
SPC	MITCHELL, GEORGE	1SG	RASMUSSEN, JOSEPH K.
CPT	MITCHELL, LUCIOUS JR.	MAJ	RATIGAN, PATRICK
CPT	MOLFINO, JEFFREY S.	1LT	REDMON, JASON
SFC	MOLINA, KENNETH	SFC	REDMOND, MORRIS A.
PFC	MONEY, JAMES	CPT	REGENNITTER, CHRISTOPHER
SSG	MORALES, CLAUDINO	CPT	REYNNELLS, STEVEN R.
CPT	MORGAN, MATTHEW T.	MAJ	RICE, PHILLIP D.
PFC	MORRIS, DAVID M.	SSG	RICHARDSON, MARCUS
MAJ	MORRIS, TODD B.	SPC	RICKS, BENJAMIN
1LT	MORRISSEY, BRIAN	MAJ	RIDEOUT, KENT
MAJ	MULLEN, SEAN F.	SSG	RIVERA, EDDIE
CPT	NIXON, CHRISTOPHER	CSM	RIVERA, FRANCIS
MAJ	NUSSIO, RICKY J.	SSG	ROBB, IAN
1LT	NYE, ERIC	SSG	ROBINSON, LANCEY L.
CSM	OGGS, DENNIS L.	1SG	RODGERS, JOSEPH B.
1SG	ORTIZ, REINALDO	LTC	ROTH, ROBERT
SFC	PARKER, COLIN	CPT	SABATINI, JEFFERY J.
MAJ	PASSAMONTI, MARK	MAJ	SANDERS, TERRANCE
CPT	PAYNE, MATTHEW C.	SFC	SANTEE, JOE S.
MAJ	PELOQUIN, MICHAEL	SSG	SANTIAGO, JOSE
SFC	PHILLIPS, VINCENT	SSG	SARGENT, DELL L.
1LT	PHINNEY, BENJAMIN	SSG	SAUCEDO, JOSE
SSG	PINKSTON, RANNULF D.	CPT	SCARBERRY, TOM
SSG	PISCIOTTA, ROBERT	1SG	SCHEHL, KEVIN S.
CPT	POLSGROVE, ARRON	CPT	SCHOBITZ, ERIK
CPT	POWELL, JEFFREY H.	CPT	SCHONBERG, EARL B. JR.
SFC	POWELL, RICHARD	LTC	SCHWARTZ, ERIC

1LT	SCHWIMMER, EVAN W.	CW3	VICENTE, FELIPE B.
SSG	SCOTT, DARYL	1SG	VOGEL, BRIAN
SSG	SCRUGGS, SOLOMON	CPT	WALDEN, FOY S.
1LT	SELLERS, CHRISTINE	SFC	WALKER, ROBERT J.
MAJ	SHUCK, ROGER L.	CW2	WALKER, STEVEN K. JR.
SSG	SLAUGHTER, DERRICK	CPT	WALKER, WILLIAM M.
CPT	SMITH, MICHAEL S.	SFC	WATERHOUSE, DONALD B.
CSM	SMITH, OTIS JR.	CSM	WATKINS, GREGORY
SSG	SMITH, ROBERT E.	MAJ	WATSON, CHARLES
CPT	SMITH, WILLIAM T.	CPT	WATTENBARGER, JACOB A.
SSG	SNELL, JOSEPH	SSG	WATTS, COREY
CPT	SOMERS, DEAN	SSG	WEAVER, CHARLES
CPT	SPONSLER, WARREN E.	SGT	WEBB, DAVID B.
SFC	STANZIOLA, FELIX	1LT	WEBER, AMY
CPT	STEINHOFF, ROBERT H.	MAJ	WEBER, MICHAEL A.
1LT	STEPHENSON, TIMOTHY	MAJ	WEINERTH, MARK
SSG	STEVER, ROBERT	SFC	WELCH, DARRELL
MSG	SWEITZER, JUDD R.	SSG	WELLS, JAMIE
1LT	SZYDLIK, BRIAN D.	LTC	WESLEY, ERIC J.
SFC	TAYLOR, ROBERT JR.	1SG	WEST, DONALD K.
SFC	TERRELL, XAVIER D.	SFC	WETTSTEIN, STEPHEN J.
SGT	THOMPSON, DANIEL R.	SGT	WHITLOCK, JOHN A.
CPT	THOMSOM, SCOTT K.	SFC	WILCOX, JOHN A.
1SG	TOLBERT, ROBERT	SFC	WILDER, JACK
1LT	TOMLINSON, MARK S.	CPT	WILES, TODD A.
SGT	TORRES, LUIS	1LT	WILLIAMS, SHANE
SSG	TOUCHET, CHAD D.	MAJ	WILLIAMS, STANLEY T.
SFC	TROUTMAN, MICHAEL A.	LTC	WILLIAMS, WILLIE JR.
CPT	TUCKER, JOHN T. III	SFC	WILSON, KENNETH
LTC	TWITTY, STEPHEN M.	SSG	WILSON, ROBERT
SFC	VAN ESS, DANIEL	CPT	WOLFORD, PHILLIP E.
SSG	VANDEGRIFT, JASON F.	1LT	WOODRUFF, JOSHUA
1SG	VANORMER, DALE B.	1LT	WOODRUFF, ROBERT

CPT	WOODWARD, SCOTT
CPT	WRIGHT, JOSHUA D.
SFC	YEATTS, GARY M.
CPT	YOUNG, CHRISTOPHER T.
1LT	ZEIBER, KEITH A.
1SG	ZITO, WILLIAM JR.

PURPLE HEART

RANK	NAME
CW3	ACEVEDO, ANGEL R.
SPC	ADAMS, PETER
CPT	ALMAGUER, FELIX J.
SPC	ATTKINSON, STEVEN
SPC	BEAMAN, STEVE A.
CW2	BISCHOFF, RAY M.
SSG	BOOKER, STEVON A.
SGT	BOWEN, RANDOLPH
PFC	BOXLEY, CHARLES
SPC	BRANCHE, ONICA P.
PFC	BRONS, KENNETH C.
SPC	BROWN, BENJAMIN
CPL	BROWN, HENRY
PFC	BROWN, JEREMY
PFC	CALIFANO, JOSEPH
PFC	CAMP, CONRAD
SPC	CARSON, DANIEL
SPC	CARSON, JOSEPH
SSG	CHANDLER, DON E.
1LT	CHEN, DAVID
SPC	CLARK, KENNETH R.
CPT	COOPER, DAVID E.
SFC	CORNELL, PHILLIP

SSG	DAVIS, WILBERT
SFC	DEAS, WILLIAM R. JR.
SGT	DEWITT, MATTHEW
PFC	EPPINETTE, CHAD
1SG	EYNON, DONALD
PFC	FOOR, CRAIG
CSM	GALLAGHER, ROBERT
SPC	GARRETT, JOCOBY L.
SSG	GILLIAM, WILLIAM
PFC	GOGGIN, CHRISTOPHER
SGM	GONGORA, ALEXANDER
PFC	GRAY, JOSHUA
SSG	HALL, JASON S.
CPT	HENDERSON, MCKELLE L.
CPT	HIBNER, DAVID
PV2	HO, VAN
SPC	HORTON, MATTHEW
SPC	HORTON, PATRICK C.
SPC	HUTH, ERIC
SGT	JOASSAINT, ANTHONY
SGT	JOHNSON, KEVIN
CPT	KORN, EDWARD
SPC	LEDFORD, CHARLES
SGT	LUCAS, DUSTIN
SSG	MAO, CHHAY
SFC	MARSHALL, JOHN
SGT	MATHIS, JEROME R.
SPC	MCDANIEL, BRIAN C.
SSG	MIDDLETON, JAMES
CPT	MILLER, AARON
PV2	MILLER, ANTHONY
SPC	MITCHELL, GEORGE
SGT	MITCHELL, MICHAEL

SFC	MORALES, JOHN N.	MAJ	SHUCK, ROGER L.
PFC	MORRIS, DAVID M.	SSG	SLAGO, THOMAS W.
MAJ	MULLEN, SEAN F.	PFC	SMITH, SYNQUOIRY
PV2	NAUMAN, CHRISTOPHER	SSG	STEVER, ROBERT
SPC	NERIO, JOSE M.	PV2	STONE, DANIEL
SPC	NOCK, JAMES A.	SPC	STRATON, PAUL N.
PFC	NORTHCUTT, ADAM	PFC	SUNDAY, SEAN P.
SPC	NORTHROP, CHRISTOPHER	MSG	SWEITZER, JUDD
SGT	PERDUE, JOHNNY	PFC	TANIGUCHI, DAVIN K.
SPC	PHIMMASING, RATTANA	PFC	TATE, BENJAMIN
CPT	REGENNITTER, CHRISTOPHER	SPC	TECHUR, GARY M.
SPC	ROBICHEAU, MOUNTAIN S.	SGT	TYLER, DALOME
SPC	SANDERS, GREGORY	PFC	WEST, SHAWN
SPC	SCHAFER, DONALD	SGT	WHITAKER, JESSIE L.
CPT	SCHOBITZ, ERIK	SSG	WOOTEN, CHARLES L.
PFC	SCIRIA, ROBERT F.	SGT	YAW, DANA
PFC	SHIPLEY, CHRIS L.		

NOTES ON SOURCES

Just before dawn on April 4, 2003, a troop transport truck assigned to the 101st Airborne Division plunged into a canal outside the Iraqi holy city of Karbala. The truck sank to the bottom, taking with it weapons, food, and equipment. All twenty-four soldiers aboard, plus a lone embedded reporter, were fished out of the canal alive. That reporter was me.

The wreck of the truck robbed me of everything I owned at that moment—two satellite phones, a laptop computer, notebooks, cash, a tape recorder, and clothing. Soaking wet, I was tossed into the back of another 101st Airborne troop truck bound for Baghdad. More than twenty hours later, we arrived at Baghdad's international airport, which had been seized the day before by the Third Infantry Division (Mechanized).

This book is the indirect result of that truck plunge, which in turn resulted in my chance encounter the morning of April 5 with the officers and soldiers of the Third Infantry's Second Brigade. I was on the airport tarmac, trying to dry out in the morning sun, when the tanks and Bradleys of the Desert Rogues battalion rolled in at the close of their thunder run through the southwestern corner of the capital. The armored vehicles were smoking and streaked with blood, and the crews inside were drenched in sweat and covered with a fine gray dust.

The first soldier I encountered was Staff Sergeant Jason Diaz, whose tank had been burned and abandoned on the highway into Baghdad. Diaz and his crewmen described a seventeen-kilometer armored charge and firefight along the highway—the first American incursion into the capital after more than two weeks of war. It was a remarkable story, and it intrigued me. Over the next several months, I interviewed more than a hundred men from the Second Brigade, whose accounts form the core of this book.

Thunder Run is a work of nonfiction. The events described in these pages represent my best professional attempt to produce a thorough and accurate account of the battle for Baghdad. My interviews with the men who fought and directed the battle were buttressed by combat histories of the units involved; the contemporaneous notes and journals of soldiers; written logs of combat radio conversations; photographs and videos taken by soldiers during the battle; and my own experiences and observations while embedded with Cyclone Company of Task Force 4-64 for the duration of the battle and the "postcombat" period. In cases where these sources produced conflicting versions of events, I reinterviewed soldiers involved to obtain a more precise understanding of what had transpired. Many officers and men were interviewed several times, and these sessions served to enrich and sharpen the book's narrative.

The descriptions of actions taken by Iraqi commanders, soldiers, and civilians were based on my detailed interviews of these sources, conducted in Baghdad with the aid of interpreters. For the descriptions of Iraqi civilians killed during the battle, I relied on my interviews with their survivors.

In certain instances, I have relied on the work of others to supplement my own reporting. The account of television interviews of Colonel David Perkins and other commanders on April 7 are taken from a Fox News videotape of the interviews. Some descriptions of events at the Fourteenth of July Bridge on April 7 were graciously provided by my colleague at the *Los Angeles Times* Geoffrey Mohan, who was embedded with Cyclone Company. The description of the wounding of two Rogue battalion crewmen near the airport on April 5 is based on my interviews of the two wounded soldiers, with additional details taken from a first-person account in *Embedded: The Media at War in Iraq— An Oral History,* by Bill Katovsky and Timothy Carlson, with permission granted by Katovsky. The description of the April 14 discovery of the body of Sergeant First Class John W. Marshall is based on my interviews of officers from the Second Brigade, with several details also provided by a *Kansas City Star* account of a postwar speech by Rick Atkinson, an author and *Washington Post* reporter who was embedded with the 101st Airborne. The account of the technician at the Baghdad airport who insisted that the army's combat computer system was accurately depicting Second Brigade units in downtown Baghdad was provided by Major Dane Childs, a U.S. Army historian who is perhaps the world's leading authority on the battle for Baghdad.

INTERVIEWS IN IRAQ AND THE UNITED STATES

Specialist Benjamin Agee
Captain J. O. Bailey
Lieutenant Robert Ball
Captain Edward Ballanco
Captain Steven Barry
Staff Sergeant John Beck
Staff Sergeant Joe Bell
Lieutenant Colonel Michael Birmingham
Major General Buford C. Blount III
Marine Gunnery Sergeant Daniel Brown
Lieutenant Mark Brzozowksi
Captain Larry Burris
Captain Anthony Butler
Captain Christopher Carter
Major Rod Coffey
Captain Jason Conroy
Marine Captain David Cooper
Sergeant First Class Phillip Cornell
Private First Class Angel Cruz
Sergeant Walter Daniel
Sergeant Robert Davis
Marine Gunnery Sergeant William (Butch) Deas
Lieutenant Colonel Philip deCamp
Sergeant Jason Deming
Staff Sergeant Jason Diaz
Major Michael Donovan
Sergeant Jeffrey Ellis
Air Force Major Jim Ewald
Sergeant First Class Robert Ford
Sergeant First Class Ronald Gaines
Command Sergeant Major Robert Gallagher
Lieutenant Colonel Kenneth Gantt
Sergeant David Gibbons
Staff Sergeant Shawn Gibson
Private Joseph Gilliam

Captain William Glaser
Private First Class Adam Gregory
Lieutenant Roger Gruneisen
Sergeant Eric Gubler
Staff Sergeant Eric Guzman
Lieutenant Matthew Hanks
Marine Corporal Trevor Havens
First Sergeant Robert Hay
Sergeant John Heath
Sergeant Carlos Hernandez
Specialist Joe Hill
Captain Andy Hilmes
Specialist Shaun Holland
Captain Stephen Hommel
Captain Harry (Zan) Hornbuckle
Captain Daniel Hubbard
Captain Shannon Hume
Marine Major Mark Jewell
Captain Ronny Johnson
Special Joseph Kalinowski
Sergeant Shawn Kemmer
Major Everett Denton Knapp
Specialist Kenneth Krofta
Specialist Mason Lowery
Staff Sergeant Michael Lucas
Sergeant First Class Jonathan Lustig
Captain Philip Xuan Luu
Lieutenant Jeffrey McFarland
Private First Class Jacob McLaughlin
Private First Class Jarred Metz
Lieutenant Maurice Middleton
Lieutenant Matthew Miletich
First Sergeant Jeff Moser
Captain Christopher Nixon
Major Ricky Nussio
Staff Sergeant Matthew Oliver

Sergeant Quincy Oree
Private Chad Ortz
Sergeant Steve Oslin
Lieutenant Edward Panetta
Marine Sergeant Dennis Parks
Staff Sergeant Jamus Patrick
Colonel David Perkins
Sergeant First Class Vincent Phillips
Captain Aaron Polsgrove
Captain Sherman Powell
Sergeant Tony Rankin
Major Mark Rasins
Major Patrick Ratigan
Lieutenant Jason Redmon
Major Kent Rideout
Lieutenant Colonel Scott E. Rutter
Private First Class Don Schafer
Captain Erik Schobitz
Lieutenant Colonel Eric Schwartz
Private First Class Chris Shipley
Major Roger Shuck
Staff Sergeant Thomas Slago
Sergeant Michael Smith
Captain William Todd Smith
Specialist Gary Techur
Sergeant First Class Timothy Terpack
Staff Sergeant Joe Todd
Chris Tomlinson, Associated Press
Staff Sergeant Chad Touchet
Staff Sergeant Christopher Turner
Lieutenant Colonel Stephen Twitty
First Sergeant Dale Vanormer
Major Charles Watson
Lieutenant Colonel Eric Wesley
Captain Phillip Wolford
Captain Josh Wright

INTERVIEWS IN IRAQ

General Ahmed Rahal
Brigadier Baha Ali Nasr
General Omar Abdul Karim
Colonel Raid Raik
General Juawad al Dayni
Jaffer Sadiq
Nabil al Qaisy
Ahmed Sardar
Harith Ahmed Uraibi
Talal Ahmed al Doori
Hashim Mahmood
Faleh Khaiber
Mohammed Neaimi
Zubida Rida
Mervet Jawad
Salar Jaff
Ahmed Jaffer
Hassan Issam
Ziad Taha
Yusef Taha
Thafar al Kassab